DEVON AND CORNWALL RECORD SOCIETY

New Series, Vol. 28

THE HUNDREDS OF DEVON IN 1238

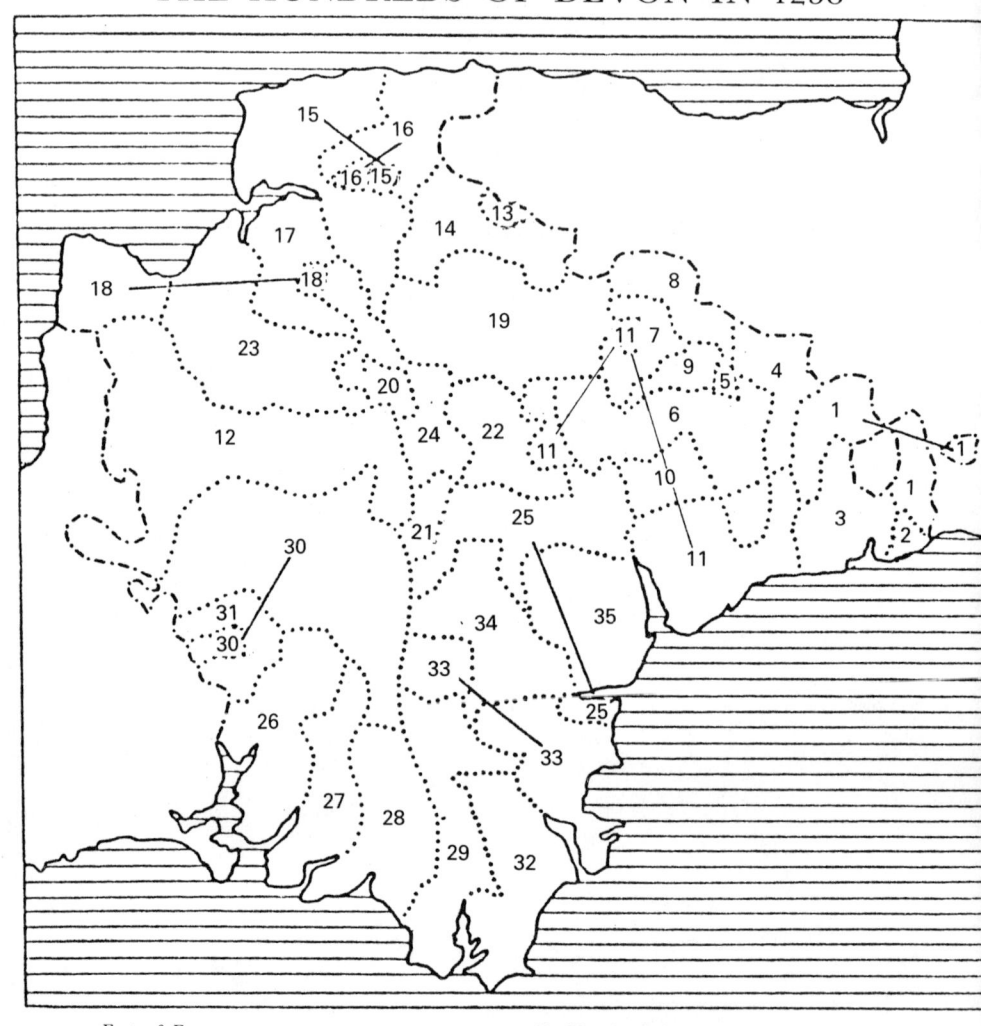

East of Exe
 1. Axminster (1–29)
 2. Axmouth (39–47)
 3. Colyton (48–68)
 4. Hemyock (75–91)
 5. Uffculme (92–102)
 6. Hayridge (103–127)
 7. Tiverton (130–140)
 8. Bampton (142–161)
 9. Halberton (162–168)
10. Cliston (169–176)
11. Budleigh (177–225)

North of the Cornish Road
12. Black Torrington (226–273)
13. North Molton (274–280)
14. South Molton (281–295)
15. Braunton (301–330)
16. Shirwell (336–343)
17. Fremington (344–355)
18. Hartland (360–367)
19. Witheridge (368–391)
20. Winkleigh (392–397)
21. South Tawton (398–410)
22. Crediton (411–422)
23. Shebbear (424–452)
24. North Tawton (457–479)

South of the Cornish Road
25. Wonford (480–519)
26. Roborough (520–533)
27. Plympton (534–543)
28. Ermington (556–578)
29. Stanborough (584–603)
30. Lifton (605–639)
31. Tavistock (644–657)
32. Coleridge (661–682)
33. Haytor (686–710)
34. Teignbridge (711–722)
35. Exminster (727–751)

(The numbers in brackets are those of each hundred's pleas in the text)

DEVON & CORNWALL RECORD SOCIETY

New Series, Vol. 28

CROWN PLEAS OF THE DEVON EYRE OF 1238

Edited with an Introduction by

HENRY SUMMERSON

Printed for the Society by
THE DEVONSHIRE PRESS LTD.
TORQUAY
ENGLAND

1985

© Devon and Cornwall Record Society and Henry Summerson
1985

ISBN 0 901853 28 3

Gratefully and affectionately dedicated to the memory of
Mary Kitzinger, died 7 February 1985.

CONTENTS

	Page
Figure: The Hundreds of Devon in 1238	ii
Abbreviations	vi

INTRODUCTION

The Eyre and its Record	ix
Early Thirteenth-century Devon	xiii
Peacemaking, Peacekeeping and Local Government	xv
Central Government and Local Government	xx
The Inquest into Hundreds	xxiii
The Incidence, Distribution and Causes of Crime	xxvii
Homicide	xxvii
Theft	xxxii
Suicide	xxxvi
Rape	xxxvii
Appeals and Plaints	xxxix
Crime and the Clergy	xliii
Financial Issues	xlvi
The Murder Fine	xlvii
Other Issues	xlix
Editorial Method	li
Acknowledgments	lii

CROWN PLEAS OF THE DEVON EYRE OF 1238	1

APPENDICES

I *Veredicta* for Axmouth and Tiverton Hundreds	125
II Articles of the Eyre and of the Tourn	128
III Statistics of Crime from Devon Eyres	130

INDEX OF PERSONS AND PLACES	131

ABBREVIATIONS

PUBLIC RECORD OFFICE CLASSES CITED

C60   Fine Rolls
C66   Patent Rolls
C132   Inquisitions *Post Mortem*
C144   Criminal Inquisitions
DL30   Duchy of Lancaster, Court Rolls
E159   Exchequer KR Memoranda Rolls
E368   Exchequer LTR Memoranda Rolls
E370   Exchequer LTR Miscellaneous Rolls
E372   Pipe Rolls
JUST/1   Eyre Rolls, Assize Rolls etc
JUST/3   Gaol Delivery Rolls
Devon Eyre Rolls cited:
JUST/1/174   1238 eyre, civil pleas only
JUST/1/175   1244 eyre, civil and crown pleas
JUST/1/176   1249 eyre, civil and crown pleas
JUST/1/180   1218/1219 eyre, civil pleas only
JUST/1/186   1281/1282 eyre, crown pleas only

OTHER SOURCES, PUBLISHED AND MANUSCRIPT
(includes only manuscripts cited more than once)

BIHR   Bulletin of the Institute of Historical Research
BL (British Library) Add. MS. 49359   Register of the Courtenay Family
BL Vit. D IX   Cartulary of St. Nicholas's Priory, Exeter
Bodl.   Bodleian Library, Oxford
Bracton, *De Legibus*   Bracton, *De Legibus et Consuetudinibus Angliae*, ed. G. E. Woodbine, translated, with revisions and notes, by S. E. Thorne, 4 volumes, (Cambridge, Massachusetts, 1968–77)
CCR   Calendar of Close Rolls
CChR   Calendar of Charter Rolls
CDF   J. H. Round (ed.), *Calendar of Documents preserved in France illustrative of the history of Great Britain and Ireland Vol. I 918–1216* (RS 1899)
Cal.Inq.Misc.   *Calendar of Inquisitions Miscellaneous*
Cal.Inq.P.M.   *Calendar of Inquisitions Post Mortem*
CLR   Calendar of Liberate Rolls
CPR   Calendar of Patent Rolls
Cam, *Hundred Rolls*   H. Cam, *The Hundred and the Hundred Rolls* (London 1930)
Canonsleigh Cartulary   V. C. M. Landon (ed.), *The Cartulary of Canonsleigh Abbey* (Devon and Cornwall Record Society, New Series, Vol. 8, 1965)
Chope, *Hartland*   R. P. Chope, *The Book of Hartland* (Torquay 1940)
Complete Peerage   G. E. C., *The Complete Peerage*, 2nd. Edition (1910–1959)
Cornwall FFI   J. H. Rowe (ed.), *Cornwall Feet of Fines Vol. I* (Devon and Cornwall Record Society, 1914)
CRR   Curia Regis Rolls
D & C (Dean and Chapter Library, Exeter) MS 3672   General Cartulary of the Dean and Chapter of Exeter
DB   *The Devonshire Domesday and Geld Inquest*, two volumes (Devonshire Association, Plymouth 1884–1892)
DCNQ   Devon and Cornwall Notes and Queries
Devon FFI   O. J. Reichel (ed.), *Devon Feet of Fines Vol. I* (Devon and Cornwall Record Society, 1912)
Devonshire Studies   W. G. Hoskins and H. P. R. Finberg, *Devonshire Studies* (London 1952)
Domesday Geography   H. C. Darby and R. Welldon Finn (eds.), *The Domesday Geography of South-West England* (Cambridge 1967)

DRO (Devon Record Office, Exeter) TD42   Cartulary of the Courtenay Family
DRO TD51   Cartulary of Otterton Priory
Dugdale, *Monasticon*   Sir William Dugdale, *Monasticon Anglicanum* (1846)
EcHR   *Economic History Review*
EHD   *English Historical Documents* Vol. I, ed. D. Whitelock (London 1955), Vol. II, ed. D. C. Douglas and G. W. Greenaway (London 1953)
EHR   *English Historical Review*
EMC   Devon Record Office, Exeter Mayor's Court Rolls
English Medieval Boroughs   M. W. Beresford and H. P. R. Finberg, *English Medieval Boroughs: a Handlist* (Newton Abbot 1973)
Fees   H. C. Maxwell Lyte (ed.), *The Book of Fees*, 3 volumes (1920–39)
Finberg, *Early Charters*   H. P. R. Finberg (ed.), *The Early Charters of Devon and Cornwall* (University of Leicester Department of Local History Occasional Papers no. 2, 1953)
Finberg, *Tavistock Abbey*   H. P. R. Finberg, *Tavistock Abbey* (Cambridge 1951)
HMC   Historical Manuscripts Commission
Hoskins, *Devon*   W. G. Hoskins, *Devon* (London 1954)
Meekings, *Studies*   C. A. F. Meekings, *Studies in 13th-century Justice and Administration* (London 1981)
Morey, *Bartholomew*   A. Morey, *Bartholomew of Exeter* (Cambridge 1937)
Oliver, *Monasticon*   G. Oliver, *Monasticon Dioecesis Exoniensis* (Exeter and London 1846, with supplement 1854)
PND   J. E. B. Gover, A. Mawer, F. M. Stenton, *Place-Names of Devon*, 2 volumes (Place-Name Society Vols. 8 and 9, Cambridge 1931, 1932)
Pole, *Collections*   Sir William Pole, *Collections towards a Description of the County of Devon* (London 1791)
Pollock and Maitland   Sir F. Pollock and F. W. Maitland, *The History of English Law* (2nd. Edition, Cambridge 1952)
PQW   W. Illingworth (ed.), *Placita de Quo Warranto* (Record Commission 1818)
PR   Pipe Roll, either ed. J. Hunter (1833, 1844), or publications of the Pipe Roll Society (PRS), first series 1884–1925, new series 1925–
PRO   Public Record Office
Queens 152   MS 152 in Library of The Queen's College, Oxford, Collections of Sir William Pole
Reg. Bronescombe   F. C. Hingeston-Randolph (ed.), *The Registers of Walter Bronescombe and Peter Quivil, Bishops of Exeter* (London and Exeter 1889)
Reichel S   O. J. Reichel, *The Hundreds of Devon*, ten supplements to the *Transactions of the Devonshire Association*, 1928–38
Risdon, *Survey of Devon*   T. Risdon, *The Chorographical Description or Survey of the County of Devon* (Barnstaple 1970 – reprint of edition of 1811)
RH   W. Illingworth (ed.), *Rotuli Hundredorum Vol. I* (Record Commission 1812)
Rot.Ch.   T. D. Hardy (ed.), *Rotuli Chartarum* (Record Commission 1837)
Rot.Fin.I   C. Roberts (ed.), *Excerpta e Rotulis Finium Vol. I* (Record Commission 1835)
Rot.Lit.Claus.   T. D. Hardy (ed.), *Rotuli Litterarum Clausarum*, 2 volumes (Record Commission 1833, 1844)
Rot.Norm.   T. D. Hardy (ed.), *Rotuli Normanniae* (Record Commission 1835)
Rot.Ob.Fin.   T. D. Hardy (ed.), *Rotuli de Oblatis et Finibus . . . tempore Regis Johannis* (Record Commission 1835)
RRA-N   *Regesta Regum Anglo-Normannorum* Vol. I, ed. H. W. C. Davis (Oxford 1913), Vol. II, ed. C. Johnson and H. A. Cronne (Oxford 1956), Vol. III, ed. H. A. Cronne and R. H. C. Davis (Oxford 1968)
RS   Rolls Series
Sanders, *Baronies*   I. J. Sanders, *English Baronies* (Oxford 1960)
Somersetshire Pleas   C. E. H. Chadwyck Healey (ed.), *Somersetshire Pleas* (Somerset Record Society Vol. 11, 1897)
Surrey Eyre 1235   C. A. F. Meekings and D. Crook (eds.), *The 1235 Surrey Eyre* (Surrey Record Society Vols. 31, 32, 1979, 1983)
TDA   *Transactions of the Devonshire Association*
TRHS   *Transactions of the Royal Historical Society*
Wiltshire Crown Pleas 1249   C. A. F. Meekings (ed.), *Crown Pleas of the Wiltshire Eyre, 1249* (Wiltshire Archaeological and Natural History Society, Records Branch, Vol. 16, 1960)

INTRODUCTION*

THE EYRE AND ITS RECORD

The text presented here contains the crown pleas of the Devon eyre of 1238, fully calendared in English from P.R.O. JUST/1/174 membranes 25 to 43. An eyre was a periodic visitation made to a county by royal justices for the purpose of hearing such civil litigation, usually over landed property, as had been initiated by royal writ, and of holding the pleas of the crown, those offences which were either by their nature traditionally reserved for the king or his justices or had been brought within the purview of the king's courts by a claim that the king's peace had been broken and felony committed, as well as of reviewing the maintenance of certain of the king's financial rights and of scrutinising the processes of law enforcement and the behaviour of local officials since the last eyre. Although it had a marked financial character – the proceeds of the crown pleas were reserved for the crown, and the penalties imposed on local communities and officials for their various failings and failures were invariably monetary ones – the eyre should be seen less as a financial institution than as a show of royal strength in the localities, one of the few means whereby the crown could hope to demonstrate its authority in the shires in a way that could be felt at every level of society. The workings of the eyre have been definitively analysed by the late C. A. F. Meekings.[1] This introduction will therefore describe court proceedings only where this seems necessary to an understanding of the text, attempting rather to suggest how the 776 crown plea cases can shed light both on law enforcement and local government in early thirteenth-century Devon, and on crime and disorder there in the ten years since the previous eyre, in 1228, and to show how these matters were related to that county's social, economic and political life.

The four justices appointed on 8 April 1238 to conduct eyres in Cornwall and Devon were William of York, Adam fitz William, Robert de Beauchamp and Jordan Oliver. Adam fitz William died in mid-May, however, and was replaced by William de St. Edmund.[2] The Cornwall eyre lasted from about 31 May to 15 June,[3] and two days later the Devon eyre opened at Exeter, probably in the castle. Two of the justices had Devon connections: Robert de Beauchamp, who during the eyre involved himself in an agreement to which one of his tenants was a party,[4] and Jordan Oliver, who had property in the county in his wife's right,[5] had

---

*The numbers in brackets are those of cases among the crown pleas. The notes on the text are in this edition placed immediately after the entries they are intended to elucidate. A reference to a case from the introduction is often as much to the accompanying note as to the text itself, and the two should be consulted together.

[1] In his introductions to *Wiltshire Crown Pleas 1249* and *Surrey Eyre 1235*.
[2] *CCR 1237–42* p. 125, *CPR 1232–47* p. 221.
[3] D. Crook, *Records of the General Eyre* (HMSO, London 1982) p. 96. All details about the chronology of eyres supplied here have been taken from this most useful handbook.
[4] *Devon FFI* no. 282.
[5] *Devon FFI* no. 70.

ix

served as a justice at the previous Devon eyre,[6] and had taken assizes and conducted gaol deliveries in the meantime.[7] In Devon, as elsewhere, the justices doubtless worked in pairs; Beauchamp plainly heard civil pleas, perhaps as partner to William of York, while Oliver is likely to have taken crown pleas, presumably with William de St. Edmund. The organisation of the eyre in Devon was in the hands of the sheriff, Walter of Bath, who through public proclamations and personal summonses would have had to secure the attendance of all free-holders, four men and the reeve from each vill, twelve burgesses from each burgh, all those involved in civil litigation which had either been adjourned to the eyre from a higher court or initiated with a hearing at the eyre in mind, all those involved in any way in crown pleas arising since the previous eyre, and all past sheriffs or their representatives.[8] Local officials, notably coroners and hundred bailiffs, would also have had to attend.

The hearing of crown pleas revolved round presentments made by juries. Each hundred (except for Uffculme, North Molton and Molland, all of uncertain status) was represented by a jury of twelve men (in theory – sometimes there were only eleven), who should be knights if possible, free and law-abiding men when knights were not available; they were men of local consequence, and many were probably experienced as jurors – in 1244 202 men served in the same juries in which they had served in 1238, so it is likely that a fair proportion of the jurors of 1238 had served in like fashion in 1228. As well as 35 hundred juries, there was also a jury of 24 men from Exeter and juries of between 3 and 13 men from 18 burghs and 2 manors (two more manors and a burgh answered through juries identical with those of their respective hundreds). By 1238 many more Devon communities could have claimed burghal status than were represented by juries at the eyre, and it is not clear why some were represented rather than others – size, wealth, the antiquity of their privileges and the importance of their founders were probably all taken into account. In 1244 Robert de Sydeham, whose manor of Rackenford had been granted a weekly market and yearly fair in 1234, appeared before the justices to claim that "his manor is so free that it should answer by itself before the justices for everything which happens in it",[9] but no Rackenford jury attended later eyres; the insignificance of the place, and perhaps its closeness to Tiverton and South Molton, probably told against it.

The jurors made presentments in the form of answers to the questions contained in the articles of the eyre – Appendix II(a) – answers which were both written and spoken, being enrolled as *veredicta*, of which one copy was handed to the justices and another read from by the jurors. Of these presentments, most were made under article 2, "of new crown pleas", meaning those arising since the previous eyre, which covered most of the crime and disorder, and of the accidental deaths, which came to the attention of the justices. The Tiverton *veredictum* – Appendix I(b) – together with the Bradford *veredictum* from the 1236 Shropshire eyre,[10]

[6]*Devon FFI* nos. 147–248.
[7]e.g. C66/45 m19d; C66/46 m14d; C66/48 m11d.
[8]For the summons to the 1244 eyre see *CCR 1242–47* pp. 235–6.
[9]JUST/1/175 m46.
[10]JUST/1/1589.

suggests that representatives of vills passed information required under this article on to the jurors; enrolled in the *veredictum* under the name of the relevant community, it nevertheless became the responsibility of the hundred jurors, who also made presentments under the other articles, as in the Bradford *veredictum*, where it was the "sworn knights" who made a presentment under article 15. Comparison of the Tiverton *veredictum* with the Tiverton crown pleas makes one important point about the latter, their incompleteness, since three raisings of the hue, three burglaries, three accidental deaths, the making of a ditch and an appeal went unrecorded among them, doubtless because these matters seemed unimportant and were probably not productive of revenue for the crown, though the omission of an appeal is surprising. A good deal of unimportant material must have gone untransferred from other *veredicta* to the plea roll during the eyre.

The same consideration may account for some of the omissions of material recorded on a fragment of a Devon coroner's roll of 1229;[11] altogether two accidental deaths, a suspected arsonist, a suspected thief and two men charged with harbouring a thief who had been hanged were omitted from the 1238 plea roll. The accidental deaths were presumably left out because the crown did not stand to gain from their inclusion; the other cases had probably been terminated at one of the four gaol deliveries known to have taken place in the county between 1228 and 1238,[12] leaving nothing of consequence to be recorded in the latter year. Another six killings allegedly perpetrated in Devon went unrecorded in 1238.[13] Three, perhaps four, probably antedated the eyre of 1228, another had been dealt with at a gaol delivery, but it is hard to see why the killing of Mabel de Hauekedon, for which a man had been appealed, arrested and released to bail in 1237, should not have been presented and enrolled a year later. As a record of all that was said and done at the eyre the plea roll is demonstrably incomplete, and what the jurors presented may well have been incomplete also, though as a fair number of cases known from other sources[14] *are* recorded among the crown pleas, it should not be assumed that omissions by jurors from their *veredicta* were commonly made.

The task of the jurors was not confined to the making of presentments, it extended also to making indictments and trying suspects. Suspects came into court because they had already been arrested and imprisoned or attached – obliged to find pledges for their appearance – as a result of a coroner's inquest, an appeal of felony or an accusation in a lower court (all described below), or had been indicted and arrested just as the eyre began. The process of indictment required each jury at the beginning of the eyre to make unpublicised accusations to the sheriff, naming those they suspected of serious crimes, so that these could, if possible, be arrested before they had a chance to run away. The suspects so indicted and consequently arrested appear to be those described in the roll as *rettati*, translated here as "charged", when they appeared in court. It is immediately apparent that most of them were acquitted. In itself this is

[11]R. F. Hunnisett, "An Early Coroner's Roll", in *BIHR* 30 (1957) pp. 225–31.
[12]*CPR 1225–32* p. 516; C66/46 m14d; C66/47 m9d; C66/48 m11d.
[13]*CCR 1231–34* pp. 1, 38–9, 180; *CCR 1234–37* p. 447; *CCR 1237–42* p. 122.
[14]*CCR 1227–31* pp. 158 (174), 337 (323), 487–88 (775); *CCR 1234–37* pp. 37 (203), 93 (626); *CCR 1237–42* pp. 37 (474); 68 (37); *CPR 1232–47* p. 104 (466).

not surprising – it was usual for most suspects at eyres to be acquitted.[15] Men and women arrested in obviously incriminating circumstances, killers taken literally red-handed and thieves caught with stolen goods, risked summary execution, or execution deferred only until a court could be convened to condemn them in proper form (cf. no. 13); many suspects are likely to have been dealt with at gaol deliveries, very many more ran away and could not be caught at all. All the same, it may seem strange that so many of those indicted should have been acquitted, when the same jurors were responsible for both. By 1238, following the effective disappearance of the ordeal after the fourth Lateran council had forbidden the clergy's participation in it, proof of guilt or innocence had come to be almost invariably made by a jury's verdict, and in 1238 the jury giving that verdict, in all save a few, obviously exceptional, cases (e.g. 97, 377, 473, 583), was apparently that of the hundred. But, as both Maitland and Meekings have demonstrated, the problem was more apparent than real;[16] the jurors were essentially passing on suspicions, which had commonly originated with vills or individuals rather than with themselves, and which might prove to stem from malice or greed (116), and to be unfounded or at any rate unsustainable (128).

The truthfulness of the allegations made against those indicted was not tested by the jurors alone; the justices too, according to Bracton, must make careful scrutiny of such charges.[17] Indeed, the role of the justices went far beyond a silent presidency in court, at every stage of proceedings they can be seen to have scrutinised and checked what was done, especially by juries. With the assistance of the rolls kept by the five Devon coroners, whose function it was to make an official record of the pleas of the crown, and probably also the rolls of proceedings in the County Court, kept by the sheriff, the justices detected 36 errors and misrepresentations by juries. No doubt some of these were unintentional, the failure of the Axmouth jurors to name an abjuror (44), for instance, which they had nothing to gain by concealing and which they must have known reference to the coroners' rolls would disclose, but most seem likely to have been deliberate, most obviously when withholding names to save people inconvenience, and at least three were probably serious offences (228, 346, 360).The justices could also detect error and pursue the truth by questioning jurors and others – in 1238 they can be construed as interrogating jurors and coroners (37, 317) and probably also the first finder of a corpse (463). If they sometimes failed to uncover the truth, it need not have been for lack of effort, and certainly not for lack of time.

The rudimentary timetable at the end of the kalendar of juries (p. 8) gives some idea as to the speed with which it was expected that the crown pleas would be got through. Although the eyre was said to have opened on 17 June, proceedings are unlikely to have begun at once. The earliest fine from this eyre is dated 21 June, and if the hearing of crown pleas also began then, allowing the jurors four days in which to make indictments and prepare their *veredicta*, the eleven hundreds and seven other burghs and manors of the parts of Devon east of the Exe (for their distribution see

---

[15]See *Surrey Eyre 1235* p. 128.
[16]*Wiltshire Crown Pleas 1249* pp. 95–6.
[17]Bracton, *De Legibus* Vol. II p. 404, ff.143, 143b.

Introduction   xiii

map on p. ii) would have had eight days for the hearing of their pleas (1–225). The next section of the county, that north of the Cornish road, consisting of thirteen hundreds and six burghs and manors (nos. 226–479), would have had seven days between 29 June and 6 July, while the last section, south of the Cornish road, consisting of eleven hundreds and eleven other presenting areas, would have had twelve days for its pleas (nos. 480–776) before the eyre ended on 17 July. The hundreds of the figures given here, and on p. ii above, are those of the text, in which Ottery St. Mary and Molland appear as manors, and not of the kalendar, where they are listed as hundreds. Throughout the eyre an average of two presenting areas a day would have been disposed of; they varied greatly in size and in the number of their pleas, but since such a timetable would have involved less than thirty pleas a day, on average, there is no reason to suppose that the justices could not have found time for a detailed examination of any case, had they wanted to do so. Indeed, the case of Robert de la Slade (473) suggests that proceedings got ahead of the timetable, and that the pleas from north of the Cornish road were finished by 2 or 3 July.[18] It is ultimately impossible to say how successful the justices were in the execution of their tasks, how accurate and reliable is the record of the pleas held before them. Devon was a big county, with a widely dispersed population, much of it in small and isolated communities, and there can be no doubt that under such circumstances concealment of crimes and criminals could have been very easy. On the other hand – as is argued below – the whole structure of local government and law enforcement deliberately worked against concealment, while the justices themselves had wide powers of investigation and scrutiny, powers which they clearly used. There must have been some covering up, corpses silently buried, homicides and suicides successfully passed off as accidental or natural deaths, but there may well have been much less than one might expect.

EARLY THIRTEENTH-CENTURY DEVON

The county which the justices visited in 1238 was large, isolated and still only partly settled. Cut off from Dorset and Somerset by a line of hills running almost continuously from sea to sea – only through the valley of the Axe and the gap between the Blackdown and Brendon hills, near Tiverton, could a traveller from the east make his way easily into Devon[19]– it is not surprising that fourteenth-century bishops of Exeter thought of their diocese, containing as it did Celtic Cornwall as well, as being on the edge of the known world.[20] An isolated county, Devon was also a shire of isolated communities, east of Exeter, in particular, where the land is broken up into innumerable deep valleys by the countless streams running off the granite expanses of Dartmoor. The infertility of much of the soil made the creation of large nucleated villages impracticable, a plentiful supply of water made it unnecessary.[21] Its communities

[18]Proceedings also got ahead of schedule in 1244, JUST/1/175 m49d.
[19]Hoskins, *Devon*, pp. 13–14.   [20]Hoskins, *Devon*, p. 223.
[21]Finberg, *Tavistock Abbey* pp. 29–30; *Domesday Geography* p. 235; *Devonshire Studies* pp. 289–333; W. G. Hoskins, *Provincial England* (London 1965) pp. 15–52.

cut off from one another more by the labour of going up and down the steep sides of the intervening combes than by any significant mileage measurable in terms of a crow's flight, the landscape of Devon was principally one of hamlets and farmsteads.[22] Communications within the county, moreover, were slow, hazardous and generally inadequate; in the early seventeenth century Tristram Risdon described Devon as "very laborious, rough and unpleasant to strangers travelling those ways, which are cumbersome and uneven, amongst rocks and stones, painful for man and horse ..."[23] and this is even more likely to have been the case four hundred years earlier.

The dispersal of its inhabitants and the difficulties of communication between them helped breed an inward-looking localism, inadequately counteracted by the effects of pilgrimages (159, 519), personal and commercial connections with Ireland (132), Wales (295, 611) and Gascony,[24] and the transhumance of flocks to and from Dartmoor.[25] Although the large number of deaths by drowning in the sea suggests that fishing was an important source of food and income in coastal districts, especially along the south coast, there can be no doubt that most of the inhabitants of thirteenth-century Devon lived by agriculture, that the most important and profitable form of agriculture was arable farming,[26] and that for those who had arable land to cultivate, the routines of ploughing, sowing and reaping were bound to keep them at home. The number of such arable farmers, moreover, was growing rapidly by 1238, the result of the restrictions placed on the spread of internal settlement in the twelfth century by the entire county's being placed under forest law, with its penalties for unlicensed encroachments on the royal forest, having been lifted in 1204, when John, in return for a payment of 5000 marks, disafforested the county.[27]

This was an event of cardinal importance in Devon's history, since it left the way clear for a substantial increase in land clearance and cultivation. The role of the landowning classes in this development should not be underrated, but it was above all the work of the free peasantry, for many of whom, indeed, participation in this great labour was both the cause and condition of their freedom.[28] The landscape of much of inland Devon, broken up into a network of small enclosed fields, bears witness to this day to the piecemeal work of colonisation that followed the disafforestation.[29] Besides the restraints it placed on its economic development, subjection to forest law may have had another effect on Devon. The characteristic feature of that law was that it was "not based upon the common law of the realm but upon the will and disposition of the

---

[22]Vividly illustrated in C. Taylor, *Village and Farmstead* (London 1983) pp. 178–9.
[23]Risdon, *Surrey of Devon*, p. 4.
[24]Hoskins, *Devon*, p. 60.
[25]G. M. Spooner & F. S. Russell (eds.), *Worth's Dartmoor* (Newton Abbot 1967) p. 393.
[26]Finberg, *Tavistock Abbey* pp. 156–8; K. Ugawa, "The Economic Development of Some Devon Manors", in *TDA* 94 (1962) p. 652; H. S. A. Fox, "The Chronology of Enclosure and Economic Development in Medieval Devon", in *Ec.H.R.* 2nd Series 28 (1975) pp. 185–6.
[27]T. Rymer (ed.), *Foedera* Vol. I Part I (London 1816) p. 89.
[28]Hoskins, *Devon*, pp. 58, 71.
[29]Hoskins, *Devon*, pp. 71–2; P. Flatrès, "La Structure Agraire Ancienne du Devon et du Cornwall et les Enclotures des XIIIe et XIVe Siècles", in *Annales de Bretagne* 56 (1949) pp. 124–34; A. H. Shorter, W. L. D. Ravenhill, K. J. Gregory, *Southwest England* (London 1969) p. 109.

monarch".[30] The men of Devon, having been thus exposed to Angevin government in its most capriciously exacting form, showed themselves consistently determined thereafter to be governed in a manner more in keeping with their own interests and usages, and as far as possible to keep the king's government at arm's length.

PEACEMAKING, PEACEKEEPING AND LOCAL GOVERNMENT

By 1238 the king's government was trying to establish a greater measure of control over a system of law enforcement that had evolved and consequently functioned without much active direction from the centre. In his coronation oath each king swore to maintain peace and administer justice, and there can be no doubt that the effective administration of justice would be one of the most cogent, and profitable, demonstrations of his authority that he could make. His subjects would have agreed with him that good order was highly desirable, but without necessarily wanting the king's close involvement in its achievement – they had rights and interests of their own which might be threatened by over-rigorous scrutiny and regulation, and preferred to be left alone in the enjoyment of them. They are unlikely to have seen the peace broken by a criminal act as something solely the king's, their own was at stake as well. Medieval people well knew how fragile was the fabric of their society, how easily violence and dissension could tear it apart – not for nothing did Dante reserve an entire circle of hell for the sowers of discord – and they freely resorted to means of protecting and repairing it with little reference to the courts and other formal instruments of law and order.[31] In Devon, as elsewhere, pressure was exerted on disputants at all levels of society to settle their differences peacefully, from the landowners whose disagreements were composed *mediantibus bonis viris pacis amatoribus* or *amicis intervenientibus*[32] to the many Exeter litigants whose quarrels went from the mayor's court to a loveday, the parties being at their own request allowed to adjourn proceedings in order to seek a reconciliation, on the understanding that they would reappear in court if they failed. One Exeter man who fell out with his groom was reconciled to him by the intervention of neighbours, though the reconciliation failed to last the night.[33] Parish priests, too, were required to exert themselves on behalf of peace and concord; in his diocesan statutes, enacted between 1225 and 1237, Bishop Brewer of Exeter ordered that they try to settle quarrels among their parishioners, so that the sun did not go down upon their wrath.[34]

Society could thus exert a good deal of pressure on its members to observe the law and keep the peace, while among the peasantry, in the context of the rural community – the vill – this pressure was given institutional form by frankpledge, a system of mutual responsibility

[30]*EHD* II pp. 527–8.
[31]See M. T. Clanchy, "Law and Love in the Middle Ages", in J. Bossy (ed.), *Disputes and Settlements: Law and Human Relations in the West* (Cambridge 1983) pp. 47–67.
[32]DRO TD51 f.127; BL Vit. D IX ff.148, 148v.
[33]EMC 1 m6.
[34]F. M. Powicke & C. R. Cheney (eds.), *Councils and Synods* Vol. II Part I (Oxford 1964) p. 231.

whereby each male inhabitant of a vill over the age of twelve was sworn both to keep the peace himself and to keep a vigilant eye on his neighbours; if one of them committed a crime and escaped capture, the whole community would be penalised.[35] In much of midland and southern England such frankpledge communities, known as tithings, consisted of groups of ten men or more, but in the south-west the scatter of population probably made this impracticable, and the whole vill was usually treated as a tithing. Membership of a tithing was predominantly something required of the unfree peasantry – the property of free men was probably regarded as sufficient guarantee for their good behaviour.[36] Frankpledge was a system which depended on making every vill as far as possible a watertight community; strangers and vagrants must be kept outside, if they were admitted, it must be for good and all, by enrolling them in the tithing and so subjecting them permanently to the scrutiny of their fellows and other pressures of community life. The antithesis between membership of a tithing and vagrancy outside it is perfectly brought out by the case of a Cornishman who two months before he abjured the realm for stealing oxen "withdrew from his tithing and during that time was a vagrant through the whole hundred, outside frankpledge . . ."[37]

Should social pressure and communal vigilance prove insufficient to prevent a crime from being committed, they were turned against the culprit, either by securing his arrest or, should he escape, by publicising his offence and so preventing either his return to his own community or his acceptance in any other. Crimes and criminals were advertised by a system of continuous presentments in local courts, to which were presented, by tithings or vills, all breaches of the peace that led to the raising of the hue – a call to attention and to action, putting all within earshot on the alert, and raised by shouting or blowing the horns which people often carried (107). The jurisdiction of a court might not enable it to deal with whatever offence had caused the hue to be raised, but such presentments at least gave offences wide publicity and worked against their concealment – an ever-present danger in small communities, whose enclosedness frankpledge risked enhancing. Each raising of the hue was therefore to be presented to the Hundred Court,[38] the County Court[39] and the sheriff's tourn – Appendix II(b) no. 7. Two of the most important functions of the coroner, the inquests he held on the bodies of those found suddenly, mysteriously or violently dead, and the conducting of abjurations,[40] laid a similar emphasis on publicity. The former required the presence of the four vills nearest to the scene of the death, and so inevitably entailed the dissemination as well as the gathering of information about the circumstances and causes of the death; the latter, an extension of traditional sanctuary rights in churches, whereby a

---

[35]For a detailed analysis of the system of law enforcement discussed here, see H. R. T. Summerson, "The Structure of Law Enforcement in Thirteenth Century England" in *American Journal of Legal History* 23 (1979) pp. 313–27.
[36]H. M. Jewell, *English Local Administration in the Middle Ages* (Newton Abbot 1972) p. 163.
[37]JUST/1/112 m10d.
[38]F. W. Maitland (ed.), *The Court Baron* (Selden Society Vol. 4, 1890) p. 88.
[39]JUST/1/175 m38d.
[40]See R. F. Hunnisett, *The Medieval Coroner* (Cambridge 1961) chapters II and III.

Introduction xvii

fugitive who took refuge in a church could, after confessing his crime before a coroner, abjure the realm (that is, promise to make his way to the coast and take ship out of the kingdom, on pain of speedy execution should he return), likewise took place in the presence of a large attendance of the neighbourhood, which was thereby notified of the event and so able to take appropriate action against the abjuror who left his road to the coast or returned home. Inquests and abjurations were both, moreover, tied into the system or local courts, since both were certainly presented to the County Court (e.g. 262, 322), and probably to the tourn, as well as to the eyre.

Such a system served several purposes. By bringing quarrels and affrays into the open, and so making it easier for them to be settled, in or out of court, it must often have helped defuse them before they could cause serious violence. It must certainly have made the task of jurors at eyres, as they prepared their *veredicta*, infinitely easier – they can have had little excuse for ignorance of what had been so frequently and publicly reported. And it was admirably geared to the process of outlawry, which required first the making of a formal accusation against a suspect in the County Court, then the prosecution of that accusation, in the same form, at the four sessions following, at the last of which, if the suspect failed to appear in the meantime, he was declared an outlaw; thereafter he bore the wolf's head and could be killed as soon as caught (though more regular methods came to be preferred – 441), while anyone convicted of harbouring him would be hanged. The accusation could be made in either of two forms. One was the appeal of felony, a personal accusation further discussed below (p. xxxix–xl), which could be begun at any time, but the other was normally gone through only after an eyre, when the justices ordered that those who had made themselves scarce on serious charges should be put in exigent – their presence formally demanded, or exacted, at four successive sessions of the County Court, until they were outlawed at the fifth if they failed to appear; the process was the same as with an appeal, except that there was no personal accuser. Just as the continuous presentment of crimes in a series of courts gave publicity to offences and offenders, so successive appeals or exigents let it be known what had been done and who was charged with it; presentments and appeals may even have run concurrently to this end – raising the hue was an essential part of an appeal of felony, thereby making a neighbourhood witness to the alleged offence[41] and perhaps helping discourage malicious or frivolous accusations, so that it is possible to imagine successive presentments of a raising of the hue being made in local courts while the appeal prosecuting the offence which had led to the hue being raised was in progress in the County Court (cf. Appendix I(a) no. 2). All these proceedings gave maximum publicity, increasing the likelihood of arrests being made both before and after outlawry, while also giving the suspect every chance of appearing in court and clearing himself.

In the context of such a system, the eyre could be seen as just another public court, with presentments to it paralleled by those made to local courts. Amercements imposed in 1238 and 1244 show that to the County Court, held every four weeks, vill presented accidental deaths, wrecks at

[41] Pollock and Maitland Vol. II p. 606.

sea, abjurations, diggings for treasure, homicides, burglaries and raisings of the hue, while of the articles of the tourn – Appendix II(b) – nos. 1–6, 9, 10, 11, 14, 17, 19, 20, 25, 28 and 29 have close or exact parallels among those used for the 1238 eyre. The tourn, a yearly perambulation by the sheriff through the whole shire (except those places from which he was excluded) to receive presentments and review the frankpledge system,[42] had other similarities to the eyre. An account of an abortive attempt by Eudo de Beauchamp, sheriff in 1214, to hold his tourn in that year, describing how first he questioned the knights of four hundreds, who claimed that they had nothing to present, and then interrogated the representatives of vills and tithings, one at a time, who had rather more to say,[43] suggests that, as at the eyre, the knights would normally make formal presentment of information supplied by the vills, and that the latter could also be questioned if necessary. Not for nothing was the sheriff at his tourn referred to as "justice for the day". Since on the evidence of Appendix I(b) nos. 5, 9 and 18 raisings of the hue were presented to the eyre as to local courts, the eyre can plausibly be seen as just the last, grandest and most public of a series of courts, an occasional extension of a system in operation all the time and which it served mainly to regulate and supervise.

On the face of it such a system left little scope for the direct exercise of royal power in matters of law enforcement. There is no doubt that the king's courts were widely respected, and that for those who could get it the king's justice was regarded as the best to be had.[44] But in a county as remote as Devon access to the royal courts at Westminster was restricted by distance, while assizes for land actions, though held regularly within the county, were inevitably the preserve of free landowners. Criminal cases, if they were to be heard in the king's court, tended to be kept for the eyre. Throughout his realm the eyre made manifest the omnipresence of the king's peace, and enhanced the king's position as the fount of justice, while also giving him access to revenues which that position traditionally conferred on him, but though by doing so it gave an important and imposing demonstration of royal authority, it was of its nature only temporary, and effective power in a county like Devon continued to lie less in the hands of the king and his representatives than in those of local lords and landowners. There were few great lords in thirteenth-century Devon, but a great many squires and gentry,[45] linked to one another by tenurial and marital ties.[46] These men were the "community of the shire", the suitors to the County Court;[47] it was they who made the bargain with the crown which in 1204 led to the disafforestation, and the county could not be governed without their cooperation. Their local authority stemmed from their wealth as landowners, reinforced by their judicial powers, and the control over lesser men these two factors gave them. The powers of jurisdiction claimed by Devon landowners were rarely very impressive in themselves; in 1281/82 only two lords claimed to have the major franchise

---

[42]Cam, *Hundred Rolls*, pp. 118–28.
[43]*CRR* III pp. 158–9.
[44]Pollock and Maitland Vol. I pp. 202–3.
[45]Hoskins, *Devon*, pp. 74–5.
[46]As can be seen in Pole, *Collections, passim*.
[47]R. C. Palmer, *The County Courts of Medieval England 1150–1350* (Princeton 1982) p. 78.

of return of writs (a franchise was a royal privilege enjoyed by a subject, usually relating to powers of government, in this case the right to administer royal writs, to the complete exclusion of the sheriff and his staff)[48], and one of these was disclaimed. But 78 had the right to hold a view of frankpledge and 65 had private gallows – many had both.[49] View of frankpledge, a franchise held by most, probably all, the lords of the Devon hundreds, gave its holder jurisdiction over the business otherwise dealt with by the sheriff when presented to him at his tourn. Presentments of crown pleas and other royal rights could only be recorded by the coroners with a view to later consideration in a higher court, usually eyre or gaol delivery; orders would be given for the arrest of suspected criminals, but there should be no trial of such cases at the tourn. Nonetheless a good deal of material would remain for immediate scrutiny; of the articles of the tourn in Appendix II(b), it seems likely that presentments under nos. 7, 12, 13, 15, 16, 18, 23, 24, 27, 30 and 31 were always, and under nos. 8, 28 and 29 at least sometimes, dealt with on the spot – a fairly wide range of business, profitable to the lord with jurisdiction over it.

With the view of frankpledge, for lords who held a hundred or its manorial equivalent (manors which had acquired independent hundredal jurisdiction by obtaining their own view of frankpledge were often themselves informally referred to as hundreds, cf. no. 265), went the ordinary business of the Hundred Court, which in 1234 was said to have cognisance of "pleas of battery and brawls that do not amount to felony, of the wounding and maiming of beasts, and of debts that can be collected without a royal writ."[50] Felonies were those crimes made "hateful to God and man" by their heinous nature;[51] certain crimes, notably homicide and grand larceny, were always felonies and so were always justiciable in the king's courts (larceny could also be dealt with in privileged private courts). But lesser offences only came under royal jurisdiction if a plaintiff chose to allege breach of the king's peace and felony, something he was under no obligation to do, and it seems certain that very many such offences – trespasses in medieval, torts in modern, parlance – were prosecuted in local courts. Hundred and County Courts had broadly similar jurisdictions in criminal cases,[52] but it seems likely that for most plaintiffs with personal injuries to complain of, especially among the peasantry, the Hundred Court, for all that it met less often than the County,[53] would usually have been their preferred source of redress, both because in a county as large as Devon it must often have been easier of access than the County Court at Exeter, and because of the place it occupied in the structure of local seigneurial power.

Taken together, the ordinary business of the Hundred Court, and the extra business provided by a view of frankpledge, must have covered a substantial proportion of the quarrels, lawsuits and business concerns of

---

[48]See M. T. Clanchy, "The Franchise of Return of Writs", in *TRHS* 5th Series 17 (1967) pp. 59–82.   [49]Figures from *PQW* pp. 164–80.
[50]Cam, *Hundred Rolls*, p. 181.
[51]Pollock and Maitland Vol. II. p. 466.
[52]For the County Court's jurisdiction see Bracton *De Legibus* Vol. II p. 436, f.154b.
[53]In 1258/59 Shebbear hundred had ten sessions and the tourn, while the County Court met thirteen times – E370/5/25 mm2–5.

those who came within their jurisdiction, and allowed the privileged possessor of that jurisdiction to exercise an important degree of social and judicial control over his tenants, a control which the franchise of gallows, of the right to hang thieves taken in possession of stolen goods, can only have enhanced. These franchises and powers of jurisdiction were highly valued, carefully organised – around 1270 four tenants of Newenham abbey were performing executions in return for their tenements, with one taking the prisoner to the gallows, another putting the gallows up, a third supplying the ladder and the fourth doing the hanging[54]– and jealously protected. It was one of the peculiar customs of Devon that the sheriff should hold only one tourn yearly instead of the two usual elsewhere[55]– since it was at his tourn that the sheriff administered the view of frankpledge it may have been regarded with particular suspicion as a potential rival to private jurisdictions. Certainly the tourn was more than once a source of contention between sheriff and landowners,[56] while the sheriff who held more than one tourn found himself the subject of vociferous complaint.[57] The inward-looking localism of the county was thus reinforced by the concentration of judicial power in the hands of its leading landowners; the authority of the sheriff, and of the king whose power was thus nominally exercised, is likely to have been commensurately restricted.

CENTRAL GOVERNMENT AND LOCAL GOVERNMENT

It needs to be said that there is no evidence that the crown aspired to any minute supervision of the day-to-day processes of law enforcement – a policy utterly beyond the capacity of any medieval government. The king may have been ultimately responsible for law and order within his realm, but as Henry III himself observed in 1249, "I am only one man and am neither willing nor able to bear the burdens of the whole realm without assistance",[58] and where law enforcement was concerned, as his legislative enactments showed, he expected such assistance from every able-bodied man, free and unfree alike. By the 1230s, however, the central government was beginning to aim at a greater and more immediate measure of control over the localities, both to ensure peace and justice for the king's subjects and to ensure the king's own rights and revenues – justice was a major source of income as well as a means of exercising power. The 1238 Devon crown pleas refer to several of the ways whereby the king involved himself directly in the processes of law enforcement and local government, to the writs by which he made his wishes known (323, 433), to the commisions of gaol delivery – groups of justices appointed to try the suspects imprisoned in a gaol – of which four are recorded as issued for Exeter between 1228 and 1238, and which helped to keep the processes of accusation and arrest ticking over (86, 255, 441), and to the granting of pardons and bail (37, 174, 203, 323, 466, 474, 626). They shed

[54]BL Arundel 17 f.36v.
[55]Authorised by the charter of 1204, see n. 27 above.
[56]*CRR* III pp. 158–9; E159/10 m9d.
[57]Bodl.Dodsw.MSS Vol. 76 f.33, *RH* pp. 63, 66, 79, 81.
[58]Matthew Paris, *Chronica Majora* ed. H. R. Luard Vol. V (RS 1880) p. 57.

light on the behaviour of local officials, and, above all, they illustrate with great clarity the use of the eyre as a means of investigation and control, through the inquest into hundreds.

The king had his permanent agents in the shires, in the shape of a wide range of officials which he could hope to use as a counterbalance to the power of the county landowners; there were, however, serious problems of control. There were obvious dangers that officials would be corrupt and extortionate, and that they would come to take on too much of the colour of their surroundings, consequently putting local or personal interests before royal ones. At the bottom end of the hierarchy of officials came beadles and bailiffs, performing mainly admonitory and coercive functions, delivering summonses and making distraints (220). Since these men might have had to buy their posts, in the expectation that they would subsequently recoup their outlays as best they could (the beadle of Wonford was paying 30s. yearly for his office by 1285[59]) small-scale corruption among them was probably both inevitable and continuous, while their outlook is likely to have been uninhibitedly local. The position of the coroner was less clear-cut. His functions, to keep, to record, the pleas of the crown, which meant above all holding inquests on dead bodies, conducting abjurations and recording proceedings in the County Court, made him both a link between the structure of local law enforcement and the eyre – his rolls were a vital source of information for the justices, who used them as checks on juries' presentments (549) – and an important part of the former. There were five Devon coroners in 1238, one for Lifton and four for the rest of the shire – perhaps, as in 1281/82, one served in the parts east of the Exe, one south of the Cornish road and two north of it.[60] They were all local landowners, but they seem more likely than the beadles and bailiffs to have been aware of their wider responsibilities, not least because they all served the crown in various other capacities, as assize commissioners, gaol delivery justices, tax assessors and the like. In 1238 few faults, and mostly unimportant (8, 29, 34, 615, 631), were found with them, possibly because jurors were reluctant to expose the shortcomings of men who were their social peers or superiors, possibly because the coroners were genuinely conscientious – the insults offered to them by the abbot of Tavistock's steward over the valuation of chattels belonging to one of the abbot's tenants (255) suggests that at least sometimes they were capable of putting the king's interests before local ones.

But the linchpin of local government, and the point where the need for central control was greatest, was the sheriff, the crown's principal executive and peace-keeping officer in a shire. The need for control may have seemed greater in Devon than in most other counties – after the disafforestation of 1204 a desire for independence seems to have asserted itself there, culminating in a payment in 1225 of 200 marks "for having a sheriff from themselves" for the next three years.[61] Since most, if not all, the recent sheriffs had been local men[62] (William le Pohier, sheriff from

[59]JUST/1/194 m2.
[60]JUST/1/186 m47d.
[61]E372/70 m13d.
[62]Details of Devon shrievalties from *PRO Lists and Indexes no. 9* p. 34. See also the notes on individual sheriffs, as indicated by the case-numbers in brackets.

1222 to 1224, may have been an outsider), what the men of Devon meant by "a sheriff from themselves" was probably really "a sheriff like themselves", one who would run the shire with their interests in mind, unlike, it may be assumed, William Brewer the younger, who was sheriff when the bargain was made, and who, like his redoubtable father, was probably too much of a royalist for local tastes. Devon's anxiety to have a local man as sheriff underlines the crown's problem in its relations with the shires, at a time when it was increasingly concerned to extract as much revenue as possible from them. It could not do without local cooperation, but if it sought that cooperation on a locality's own terms, it might lose effective control. The best sheriff, probably, was local but not too local, perhaps a man who had interests or had gained experience elsewhere, and was thus responsive, without being over-amenable, to the wishes of those he governed.

Devon had eight sheriffs between 1228 and 1238, of whom the first, William de Ralegh (the county's choice of three years earlier, a fact which in itself makes it extremely unlikely that this was the future royal justice), was replaced shortly after the 1228 eyre, and another, Peter de Rivaux, played no active part in the administration of the shire. But the remaining six were men whose differing qualifications illustrate some of the options open to the crown in its efforts to find a suitable sheriff for a remote and imperfectly tractable county. Two of them, Roger la Zuche (280) and Robert de Vallibus (513), had important properties in Devon, but most of their estates lay elsewhere – perhaps it was hoped that such a division of interests would make these men acceptable in Devon but not too malleable under local pressure. But Robert de Vallibus only served for a few months, while Roger la Zuche appears to have left routine administration largely to his subordinate Rannulf de Cerne (50), whose record in 1238 suggests that he made himself profoundly unpopular. Thomas de Cirencestre (3), who had estates in Devon and had previously served there in other capacities, may also have been meant to prove acceptable through non-residence, since he was also sheriff of Somerset and Dorset for most of his term in Devon, but the fact that he too operated in the latter shire through an unpopular underling, Thomas de la Wyle (187), probably nullified any gains his inevitable absences might have secured.

The charges against de Cerne and de la Wyle in 1238 help explain why such men, essentially professional administrators, were disliked in the shires,[63] and why counties like Devon wanted their own men as sheriffs. It was not just social snobbery, the landed gentry's distaste for career officials; rather because the latter were professionals they were efficient, because they were men of little standing or substance they were always liable to feather their own nests, in either capacity they were bound to seem grasping. From the crown's point of view they probably gave satisfaction, but in the aftermath of Richard Marshal's revolt such satisfaction may have seemed too dearly bought. Peter de Russeaus, sheriff between January and May 1234, appears to have been another such professional – he had been constable of Bridgwater castle and an

---

[63]D. A. Carpenter, "The Decline of the Curial Sheriff in England 1194–1258", in EHR 91 (1976) p. 20.

agent of Peter de Rivaux[64]– but his successor in office, Nicholas de Molis (596), was by contrast a man of varied talents and of considerable importance at court and in the king's service generally. Appointed in the aftermath of the fall of Peter de Rivaux, he seems to have devoted little time or attention to Devon, but this did not matter, since his undersheriff, Walter of Bath, made himself so far agreeable to both county and crown that, having succeeded Nicholas as sheriff in 1236, he remained in office until 1251. Few and unimportant were the shortcomings laid to his charge in 1244 and 1249, and although after his replacement as sheriff inquiries into his alleged malpractices led to his having to make fine for ten gold marks, the fact that he was subsequently pardoned this sum suggests that the crown responded gratefully to his long term of office.[65] Yet the fact that there had been little complaint against him during his shrievalty, in contrast to the allegations of "trespasses and injuries" made after it, and his personal advancement while he was sheriff, show how difficult it was for the crown to exercise control over and through its officials in a shire like Devon; in 1237 Walter had found himself at loggerheads with many of the leading knights of the county,[66] but thereafter he did rather more than just make his peace with them, since he married the sister of Robert Giffard of Bickington and ended his days as lord of the manor of Colebrooke and much else besides.[67] His origins are uncertain – he may have come from Somerset, as his name suggests[68]– but if he was not a Devon man at the outset of his career he was surely one at the end of it, and as such he is likely to have been ultimately less useful to the crown.

THE INQUEST INTO HUNDREDS[69]

Extending royal authority through the activities of royal officials was thus likely to be a slow, laborious and uncertain business. The inquests into the holding of hundreds conducted in 1238 show how the eyre could be used to the same end, but in the hope of quicker and greater gains. These inquests need to be placed in the context of government policies in the 1230s. It was a period of "consistent attention to detail and of persistent endeavours to supervise localities"[70] on the part of the central government, of attempts to exploit the crown's resources to the utmost and of continuous efforts to recover royal rights and revenues which had passed into private hands. In the brief period of the ascendancy of Peter de Rivaux (1232–1234) there may have been investigations made into the warrants by which holders of franchises enjoyed their privileges – at the 1232 Buckinghamshire eyre the king could take it for granted that the justices would be inquiring into "encroachments by liberties and others at his expense"[71]– while later in the 1230s rigorous and extensive scrutiny

---

[64]*CCR* 1231–34 p. 346; *CPR* 1232–47 p. 95.
[65]*CPR* 1247–58 p. 112.
[66]*CRR* XV no. 1983.
[67]*Devon FFI* nos. 367, 457, 458, 477, 480, 510, 554, 563.
[68]*Somersetshire Pleas* no. 750.
[69]For what follows I am heavily indebted to Drs. M. T. Clanchy and R. C. Stacey for information and advice.
[70]M. T. Clanchy, *England and its Rulers 1066–1272* (London 1983) p. 223.
[71]F. M. Powicke, *King Henry III and the Lord Edward* (Oxford 1947) pp. 110–11; JUST/1/62 m8.

was made of the tenure of the royal demesne manors and forests. Thus in Devon William le Flemeng was challenged in his possession of the manor of Holditch,[72] though he ultimately secured himself in it, while the citizens of Exeter found it necessary to pay 25 marks for a confirmation of their charters.[73] Although no direct evidence survives to explain why an inquest into hundreds was called for, or why Devon was chosen as the proper county for it, it may be surmised that such inquests were both in keeping with the main trends of government policy and of a sort to reflect the part played in the direction of that policy by William de Ralegh, whose position as the king's leading councillor is amply attested by his appearance as royal spokesman at the Westminster parliament of 1237.[74] A Devon man, treasurer of Exeter cathedral, Ralegh had served as a justice both of assize and gaol delivery in the county in the 1230s,[75] and must have known it well. He was well placed to suggest a programme of inquests into hundreds in Devon as a possible test for future inquests elsewhere, knowing, as he surely did, how important a part the Hundred Courts played in the local government of the shire, how many of them were in private hands, and not least, how few of them were held by royal charter. If there was to be a substantial advance in royal authority, Ralegh may have reasoned, the deeply entrenched positions of local oligarchies like the gentry of Devon would have to be undermined. That the county chosen for this experiment was also geographically isolated and relatively lacking in great lordships may also have occurred to him.

The hundred in its pre-Conquest origins was a territorial unit grouped round a royal manor, to which its inhabitants delivered such produce as was required of them for the maintenance of the king and his retainers, and which also served as a centre of government and jurisdiction.[76] In 1086 the great majority of the hundred-manors of Devon were held by the king, but thereafter successive monarchs were extremely generous with them,[77] and by 1238 only one was still in the crown's possession (452). The fact that its origins could make possession of a hundred seem an especially royal right was no doubt a principal justification of the inquiries into the warrants by which private individuals now held the Devon hundreds. The jurisdictional value of those hundreds is more obvious than their financial worth. When at the 1249 eyre an assessment was given of the value of each hundred, the figure was always a low one, and the Hundred Rolls invariably put a far lower value on the hundred than on its hundred-manor. The manor of Bampton, for instance, was valued at £20 yearly in 1274/75, the hundred at only 13s. 4d.[78] Such assessments of hundreds may, however, have been fossilised at artificially low rates, related to ancient valuations rather than to their true worth, and how unrealistic they could be is vividly brought out by the presentment of the Black Torrington jurors in 1249 telling how Alan la Zuche, who held that

---

[72] E159/11 mm8, 9; E159/12 m13.
[73] E372/81 m6.
[74] Matthew Paris, *Chronica Majora* ed. H. R. Luard Vol. III (RS 1876) p. 380; see also the introduction to Bracton, *De Legibus* Vol. III, especially pp. xxxv–xlii.
[75] Meekings, *Studies*, chapter XI; *CPR 1225–32* p. 516; C66/45 m5d.
[76] H. Cam, *Liberties and Communities in Medieval England* (London 1963) pp. 64–90.
[77] The histories of the individual hundreds are discussed in footnotes to the text.
[78] *RH* p. 64.

hundred, had farmed it to Richard de Wanford for one mark yearly; Richard had in his turn farmed it to Henry de Tracy for seven marks *per annum*, while Henry had made it over to his bailiffs for twelve.[79] Ralegh could have had grounds to hope for financial gains if any hundreds were recovered as a result of the justices' inquiries.

How the inquests were organised, how much notice was given to the holders of hundreds that they must be ready to justify their tenures, is obscure. In a few cases juries made rather cursory presentments (176, 218, 280, 707), which may have helped make up for the absence of the lords of the hundreds in question, but which hardly amounted to a satisfactory claim on those lords' behalf, and do not argue that the jurors had come prepared to make one. The fact that in the absence of Gilbert de Turberville, lord of South Molton, no claim at all was made, may suggest that both Gilbert and jurors were unprepared for the justices' inquiries. The ability of the lords of Colyton (68), Halberton (168), Axminster (224), Black Torrington (273) and Braunton (301) hundreds to produce charters in support of their rights, makes it likely that some notice was given, but it may not have been very much. Richard Burdun, lord of half of Teignbridge hundred, claimed to have a charter from Henry II, but was unable to produce it (720), and may have set off for the eyre before he learnt he would need it, and it is probably significant that the lord of Shirwell hundred was not present on the first day of the eyre, but came later to claim his hundred (342, 343); he may have intended at first to stay away, only to change his mind when he learnt what the consequences of absence might be. Ralegh may well have been anxious not to give too much advance warning of his intentions, for fear of meeting concerted opposition, but to have given none at all might have made the entire enterprise futile.

As a means of persuading the lords of the Devon hundreds to appear and show their warrants, the eyre was a success. The earl of Devon, who was a minor, naturally did not attend to claim his six hundreds, though in three cases (518, 532, 543) a claim of sorts was made for him, and North Molton was in the king's hand because the young Alan la Zuche had yet to pay his relief for possession of his father's lands (280); otherwise only Gilbert de Turberville neither came himself nor made any arrangement to be represented in his absence, and his hundred of South Molton was taken into the king's hand (295). Of the hundreds which were claimed, by or for their lords, fourteen were said to be held on the strength of ancient tenure only. Occasionally a note was made that further discussion of a claim seemed called for, but usually the justices made no recorded comment. No doubt it was intended that their findings should be scrutinised by Ralegh and his colleagues back at Westminster, and that scrutiny should be followed by action, either in the form of resumptions or in demands that ancient prescriptive right be replaced by expensive royal charters. In the end, however, no action was taken. The evidence is purely circumstantial, but it is possible to point to a number of events which together are likely to have led to a reversal of policy. In the first place, and of prime importance, the dominance of William de Ralegh, already shaken by the revolt of Richard of Cornwall early in 1238, was almost certainly further

[79] JUST/1/176 m42d.

undermined by his breach with the king after his (near) election to the see of Winchester later that year, following which he left the royal council to become bishop of Norwich in 1239. As Ralegh lost ground, and was replaced by Stephen de Segrave, who reversed most of Ralegh's policies, so the pressure for action on Devon must have been markedly reduced.[80]

At the same time, resistance in Devon is likely to have been building up, crystallising round the figure of Baldwin de Redvers, earl of Devon, who probably came of age late in 1238.[81] The earl, who would in any case have been the natural leader of county society, had strong personal motives for opposing the crown's policy with regard to hundreds – he held six of them, far more than anyone else, and was jealous of his rights in them (his earliest recorded action after his coming of age was to litigate in the Bench for suits to his hundred of Hayridge),[82] but does not appear to have had a charter for any of them. Nor did Baldwin lack influential allies, for he is likely to have had the support of Richard of Cornwall, the king's brother, whose ward he had been and whose friend he remained – it was Richard who secured Baldwin's formal investiture as earl of Devon on Christmas Day 1239.[83] Earl Richard appears to have been a careful protector of his ward's interests, appointing one of his own servants to manage Baldwin's Devon estates (16). At a time when Ralegh's policies were everywhere being reversed, the two earls probably found it easy to prevent action being taken on the hundreds of Devon. Consequently the holders of those hundreds remained undisturbed in their tenures. Gilbert de Turberville recovered South Molton – there is no evidence that he had to pay for it – and nobody who held a hundred by ancient tenure only seems to have felt obliged to obtain a royal charter to confirm him in his possession. At the time of the *Quo Warranto* inquests in 1281/82 most of the hundreds of Devon were held by members of the same families that had held them in 1238, and exactly the same claims were made to justify tenure on both occasions; if anything, even less documentary evidence was presented at the later date, since Thomas de Waninforde, on whose behalf a charter was produced in 1238, pleaded ancient tenure alone in 1281/82, and Roger de Mules, to whose father Henry III had given Haytor and Stanborough (596, 707), though he claimed to have a charter, found that he could not lay hands on it, and therefore referred the justices to the Chancery rolls.[84] Whether as a means of recovering royal rights, or of forcing the leading men of Devon to purchase documentary titles for their hundreds, the eyre of 1238 was a failure.

That this should have been so illustrates the difficulties under which the crown laboured rather than the futility of the eyre. The latter was periodic and occasional, as well as liable to diversion from its purposes by political interests, whereas the local gentry were all too permanent. It was the sheriff's own permanence which in the end made him probably more useful than the eyre as a means of extending the king's authority in a county like Devon; he was always there, with traditional functions and responsibilities whose general acceptance gave him the power to make his

---

[80] Information from Dr. R. C. Stacey.
[81] *Rot.Fin.I.* p. 318.
[82] *CRR* XVI nos. 1023, 1035.
[83] Matthew Paris, *Chronica Majora* ed. H. R. Luard Vol. IV (RS 1877) p. 1.
[84] *PQW* pp. 164, 173–4.

presence felt – if his office had been a sinecure the men of Devon would not have cared who held it – and the exchequer behind him to keep him under supervision. Indeed, it was the steadily increased pressure from the exchequer during the 1240s and 1250s, acting through the sheriff and his underlings, which did most to secure for the crown what it wanted, a greater control of the shires and a much fuller exploitation of its own resources in them.[85] But achieving this was a slow business, and the local power of the country gentry was arguably not truly shaken until the coming of the railways and the repeal of the Corn Laws. Walter of Bath, whatever his merits, seems to have been absorbed into county society in the end, and Devon's localism, not least with regard to the king's representative in its midst, certainly persisted after his shrievalty – in 1272 the knights of the county petitioned that Roger de Pridias be dismissed, to be replaced by "another knight of their own county".[86]

THE INCIDENCE, DISTRIBUTION AND CAUSES OF CRIME

Homicide A maximum of 151 killings was presented in 1238, though as already noted, there were probably a few more, while at least two of those presented had been committed before 1228 (323, 577) and another had been committed in Somerset (664). Such figures present considerable difficulties of interpretation. In eighteen cases people were charged and acquitted of homicide without others being described as convicted, so leaving doubt as to whether anyone had been killed, or was even dead (cf. 174). On the whole it is likely that such cases represent deaths in suspicious circumstances, but homicide cannot be taken for granted. A further difficulty is that even where there is no doubt that someone had been killed by violence, jurors and justices made no discernible distinction, as their modern counterparts would do, between premeditated murder and manslaughter,[81] that is, homicide which, though culpable, had not been committed by deliberate intent. The fact that most of those named as suspects had fled, and that fugitives were almost always treated alike, is certainly the principal cause of this failure to make such distinctions. The figures are without much doubt also distorted by primitive medicine; men and women died when wounds turned gangrenous well after the brawls in which they had received them, the woman who died seven weeks after such an injury (332) being only an extreme example.

These figures suggest an average number of 15 killings *per annum* in Devon between 1228 and 1238. By comparison figures from the next two Devon eyres, of 1244 and 1249, show 80 killings at the former and 69 at the latter, a total of 149 over eleven years, or a small decline to an average rate of 13.5 *per annum*.[88] This may attest the usefulness of the eyre, which had been coming at nine or ten year intervals between the beginning of

---

[85]See Carpenter, art. cit. n. 63 above, pp. 21–31 [86]Bodl. Dodsw.MSS Vol. 76 f. 33.
[87]See T. A. Green, "The Jury and the English Law of Homicide 1200–1600", in *Michigan Law Review* 74 (1976) pp. 414–99.
[88]For figures from some other counties during the 1230s and 1240s, see H. R. T. Summerson, *The Maintenance of Law and Order in England 1227–1263* (Unpublished Cambridge Ph.D. Dissertation, 1976) chapter 5.

Henry III's reign and 1238, but now came three times between 1238 and 1249, and probably also reflects the value of administrative continuity, with a single sheriff in office during all three eyres. The distribution of homicides in 1238 suggests that local government in some parts of the county needed tightening up. One might expect the parts east of the Exe, a generally fertile and prosperous region,[89] likely to be relatively heavily populated, to have had the highest homicide rate, but in fact it had the lowest. In particular it is surprising that more killings should have been reported from the regions north of the Cornish road, which included many of the poorest parts of the county, while though the regions south of the Cornish road contained the richest lands in all Devon, they also included almost the whole of Dartmoor. Since in both 1244 and 1249 the distribution of homicides was in fact as might be expected,[90] with more homicides east of the Exe than in the other two subdivisions, it may well be that eyre and sheriff between them had indeed brought about an improvement in local government west of the Exe. It is noteworthy that at all three eyres killings by unknown criminals were most numerous in the parts east of the Exe; to vagrants and bandits this was clearly the most attractive region in Devon, as well as the most accessible from the rest of England. It was not these men who killed west of the Exe, but those who lived there already, and the homicide rate among the latter may have fallen when and because the ordinary processes of law enforcement had been brought more effectively to bear upon them.

The killers named at the 1238 eyre were almost invariably men – only five out of a total of 146 people described as killers were women. Details bearing on the status of these men are not always given, but 88 were said to be in tithings and fifteen in mainpasts (see no. 31), so they were either unfree or in a humble state of dependence. Six were said to be vagrants, three had been harboured by communities without being obliged to join tithings, one was a free man (650) and three were clerks, one of whom was convicted in court (103). 59 of them had no chattels, 23 had chattels worth less than 3s. 4d. – the minimum value of property on which the thirtieth of 1237 had been levied,[91] used here as a rough yardstick for poverty. Juries often undervalued chattels, and men who knew that they were suspected of serious crimes sometimes fled taking their moveables with them (Appendix I(a) no. 4), while since prisoners awaiting trial were maintained out of their own property, a suspect could easily be considerably poorer by the time he was convicted in court than he had been when he entered prison. But on the whole it seems legitimate to conclude that most killers were poor men, of low social status, living in the countryside. The low number of killings committed in urban communities is indeed one of the most striking characteristics of all thirteenth-century plea rolls.[92] In 1238 fifteen homicides, at the most, were presented as committed in Exeter and other burghs (it is impossible to tell how many were committed in Tavistock, as burgh and hundred answered together), a tenth of the whole. A high proportion of the Exeter presentments

[89] See *Domesday Geography* pp. 290–4.
[90] See Appendix III.
[91] W. Stubbs, *Select Charters* (9th Edn., Oxford 1921) pp. 358–9.
[92] J. B. Given, *Society and Homicide in Thirteenth-Century England* (Stanford, California 1977) p. 175.

concern strangers, particularly thieves, and it is certainly possible that civic *esprit de corps* sometimes caused the citizens to unite to protect one another by concealing crimes committed by their fellows. Yet the homicide rate in Exeter, at least, may have been genuinely low. Better-than-usual policing may have contributed to this. The assize of the watch of 1233 had laid down that there must be watchmen at night in every vill throughout the summer months,[93] but by December 1240 Exeter was apparently being patrolled by watchmen all the year round.[94] But equally valuable, probably, were the opportunities for settling quarrels and obtaining redress which the mayor's court provided – since it met every Monday, anybody with a grievance could hope to obtain redress, or at least set in motion the process of obtaining it, within a week of the initial injury. As well as charges of theft, sexual assault and wounding, its early rolls record actions on insults, brawls and threats to life and limb, and show it to have been competent to take pledges from those involved for their keeping the peace in future, to reconcile them to one another and probably, since they were often claimed, to award damages as well. Such functions were important because they could stifle at birth precisely the sort of quarrels which, if left unchecked, could easily lead to violence.

All the signs are that most killings resulted from disputes between peasants, from quarrels between labouring men. Homicide in the home is rarely reported in 1238. The case of the man who burnt his home with his wife and children inside it (671) certainly argues a measure of disillusion with domestic life, to put it mildly, and two cases were reported of wives abetting the slaying of their husbands (184, 579), while two other women were acquitted of killing their husbands (291, 756). The case of a man who killed his sister (560) is the only other killing within the family recorded in 1238 – although a priest's son was alleged to have killed his brother, the death was subsequently found to have been accidental (392). One reason why husbands and wives rarely killed one another is likely to have been the severity of the penalties for doing so. The wife who killed her husband did not just commit felony, she had committed petty treason against her lord, and on conviction was liable to be burnt,[95] while it was not entirely unknown for the husband who killed his wife to be condemned to undergo the penalties for petty treason also, in his case being dragged on a hurdle to the gallows for execution.[96] Another reason was certainly the strength of family ties, reinforced as they were by religion and social custom. Excessive violence within the family was disapproved of, and neighbours and relatives might interfere to stop it – in 1281/82 the defence offered to an appeal of abduction and assault, that "the woman went of her own good will with Hugh her nephew as her husband often beat her", was largely upheld by the trial jury.[97] The high value placed on children probably accounts for the rarity of reported infanticides – the only one mentioned in 1238 may have been accidental (333), though three were presented in 1249, two of them babies drowned by their mothers.[98] It is

---
[93] *CCR* 1231–34 pp. 309–10.
[94] JUST/1/175 m50.
[95] F. M. Nichols (ed.), *Britton* Vol. I (Oxford 1865) p. 42; JUST/1/186 m5d.
[96] JUST/1/759 m15d.
[97] JUST/1/186 m23d.
[98] JUST/1/176 mm36d, 44, 45, cf. Given, op. cit., p. 61.

possible, however, that the early age at which children might be put to work may have led to some killings of the very young passing unrecognised as such – in all the Devon rolls there is no case more pathetic than that of nine year old Matilda, daughter of Gilbert de Stodlegh, who fell asleep while guarding William de Wolmereswurthy's beasts, and was so severely beaten by William's wife that she died six weeks later.[99]

Most killings were the work of men, their victims almost always other men, those they came into contact with as they worked and in the other routines of daily life. Six killings were the work of a group of three people or more (16, 57, 152, 232, 310, 473), another fifteen of two people, but the great majority undoubtedly involved one individual killing another. This is in sharp contrast with Professor Given's finding that homicide in thirteenth-century England had a "markedly collective character",[100] but reasons can be suggested for it, reasons as much procedural as social. Juries naming suspects, particularly those who had, for whatever reason, made themselves scarce, must always have been tempted to point an accusing finger at everybody who could plausibly be accused, in the hope that such a blanket coverage would at any rate make sure that the guilty were included in the charge;[101] in the 1230s, however, the appeal was still a highly important means of prosecuting homicide – 53 appeals of homicide are recorded at the 1238 Devon eyre, and 68 killers were said to have been already outlawed, compared with the 50 whose exigents were ordered during the eyre – and the personal nature of the appeal made it much more likely to be limited and precise in its scope, since bereaved kinsmen would usually know exactly who they wanted to bring retribution upon and would not extend their appeals wider than was necessary. Such an outlook may in these years also have communicated itself to jurors, who consequently also restricted their charges as far as possible to the obviously guilty. In the small communities of much of thirteenth-century Devon it must often, in fact, have been unnecessary to make wide-ranging accusations, since it would be perfectly clear from the first who had killed his neighbour, but there may also have been a general determination, perhaps *because* so many communities were small and therefore especially vulnerable to internal frictions, to limit the damage a homicide could inflict, by pinpointing the killer and getting rid of him through arrest or outlawry, but curbing further accusations and proceedings thereafter.

The motives which prompted acts of violence among people dead for some 650 years can hardly be other than elusive, but it can at least be pointed out that the emotions of medieval men and women were always close to the surface and that the prevailing conditions of peasant life, in particular, were anything but conducive to a relaxed state of body or mind, with the discomforts of domestic life, in badly-built, draughty and smoke-filled houses,[102] being surely exacerbated, in commonly insanitary conditions, by the more intimate pains of ill-health – the twelfth-century miracles of St. Nectan at Hartland, and the miracles attributed in 1361 to

---

[99] JUST/1/186 m13d.
[100] Given, op. cit., p. 43.
[101] A suggestion I owe to the late Professor R. B. Pugh.
[102] See G. Beresford, "Three Deserted Medieval Settlements on Dartmoor", in *Medieval Archaeology* 23 (1979) pp. 98–158.

the late vicar of Whitstone in north Cornwall, give an impression of a countryside full of men and women crippled, blind, paralysed and insane.[103] Pain and discomfort helped breed irritability, and did so among people who were not only easily moved emotionally but whose way of living probably promoted a frame of mind according to which all problems were solved by physical means. The man who did anything – felling trees, ploughing, digging, reaping – did it first and foremost by the exercise of his physical strength. Such a life was dangerous in itself, and fatal accidents at work were common (e.g. 10, 113, 216, 435, 573). Nor were the other activities of daily life much safer. Travelling, by land or sea, claimed many lives; people died when they fell from ladders (358), when they fell on their own axes or knives (331, 392), when their houses caught fire (372) and when their roofs fell in (675, 699). A rough, hard and dangerous life bred a rough, hard and dangerous people, who had to be stoical about their own sufferings and misfortunes, and had little sympathy to spare for those of others – when the house of a peasant who had refused hospitality to one of the canons of Hartland mysteriously burnt down one night, "he was more annoyed by the reproaches and mockery of his neighbours than by the burning of his house."[104]

The countrymen of thirteenth-century Devon were aggressive, vindictive, acquisitive and suspicious. They were also, in a century in which average life expectancy in England has been estimated at only 35 years,[105] for the most part young, and youth, which for medieval aristocrats has been described as "a time of impatience, turbulence and instability",[106] is not likely to have been a season of greater sobriety and self-restraint among the peasantry, who in Devon, as elsewhere, showed themselves quick to respond to injuries, to meet violence with violence, as with the forceful resistance sometimes offered to the taking of distraints and the impounding of beasts (55, 467, 494), and to quarrel when they felt themselves aggrieved. A sense of grievance could indeed generate a passion for revenge, which might in turn breed a terrible cruelty, even among those who might have been expected to show more restraint. A quarrel which broke out in Exeter on 9 June 1271, among a group consisting mainly of churchmen, led to the parson of Quantoxhead in Somerset threatening Master Thomas de Graham "that he would be revenged on him within three days", and far from letting not the sun go down upon his wrath, he was as good as his word, for on the very next day Master Thomas was set upon at Thorverton by men who killed him and his groom and cut out his tongue for good measure.[107] The professions of killers and their victims are rarely mentioned in the 1238 roll, but it is noteworthy that three millers were among those killed, and eight millers among those named as killers. The frequency with which millers were involved in homicide has been commented on elsewhere.[108] They practised an essential trade, which gave them control over food production at an

---

[103]Chope, *Hartland* pp. 226–32; G. G. Coulton, *A Medieval Garner* (London 1910) pp. 535–37.
[104]Chope, *Hartland* p. 231.
[105]By R. S. Lopez, *The Birth of Europe* (London 1967) p. 398.
[106]G. Duby, *The Chivalrous Society* (trans. C. Postan, London 1977) p. 113.
[107]JUST/1/186 m34d.
[108]Given, op. cit., pp. 86–7.

especially vital point which they were universally suspected of exploiting for dishonest purposes; tension between them and their customers must have been more often the rule than the exception to it, and when, for instance, we read that William the miller had killed William the baker (670), it is easy to imagine how this had come about.

The great majority of those who came to the eyre on homicide charges appear to have been poor men, but the upper orders make some interesting appearances. Their treatment shows that they were favoured, but not usually outrageously so (the case of Simon son of Herbert de Pinu may be an exception, but the plea roll leaves obscure the problem of whether he killed Dolwyn Veg by accident or in a moment of anger – 37). Two bailiffs of hundreds were accused of homicide; judgment by peers in such cases involved a considerably enlarged jury, but the fact that proof came in the form of a verdict by the juries of five hundreds with three vills did not save Robert de la Slade, bailiff of North Tawton, from being convicted and hanged (473). Robert Mercator, bailiff of Witheridge, was acquitted of killing a woman by the verdict of three juries and four vills (377), while the far more eminent Hugh Peverel, lord of Ermington hundred, was cleared of killing Alfred the cook by four juries reinforced by twenty-four knights (583). But the most revealing case in this context involved one of the greatest men in Devon, Henry de Tracy, lord of Barnstaple, who was found to have knowingly harboured one of his servants after the latter had commited homicide (494). The man who harboured a felon, himself committed felony. At this same eyre Roger de Falklefelde was convicted and hanged for harbouring his brother Walter, a suspected thief (267). But Henry de Tracy was not hanged; instead he was able to make fine for the substantial sum of 400 marks. The attitude of the king and his justices was probably not so much one of outright social favouritism and class solidarity as informed by a belief that, as Dr. Clanchy has written, "wrongdoers should indeed be punished with equal severity, but that did not mean that all punishments would be the same."[109] Each man gave what he had to make up for his offence against the peace of God and the king. Roger de Falklefelde had chattels worth only 40s. 8d., so he must give the ultimate forfeit; Henry de Tracy, who had greater resources, incurred a debt which was not discharged until 1247. There is no way of telling whether Hugh Peverel was guilty or not; but his fine of 200 marks, whether it was made for trespass, as recorded in the plea roll (581), or for having a jury, as recorded in the pipe roll, may have been regarded as a sort of fine before judgment (see p. xlvii below), a settling of accounts in advance; since he had already incurred a penalty in keeping with his alleged offence, the jurors may thereafter have felt free to acquit him of it. Rich and poor were obviously not treated exactly alike under the law, but the differences in their treatment were not such as to mean that the rich man could, any more than the poor man, by an act of homicide break it with impunity.

Theft The number of homicides may seem high, and the danger of falling victim to it considerable, but the crimes of which medieval people were

---

[109]M. T. Clanchy, "Highway robbery and trial by battle in the Hampshire eyre of 1249", in R. F. Hunnisett & J. B. Post (eds.) *Medieval Legal Records edited in memory of C. A. F. Meekings* (HMSO, London 1978) p. 46.

most afraid were robbery and theft.[110] They dreaded the brigand who haunted the roadsides, and the bandit who broke in to rob and kill by night, rather than the neighbour they worked alongside by day, even though they might appear more likely to meet a violent death at the hands of the latter than of the former, while slanderous allegations of theft were bitterly resented by those at whom they were directed, as the Exeter mayor's court rolls make abundantly clear.[111] It is not in fact possible to tell how many crimes of theft there were in Devon between 1228 and 1238, since the plea roll makes no attempt to record them all; individual thieves are named, but not the thefts each had committed. The Tiverton veredictum – Appendix I(b) – shows that more burglaries were presented at the eyre than were eventually recorded on its roll, and it is also certain that more thieves were hanged in private courts and at gaol deliveries than the plea roll reports, but there is no way of assessing the extent of the omissions. Such statistics as can be supplied give the impression that thieves were most numerous in the parts east of the Exe; this may have been so, but it would be unwise to rely on the 1238 plea roll for proof of it, as the figures are seriously distorted by the inclusion of seven thieves hanged in two private courts, in separate incidents which would never have been recorded had not the justices detected procedural irregularities in one case (13), and wanted to know by what warrant thieves had been hanged in the other (47). A more reliable deduction would probably be that on the whole thieves were as likely to be found in one part of Devon as another.

Rather more, however, can be said about the thieves themselves. 92 were named in the course of the 1238 eyre, of whom six were women and two were clerks – theft, like homicide, was nearly always committed by men, possibly a reflection of the obvious premium put on masculine strength in such tasks as burgling houses and rustling livestock. 33 of those named as thieves were put in exigent, which ostensibly meant only that they were of ill fame, and left it possible for them to return to the king's peace to stand trial. Such cases were usually dealt with at gaol deliveries, but after the Norfolk and Suffolk eyres of 1234/35 so many returned or were arrested that in August 1235 a special session had to be held to deal with them, and the record of this gives some indication as to the likely guilt or innocence of those put in exigent.[112] A total of 50 names is recorded, of whom one was already outlawed and four, who had been released to pledges, did not attend and were put in exigent again, while three more failed to appear. Of the remaining 42, twelve were hanged and seven were convicted of petty theft. Thus only a minority, though quite a large one, was either guilty or too disreputable to face trial. Those fifty, however, were probably only a small proportion of the total number of exigents, most of whom are likely to have been outlawed. In Devon, where no gaol delivery is recorded as having been ordered between 1238 and October 1242,[113] there was probably no such influx of suspects awaiting trial, and no-one put in exigent in 1238 was cleared at the eyre of 1244.

[110]Given, op. cit., pp. 130–1; B. A. Hannawalt, *Crime and Conflict in English Communities 1300–1348* (Cambridge, Massachussetts, and London 1979) pp. 60, 271.
[111]e.g. EMC 1 mm16, 16d, 18d; EMC 2 m10.
[112]JUST/1/1173 mm6d–7d.
[113]C66/51 m3d.

Most of the thieves put in exigent seem likely to have been outlawed. To be put in exigent was not an infallible sign of guilt, but it may be regarded as a strong pointer in that direction. Of the male thieves recorded in 1238, eighteen were members of tithings and twenty-five were described as vagrants; twenty-eight had no chattels and nine had chattels worth less than 3s. 4d., but in many cases no details are given, probably because none were available, and the true numbers of indigent wanderers were probably a good deal higher.

Contemporaries did not doubt that there could be a direct connection between poverty and theft; in 1246 the English clergy, trying to show why they should not have to pay a papal subsidy, argued that if they did, they would have less to give to the infinite numbers of poor people, some of whom, before dying of starvation, would turn to crime, with horrendous consequences for public order.[114] Theft only became a capital offence when the value of the goods stolen exceeded 12d., because, it was later argued, that was the sum sufficient to keep a man alive for a week,[115] and it would be wrong to hang anyone for stealing it, at least for the first offence. Petty thieves, like Alice the Cornish weaver who stole two pairs of shoes (555), might lose an ear, both as a punishment and as a way of marking them for the future. Thirteenth-century Devon must have contained many desperately poor people living on the very fringes of society, their lives a series of expedients to keep going, maintaining themselves by seasonal labour, mendicancy (262, 275, 286) and crime. When in 1261 Bishop Bronescombe appropriated Dean Prior church to Plympton priory "to mitigate the needs of the paupers and pilgrims converging upon you . . ."[116] this may not have been mere rhetoric.

Some wanderers were probably travelling craftsmen, hawking their talents and their wares round isolated communities which could neither afford to maintain specialist craftsmen nor be entirely self-sufficient. It is tempting to believe that many of the men described as "harboured outside frankpledge" came into this category. In fact, conditions in thirteenth-century Devon seem to have been such as to encourage vagrancy, or at least mobility, thanks to the opportunities offered, in a period of economic advance, by land clearance on wastes and woodlands, by life in one of the small burghs which proliferated after 1204 (three fairs, eight markets, and nine fairs *and* markets were granted to Devon communities by the crown between 1216 and 1238 alone[117]) and by tin mining.[118] But though there were possibilities of prosperity in all these things, there were at the very least equal opportunities of failure – small burghs, for instance, often failed to develop into towns, while clearing wasteland was certainly no guarantee of affluence – and those who so failed, having cut themselves adrift from settled communities, would often have had to keep wandering thereafter, needy, wretched and dangerous.

[114]*Councils and Synods* Part II Vol. I p. 400.
[115]*Britton* Vol. I p. 56 n.i.
[116]*Reg. Bronescombe* p. 65.
[117]Fairs: Okehampton, Brentor, Sidbury. Markets: Teignmouth, Brendon, Combe Martin, "Chirchhamton", Newton Poppleford, Bovey Tracy, Werrington, Kingsbridge. Markets and Fairs: Hatherleigh, Crediton, Bradworthy, Kenton, Dartmouth, Ottery St. Mary, Sheepwash, Rackenford, Ilfracombe.
[118] Cf. G. R. Lewis, *The Stannaries* (London 1908) pp. 36–7.

It may be possible to see differences between villagers and vagrants through comparisons of the status and wealth of suspects put in exigent and thieves who abjured the realm. Of the 33 former, nine had no chattels, but several had moveables worth more than 3s. 4d., and three had free land as well (200, 416, 418), whereas of 35 abjurors, only four had any chattels at all, and the wealthiest of them was only worth 7s. (645). Of the men in exigent at least sixteen were in tithings, whereas of the abjurors only two were in tithings, and nearly all the others were said to be vagrants or wandering thieves – one was an Irishman (322), and others came from Cornwall, Somerset, Wiltshire and Gloucestershire (34, 357, 420, 759, 771). From this it may be deduced that those put in exigent were often, like John le Fatte (128), people who seemed suspiciously well-off – the goods they were alleged to have stolen were almost invariably livestock (e.g. 193, 326, 421), so perhaps alert neighbours had noticed that their flocks and herds had become unaccountably large. Such people may have been disreputable long before they came under a definite suspicion, but they were usually people with a place in village society who had become dishonest under pressure of poverty or sudden temptation, or because their personalities led them that way. The abjurors, by contrast, as recorded in the 1238 roll, were almost all footloose thieves, making a living from whatever they could lay their hands on, until they were spotted in the act of picking and stealing and had to run for their lives to the nearest church; the whole scale of their operations was at a lower level of criminality – not for them the rustling of cows and sheep, when the goods they stole are mentioned, they almost invariably turn out to have been clothes (44, 420, 763, 764, 766).

Some abjurors may have been only occasional or part-time thieves, but others probably shared the lawless existence of the professional criminal. The latter was extremely hard to bring to book by the ordinary processes of law enforcement – how could villagers indict men whose names and whereabouts they did not know? – and was only likely to be caught by chance or through the accusations of an approver.[119] The approver was the medieval equivalent of Queen's evidence, a criminal who having made full confession of his crimes endeavoured to win for himself the right to abjure the realm, so saving his life, by securing the conviction of his associates, either through defeating them in judicial combat or through juries' verdicts. Several arrests on approvers' appeals were recorded in 1238 (35, 325, 552, 743, 746, 748, 749), and two report convictions (746, 749), but most of the approvers mentioned were said to have been already hanged – in Devon, as elsewhere, juries were clearly reluctant to accept the obviously interested stories of self-confessed criminals, and usually acquitted those charged, after which the unsuccessful approver would be hanged. The world of professional crime in thirteenth-century Devon is consequently extremely murky, and most of the evidence for it comes from late in that century. By then the fairs of Devon seem to have become meeting-places for thieves – in 1277, for instance, a man appeared at a gaol delivery who had been "arrested on suspicion at Holsworthy fair because he was found sleeping in a house among thieves";[120] it would not

---

[119]See Clanchy, art. cit. n.109 above; *Wiltshire Crown Pleas 1249* pp. 91–2.
[120]JUST/3/14/1 m7.

be surprising if they were attracted by their large attendance and the opportunities they offered for the disposal of stolen livestock. In the countryside, too, the operations of criminals made some places notoriously dangerous; Haddon Moor, for instance, south-west of Exeter, had by 1300 become so infested by robbers that the canons of Torre declined to cross it in order to attend the bishop.[121] Many of the burglaries and killings attributed to unknown criminals will have been the work of such people. It must be said, however, that thieves were as much a menace to one another as they were to the honest and law-abiding. The justices at the 1280 Somerset eyre heard a bizarre story about four thieves who, having committed a robbery in Devon, probably at Bampton fair, left the county and retreated into Somerset. On their arrival at Winscombe they quarrelled, and three of them united to kill the fourth. They then continued their journey, but soon quarrelled again, and two of them united to kill the third. Once more the survivors resumed their journey, and had crossed into Gloucestershire before they fell out yet again; one of them killed the other, and with the entire proceeds of the original robbery went on his way before being arrested and hanged at the suit of a man from Devon who had apparently been following the robbers, his task no doubt greatly eased by the trail of corpses.[122]

Suicide Suicide was a felony one committed on oneself, and as such it entailed the confiscation of lands and chattels. For this reason both suicides themselves and their chattels were frequently concealed or misrepresented (346, perhaps 762). Bracton distinguished carefully between suicides committed by suspected criminals fearful of conviction and the self-slaughter of those weary of life or in continuous bodily pain, and obscurely between the penalties of forfeiture each respective act incurred.[123] Thirteenth-century justices made no such distinctions. Although some men unquestionably took their own lives so as to forestall a certain hanging – one Dorset man, arrested for theft and put in the stocks at Bryanston, deliberately starved himself to death, a process which took eight days[124] – all suicides were treated alike, and no attempts were made to investigate their motives. Nine suicides – seven men and two women – were presented in 1238. There is no way of telling whether others were successfully hidden, though it seems likely enough – it is noteworthy that of the nine, seven chose to hang themselves, a means of suicide which can hardly be misrepresented as accidental and leaves no doubt as to the determination of the self-killer to make away with himself, whereas the death of Robert le Pestur, who drowned himself (762), was at first thought to be accidental and was only established as suicide at the eyre. It is possible that in other, similar, cases, coroners' juries, uncertain as to the cause of death, gave the benefit of the doubt to the deceased and found as accidental deaths which were in fact self-inflicted. There seems to have been an increase in the number of suicides in Devon as the thirteenth century progressed; two were presented in 1244, eight in 1249 and

[121] D. Seymour, *Torre Abbey* (Exeter 1977) p. 73.
[122] JUST/1/759 m27.
[123] Bracton, *De Legibus* Vol. II pp. 423–24, ff.150, 150b.
[124] JUST/1/213 m30d.

twenty-three in 1281/82. To some extent this must have been due to population growth, but that growth may itself have made life more competitive and more anxious, with ever more people vying for the available resources, and the number of those unable to endure the strain may have increased accordingly.

Rape Although rape, in the sense of a sexual relationship forcibly inflicted by a man on a woman, was a felony, it was almost invariably, until procedure was changed by the first statute of Westminster in 1275,[125] brought to the attention of the king's courts through a personal action, an appeal, on the part of the wronged woman. It is not possible, therefore, any more than it is with thefts, to say how many rapes were actually committed,[126] but it is certainly most improbable that every rape led to an appeal by its victim. Thirteen appeals were recorded in 1238 against twelve men, one man being the subject of two separate appeals (529, 536). Of those appealed, two were already outlawed, and one of these was later captured and hanged at a gaol delivery (441), while another had been outlawed for homicide (405). There were no other convictions. Of the appellors, one was dead by 1238, and six more failed to appear at the eyre. Of the three who did attend and failed to secure convictions, two were too poor to be amerced (585, 613) and another was found to be prosecuting her ex-lover (292). Of those who did not come, two had been unable to find pledges to prosecute, usually a mark of poverty (529, 590). The pattern, in fact, was the normal one for a thirteenth-century eyre, of a small number of appeals largely unsuccessfully brought by women who were commonly either poor or disreputable or both.[127] The same pattern emerges from the 1244 and 1249 eyres, at which a total of nine appeals were made against ten men; in 1249 one man was said to have been outlawed, but at neither was there a conviction in court. Of the appellors, five were either poor or had been unable to find two pledges.

Clearly either respectable women were seldom, if ever, raped, or some consideration inhibited them from prosecuting when they had been so injured. It seems improbable that the men of Devon had the disproportionately higher regard for female chastity than for human life that a comparison of the rape and homicide figures suggests, and the latter possibility is much more likely. Women were deterred from prosecuting by the procedure involved, which was of a sort likely to make the consequences of failing to secure a conviction very serious for themselves. To Glanvill rape was an offence for which "a woman is allowed to make an accusation just as in every case of injury done to her body".[128] In the thirteenth century, however, although the right to prosecute did not vanish, it came to be accompanied by an insistence that in making her appeal, the appellor must show that she had been a virgin until forcibly deflowered – at the 1244 Devon eyre a widow's appeal of rape was

---

[125]See J. B. Post, "Ravishment of women and the statutes of Westminster", in J. H. Baker (ed.), *Legal Records and the Historian* (London 1978) pp. 150–64.
[126]Since a rape and an attempted rape, both by the same man, were presented to the Exeter mayor's court in 1266, some rapes, for all that rape was a felony, may have been prosecuted outside the royal courts, perhaps by omitting a charge of felony – EMC 1 m16d.
[127]See Summerson, op. cit., n.88 above, p. 153.
[128]G. D. G. Hall (ed.), *Glanvill* (London 1965) pp. 175–6.

quashed on the grounds that "a woman has no appeal except for rape of her virginity and the killing of her husband in her arms".[129] In other words, in making her appeal, the appellor had to admit that she was not a virgin, and then try to convince a male jury that she had reached this condition involuntarily. If she failed, she had in effect been convicted of fornication on her own confession. Securing convictions was going to be hard work anyway. Men convicted of rape should in theory have been blinded and castrated; apart from a single case in 1222,[130] no instances of this being done are recorded, but the threat remained, and jurors may have been reluctant to expose fellow-males to it. Some men, then as now, may simply have assumed that all accusations of rape were groundless, and consequently done their best to thwart them – the Sussex knights who tampered with the record of an appeal of rape in their County Court rolls may come into this category.[131] The possibility, sometimes substantiated, that an appeal of rape had been incited or exploited by others to embarrass, intimidate or blackmail their enemies,[132] gave securer grounds for treating it with suspicion.

The appellor's path was thus a very difficult one, potentially embarrassing from beginning to end (a physical examination might be part of it), certainly embarrassing if that end was failure – the unsuccessful appellor must have risked both an amercement for unchastity in a manorial court and a citation to appear in the rural chapter, where the archdeacon presided over cases of sexual misconduct.[133] But the principal reason why women did not bring appeals of rape was surely the consequences for their reputation if they failed to secure convictions. They would certainly find it very hard to make satisfactory marriages, since men with property to transmit would be understandably reluctant to beget their heirs on women so publicly found, as it would so appear, to have been unchaste. Appeals of rape therefore were increasingly brought only by women of low status and reputation, with the inevitable result that jurors became still more reluctant to convict those they accused.

There is no means of knowing whether any of the men appealed and acquitted of rape in 1238 were in fact guilty of the assaults imputed to them, though Hugh de la Kage, appealed of rape by two women (529, 536), would appear to have been at the very least a man of licentious reputation. Nor is it possible to do more than speculate about the motives of the women who made the appeals. Some, of course, may simply have wanted justice for themselves and retribution for those they accused. Appeals of rape did quite often end in the marriage of the parties or in some other form of settlement, but no Devon appellor between 1238 and 1249 achieved either marriage or a settlement; the woman who in 1249 asked for damages did not get them, or indeed a conviction.[134] One appeal, that of Agnes daughter of Robert de Medwille (613), with its somewhat implausible account of a rape perpetrated in her own father's

---

[129] JUST/1/175 m44d; Bracton, *De Legibus* Vol. II pp. 414–19, ff.147, 147b.
[130] Post, art. cit. n.125 above, p. 152.
[131] JUST/1/909A m20d.
[132] e.g. JUST/1/230 m9d; JUST/1/778 mm50, 55; JUST/1/1581 m1d.
[133] See J. Scammell, "The Rural Chapter in England from the Eleventh to the Fourteenth Century", in *EHR* 86 (1971) pp. 1–21.
[134] JUST/1/176 m34.

house in the middle of the night, looks very like an appeal made in the desperate hope of saving a reputation that was already at risk, of persuading the world at large and the neighbourhood in particular that Almaric de Sideham had visited her at night not by assignation but for altogether more sinister purposes.[135] The jurors' task in uncovering the truth in cases of rape was rarely a simple one, and they must often have been right to acquit; that this should have been so was to a large extent the inevitable consequence of the form the action of rape had come to take, and of the social and moral standing of the women who, as a further consequence, were the ones most likely to use it.

APPEALS AND PLAINTS

Apart from receiving presentments about killers and thieves, the justices also heard a large number of personal actions, alleging offences that were almost always less serious (except in the case of rape), but brought within their cognisance by a charge that felony had been committed and the king's peace broken. The vehicle for these charges was the appeal,[136] which was also used to prosecute homicide and rape. In 1238 there were reported 53 appeals of homicide and 13 of rape, and another 135 actions, all but nine of them begun by appeal. The appeal was a highly formal action (e.g. 203, 524, though none of the Devon appeals, as recorded, are as elaborate as some of those to be found elsewhere), requiring that a detailed account of the alleged offence be made in a prescribed form, and that the appellor should offer to prove the truth of it by his body, that is, by judicial combat. In this form the appeal went back to the days when combat and ordeal were the only available forms of proof in criminal cases, and when those appealed could only either fight or, if they were women, or men who were either maimed or under twelve or over sixty years old, opt for the ordeal. In fact they would do neither if they could avoid it; the usual response on the part of the appellee was to "traverse" the appeal, to challenge it on points of detail, as by showing omissions or differences between the present and original forms of the appeal. If this was done, and few appellees found it very difficult, the justices would declare the appeal null and the appellor in mercy for a false appeal (e.g. 99). In the early years of the thirteenth century the form and the content of the appeal were still so closely linked that an error in the formulation led to the automatic dismissal of the content – when the appeal was declared null the appellee was thereby acquitted.[137] But as the century progressed, and especially after jury-trial had come to replace the ordeal, it became increasingly common for the task of prosecuting a quashed appeal to be taken over by the king, to preserve his allegedly broken peace, and since the king did not fight this meant that a jury's

---

[135]Cf. JUST/1/213 m34, when the man appealed of rape at midnight in the appellor's mother's house was found to be the appellor's lover.
[136]See *Wiltshire Crown Pleas 1249* pp. 69–88; *Surrey Eyre 1235* pp. 116–25; A. Harding (ed.), *The Roll of the Shropshire Eyre of 1256* (Selden Society Vol. 96, 1980) pp. xxxii–xlii. Unless otherwise stated, the statistics presented in this subsection cover all personal actions, whether brought by appeal or plaint, for all offences except homicide and rape.
[137]e.g. JUST/1/1 m5; JUST/1/229 m14d; JUST/1/341 m1d.

verdict had to be taken. The situation whereby an appeal declared null meant instant recourse to a jury did not come at once, however, and the 1238 Devon eyre marks an interesting stage on the road thither. Appeals were numerous, and there were no duels (though this remained a remote possibility, cf. 401), but while many appeals were quashed, verdicts were recorded as given on barely half the appellees – of the 386 people prosecuted, 123 were acquitted, while 79 were convicted on at least some part of the charge.

This was the presumably considered response of the justices to the problem of dealing with a large number of actions of which only a few dealt with genuine felonies, offences which if proved could have led to the defendant's being hanged or mutilated. Although their contents are not always easy to classify, 62 appeals and plaints alleged what was essentially injury to the person – wounding, beating, maiming and imprisonment – and another fourteen alleged injury aggravated by robbery. Thirteen involved charges of robbery, housebreaking, burglary and the like, 23 brought accusations of felony or breach of the king's peace, without further elaboration, and in fourteen cases the nature of the appeal went unrecorded. Of these actions, with a few others not included in the totals above, only five had been prosecuted to the extent of outlawing at least one appellee (405, 557, 571, 618, 740) and may have been concerned with genuine felonies. Similarly in those four cases where the appellors were instructed to continue proceedings against absent appellees (201, 492, 550, 557), the alleged offences may have seemed serious enough to warrant outlawry, as where a dangerous wound was said to have been inflicted (201, 550) – since in all 74 appellees failed to appear in court, some such criterion must have been used to decide that proceedings should continued in these cases only. But the great majority of appeals were concerned with offences of the sort that would later be defined as torts, that is, as "acts wrong in themselves and not as breaches of a prior agreement, but subject to damages to the injured man rather than criminal punishment".[138]

The appellors who brought such actions are likely to have had a variety of motives. Some will have wanted only to bring to book those who had injured them, and may have hoped that hundred jurors and the king's justices would give them a more equitable judgment than they had reason to hope for from a local or manorial court; others acted out of malice, vindictiveness or greed (125, 170, 467). The two women, both poor, who were told that their actions, both alleging the removal of grain by night, would be better proceeded with by writs of novel disseisin (163, 190), may have been taking advantage of the fact that there was no hard and fast distinction between criminal and civil actions to try to obtain the benefits of royal justice without going to the trouble and expense of obtaining royal writs. But many appeals, to judge by the justices' treatment of them, though probably related to genuine disputes, represented attempts to exploit the long drawn-out procedure involved in the making of appeals (see above p. xvii) to force the accused to settle those disputes, rather than to obtain the judgment of a royal court on them. The great majority of

---

[138]A. Harding, *A Social History of English Law* (Harmondsworth 1966) p. 98.

those appealed came to the County Court and were there attached to appear at the next eyre, and it was probably at this moment that negotiations to settle the dispute often began, either directly between the parties or through intermediaries; when William Doggefel wounded Richard Niger, it was William's father who took steps to reconcile the parties and so persuade Robert to desist from his appeal (395). That the appeal was used for such purposes is argued not just by the fact that 27 appeals were said to have entailed settlements, but also by the considerable number of occasions where finding out whether or not a settlement had been made was apparently all the justices felt was required of them (e.g. 284, 429).

The justices' interest in settlements may have been in part prompted by concern that potentially serious matters should not be concluded without reference to the interests of the crown – the settlement of an appeal of homicide, like that made between Emma daughter of Richard de Besseheie and her father's killer (29), obviously comes into this category. But they were probably equally concerned to discourage what they would certainly have regarded as the misuse of appeals alleging felony and breach of the king's peace for the purpose of settling parish-pump quarrels over trivial matters. There is no evidence that the legal reforms of the twelfth century had been intended to draw everybody's business into the royal courts.[139] What is probably the earliest record of any Devon plea, from 1169/70, shows a land action being begun in the Totnes honour court and then transferred to a session of the king's justices at Exeter, who sent it straight back to Totnes,[140] and thirteenth-century justices were probably just as reluctant to concern themselves with the affairs of the unimportant, which could perfectly well be disposed of elsewhere. So they inquired into out-of-court settlements, penalised them when discovered, and refused to award damages. If they hoped to discourage the use of the appeal for tortious offences, they appear to have been successful; though there were 92 appeals in 1244, by 1249 the total had fallen to 53, while at the 1281/82 eyre only seventeen appeals for offences other than homicide and rape were recorded. The figures for 1249 are also of interest in that they show that a more consistent attitude towards the giving of verdicts had evolved; of the 136 people appealed, 49 were acquitted and 67 convicted on some part of the charge, leaving only twenty unaccounted for. From the justices' point of view, a situation in which there were fewer appeals to be heard, but those made were definitively dealt with, must have been a far more satisfactory one.

People did not cease, however, to want access to the king's courts, for the chance of better justice there, together with the coercive power the processes of royal justice could bring to bear on their opponents and the hope of extracting damages from the latter. In the end the action of trespass supplied all these things, but not till much later in the century, and in the meantime there were experiments with modifications of appeals and with plaints.[141] A plaint, an informal complaint of an injury, to come

---

[139]A point I owe to Dr. P. R. Hyams.
[140]Bodl.MS James 23 pp. 159–60.
[141]See H. G. Richardson & G. O. Sayles (eds.), *Select Cases of Procedure without Writ under Henry III* (Selden Society Vol. 60, 1941); A. Harding, "Plaints and Bills in the History of English Law", in D. Jenkins (ed.), *Legal History Studies 1972* (Cardiff 1975) pp. 65–86.

within the competence of the eyre must usually relate to an injury recently committed, within twelve months at the most; otherwise the would-be plaintiff must proceed by appeal or writ of trespass (the latter only rarely used in the 1230s). At the 1238 eyre nine actions were begun or continued by plaint (94, 163, 314, 377, 448, 480, 558, 617, 768). At least three of these may have been genuine plaints of recent offences (448, 480, 558), while the complaint against the serjeant of Witheridge hundred of fatally injuring the plaintiff's wife (377) seems most readily comprehensible as the husband's response to a death that apparently occurred while the eyre was still in progress – it is hard to see why otherwise neither defendant nor justices objected to the procedure used. No. 94, on the other hand, had begun as an appeal but was now continued as a plaint; the appeal had probably been allowed to lapse at some point, and was now being informally resumed, a formal appeal having become pointless.

A particularly interesting plaint is that made by Robert de Lanteprei against Joel de Buketone (617), interesting both for its content and for the fact that although the alleged offence had taken place fifteen years ago the defendant made no demur about answering the charge. It was one which it would in fact have been hard to fit into an appeal of felony; its substance was really an alleged official malpractice, and as such this case is a forerunner of the complaints that would come before justices itinerant in growing numbers from the 1250s onwards, as the king extended his efforts to bring his local officials under control.[142] Thirteen plaints were made at each of the 1244 and 1249 eyres; of the total of 26, eleven were made by women, perhaps hoping in this way to get round the restrictions theoretically placed on their rights in the use of the appeal, and though certainty is hard to come by, up to five seem to have been directed against local officials. The usual purpose of the plaint is made particularly clear by the 1249 eyre, where eight plaintiffs asked for damages, hoping to get thereby what the appeal itself did not give and what the process of the appeal, thanks to the vigilant hostility of the justices, gave no longer. But there is no sign that they received what they wanted. By 1281/82, when the crown plea roll concludes with five membranes devoted solely to plaints,[143] such actions had become a regular part of the eyre, and damages were consistently awarded. But this was due to the events of the 1250s and 1260s, in particular to the period of baronial reform, and in the 1230s and 1240s plaints very rarely obtained damages; rather they tended to be regarded as eccentric appeals, and the justices handled them with uncertainty and reluctance.

The background to appeals and plaints is rarely described, but a few exceptions show Devon men and women falling out over the same sorts of issues that in other cases led to homicide. The rough and ready means of coercion which the law made available, when beasts were impounded (55, 467) or distraints taken (433) could lead to violence and thence to legal action. Some appeals were related to disputes over land (132, 528, 773, 775), or were apparently extensions of quarrels between lords or their retainers (263, 373). Some interesting appeals relate to villeinage and to the attempts of lords to control and exploit their villeins (125, 429, 448,

[142]Harding, art. cit. n.141 above, pp. 66–8, 73–4.
[143]JUST/1/186 mm48–52.

527, possibly 282). Devon was a county whose economy and geography probably always made it favourable to freedom; the substantial expanses available for cultivation, the wide scatter of population, the development of tin-mining and the growth of burghs, all gave the peasant opportunities for escape from the status and stigma of the villein. Labour services were never very onerous there, and there was much personal freedom even before the disafforestation of the county gave still more opportunities for enterprising pioneers to set up for themselves, with or without their lords' connivance.[144]

But of course the opportunities given by the disafforestation applied to lords as well; they too could bring land under the plough, and as the population grew they could expect a greater demand for the produce of their estates. A labour force for the task was obviously essential, and there are signs that lords who had villeins became anxious to keep them. The Otterton cartulary, compiled in 1260, contains a number of recommendations for dealing with the priory's tenants, free and unfree; for the latter they include restrictions on marriage, on taking holy orders and on holding land by charter, since in the last case a villein who so holds at once claims to be free, and "if anything is claimed of them they will not answer for their free tenements without the king's order, and then before the justices or in the County Court".[145] The civil pleas section of the 1238 eyre roll records many suits whereby lords claimed villeins or villeins tried to prove their freedom,[146] and the crown pleas contain such cases as that of Walter Lupus, seizing two alleged villeins at Shebbear and taking them to Kentisbury (a considerable distance), pointlessly in the end, since they proved their freedom (448), and that of Hamelin de Havecumbe, who refused to act as reeve to Roger de Ferrariis and had to be coerced (527). The case of Ralph son of John, said in 1244 to have been imprisoned by his lord "for trying to leave his land" and forcibly rescued by his brother "with a great following",[147] and still more the death of Philip de Seynte Mariecherch, recorded in 1281/82, who was killed by a group of his villeins and his body thrown into the sea,[148] point to the tensions that could arise.

CRIME AND THE CLERGY

The Church had a substantial presence in Devon, with 21 religious houses in the county by 1238 (including Ford, which is now in Dorset).[149] The parish system had probably been completed by the end of the twelfth century,[150] though the parishes were often very large ones, and the spread of population within them sometimes made further sub-division or adaptation necessary,[151] while men of substance began to acquire private

[144]Finberg, *Tavistock Abbey* pp. 70–5; J. L. Bolton, *The Medieval English Economy 1150–1500* (London 1980) pp. 28–9.
[145]DRO TD42 ff.62–5.
[146]JUST/1/174 mm21, 22, 24, 24d.
[147]JUST/1/175 m42.
[148]JUST/1/186 m24d; JUST/3/14/1 m1.
[149]Figures from D. Knowles & R. N. Hadcock, *Medieval Religious Houses: England and Wales* (2nd. Edn., London 1971).
[150]Hoskins, *Devon*, p. 224.
[151]cf. *Reg. Bronescombe* pp. 204–5.

chapels to save themselves long and wearisome journeys (100). The Church was in two senses an alternative jurisdiction, in that it claimed authority over the laity in certain spheres closely related to its spiritual office – perjury and breaches of faith, disputes relating to ecclesiastical property and rights and to marriage, and, most obviously and obtrusively, sexual morals, which came within the competence of the rural chapter presided over by the archdeacon – and also over men in orders prosecuted in the king's courts. The issue of jurisdiction over men in orders who came before royal justices had been effectively settled by Becket's murder;[152] thereafter such men were handed over to Court Christian, where they were required to clear themselves by purgation, by finding a set number of people willing to swear in proper form to the suspect's good character. Initially it had been sufficient for the accused clerk to claim benefit of clergy, and for the bishop or his representative to claim him in their turn as a clerk. From the late 1220s, however, there was a growing tendency for juries to be asked to give verdicts on suspected clerks before they were handed over, probably in the hope of preventing clerks so convicted from securing too easy a purgation in the church courts.[153] At the 1238 Devon eyre verdicts (in the case of appeals sometimes amounting to no more than a statement that an agreement had or had not been made) were given on all save one (533) of the clerks who appeared in court (103, 104, 105, 107, 292, 296, 374, 585), a process which may have been facilitated by the fact that not all of them appear to have claimed benefit of clergy.

Of the clerks mentioned in the course of the 1238 crown pleas, one was convicted in court (103), one abjured (291) and one was put in exigent (683) for homicide; a chaplain had been outlawed for wounding (576), for which another clerk was convicted in court (296), and one clerk was put in exigent for burglary (470). A man who was probably a clerk had abjured the realm for forging the king's seal (622). Several clerks were involved in quarrels and brawls (43, 107, 187, 374), others were acquitted of various charges of homicide and assault (104, 105, 474, 524), sometimes in their absence. None of the three clerks appealed of rape was convicted (120, 292, 585). The clergy could also be the victims of crime; three of them met violent deaths (360, 491, 650), and the house of the priest of Cotleigh was burgled (61). Numerically the involvement of the clergy in crime and violence was not disproportionately large, a total of seven convicted felons, at the most, does not suggest that their contribution to disorder in Devon was substantial; obviously they might be violent and quarrelsome, but then so might anybody else. In the overall context of any county's crime, however, the clergy's role cannot be considered solely in terms of its statistical contribution. The moral code which proclaimed most emphatically that it was wicked to kill and to steal was Christian, authoritatively embodied in the Ten Commandments; such acts were mortal sins, and the conscientious priest's responsibility for the salvation of his flock should therefore have involved trying to prevent them. Bishop Bartholomew's late twelfth-century penitential, with its call for love of one's neighbour, its

---

[152]See L. C. Gabel, *Benefit of Clergy in England in the Later Middle Ages* (Smith College Studies in History no. 4, 1928); C. R. Cheney, "The Punishment of Felonous Clerks", in *EHR* 51 (1936) pp. 215–36.
[153]JUST/1/775 m22 provides a good illustration of this point.

insistence that those who have injured others must be reconciled to them and give them satisfaction, its awareness of the possible consequences of sins of anger and avarice (described as including bloodshed, homicide, lust for vengeance, theft and perjury) and its hostility to hatred and drunkenness (cf. 58), laid down lines on which spiritual counsel could profitably have been given with this end in mind.[154] The extent to which the clergy actually did try to restrain the criminally-inclined, whether by word, deed or good example, and how much success their efforts enjoyed, is, however, extremely hard to ascertain.

One problem is that it is impossible to say how far the articles of the Christian faith were known or accepted. There can indeed be no doubt about the religious convictions of a man like William Buzun, who confirmed to Buckfast abbey a grant of seven acres in Churston Ferrers and then gave five more to make the total up to twelve "in honour of God and of Christ's twelve apostles . . ."[155] Much harder to interpret is the behaviour of five Dorset men who, meeting a youth from Devon at Yetminster, took him with them to Ryme, where "they bound his head with a knotted cord, and tormented him, and put him on a cross, and kept him there all night, and in the morning paid him and let him go".[156] Presumably they knew they were staging an imitation of the Crucifixion, but what that event meant to them is anyone's guess. As for the vagrants on the roads, fear of punishment in this world – a servile fear, according to Bishop Bartholomew, and not to be compared with a wholesome dread of hell-fire[157]– seems more likely to have inhibited them from evil courses than religious doctrines of which they were probably largely, if not wholly, ignorant. The spiritual authority of the Church may therefore not have been entirely secure, its ability to compel obedience through its control of the sacraments less than complete – one Cornishman refused to take the sacraments for over three years because he had quarrelled with his parish priest.[158]

The fact that most priests appear to have been men whose birth and upbringing differed little from that most of their parishioners,[159] though not without its advantages, in that there should have been no social barrier between a parson and his parish, carried with it the obvious risk that both might have the same standards, and that these might not be unequivocally the priest's. A preacher like the Dominican Jordan of Saxony, visiting England in 1229, might call on the clergy to persuade the laity to virtue "by holy living and good example",[160] but there was little of either to be learnt from Arnold the deacon, so embarrassingly appealed of rape by his ex-mistress (292), or from the likes of John le Cornu, parson of Thornbury, said in 1281/82 to have killed his servant in a quarrel over a horse.[161] Even when they did order their lives with propriety and restraint

[154]Morey, *Bartholomew*, pp. 177, 181, 204–5, 269–71, 274.
[155]DRO 123M/TB/109.
[156]JUST/1/201 m3d.
[157]Bodl. Bodley MSS 449 f.84.
[158]C144/7 no. 32.
[159]cf. J. R. H. Moorman, *Church Life in England in the Thirteenth Century* (Cambridge 1946) pp. 24–5.
[160]A. G. Little & D. Douie, "Three Sermons of Jordan of Saxony", in *EHR* 54 (1939) pp. 1–19.
[161]JUST/1/186 m5d.

(and serious crimes like John le Cornu's were rare among the clergy of thirteenth-century Devon), it was difficult for the clergy not to find themselves at least occasionally at odds with the laity, since so much of the former's income came in the form of compulsory dues supplied by the latter. Tithes, in particular, were a common cause of discord,[162] while friction could also arise from the practice whereby the second-best beast of a dead parishioner was customarily given to his parson as a mortuary, in compensation for all the tithes he must inevitably have withheld; in 1267 Bishop Bronescombe, having first excommunicated and then absolved the parishioners of Okehampton, bound them over to give mortuaries in future, on pain of paying 100s. to the vicar should they transgress in like manner again.[163]

All this does not mean that the Church's teaching had to have little or no effect, only that it was bound to make it more difficult for the clergy to dissociate themselves sufficiently from secular affairs to be able to convey a spiritual message with authority and conviction, and in particular to be able to contribute to the keeping of the peace by preventing quarrels and reconciling parishioners who fell out – a degree of detachment is generally regarded as essential to successful peacemaking. In fact there are signs that in some spheres, at least, the Church's message was heeded. Suicides, and recorded burglaries of churches – always tempting targets for thieves for the treasures they might contain, like the "silver and gold plates" which robbers one night stole from the "shrines encrusted with gold and silver" in Hartland abbey church[164] – though both probably under-reported, were still significantly few in number in Devon.[165] Although it is ultimately impossible to say how effectively the Church worked in restraint of crime, it can at least be said that the means existed for it to work to that end, and that Bishop Bartholomew's penitential and Bishop Brewer's diocesan statutes (see above p. xv) show that efforts were made to use them. A homicide or a burglary was a sin against God as well as a breach of the king's peace and a threat to the social fabric. In thirteenth-century Devon, as elsewhere, the actions and teachings of the Church helped supply a moral and spiritual dimension to the parallel efforts to prevent crime embodied in a system of local government which, like the Church itself, was largely self-regulating and was in operation all the time.

FINANCIAL ISSUES

The financial issues of the pleas of the crown were made up of criminals' chattels, fines, amercements and any revenue arising from royal rights like treasure trove and wreck. A few highly privileged lords were entitled to receive the issues from their own lands – at the 1228 eyre, the last occasion on which their names were recorded for Devon, these were the abbot of Glastonbury, the monks of Bec and the Knights Hospitallers, while the

---

[162]e.g. JUST/1/278 m48; JUST/1/776 m26; JUST/1/921 m15d.
[163]*Reg. Bronescombe* pp. 211–12.
[164]Chope, *Hartland* p. 227.
[165]JUST/1/176 m34 and JUST/1/186 m13d record the only robberies of churches noticed in thirteenth century court records for Devon.

same privilege was granted to Richard of Cornwall, and Henry de Trublevill was pardoned the sums due from his manor of Bradninch and his contribution to the county's common fine.[166] This last was a lump sum invariably raised from each county during a thirteenth-century eyre, either on the grounds of a particular shortcoming or to cover such shortcomings as were bound to be revealed.[167] It was paid by the suitors to the County Court, and by 1270 was levied by means of a hidage, at the rate of 3s. per hide[168] (usually rated at 120 acres, but possibly as little as 40 or 48 acres in south-west England[169]), perhaps, as in 1282, under the supervision of four assessors appointed at the end of the eyre.[170] Devon's common fine had been only £40 after the eyre of 1218/19,[171] but it rose to £100 in 1228 and to 200 marks (£133. 6s. 8d.) in 1238, at which it remained for at least the next three eyres.[172] During the nationwide circuit of 1246–1249, Devon's common fine was the highest to be raised from any English county.[173]

The Murder Fine Little or no effort was made to conceal the fact that the common fine was a device whereby the crown used the eyre to raise money in the localities, and long before 1238 this had become equally true of another form of fine, the Murder fine. This originated in the years after 1066, as a means of protecting William I's French followers from the homicidal attentions of unreconciled Englishmen.[174] A man found dead by violence was assumed to be French, and a substantial sum of money consequently became due from the neighbourhood of his death, except when a sufficient number of the near kinsmen of the deceased – in Devon two on both his father's and his mother's side (1) – could prove, by what became known as presentment of Englishry, that he was English. The 1130 pipe roll shows Murder fines of as much as 25 and 15 marks as having been levied in Devon,[175] but subsequently the rate was reduced, usually to sums of between £2 and £5; but though the rate was reduced, the incidence became wider, for as the 1238 crown pleas show, it was frequently found to be due when death resulted from misadventure as well as from felony (e.g. 11, 149, 522), while as it had long been impossible to distinguish Normans from Englishmen the number of potential incidences of the fine had become much higher. The Murder fine was clearly related to Murder in another, broader, sense, that of underhand, undetected, killing;[176] it was especially likely to be due in cases of felony when the killer was unidentified (6, 23, 54, 60, 95, 150, 436, 605, 625), and also in cases of misadventure where there was no bane, no tangible cause of death like horses, mill-wheels and boats. At the 1244 Dorset eyre it was said that

[166] E372/72 m3d; E372/73 m11d.
[167] Hence its alternative name of fine before judgment. *Surrey Eyre 1235* pp. 136–8.
[168] *RH* p. 72.
[169] R. Welldon Finn, *An Introduction to Domesday Book* (London 1963) p. 104.
[170] JUST/1/186 m47d.
[171] E372/65 m5.
[172] See Summerson, op. cit., n.88 above, Appendix I.
[173] *Wiltshire Crown Pleas 1249* p. 114.
[174] Pollock and Maitland Vol. II p. 487; F. M. Stenton, *Anglo-Saxon England* (2nd. Edn., Oxford 1947) p. 676; *Wiltshire Crown Pleas 1249* pp. 61–5.
[175] *PR 31 Henry I* pp. 155, 157.
[176] *Wiltshire Crown Pleas 1249* pp. 61–2.

"nor is it (i.e. Englishry) presented on anyone whose banes are present, but it is presented on all misadventures whose banes are not present, except for those drowned in the salt sea";[177] such banes were known as deodands because, as an act of propitiation, they were given to God, that is, to charity, and it was unusual for a Murder fine to be imposed when there was a deodand to be accounted for – at the 1247 Leicestershire eyre one was cancelled precisely because a deodand, in the shape of a millwheel, had come to light.[178]

Only free men were said to be liable to Murder fines, doubtless on the assumption that to be French was to be free;[179] thus in 1244 the coroners and knights of Devon presented that "Englishry was not wont to be presented on any free man of the county".[180] Analysis of the deaths of men in orders – the only ones of whose free status it is possible to be sure – shows how Murder fines were imposed in such cases. At the Devon eyres of 1238, 1244 and 1249 the deaths were recorded of sixteen clerks and a monk, of whom eight died by felony and nine by misadventure. For the former Murder was awarded in one instance, a killing by unknown criminals, for the latter, on three occasions, for all of which there was no deodand – there were deodands in five other instances, while the sixth was concealed right up to the time of the eyre and appears to have been entirely natural anyway. So in these cases Murder was awarded where one might expect, on free men where the cause of death could not be produced or accounted for, on what, in fact, by thirteenth-century standards could plausibly be described as murder, only with the latter's criteria extended to deaths by misadventure.

The same criteria usually (though not invariably – 131) apply to the other deaths where in 1238 a Murder fine was imposed. Nothing here can be said about the status of the deceased, and though freedom was widespread in Devon (see above p. xliii), it would be rash to assume that they were all free men; indeed, the fact that Englishry was successfully presented in one case (338) and unsuccessfully in three more (77, 169, 741) argues the contrary, and there were almost certainly villeins among them, on whom Englishry could have been, but was not, presented. There is plenty of evidence that people resented having to pay Murder fines and tried to avoid doing so; in 1244, for instance, the body of a man found killed within the manor of Exminster was said to have been carried over the manor's boundaries "so as to free Exminster manor from the Murder fine ..."[181] What the unfree and their kinsmen did not do, however, was present Englishry.

More than one explanation can be suggested for this. In the first place, not only was presenting Englishry a lengthy and time-consuming business, to be gone through at coroner's inquest, County Court and eyre, but it may also have become so complex and antiquated that the rules were no longer properly understood; thus when at the 1244 Devon eyre, after it had been declared, on behalf of the whole shire, that Englishry was

[177] JUST/1/201 m1.
[178] JUST/1/455 m7.
[179] *Wiltshire Crown Pleas 1249* p. 62; *EHD* II p. 523.
[180] JUST/1/175 m40d.
[181] JUST/1/175 m45.

Introduction xlix

not presented on women, the South Tawton jurors nevertheless presented Englishry on a woman found dead in a wood,[182] it is hard to believe that they knew what they were doing. Then there was the possibility that Englishry went unpresented because there was no certainty that a Murder fine would be avoided by presenting it. The amounts the Devon hundreds had to pay for Murder in 1238 are unrecorded, except in the case of Budleigh, which agreed on its fine in advance (177). In 1244, however, four Murder fines were imposed on Witheridge hundred, which consequently had to pay seven marks (£4. 13s. 4d.);[183] in 1249 only one fine was imposed, yet the sum demanded for Murder rose to £5.[184] After the 1263 Surrey eyre, Godalming hundred was required to pay 40s. "for Murder and trespass",[185] although the plea roll records no Murder fines at all in that hundred. Murder may have become a hundredal equivalent of the common fines imposed on counties, rated according to a hundred's size and wealth rather than to the number of Murder fines falling due within it, in which case presenting Englishry would be pointless. Finally, presentment of Englishry may have been shirked because of its social implications. If Murder fines were reserved for the free, then proving that a dead man was English meant proving that he and his kin were unfree. At a time when lords were apparently struggling to keep a grip on their villeins (see pp. xlii–xliii above), the price of such a proof might easily turn out to be a great deal higher than an amercement of a few marks, perhaps leading to the servitude of those involved over many generations. Under such circumstances reluctance to present Englishry becomes very understandable.

Other Issues Along with fines among the issues of the eyre went amercements, the money raised from individuals, groups and communities that had fallen into the king's mercy for failings and transgressions presented or committed during the eyre. These were assessed in the closing stages of the eyre. At the end of the 1228 eyre the justices had been assisted by "the bailiffs and serjeants of hundreds",[186] who would have been well qualified to know how much people could afford to pay, and perhaps these men acted in a similar role in 1238. From the 1228 eyre the pipe rolls record large numbers of small debts, mostly of sums between 6s. 8d. and 20s., and nearly all from individuals, though a few were from vills (up to 237 individual debts were recorded). The sum total due from the issues of this eyre was £964. 2s. 10½d., of which £57. 10s. went to Earl Richard and £13. 7s. 2d. could not be collected, while another £7. 3s. 4d. went to the privileged lords mentioned above. By 1238 exchequer procedure had been altered; the sheriff now accounted for all the lesser amercements and fines in undifferentiated lump sums, and only a few debtors accounted individually at the exchequer, mostly for large sums.[187]

The exact issues of this eyre cannot be known, the absence of the sums received by privileged lords probably making much less difference than

[182]JUST/1/175 mm37, 49d. For another example of confusion see JUST/1/62 m4.
[183]JUST/1/175 m46; E372/90 m11d.
[184]JUST/1/176 m44d; E372/94 m4.
[185]E372/111 m23d.
[186]E159/15 m16.
[187]Meekings, *Studies*, chapter XX pp. 228–32.

the king's grant to Richard of Cornwall of "the amercements of Exeter vill, Kenton and Lifton hundred" before these could be accounted for to the exchequer.[188] Richard's receipts from amercements proper are unquantifiable, but since the recorded fines from civil and crown pleas in Exeter, Kenton and Lifton amounted to £185. 3s. 8d., the issues of the eyre are likely to have been reduced by at least £200. In spite of this loss, the crown's receipts were still substantial, with a total of £1600. 6s. 4d. being accounted for at the exchequer.[189] £133. 6s. 8d. of this came from the county's common fine, while the sheriff accounted for £735. 12s. 4d. in three lump sums. The remaining £731. 7s. 4d. were almost entirely covered by four large fines, of 100, 200, 300 and 400 marks from Robert de Bulkewurth (476), Hugh Peverel (581), Walter Giffard and Henry de Tracy (494) respectively, amounting to a total of £666. 13s. 4d. Of those fines two resulted wholly and one at least partly from crown pleas proceedings; since no list of individual amercements has survived, however, there is no way of telling the relative overall contributions of crown and civil pleas to the grand total, but it is likely that the crown pleas made considerably the larger contribution – at the 1241 Surrey eyre, from which an amercements roll has survived, the total issues of the eyre, as recorded, came to £350. 1s. 9d., of which £248. 18s. 5d., over two thirds, came from the crown pleas.[190] How many of those put in mercy in 1238 actually found themselves debtors to the king, or, having become debtors, paid all, or any, of what they owed, cannot be assessed either, but it seems likely that on each count many escaped. If the 1241 Surrey eyre is typical, it suggests that over a fifth of the sums listed on the amercement roll might not reach the exchequer – the sheriff and individual debtors recorded on the pipe rolls together accounted for a total of £256. 14s. 2d. from this eyre, making a shortfall, after £15. 13s. 4d. due from foreign pleas (civil pleas from other counties adjourned to and terminated at the Surrey eyre) have been deducted, of £77. 14s. 3d. compared with the amercements roll, a lot more than can be attributed to the sums due to such lords as had the right to the profits of royal justice from their own lands. Making up for such deficiencies may have been one justification for the common fines levied on counties as a whole.

The total issues of the 1238 eyre were higher than those of 1244, 1249 or 1256, but those of 1244 and 1249 are likely to have had a far wider impact than those of 1238, since there were none of the big fines on individuals of the 1238 eyre. In 1244 the total amount accounted for was £1273. 18s. 11½d. (of which £43. 19s. 11d. went to Earl Richard), in 1249 £1077. 0s. 10½d. Only in 1256 was there a notable fall, to £944. 10s. 6d., and even that was only £20 less than the sum raised in 1228, at an eyre which had covered nine years, compared with the seven covered by the eyre of 1256. From the financial angle the eyre may have been closer akin to a periodic foray than to a regular part of the central government's fiscal apparatus, but the fact remains that even from a county as remote and potentially impenetrable as Devon the crown was able to extract nearly £4000 by

[188]*CCR* 1237–42 p. 70.
[189]Details for the 1238 issues from E372/83 m10; E372/84 m5; E372/85 m14; E372/86 m16d; E372/87 m9; E372/88 m11d; E372/89 m12; E372/90 m11d; E372/91 m11. Figures for other eyres as in n.172 above.
[190]Figures from JUST/1/869 mm6–8.

means of the three eyres between 1238 and 1249, and over £5800 through those between 1228 and 1256, and that it could do this is arguably the strongest evidence available for the effectiveness with which it was able to make its authority felt, at least at well-spaced intervals, in the localities. Not that this was accomplished easily – a case from the 1244 eyre illustrates the problems that might arise. One Adam Praunte appealed nine men that on 22 March 1239 they arrested, ill-treated and imprisoned him, and took 26 of his cattle. It transpired, however, that Adam had previously been distrained for his contribution to the common fine made by the county at the 1238 eyre, but on that occasion had rescued his beasts and beaten up the sheriff's officer who took them, and that the sheriff had then ordered another distraint to be made, with the results that Adam was now complaining of. Only grudgingly did the shires allow their penetration by royal power, and they continued to cherish their privileges and traditional usages. Adam Praunte was eventually compelled to make his due contribution to the common fine paid to the king; he also had to make another, more unexpected, contribution elsewhere. One of his oxen, one of the best he had, so he complained in 1244, had not been returned to him with the others taken in distraint; to this the knights of the county made unanimous reply. The ox would remain in the keeping of those who had made the distraint, "to be eaten, for such is the custom of the county of Devon".[191]

EDITORIAL METHOD

What follows is a slightly abbreviated translation from the Latin (see specimen of original text and literal translation below). A premium throughout has been placed on the production of an English text as comprehensible as possible, even at the risk of an occasional inconsistency.

The word *judicium*, when used to accompany findings of misadventure and the like, has been omitted throughout. The phrase *unde ... respondebit/respondebunt*, meaning that he/they will answer where chattels, wreck or deodands are to be accounted for, has been replaced by 'etc.' throughout (e.g. 10). All marginalia have been omitted, except that marginal notes of hangings have here replaced the 'etc.' of the text (e.g. 16). Christian names have been translated, if an English equivalent exists, professional and locative names (e.g. Welshman for *Walensis*) if their descriptive meaning seems clear; thus *molendinarius* has been rendered as miller, but a word like *serviens* is left in Latin if it is unclear whether servant or serjeant is meant (93).

Place-names are given in their modern form, where identified (unidentified place-names have been placed in inverted commas), except when they form part of a personal name, when they have been left in their original form, even if a professional name has been translated into English (e.g. 103). In such cases final "es" indicated by suspension marks have been supplied, but not larger abbreviations; so Thomas de Cirencestr' has been rendered as Thomas de Cirencestre, but Walter de Bathon' left as such.

[191] JUST/1/175 mm47, 47d.

The manuscript of the plea roll is in good condition, that of the Tiverton *veredictum* very much less well preserved. Illegible passages are indicated by three dots, blanks deliberately or accidently left in the manuscript by dashes.

Words and phrases which are interesting, unusual or difficult of translation are supplied, in Latin, in brackets after their English renderings in the text.

SPECIMEN OF LATIN TEXT WITH ITS LITERAL TRANSLATION:

114 *Bartholomeus de Uphexe et Rogerus Cal utlagati sunt pro morte Thome de Ferrariis per sectam Serlonis de Bikebire. Et Rogerus Cal fuit manens in tethinga de Torvertone ideo in misericordia. Et Bartholomeus fuit de manupastu Henrici de Tracy et non habuit ipsum ideo in misericordia. Nulla habuerunt catalla. Et predictus Serlo appellavit de eadem morte Walterum de la Rodeweie et modo veniunt ambo sed Serlo non sequitur versus eum ideo ipse et plegii sui de prosequendo in misericordia scilicet Henricus de Hyne and Ricardus de Clive. Et juratores testantur quod Walterus non est culpabilis ideo quietus et predictus Serlo custodiatur. Post venit Serlo et finem fecit pro se per dimidiam marcam per plegium Wydonis le Bret et Hugonis de Loges.*

Bartholomew de Uphexe and Roger Cal were outlawed for the death of Thomas de Ferrariis by the suit of Serlo de Bikebire. And Roger Cal was living in Thorverton tithing so in mercy. And Bartholomew was of the mainpast of Henry de Tracy and he did not have him so in mercy. They had no chattels. And the aforesaid Serlo appealed of the same death Walter de la Rodeweie, and now they both come, but Serlo does not make suit against him, so he and his pledges for prosecuting in mercy, namely Henry de Hyne and Richard de Clive. And the jurors testify that Walter is not guilty, so quit, and the aforesaid Serlo is to be taken into custody. Later came Serlo and made fine for himself by half a mark, by pledge of Guy le Bret and Hugh de Loges.

ACKNOWLEDGMENTS

My greatest debt is to Mrs. Audrey Erskine, for the patient and benevolent vigilance with which, on behalf of the Devon and Cornwall Record Society, she has supervised the production of this edition over several years and the painstaking care with which she has prepared it for the press. My thanks are due to the staffs of the Public Record Office and British Library in London, of the Bodleian Library and the Library of The Queen's College in Oxford, and, in particular, to Mrs. M. M. Rowe and the staff of the Devon Record Office in Exeter, whose good offices enabled me to make the most of the limited time at my disposal there. Finally, I am grateful to Drs. M. T. Clanchy, R. C. Stacey and P. R. Hyams, Mr. J. M. Kaye and Mrs. Jean Scammell for their advice and assistance, to Dr. David Crook of the Public Record Office for help on points of decipherment and translation, and to Mrs. Carrie Cocke for help with the typing.

Translations of Crown-copyright records in the Public Record Office appear by permission of H.M. Stationery Office.

LONDON, FEBRUARY 1985   HENRY SUMMERSON

CROWN PLEAS OF THE DEVON EYRE OF 1238

[KALENDAR OF JURIES]

(m 25)
These were coroners in Devon after the last eyre
William de la Bruere
Roger Giffard
Guy de Bretteville
William de Wydewrth
Rannulf de Albemarle, coroner of Lifton

These were sheriffs in the same county after that time
Sir William de Ralegh
Roger la Zoche who has died, Rannulf de Cerne answers for him
Thomas de Cirencestre
Thomas de la Wyle, through [*recte* for] Peter de Oryvalle
Robert de Vallibus
Peter de Russelle
Nicholas de Molis
Walter de Bathon' who is now sheriff

Ausemenistre Hundred (Axminster). Alice de Moun has the hundred.
Serjeant Adam Hunte. Electors Richard de Manbire, Henry de la Gate. Nicholas de Cumba Henry de Laforde William de Hauville Nicholas de Yae Ralph de Muntorie Robert de Huppehaie Philip de Greneweie William Pain Andrew de Luneput Ralph de Candebec Walter de Yale

Axemue Hundred (Axmouth). The prior of Axmouth has the hundred.
Serjeant Thomas de Byendone. Electors Adam de Dune, Ralph de Dune. Philip the marshal Jordan de la Hille David Pelecoke Henry de Clanemere Robert Poke Roger de Ver Walter Warin Adam de Aure Gilbert de Hupperiche William Cailli

Culitone Hundred (Colyton). Reginald de Valle Torta and John Byset have the hundred.
Serjeant Robert Casewolde. Electors William de Leghe, Robert de Helion. Robert de Bulkiwrthe Martin de Eveforde William de Winburnefort William de Colevile Stephen de Ofwelle Benedict de Lesbocke John de Leghe Thomas le Rus Thomas de Bramlee Luke de Setone

Hemiok Hundred (Hemyock). Richard de Hydone has the hundred.
Serjeant Peter son of Vincent. Electors Geoffrey Cophin, Andrew Terry. Robert fitz Pain John de Prestcote Richard le Daneis Walter de Perville

Peter de Hinteberghe Richard son of Godfrey Roger Suethogge William Alexander William Moun William le Deveneis

Uffculum Hundred (Uffculme). Alice de Moun has the hundred.
Serjeant William Godegrom. Electors Roger de Goddeleghe, John de Yepy.
Hugh de Heighe William de Brok Osbert de Bosco William de Molendino

Harigge Hundred (Hayridge). Baldwin de Rivers has the hundred.
Serjeant Richard de Prestecote. Electors Philip de Sicca Villa, Philip de Kingesforde.
William Malherbe Gilbert de Grucy Nicholas de Burne Hugh de Bodlai Henry de la Heie John de Cherltone Thomas de Horwaie Richard Freschet Ralph Butyn Robert del Estre

Twyvertone Hundred (Tiverton). Baldwin de Rivers has the hundred.
Serjeant Richard de Prestecote. Electors Thomas de Bradele, Thomas le Paumer.
Robert de Leie Walter Passemer Thomas le Norreis Anthony de la Pole William Tracy Richard de Chivethorn William de Chivethorn Robert de Chirchehille Hervey de Kerselake

Bauntone Hundred (Bampton). Herbert son of Matthew has the hundred.
Serjeant Walter Russel. Electors John de Hocforde, Roger de Barneville.
William de Leghe Hugh de Morba Robert le Paumer Richard de Cornwde Michael de Wadeheghe Alan de Morba Maurice de la Hele Nicholas de Nutcumbe Simon Lanpreie Walter Wade

Haubetone Hundred (Halberton). William Peverel and William de Bosco have the hundred.
Serjeant Roger de Moristone. Electors William de Claville, William Cailloel.
William de Bosco Richard de Bosco Walter le Carpenter Roger de Morstone Gilbert Longus William de Pilketin Thomas de Eshe William de Manileghe William Blundel William le Franckelein

Clistone Hundred (Cliston). Isabel countess of Oxford has the hundred.
Serjeant Richard de Puridone. Electors William de Clyt, John de la Verge.
Thomas Pulein William de Marisco Walter de la Hope Thomas de la Bere William Sangwin Gerard de Clit Richard Pudding Richard de la Pitte Humphrey de Limbire John Longus

Buddeleghe Hundred (Budleigh). Robert de Hoxham has the hundred.
Serjeant Jordan de Radeslo. Electors John Tybaud, Tholomeus de Oteritone.
Robert le Peitevin William de la Hialestone Robert de Hortone Roger de Alneto Peter le Franceis William de Sande Alexander Wither Philip de Bosco William de Fendone William del Cumbe

Sancte Marie Otery Hundred (Ottery St. Mary). The dean and chapter of Rouen have the hundred.
Serjeant Geoffrey de la Stone. Electors William de Cadeheghe, Roger le Poher.
Robert Buzun William de Strethede John de Blakelake Daniel de

Knittestone Roger de Spina Edward de Essche Richard de Essche Peter de Morcumbe Henry Cobba Alfred de Knittestone

Wnforde Hundred (Wonford). Baldwin de Revers has the hundred.
Serjeant Ralph de Chieurestone. Electors Robert de Beville, Eudo de Serintone.
Robert de Baltforde William de Stokes Ralph son of Bernard Hugh de Chakeforde Richard Corbin Tholi de Bosco Reginald de Holleham Peter de Albemarl Bartholomew de Pultimor John de Ridone

Exemenistre Hundred (Exminster). Richard le Horder has the hundred and is its serjeant.
Electors Ralph de Dotescumbe, Joyre de Teigne.
Alfred d'Harecumbe William Lupus Roger Coterel Roger le Butor Osbert de Keneforde Gerard de Bromhille Robert de Mulehiwis Roger de Rixtiville William de Langgedone Godfrey Caillou

Teignebrigge Hundred (Teignbridge). Richard Burdon and Theobald de Englescheville have the hundred.
Serjeants William de Gatepathe and William de Ringeslade.
Electors Richard de Treminettes (Richard de Hundetorre *deleted*). Michael de Hugotone Martin de la Torre Richard de Walemere William de Wrei Richard de Hugetone William de Halebem William de Sumerhille Thomas de Winesthorre Geoffrey de Chintellesbere John de Bacbake Adam de Historre. William de Gatespathe is in mercy for not coming

(m 25d)
Heytorre Hundred (Haytor). Nicholas de Molis has the hundred.
Serjeant Gilbert de Tywe. Electors Michael de Spichwik, Stephen de Hacumbe.
Robert de Morcellis Peter de Cunitone Elias de Stantor Ralph son of Ralph John Paz Richard le Barun Jordan de Hacumbe Richard de Dageville Roger de Cokintone Hugh Doo

Stanberghe Hundred (Stanborough). Nicholas de Molis has the hundred.
Serjeant Gilbert de Tywe. Electors Gerard de Spineto, William de Morle.
Richard Crespin John de Alnethistone Peter le Franceis William Norreis Henry de Altaribus William Fichet (Nicholas de la Ya *deleted*) Alfred de Duddewrth William de Bradeleghe Richard de Cumbe Elias le Goiz

Curigge Hundred (Coleridge). Herbert son of Matthew has the hundred.
Serjeant Richard de la Forde. Electors William de Praule, Lawrence le Flemeng.
Durandus son of Richard Gilbert Crespin Michael de Cumbe William de Bikeleghe Ralph de Godesaltre Andrew de Totefen Guy de Wasseburne William de Bimelee Henry de Tidewrthi Hugh de Mallestone

Ermintone Hundred (Ermington). Hugh Peverel has the hundred.
Serjeant David de Holecumbe. Electors Geoffrey de Pridias, William de Omnibus Sanctis.
Stephen de Luddebrok Thomas Daniel Walter de Minminlande John de Shirvestone William de Modecumbe Reginald de Baucumbe William Spridelle Ralph de Stanebire Gilbert de Addestone Roger de Scotia

Plimtone Hundred (Plympton). Baldwin de Revers has the hundred.
Serjeant Serlo le Harpur. Electors Alexander de Henemeredune, Guy le Bret.
William de Spridlestone Ralph de Backemores William de Wlrivetone Walter de Lineham William de Briteristone Nicholas de Fernhille Thomas son of Joel Roger Trace Adam de Wenbire

Rugheberghe Hundred (Roborough). Baldwin de Revers has the hundred.
Serjeant Serlo le Harpur. Electors Walter Giffard, Roger de Cadewrthy.
Robert Giffard Hamelin de Leghe Roger de Nutleghe Baldwin de Sucumbe Alan de Buthkeshide Roger de la Torre Richard de Mewy Ralph de Valletorta Richard de Godeswrthi Colin Bastard

Tavistoke Hundred (Tavistock). The abbot of Tavistock has the hundred.
Serjeant Ralph Osmer. Electors Ralph Gurdac, Roger de Ogbere.
John de Lawike William Furel Robert de Vado Roger Bugkedone Angerus de Milmed John de Kerdewelle Godfrey de Wdehevese Odo Wille Vivian de Wdehevese

Liftone Hundred (Lifton). Agatha de Gatesdene has the hundred.
Serjeant Richard de Cokewrthy. Electors Richard de Veteri Ponte, Geoffrey de Culitone.
John de Huntessor Joel Giffard Roger de Brente Philip Talebot John de Arkeswrthi Godfrey Ivaus Geoffrey de la Hoke John de Wrwildic Roger le Parc William de Brente

Blaketoritone Hundred (Black Torrington). Henry de Byamaunt, guardian of Richard de Wangeforde, has the hundred and is its serjeant.
Electors Alan de Aleswrthy, Philip Perrer.
William Cornutus William de Leghe William de Albernon Thomas de Hortone John de Witefelde Angerus de Wile Jordan le Spicer Richard Passemer Osbert de Wisdom Thomas de Hollecumbe

Shefbere Hundred (Shebbear). The lord king has the hundred.
Serjeant William le Venur. Electors Henry de Mertone, Robert Miles.
Richard de Crus Henry Bacun Baldwin de Halbiri Robert de Holne John Goding Adam de Faddecote Richard de Spekecote William de Culeleghe William de Hunteneforde Thomas de Wynescote

Hertilande Hundred (Hartland). Geoffrey Dynant has the hundred.
Serjeant Oliver de la Hole. Electors Geoffrey de Fattecote, Joel de Langfurlang.
William de la Weie Robert de Wlfereswrthi William de Leghe Henry de Shirewode Robert de Notecote John de Clifford Peter de la Bare Robert Herbiz Robert de Buchiwises Stephen de Almerstone

Fremitone Hundred (Fremington). Henry de Tracy has the hundred.
Serjeant Roger Oysel. Electors Robert de Whitesleghe, Walter Bernus.
Robert de Tappeleghe Alexander de Clugnie Richard de Alebrigge Geoffrey de Leghe John de Rothebare William de Wanteleghe Simon de Bosco Walter de Via John de Winnescote William Chastel

Brangtone Hundred (Braunton). The abbot of Cleeve has the hundred.
Serjeant William de la Weye. Electors Nicholas de Fileleghe, William Fauvel.

Thomas le Bretone Ralph de Pinu Richard de Biccadewe Reginald de Charterai Richard de Witafelde Richard de Punchardone William de Punchardone Eustace de Merewde Philip de Loppa Richard de Porta

Shirewelle Hundred (Shirwell). Philip de Bello Monte has the hundred.
Serjeant William de la Weye. Electors Robert de Pidekeswelle, Philip Luvet.
Thomas Terri Robert Caillo Thomas de Luvese Stephen de Sancto Albino Robert de Stapestote Roger le Pig Hugh Coffin Ogerus de la Birche Malerus de Spelangre Humphrey de Logeshore

Sumotone Hundred (South Molton). Gilbert de Turbeville has the hundred.
Serjeant Geoffrey de Gambun. Electors William de Revetone, Vincent de Norwelle.
Reginald Archiepiscopus William le Franceis Jordan de Heyle Richard le' Tirant Thomas Derneburne William de Froudetone Robert de Molendino Richard de Cumba Robert de Brademore Philip de Stafford

Normotone Hundred (North Molton). Alan la Zoche has the hundred.
Serjeant Archebald de Cruce. Electors Jordan de Poleham, Martin de Swanecote.
Herbert de la Mersa Richard de Molland Richard de Roberdescote Robert de Shopilande

Mothlande Hundred (Molland). Albreda de Boterelle has the hundred.
Serjeant Everard de Knostan. Electors William de Knustone, Geoffrey de la More.
Robert de Sicca Villa Robert de West Mollande Nicholas de Witefel Adam de Godcumbe

Wytherigge Hundred (Witheridge). Robert le Marchand has the hundred and is its serjeant.
John le Despenser Roger Fromind Jordan de Wodeburne Richard Vassel Richard de Chedeledone William le Rus Robert le Copener Robert de la Bere Rannulf de Wike Guy Crespin Thomas de Sepwassy Walter de Blakewrthi

(m 26)
Nortautone Hundred (North Tawton). Joel de Valle Torta has the hundred.
Serjeant Robert de la Slade.
Alexander de Wike Richard de Riwe Daniel le Bretone Robert de Stoddone John de Reingni Thomas de Helleredune Robert de Champeus Geoffrey de Northcote Robert de Affatone Miles Corbin William de Argentein Robert Burnel

Sutautone Hundred (South Tawton). Ralph de Thony has the hundred.
Serjeant Alfred de Colebere.
Walter de Wike Roger de Wike William de Minet Roscelin de Bosco William Tremenet Reginald de la Sele Hugh Cobe William de Tau John de Colebere John Burnel Robert Champeneis Robert de Wikedone

Winkeleghe Hundred (Winkleigh). Henry Curant has the hundred.
Serjeant Osbert le Gydie.
Michael de Sucote Nicholas Lug Richard Blundus William de Baisdone

Walter Niger William Tracy Wermund de Portmora Walter Collecote Roger de Lamasne Richard de Sucote John de Collecote Nicholas de Colecote

Criditone Hundred (Crediton). The bishop of Exeter has the hundred. Serjeant Rannulph de la Were.

Richard de Hidone Sampson Coterel Osbert de Hollecumbe Geoffrey de Estennestone Robert de Bononia Robert Wanci Deodatus de Nortone Peter de Cadewrthi Richard Mercator de Cumba Hugh son of William John de Denrighe Richard de Alneto

City of Exon' (Exeter)
Electors Walter la Chowe Adam de Rifforde Philip le Paumer Thomas Rof

John Turbert John de Okestone Philip the dyer Walter Speare Martin Rof William Boschet John the goldsmith Paul the Irishman Geoffrey Strange Peter Quinel Reginald le Steimur William Busse Walter le Granger Robert Spowe Richard le Paumer Richard the clerk Richard Stranga Reginald Crane Walter de Moutone William Hog

Hunetone Burgh (Honiton).
Richard de la Berne Robert Hopere William de Leghe Walter le Bel Robert le Taliur Thomas Page Walter Bellestane Walter de Cruce Walter Blakebene John Serviens William de Eswaie Robert Mareis

Twvertone Burgh (Tiverton).
Richard Butehors Richard de Mokeforde William Languil William Tranze Richard le Turnur Adam Lithebi Henry le Turnur Roger Viel Robert Burri Robert de Hunnesham John de Molins Roger Vito

Okemantone Burgh (Okehampton).
Richard Coldmere Walter son of the dean William de Ponte Alan de Meledone William Ruwilin Ruwelin Chete Richard Barat Gilbert de Capella John son of Jordan Robert de Holleweie William Cumpaniun William de Glindone

Braaneys Burgh (Bradninch).
John le Taliur Robert Lifrere William Porteman Warin de Sicca Villa Henry le Taliur John le Peitevin

Totenesse Burgh (Totnes).
Robert Niger the smith William de Route Geoffrey de Cotemore Richard Stile Andrew le Scot Geoffrey son of Sarah Robert de Dertemue Geoffrey Rugge Richard son of Humphrey Richard son of Adam Richard de Fonte Richard de Clautone

Plimtone Burgh (Plympton).
Reginald the smith Humphrey de Duningtone Serlo de Bosco Thomas de Greneslade Roger de Cadewrthe Richard Herbert Jocelin de Vado John de Shirewelle Robert de Hekewrthi Geoffrey le Pottere Robert Wayfrac Godfrey de Bosco

Mobire Burgh (Modbury).
Philip Girard William Grob Gilbert Turpin William the tailor Walter de Buttelonde Ralph de Iharnecumbe Walter Grocy Siward Thomas the tailor Adam le Bois Walter Bulefen Rannulf de Harwdetone

Kalendar of Juries

Tavistoke Burgh (Tavistock).
Joel le Mazun William de Fonte Walter le Tanur David le Bloye Walter Hopetrede Richard Sehive Eustace del Soler Walter Fulco Nicholas de Fosseto Nicholas de Bosco William Cobern Walter Fulke

Lideforde Burgh (Lydford).
Richard Ettard Robert Colbern Reginald Cruch Richard the clerk Philip Kainges William Doget Adam Brun Jordan de Monte Martin de Werwale Ralph Pullus Ralph de Warwale William Blundus

Toritone Burgh (Torrington).
Germanus Wisdom Osbert de Anerie Robert le Gylene Reginald Leicestre Anketill de Cappella William Vluesgrave Thomas le Bret Robert the smith Walter Gurand John de la Thithene John Leicestre

Bernestapele Burgh (Barnstaple).
Richard de Langeleghe William Lowis Thomas Crestien Walter Hog William le Cordewaner Thomas Burel Adam de Culeleghe Durandus the tailor Roger Pulein Nicholas Pulein Roger Coc William Bonus Homo

Kentone Burgh (Kenton).
Richard de Hokestone Luveric de Colerole Reginald de Middilkote Roger de Semechille William de Cocforde Walter Bisudebrok Roger de la Forde Walter de Cocforde Richard de Hoggehulle Arlewin de Wike Ailmer de Lamer Roger the smith Richard the smith

Sutmoltone Burgh (South Molton).
Peter de Pilefen Jocelin de Moutone Arnold de Cobetone Ralph the reeve William the clerk Robert Cokeman Robert le Balle Roger the smith Arnold Blundus Robert de Lubalde John de Brai Robert le Taverner

(m 26d)
Aspertone Burgh (Ashburton).
Martin Crock William de Tautone Robert the smith Henry the smith Edward son of John William Greistone John Prige Henry Smok Ralph the marshal Joel Kyde Hamelin son of Angerus Bartholomew the marshal

Bydiforde Burgh (Bideford).
Stephen Sciria John Tirel Robert le Bule William le Turnur Walter le Bretone Walter de Hafrige

Normotone Burgh (North Molton) answers with North Molton hundred.

Molande Manor (Molland).
William de Cnutstane Robert de Sicca Villa Adam de Godcumbe Geoffrey de Mora Nicholas de Whitefelde Robert de Westmorlande

Ialmetone Manor (Yealmpton).
Bartholomew de Linham William Tranipreye John Tyrant

Critone Burgh (Crediton).
Walter le Taliur Matthew Juvenis Roger le Taliur Walter Blundus Richard de Cumba John de Paz Osbert le Poter

Culiforde Burgh (Colyford).
Thomas son of William Henry de Unetone Matthew de Culiforde Roger Poyt Roger the vintner Odo de Culiforde

Kingbrige Burgh (Kingsbridge).

Hunetone Manor (Honiton).
Ralph de Hale Walter Bowewode Robert Truttup Robert de Northcote Henry Blanecumbe Ailmer Attestute William de la Forde Philip de la Strete Roger de la Cumbe Robert de la Dune Ralph de Middilhille William de Coppeshore

Whyteforde Burgh (Whitford).
Gilbert de Lokinge Richard Lideman Luke de Shete William de la Hulle Ralph de Mora Peter Blundus

Free Manor of Plimlande answers by the same twelve as answer for Plympton Hundred.

The Eastern Part is to begin at once.
Let the Northern Part come on the Tuesday next after the feast of St. John the Baptist (June 29).
The Southern Part on the Tuesday next after the Octave of St. John the Baptist (July 6).
Whitford vill is in mercy for manifest trespass.

Axminster

(m 27)
CROWN PLEAS OF THE COUNTY OF DEVON TAKEN AT EXETER BEFORE WILLIAM DE EBOR' AND HIS FELLOW JUSTICES ITINERANT, IN THE 22ND YEAR OF KING HENRY SON OF KING JOHN.

AXMINSTER HUNDRED ANSWERS BY TWELVE JURORS

1   In this county Englishry is presented by two on the father's side and two on the mother's.
> The presentment of Englishry and the workings of the Murder fine are discussed in the introduction. In 1244 and 1249 Englishry was described as being presented as here, with the additional information that it was not presented on women, on anybody drowned in the sea, or on males less than seven years old, but in all other cases it was presented, whether death resulted from felony or accident. At the 1281/82 eyre, however, Englishry was said not to be presented in the county. JUST/1/175 m37; JUST/1/176 m34; JUST/1/186 m.l.

2   Nicholas de Cumbe, one of the jurors, is in mercy for not coming with his fellows before the justices to answer for their *veredictum*.

3   To judgment on Thomas de Cirencestre for not coming to answer for his time as sheriff of Devon.
> Thomas de Cirencestre was sheriff of Devon from April 1231 to July 1232, and again from Michaelmas 1232 to Michaelmas 1233. He had lands in Woodhuish, St. Mary Church and Hareston – *Fees* pp. 767, 768, 796 – and his previous administrative experience included service as bailiff of the earl of Devon's lands during the latter's minority, *Rot. Lit. Claus.* II p. 46. "To judgment" is a literal translation of *ad judicium*, a phrase which seems to have represented a call by the justices to the suitors of the County Court and other notables present at the eyre to pronounce on a matter which seemed to the justices blameworthy, but which might be differently interpreted, as here – Thomas was also sheriff of Dorset and Somerset through much of the 1230s, and had been served in Devon, at least for some of the time, by deputies, notably by Thomas de la Wyle (see no. 187 below), whom he may have expected to answer for him. He cannot be shown to have been amerced for his failure to appear, so perhaps the circumstances were ultimately found to be sufficiently extenuating.

4   Likewise to judgment on Thomas de Blakeforde, Alice de Mohun's steward, who acts as sheriff, for not coming to answer for his time.
> That Axminster hundred claimed special status is suggested by presentments at later eyres, describing how an appeal of theft led to a wager of duel, though ultimately the appellor retracted, and how a thief turned approver and a duel was waged, both in the hundred court – JUST/1/175 m37d; JUST/1/176 m34. The approver was normally a royal monopoly. At the 1281/82 eyre the abbot of Newenham, to whose house the hundred had been granted by Reginald de Mohun, its founder, was summoned to show by what warrant he held the sheriff's tourn in the hundred. Unfortunately, the abbot vouched to warranty John de Mohun, Reginald's grandson, who being under age could not be summoned to warrant him, so no verdict was given, *PQW* p. 171. But the reference to the tourn, as to the sheriff's functions which Thomas de Blakeforde was said to be performing in 1238, suggests a considerable degree of administrative autonomy, which it is tempting to attribute to the hundred's period of tenure by the immensely powerful William Brewer – see below, no. 224.

5   East Membury vill is in mercy for not coming fully before the justices and not presenting to the County Court a case of a mound being dug into.

6   A beggar was found killed on John Capie's land, it is not known who killed him. No Englishry so Murder fine.
> In 1242 John Capy shared with William de Aqua one eighth of a fee in Membury of the

honour of Plympton, *Fees* p. 788. His family gave its name to Capiehayes in Membury parish, *PND* p. 644.

7   Another unknown man was found dead on 'Giseweie' road. No Englishry so Murder fine.

8   William de Oteri Sancte Marie fled to 'Cumbe' church, admitted to being a killer and thief, and abjured the realm. To judgment on the coroners for not presenting the name of him he killed.

9   Unknown criminals burgled the house of Elias Palmer, wounding him, his wife Cecilia and his whole household. Elias, attached for this, comes, but Cecilia does not. She was attached by Reginald Uphothedune and Alan Pigace, who are in mercy.

10   A miller was drowned at Upottery mill. No-one is suspected, misadventure. Later it was testified that he was drowned by the mill wheel. Value of the wheel 12d, the sheriff etc. The jurors are in mercy for not presenting the drowned man's name.

11   Adam de Eddileghe was found dead at 'Eddicumbe' in Holloway road. No-one is suspected. No Englishry so Murder fine. Thomas de la Cumbe, attached for the death, does not come, so he and his pledges, Richard de la Cumbe and Roger de Digerestone, are in mercy.

12   Criminals killed two women at Knightshayne. It is not known who they were. Knightshayne vill is in mercy for not pursuing them.

13   Two men were arrested for theft and taken to Axminster. The prior of Yarcombe came and claimed his court on them, on account of the liberty which he said he had, and they were handed over to him. Harding Shene, charged with harbouring those thieves, comes and puts himself on the country. The jurors testify that he is guilty, so he is hanged. He had no chattels. And as it is testified that the men of Axminster hundred and the bailiffs of Alice de Mohun, who holds the hundred, handed those two thieves over to the prior, the hundred is taken into the king's hand. To judgment on the men of the hundred and also on Alice de Mohun. And it is testified that the two thieves were hanged by judgment of the prior's court without any suit being made against them for any theft or any stolen goods being found on them, so to judgment on the prior's court. And as John the huntsman, an associate of the thieves, who was arrested and taken to the County Court, where he became an approver but later retracted, was handed over to the prior's court and hanged, without suit by anyone and without stolen goods being found on him, to judgment on the court.

>   In the light of what was said about them later in this entry, the thieves, not having been found in possession of stolen property, should have been sent to the king's gaol at Exeter. The legitimate use of the franchise of gallows, which the prior claimed to have, required that suit, prosecution by the owner of the goods allegedly stolen (which must be worth more than 12d.), supported by the testimony of neighbours, should have been made against the thief arrested "with the mainour", in physical possession of his plunder (DL30/1470/104 m6 provides a good example, from Norfolk in 1273). Neither of these conditions was met in this case.
>   William I gave the manor of Yarcombe to the Norman abbey of Mont St. Michel – Oliver, *Monasticon* p. 250 – which in turn gave it to its own daughter-house at Otterton, though not until the reign of John, Reichel S4 p. 168. At the 1281/82 eyre the Axminster jurors presented that the abbot of Mont St. Michel claimed to have assizes of bread and ale, gallows and tumbrell in Yarcombe – JUST/1/186 m33 – and the grants of land in

Yarcombe recorded in the Otterton cartulary are all formally made to Mont St. Michel, but these nonetheless provide ample evidence for Otterton's practical possession, DRO TD42 f.90. Since no reference to a prior of Yarcombe has been found elsewhere, it is reasonable to assume that the prior of Otterton is meant, here renamed from his property in this hundred, just as elsewhere the prior of Loders was renamed as prior of Axmouth – see below, no. 47.

14 A boy named Robert was found drowned under Rawridge mill wheel. Misadventure. Value of the wheel 2s., the sheriff etc.

15 Ralph de la Penne's house was burgled by unknown criminals. Reginald and Peter, sons of John the clerk, and Ralph's daughter Alice, attached for the deed, come. Reginald and Peter deny all and put themselves on the country. The jurors testify they do not suspect them or anyone else of the burglary, so they are quit. Luppitt vill is in mercy for not pursuing the criminals.

16 John de Pessy was found killed below Northcote vill. It is testified that Adam the miller and Walter son of Cole were with him when he was killed and were wounded there. They do not come and were not attached, so let them come tomorrow. And Alice the widow of Northcote, Ralph, Roger and Robert her sons, and William son of Stephen de Blanecumbe are charged with the death. Later Adam and Walter come, and Alice also, but the others do not. Alice puts herself on the country, and the jurors testify that she is guilty, so she is hanged. Likewise all her sons are guilty, so let them be exacted and outlawed. They were in the free manor of Honiton, which is in mercy for not producing them. The jurors also testify that William is not guilty, so he is quit. Alice and her sons had chattels 116s., John le Bretesche etc. The men of Northcote are in mercy for not capturing these criminals, later they, that is, just three of them, come and make fine for 10s., pledges Ralph de la Hale and William de la Forde. Later it was found that the king should have the money, so John found the following pledges, Ralph de Lahale, William de la Forde, Robert Hugun, Stephen de Blanecumbe, Philip de Strete, Robert de la Putte.

> Honiton manor was held by the earls of Devon. John le Bretesche, who appears elsewhere (nos. 515, 518) as acting on behalf of Baldwin de Redvers, and who was described in 1249 as having been his steward at Tiverton – JUST/1/176 m9d – by 1241 was steward of the honour of Berkhampstead, held by Richard of Cornwall, Henry III's brother, who in 1233 had been granted Baldwin's wardship, *CCR 1237–1242*, p. 270, N. Denholm-Young, *Richard of Cornwall* (Oxford 1947) p. 27. No doubt it was in that capacity that he appeared in the Oxfordshire eyre of that year as his lord's bailiff in a case involving dower in Somerset, while later in that year he also appeared for earl Richard in the *coram rege* court in a plea concerning a wardship in Cornwall, *Somersetshire Pleas* no. 420d, *CRR* XVI no. 1703. In 1238 he must have been the agent appointed by earl Richard to administer his ward's Devon lands.

17 Robert Coche and his sons Henry and Ralph appealed John Bal and William Luunge of peace etc. and wounding. Robert comes now but does not make suit, so he and his pledges, Matthew Morcok and John le Bunz, are in mercy. Henry does not come, and he had the same pledges, so as before. Ralph has died. John and William come, and the jurors testify that they are not guilty, but that they have made an agreement, so let them be taken into custody. Later appellor and appellees came and made fine for one mark, pledges William de Lahille and Richard Litelman.

18 John le Heine hanged himself in his home in Luppitt. Matilda his

wife, who first found him, has died. No-one is suspected. Felony *de se*. He had no chattels.

19 William de Dorsette was with Painetus his son when he was drowned. He was therefore attached by Gervase de Brutham and William the merchant, who are in mercy for not producing him.

20 Thomas Anderbode was drowned in the river Yarty. His nephew Thomas, from Dorset, first found him. The jurors are in mercy for presenting this case falsely. Membury vill is in mercy for not presenting this case to the County Court.

21 Swetricus Segar was charged with theft. Kilmington tithing, which mainprised to produce him before the justices, is in mercy for not doing so. The jurors testify that he is a thief, so let him be exacted and outlawed. He had no chattels. Later Nicholas de Bona Villa came and made fine for 6s. 8d., himself as pledge.
> To mainprise was to guarantee, to give pledges, most often, as here, for the appearance of a person or persons in court.

22 A boy named Roger was found drowned under the wheel of Axminster mill. Misadventure. Value of the wheel 2s. Walter the miller, who first found him, does not come, and he was attached by Henry de Buggepattesheie and Jocelin de Greihille, who are in mercy.

23 A stranger was found dead on the abbot of Ford's land in Membury. No Englishry so Murder fine. It is not known who killed him.
> No mention has been found elsewhere of Ford Abbey's holding property in Membury. There is nothing under that name in Richard I's confirmation charter, Oliver, *Monasticon* p. 346.

24 William Angot appealed Richard le Mus, otherwise known as Richard le Veutrer, and Walensis Leveneurda of breach of the king's peace, robbery and wounding. William does not come, so he and his pledges, Richard de Hundetorre and William de Godesaltre, are in mercy. Richard does not come, so he and his pledges, Robert de Capella, Robert de Ivedone, William le Brun and Osbert de Northdone, are in mercy. Walensis comes, and the jurors testify that he is not guilty, nor have they made an agreement, so he is quit.

25 Edmund de Witecroft appealed the said Richard and Walensis of the same. He does not come, so he and his pledges, William de Praule and Michael de Iseni, are in mercy. Richard does not come, so he and his pledges are in mercy as before. Walensis comes, and the jurors testify that he is not guilty, nor have they made an agreement, so he is quit.

26 A tun of wine came to land at Uplyme from a wreck at sea. John le Brokere, Gilbert Hamund, Alan Kerl, Geoffrey Coppe, William Giuwold and William Gutt, all from Lyme Regis in Dorset, took the tun and drank more than half of it, and the abbot of Glastonbury without warrant took the rest of the wine with the tun, so he is in mercy. Uplyme vill is in mercy for not presenting this case to the County Court.
> A presentment under article 33, of wrecks at sea. An ancient royal right, wreck had been the subject of a proclamation by Henry I, decreeing that it should become the property of any survivors from a shipwreck, and although this seems to have lapsed after his

death, it was apparently renewed later, since to Bracton "if a ship is broken and no living soul escapes from it, that may properly be called wreck", Bracton, *De Legibus* p. 339, f. 120; A. Gransden, *Historical Writing in England c.550–c.1307* (London 1974) p. 277. No survivors are reported from any of the numerous wrecks reported in 1238, in one instance the jurors were at pains to present that all the sailors in a wrecked ship had drowned (700). Glastonbury abbey held the manor of Uplyme, and had done so since the early tenth century, Finberg, *Early Charters* no. 27.

27 The jurors present that Lady Alice de Mohun is in the king's gift, and her manor of Axminster which she holds of the king is worth £20.

Alice de Mohun was the fourth of the five daughters of William Brewer, among whom or among whose heirs William's estates were divided on the death of his only son in 1233. Her share included Axminster and other manors in Devon. By 1238 she had outlived two husbands, Reginald de Mohun and William Paynel, and so, as a tenant-in-chief, her marriage was in the king's gift. Sanders, *Baronies* pp. 122–123; *CCR 1231–1234* p. 228.

28 Of defaults they say Alice de Mohun, Geoffrey de la Pomerei, Wymund de Raleg', Ralph de Monte Sorello, the abbot of Glastonbury who is lord of Uplyme and Sir Robert de Curtenay did not come on the first day of pleading, so they are in mercy.

A presentment under article 27. Attendance at the eyre was required of all the county's freeholders. The Axmouth jurors – Appendix I(a) no. 8 – appear to have believed that it was still possible, as it had been at the last eyre, to essoin, to excuse oneself, on this summons, but the plea roll (no. 46) shows that they were mistaken, *Surrey Eyre 1235* p. 21.
For Alice de Mohun, who held the hundred, see nos. 27 above and 224 below. Geoffrey de la Pomerai was lord of Upottery, held of the honour of Berry, Reichel S4 p. 155.
Wymund de Raleg held half an ancient fee in Smallridge, *Fees* p. 791.
Ralph de Monte Sorello in 1249 witnessed a deed relating to the Glastonbury abbey manor of Uplyme, so he was probably one of the abbey's tenants in that manor, *The Great Cartulary of Glastonbury*, ed. Dom Aelred Watkins Vol. III (Somerset Record Society Vol. 64, 1956) no. 1069.
For the abbot of Glastonbury see no. 26 above.
Sir Robert de Curtenay was lord of the barony of Okehampton, and as such held Musbury, Thorncombe, Great Trill and Ford next Trill in Axminster hundred, Reichel S4 pp. 151–5

29 William Cude, suspected of the death of Richard de Besseheie, comes, denies Richard's death and puts himself on the country. The jurors testify that he is guilty, so he is hanged. Richard's daughter Emma, who previously made suit against him for her father's death, come but does not prosecute, and the jurors testify that they have made an agreement, so let her be taken into custody. He had chattels worth 65s., Nicholas de la Iae etc., pledges Guy de Bretteville and Roger Giffard. Holditch vill is in mercy for not presenting this case to the County Court. William de Wideworthe, the coroner who saw Richard when he had been wounded, is in mercy for neither attaching William nor having him attached. Later Emma came and made fine for 6s. 8d., pledges John de la Roche and William Hubbert.

HONITON BURGH ANSWERS BY TWELVE JURORS

30 Hugh le Taliur de Hunetone, charged with associating with a thief who abjured the realm, comes, denies all and puts himself on the country. The jurors testify that he is not guilty, so he is quit.

Honiton burgh, described as a member of Plympton manor in 1274/75, was founded by William de Vernun, fifth earl of Devon, between 1193 and 1217, *RH* p. 74. By 1224 its revenues included burgage rents amounting to 13s. 10½d. – *English Medieval Boroughs* p. 92 – and in 1245 its total annual value was assessed at £5. 15s. 4d., C132/3 no. 10(3).

31   Thomas le Gaoler killed Robert le Soper and fled, so let him be exacted and outlawed. He had no chattels, but was in the mainpast of Thomas de Cirencestre, who is in mercy for not producing him. Hugh le Syneker, who was with him when he killed him, comes, and the jurors testify that he is not guilty, so he is quit. And as the jurors presented Hugh's name as William, they are in mercy for a false presentment.

> A mainpast was an alternative to frankpledge for some of the poor and unfree. A lord like Thomas de Cirencestre could become responsible for his immediate dependents or mainpast – literally those who ate his bread – and if, as here, one of these committed felony and ran away, his lord would be amerced for failing to produce him in court just as his tithing would have been had he belonged to one, Pollock and Maitland Vol. I p. 568; W. O. Morris, *The Frankpledge System*, (New York 1910) p. 131.

32   Herbert le Pinu makes fine for five marks for having a respite so as to speak with the king about his son, who is charged with killing a man, pledges Robert Fitzpain and Richard de Hidone.

33   Robert son of Bernard struck John Pinhochet on the head with a stone, so that he died within three days, so let him be exacted and outlawed. Honiton burgh is in mercy for not raising the hue or pursuing him. And Thomas de Brumlege, Roger Osmund, Gilbert de Farewei and John de Appelthorn, who were in John Pinhochet's company, come and are not suspected, so they are quit. Robert son of Peter, who was in Robert's company, comes and is not suspected, so he is quit. William Wittawere, who was in Robert's company, does not come, but he is not suspected, so he may return if he wishes. Thomas, Roger, Osbert (sic) and John, though they were present, did not arrest him, so they are in mercy; they made fine for two marks, pledges Philip de Greneweie and Adam de la Cnolle. Robert the killer was in the mainpast of his father Bernard, who is in mercy, and had no chattels.

(m 27d)

34   Emelota, a thief from Cornwall, fled to Honiton church for theft and abjured the realm before the coroners, who do not have this case enrolled, so to judgment on them. The vill is in mercy for not presenting this case to the County Court.

35   John de Hindone, arrested on the appeal of John de Berghe who was hanged in London, comes, denies all and puts himself on the country. The jurors testify that he is not guilty, so he is quit.

> John de Bergh, described in June 1238 as "lately hanged at London" – *CCR 1237–1242* p. 67 – was probably the approver whom the sheriff of Devon was ordered to send to London "with all speed" in April 1238 – *CLR 1226–1240* p. 327. See also nos. 743, 745, 746 below.

36   Robert de Hindone, Roger son of Henry de Exon' and Robert Mareis are in mercy for selling wine contrary to the assize in Honiton.

HONITON MANOR ANSWERS BY TWELVE JURORS

37   The jurors of this free manor, together with the twelve jurors of

Honiton burgh, present that William Peverel gave them to understand that Simon son of Herbert le Pinu struck Dolwin Veg, a servant of Lady Joan de Briuwere, in the throat with a spear, so that he died next day. But none of them saw this, and they say it happened after a tourney (*burdeicium*) in Honiton. The coroners testify that at an inquest they held into Dolwyn's death they were given to understand that, after the tourney, Ralph de Albemarle, John son of John and Luke de Alneto his squire left the house of Thomas Page with two iron-grey (*ferantos*) horses and carrying two lances, and one of those riding told Dolwyn to put a girth on his horse and, because he would not, struck him in the throat as aforesaid. But they do not know which of them it was. Asked how those who attended the inquest knew this, they say through Dolwyn and in no other way, and they could not find out whether Simon was with Ralph and the others. And because it could not be established by the country that Simon was not guilty of the death, save only through the assertion of his father, who later admitted this, the case was respited until the king's wish on it should be known. Later the king sent his writ to the justices in the following words: H by God's grace etc. to his beloved and faithful William de Ebor' and his fellows etc. Since we have learned that Simon son of Herbert de Pinu by accident and not by malice aforethought killed Dolwyn Veg, the servant of Joan Briuwerr, we have pardoned Simon the death as far as pertains to us, as long as he stands to right if anyone wishes to proceed against him for the death. And so we order you to cause Simon to be quit of the death before you, as far as pertains to us, as aforesaid. And the justices by virtue of their office had it three times publicly proclaimed before them that if anyone wishes to proceed against Simon for the death he should come at once. And since no-one comes who wants to proceed against him it is ordered that he have peace perpetually for it. And Ralph de Albemarl, Luke his servant and John son of John, attached for this, are quit in perpetuity.

> Several presenting areas were described as manors in kalendar, or text, or both – Honiton, Colyford, Whitford, Ottery, Molland, Plimland and Yealmpton. They would appear to have become privileged by reason of their long tenure in the hands of king or earl, and may, indeed, have once been centres of royal estates – all except Molland are in the rich lands east of the Exe, and along the south coast which were probably taken over by the kings of Wessex during their conquest of the south-west, and Molland also seems to have been a royal estate – Reichel S9 p. 527. Honiton manor, however, was held by the Count of Mortain in 1086, and was said then to have paid 30d. *per annum* to the king's manor of Axminster until the Count acquired it, when payment ceased. *DB* p. 14. It obviously retained its *de facto* independence after it had been given to the earls of Devon – Reichel S4 p. 150. Simon's pardon is dated 27 June 1238 – *CCR 1237–1242* p. 68. His father gave ten marks and a mewed hawk for the pardon as well as five marks for the respite (no. 32 above) – E 372/88 in 10. In 1239 he was licensed to pay off his accumulated fine at four marks yearly, E159/17 m7. At the back of this killing may have lain tensions arising out of the dispute between William Brewer, father-in-law of Dolwyn's employer Joan, and Herbert de Pinu, who had been his steward, about arrears allegedly owed by the latter to the former, *CPR 1225–1232* pp. 73–4.

38 Walter de Boteilerheie killed Nicholas de la Furse and fled, so let him be exacted and outlawed. He lived in Waringstone tithing in Hemyock hundred, which is in mercy, and had chattels 20s., the aforesaid tithing to answer for 13s. and Battishorne tithing for 7s. Nicholas Avenel took two bullocks from Walter's chattels so that the coroners could not view them, so he is in mercy. Walter's wife Wymarcha, whom Nicholas is said to have slept with, went away with Walter her husband, but she is not suspected,

so she may return if she wishes. And since it is not fully clear to the justices about Walter's chattels, nor whether he had free land or not, inquire more fully in Hemyock hundred.

AXMOUTH HUNDRED ANSWERS BY TWELVE JURORS

39 The house of Roger de Wachcumbe was burgled by unknown criminals. 'Dunesibille' vill is in mercy for not pursuing them as it should have done.

40 William Ernewei was outlawed for the death of Richard Curlepeis by the suit of Richard's wife Cristiana. He was living in Colyford manor, so inquire there about his chattels.

41 A tun with a little wine in it from a wreck at sea was found at Axmouth. The coroners valued it at 3s., the prior of Axmouth etc.

42 Robert de Bendone was outlawed for the death of Peter de Bonon' by the suit of Peter's brother Robert. He was in Bindon tithing, which is in mercy, and had chattels 2s., the prior of Axmouth etc.

43 Walter the chaplain of Cumba wounded Philip de Witeford and made himself scarce. Philip recovered from the wound and does not make suit against him. Walter left behind chattels worth 4s. Discuss who should have those chattels.

> The man who fled from justice forfeited his chattels even if he later appeared in court and was acquitted.

44 William Makerel stole clothes at Osbert Hose's house. He fled to church, where he admitted to the deed and abjured the realm before the coroners. The jurors are in mercy for not presenting William's name. Robert de Shete's tithing of Combe is in mercy for not pursuing him.

> This must be Combe Pyne which on 9 July 1238 Alice Coffin gave in marriage with her daughter Roesia to Robert, son of Luke de Shete. Reichel S4 p. 180, S7 p. 347.

45 Three men drowned by falling into the sea from a boat. Misadventure. Value of the boat 30d., the sheriff etc.

46 Of defaults they say William le Flemeng did not come on the first day as summoned before the justices, so he is in mercy.

> William le Flemeng had land at Rousdon and 'Slade' in Axmouth hundred. At the time of the eyre he was on pilgrimage to Santiago di Compostella, having entrusted his Devon lands to Geoffrey de Mandevill – JUST/1/175 m3 – but he had returned by 3 August 1238, when he gave his Axmouth properties to Loders priory, L. Guilloreau (ed.), *Cartulaire de Loders* (Evreux 1908) no. 70.

47 Four thieves were hanged by judgment of the prior of Axmouth's court as they were arrested with stolen goods. Whereupon the prior of Axmouth comes and says he can do this through the liberty he has, but he shows no warrant, only says he has used such a liberty for a long time.

> Although there are occasional references in thirteenth-century sources, as here, to a prior of Axmouth (e.g. *HMC Various Collections* Vol. IV p. 57, D & C 3672 ff. 160–1), this was certainly, like the prior of Yarcombe (no. 13 above), a substitute title for the ecclesiastical lord of the manor, in this case the prior of Loders in Dorset. The identity of the two prelates is placed beyond doubt by William le Flemeng's grant of his lands in

Axmouth hundred to Loders priory (for the reference see no. 46 above), whereby he gave seisin "*Ricardo de Cesarisburgo, tempore huius donationis Priori de Lodres et de Axemue*". The manor of Axmouth was granted before 1107 to Montebourg abbey in Normandy by Richard de Redvers – *RRA–N* II nos. 825, 826; *CDF* no. 879 – but came to be held by Montebourg's daughter-house of Loders. It gave its name to a small hundred, later absorbed by Axminster, *PND* p. 633.

COLYTON HUNDRED ANSWERS BY TWELVE JURORS

48 Robert de Helion and Thomas de Bramlege, two jurors of this hundred, did not come with their fellows to answer for their *veredictum*, so they are in mercy. Each is amerced of 6s. 8d.

49 A tun of wine came to land at Seaton from a wreck at sea, and Robert de Helion had it by view of coroner and sheriff. Value 6s., Gatcombe tithing etc.

50 Alan de Bere and William de Rocforde came from Exeter with Henry de Dene. Henry, in going home, fell ill, and Alan and William took him to the house of Henry de Furse, where he died that night. No-one is suspected. Rannulf de Cerne, then sheriff, took 50s. from Alan and William because of that, so to judgment on him. Inquire more fully about this case in Budleigh hundred, because Henry de Furse lives in that hundred.

> Rannulf de Cerne was clerk to Roger la Zuche, and seems to have been largely responsible for routine administration during Roger's shrievalty, from November 1228 to April 1231. A small landowner in Dorset – E. A. & G. S. Fry (eds.), *Dorset Feet of Fines* (Dorset Records, Vol. 5, 1896) pp. 70–1 – who later made a brief appearance as under-sheriff of Yorkshire, he seems to have been the sort of professional administrator counties hated – D. A. Carpenter, 'The Decline of the Curial Sheriff in England 1194–1258', in *EHR* 91 (1976) p. 20. His other appearances in this roll suggest that he was abrasive and officious (189, 300, 645, 654), possibly corrupt (86) and not always efficient (323). All this could have been no more than a testimony to the resentment aroused by his administrative skills, were it not that subsequent inquiries suggested that money paid to him as Zuche's clerk had been sticking to his fingers, E159/12 m16.

51 Walter Spere of Colyton hundred went towards Exeter with cloth and was killed on 'Blakedone' in Budleigh hundred, so inquire more fully there. Geoffrey the forester, charged with the death, was arrested and imprisoned at Exeter, where he died in prison. No-one else is suspected.

52 A tun of wine came to land at Branscombe and was handed over to Branscombe tithing. Value 11s., that tithing etc.

53 A mare belonging to Absolon de Laneweie, who lives in this hundred, was found at Sidbury mill in Budleigh hundred, so inquire more fully there. The twelve jurors of Budleigh hundred come later and say they know nothing besides what is aforesaid.

54 Unknown criminals killed Rannulf de Littelcombe by night in his home. It is not known who they were. No Englishry so Murder fine. Miles de Littelcumbe and his son Robert, attached for the death, come and put themselves on the country. The jurors testify they are not guilty, so they are quit.

55 Robert de la Slade and Robert de Erthi appealed Ralph de la Hille

that he, with abettors, badly beat them, but they do not mention a sword or any other kind of weapon. And they appealed Hugh de la Hille of abetting. Hugh and Ralph come, and since the appeal is null, let the country inquire. The jurors say that Ralph took beasts of Robert de Bulkewrthi's which were causing him damage and wanted to impound them, and the two appellors wished to take the beasts away, and he, in repelling force by force, struck them. So it is decided that the appellors are in mercy, they made fine for one mark, pledge Robert de Bulkewrthi.

> In 1242 Robert de Bulkewrthi held Sutton Lucy in Colyton hundred Reichel S7 pp. 350–1.

56 Ralph de Williamestone's cart with six oxen crushed a child to death. Misadventure. Value of the cart and oxen 18s. 10d., the sheriff etc.

57 Richard Juvenis de Forwde, Wimund Wittinge and Hugh Burelle killed Geoffrey de Sulleie and were outlawed for the death by the suit of Robert Collop his brother. They were in the abbot of Quarr's mainpast, he is in mercy for not producing them. Later it was testified that Wimund was in Northleigh tithing, which is in mercy, and had chattels 12s., that tithing etc. The others had no chattels. The twelve jurors are in mercy for presenting this case falsely.

> Quarr abbey on the Isle of Wight was founded in 1132 by Baldwin de Redvers – D. Knowles and R. N. Hadcock, *Medieval Religious Houses; England and Wales* (2nd edn., London 1971) p. 123 – and it was from the de Redvers honour of Plympton that Hubert de Vallibus gave Farwood to the abbey, which also received lands in Farway and near Whitley, both in Colyton hundred – Reichel S7 p. 351; *Canonsleigh Cartulary* no. 181; *Devon FFI* nos. 29, 222. By 1249 Quarr also had a sheep run at Watchcombe, JUST/1/176 m34d.

58 Nicholas Pain was mortally wounded as he returned from an ale-feast in Dorset. Roger the miller, who killed him, was outlawed for the death by the suit of Nicholas's wife Ascelota. He had no chattels and was in Offwell tithing, which is in mercy.

> The hard drinking to which medieval Englishmen were notoriously prone was clearly as prevalent in Devon as elsewhere, as may be deduced from the stipulation that a corrody conferred on two men, probably ex-employees, by Newenham abbey in 1279 should include five gallons of conventual ale and five gallons of second ale each week – DRO 49/26/2 ff. 39v – 40r. Alcohol was continuously productive of violence and disorder, and was for that reason, among others, repeatedly condemned from the pulpit – G. R. Owst, *Literature and Pulpit in Medieval England* (2nd edn., Oxford 1966) pp. 425–41. In his Penitential, Bishop Bartholomew of Exeter ordered the excommunication of those who drank too much – Morey, *Bartholomew* pp. 269–71 – and in 1260 people were said to have been excommunicated *propter communes potaciones que sociales vocantur* – *Reg. Bronescombe* p. 92. See also nos. 94 and 384 below and for other, similar cases at Devon eyres, JUST/1/175 m 38; JUST/1/176 mm 35, 39d; JUST/1/186 mm 5, 8d, 9d, 10, 13.

59 A mound was dug into on the boundary between Whitley Farm and Netherton. These two vills are in mercy for not presenting this case to the County Court.

> A presentment under article 13, "of treasure trove" – an ancient royal right. It is clear that the mounds so often dug into were prehistoric barrows of which large numbers survive in Devon to this day. Many more must have been destroyed, either by treasure-hunters or by farmers levelling land for the plough. The large number of such presentments in 1238 may be a reflection of Henry III's interest in barrows as a source of treasure; in the previous year he had instructed his brother to have the barrows in Cornwall and the Isle of Wight dug into, "to look for treasure in them", *CCR 1234–1237* p. 433.

60 Offwell vill is in mercy for not pursuing criminals as it should have

done. An unknown man was found killed in 'Werdescumbe' waste. It is not known who killed him. No Englishry so Murder fine.
>This may be a presentment under article 23, "of those over whose lands outlaws have passed without pursuing them".

(m 28)
61   The priest of Cotleigh's house was burgled, it is not known by whom. The vill is in mercy for making no pursuit.

62   Alice de Culitone who first found her son drowned does not come. She was attached by Walter Godknave and Walter son of the smith of Culitone, who are in mercy. Later Alice comes, so nothing from her pledges.

63   Hugh Bogge was found dead on the land of Colyton church. No Englishry so Murder fine.

64   Henry son of Ralph the miller was outlawed for the death of Gilbert de Spillecumbe by the suit of Alfred son of Edgar. He had no chattels and was in no tithing, so nothing. Later it was testified that he was harboured outside frankpledge in Shute, a part of Whitford, which is in mercy.
>According to Reichel – S7 p. 347 – Shute originated in a grant by John Biset and his wife Alice, lord of Whitford manor, of a free tenement within that manor to Luke de la Shete, made between 1205 and 1228.

65   Of defaults they say that Richard de la Roche, Richard de Langeforde, William Roc and Rannulf de Watercumbe did not come on the first day, so they are in mercy.
>Richard de la Roche held half a fee at Cotleigh of the barony of Cardinan, *Fees* p. 795. He was a juror for Colyton hundred in 1244 and 1249, JUST/1/175 m35; JUST/1/176 m46.
>Richard de Langeforde in 1238 exchanged lands in Branscombe for half a hide in Barcombe; both properties were in Colyton hundred, Reichel S7 p. 356.
>William Roc was a juror for Colyton in 1244, JUST/1/175 m35. Rannulf de Watercumbe – who probably took his name from Watercombe in Dorset – defaulted again in 1248, JUST/1/176 m34d.

66   The jurors present that Branscombe vill withdrew from the sheriff's aid after the shrievalty of William de Raleigh, so let this be discussed. It used to give 6s. 8d. yearly, so they say.
>William de Raleigh was sheriff of Devon from October 1225 to November 1228. Branscombe was held by the chapter of Exeter cathedral, Reichel S7 p. 348. Sheriff's aid was a customary due, levied all over England on land anciently assessed for geld, probably in origin intended to meet the sheriff's expenses and usually paid at his tourn – N. Neilson, *Customary Rents* (Oxford 1910) pp. 124–9. The name may, however, have come to be loosely applied to other dues or commutations, as in the case of North Molton manor (279) where its payment was an alternative to suit at the County Court.

67   The prioress of Polsloe's men in Colyton did not come on the first day, nor did they wish to be with the jurors in making their *veredictum*, so they are in mercy.
>The nuns of Polsloe were given lands worth 100s. *per annum* by Henry II in 1177 or 1178 – *PR 24 Henry II* p. 10; *Fees* pp. 67–68; *RH* p. 68. The estate was identified as Tudhay at the 1244 eyre – JUST/1/175 m37d.

68   Reginald de Valle Torta, asked by what warrant he holds Colyton hundred, comes and proffers a charter of King Richard, testifying that he

has given and granted to Thomas Barset, for homage etc., the whole manor of Colyton with all its appurtenances, except for 100s. of land which the nuns of Polsloe have by gift of King Henry his grandfather. So that he says that John Bisetter, who is one of Thomas's heirs, has one half and he the other, but he says that the hundred pertains to that manor. And so King Richard held that manor when he gave it to Thomas, and so he has always held the hundred until now, but he shows no other warrant. So let this be discussed.

> Colyton was held by the king in 1086 – DB pp. 18–21. In 1159 Henry II gave it to Robert de Dunstanvil – Reichel S7 pp. 342–3 – whose son or grandson Walter gave it to Thomas Basset – DRO TD 51 f. 150 – a gift confirmed by Richard I in 1198 – *Cartae Antiquae Rolls 1–10* (*PRS, NS* Vol. XVII, 1939) no. 315. Thomas Basset left three daughters, among whom his lands were divided, probably between 1220 and 1229. Philippa, then wife of earl Henry of Warwick and later of Richard Siward – *Complete Peerage* Vol. XII Part II pp. 364–5 – received lands outside the hundred, which was shared between Joan, with her husband Reginald de Valle Torta, and Alice, with her second (apparently) husband John Biset. DRO TD 51 ff. 154–5. Possession of the hundred-manor of Colyton, however, always gave Joan's descendants precedence within the hundred over those of Alice, BL Add MS 49359 f. 53v. In 1249 the hundred was valued at two marks *per annum*, JUST/1/176 m34d.

COLYFORD BURGH ANSWERS BY SIX JURORS

69   Basilia de Setona was scalded to death in a cistern full of hot water. Misadventure. Value of the cistern 3s., the sheriff etc.

> In 1207 John granted Thomas Basset a yearly fair at Colyton, *Rot. Ch.* p. 169. But he subsequently moved his new borough to the ford where the road from Dorchester to Exeter crossed the river Coly. Hoskins, *Devon*, p. 372.

70   Ralph de Rifforde is in mercy for selling wine at Colyford contrary to the assize.

WHITFORD MANOR ANSWERS BY TWELVE JURORS

71   Of defaults they say that John Biset, Gilbert Basset and Stephen Bausan did not come the first day, so they are in mercy.

> John Biset was lord of Whitford, which, like Colyton (no. 68 above), was confirmed to Thomas Basset by Richard I in 1198. Originally Thomas appears to have intended Joan to have Whitford as well as Colyton – DRO TD 51 ff. 155–6 – but ultimately it passed to Alice, John Biset's wife.
> Gilbert Basset probably held Colcombe, a sub-manor created on the waste-lands of Colyton, Reichel S7 pp. 342, 344. He witnessed the partition of Thomas Basset's lands, DRO TD 51 ff. 154–5. Stephen Bausan was said to have been granted land in Lexhayne, in Sure parish, by Peter Blundus two generations before 1260, DRO 49/26/3/1 f. 30.

OTTERY ST. MARY MANOR ANSWERS BY TWELVE JURORS

72   Richard de Crunttetone drowned by falling from his horse into the river Otter. Misadventure. Value of the horse 30d., the sheriff etc.

73   Gilbert de Dune drowned by falling from his horse into the river Otter. Misadventure. Value of the horse 4s., the sheriff etc.

74   William son of Beatrice was found dead on 'Blakedune'. No Englishry so Murder fine. No-one is suspected.

> Edward the Confessor gave Ottery manor to St. Mary's Rouen in 1061, *CDF* no. 1. It ranked as a hundred in 1244 and 1249, but as a vill in 1281/82.

HEMYOCK HUNDRED ANSWERS BY TWELVE JURORS

75   Richard son of Godfrey is in mercy for foolish speaking (*pro stultiloquio*), and likewise Roger Swethog and Peter de Hindebereghe are in mercy for not coming with their fellows to answer for their *veredictum*.

76   A boy called William was drowned under Buckerell mill wheel. Misadventure. Value of the wheel 2s., the sheriff etc.

77   Richard Bukerel was found dead in Whitley field. No-one is suspected, no Englishry so Murder fine. Buckerell tithing is in mercy for falsely presenting Englishry on this case.

78   William de Coleheia appealed Richard de Langeford, Roger the marshal, William de Wudebere, William de Sireford and John de Coleheia of breach of the king's peace and beating. He does not come, so he and his pledges, William Pincerna and William Hamelin, are in mercy. Richard de Langeford and Roger the marshal come, but William de Wudebere, William de Sireford and John de Coleheia do not, so they and their pledges are in mercy. William de Wudebere was attached by William de Wevere and Nicholas de Wevere, William de Sireford by Oliver de Sireford and Richard Beta, John by Robert Revel and Nicholas Bissop. Later William de Coleheia comes and makes fine for 40s., pledges Walter Pincerna, Hugh Fuke and Roger Swethog. Later William de Coleheia came and appealed Richard de Langeford that on the morrow of St. Gregory he came to Colhayes and knocked down his pound, badly beat him and flung him from his horse, so that his hand was wounded, and that he did this evilly and in felony he offers etc. Richard comes and asks for judgment on his accusation, but as the appeal is null the country is to inquire and William de Coleheia is in mercy for a false appeal. The jurors testify that Richard did him no harm and did not knock his pound down, so Richard is quit and William de Coleheia is in mercy, let him be taken into custody, while since no deed was done, all those appealed of abetting are quit.

79   To judgment on the jurors for presenting no Englishry.

80   Lawrence the Welshman and William the Welshman killed their colleagues Walter and Adam, metal-founders (*fundator*), and fled, so let them be exacted and outlawed. They were in the mainpast of the abbot of Dunkeswell, who is in mercy, and had no chattels. Hemyock tithing is in mercy for not presenting that case as it should have done.
    Dunkeswell abbey's holdings in Hemyock hundred included Dunkeswell itself, Waringstone in Buckerel, Bolham in Clayhidon, Bywood in Dunkeswell, Awliscombe, Stentwood and Wolford. *Devon FFI* nos. 283, 397, 541; *Fees* p. 1443; *Rot. Ch.* pp. 164–5.

81   Elena daughter of Richard Budde appealed Richard Buletrug of rape. She does not come, so let her be arrested and let her pledges, Gorwy Budde and Geoffrey de Leghe, both from Somerset, be in mercy. Richard comes, and as they have made no agreement and the jurors testify that he is not guilty, he is quit.

82   Unknown criminals stayed at the home of Robert de la Thorne, from

which they departed secretly, leaving chattels there worth 2s., 'Stantone' tithing etc.

83   Criminals burgled the house of Cristina de Matecumbe. Hemyock tithing is in mercy for not pursing them.

84   Gerald de Tottewurthe fell from his horse on Widecumbe moor and died. Value of the horse nothing as he was from Somerset. The men of Otterford are in mercy for burying him without a coroner's view, Churchstanton vill for presenting no first finder. Later the vill came and made fine for 10s.

85   William de Schabecumbe killed Thomas le Chareter and fled. Later he returned and fled to Dunkeswell church, where he admitted the deed and abjured the realm before the coroner. He was in the mainpast of the abbot of Dunkeswell, who is in mercy, and had chattels worth 3s., the abbot etc.

86   William Niwecumbe, an approver, was hanged before William de Raleghe and his fellow gaol delivery justices. The jurors testify that Rannulf de Cerne, the then sheriff, took goods worth one mark from his chattels, so to judgment on him.
    This was probably the gaol delivery ordered for 27 March 1232, at which the four justices already appointed were instructed to act on William de Raleigh's advice, *CPR 1225–1232* p. 516. The reference to Rannulf de Cerne suggests that William had been arrested at least a year before his execution – see no. 50 above.

87   Roger le Bon is suspected of stealing oxen and cows, so let him be exacted and outlawed. He was in Culm Davy tithing, which is in mercy.

88   Richard de Hidune mainprised to have Walter Brode, charged with associating with Geoffrey Ridel, a thief who abjured the realm, before the justices, so he is in mercy for not producing him. The jurors testify that Walter is not guilty, so he may return if he wishes.
    For Richard de Hidune see no. 90 below.

89   Walter Morel, charged with harbouring Osbert Morel, a fugitive, has made himself scarce. The jurors testify that he is not guilty, so he may return if he wishes. Since Walter does not come, his pledges, Mabel de Marlecumbe, Ralph son of Jocelin and William Hamelin, are in mercy.

90   The jurors present that earl Richard de Rivers, who was enfeoffed with Hemyock manor, together with the hundred, gave manor and hundred to one Robert Foliot, ancester of Richard de Hidone, and the right (*ius*) to the manor and hundred descended from him to the same Richard, being one of Robert Foliot's heirs, as his share. But he shows no warrant besides ancient tenure.
    The hundred manor of Hemyock was Madford or Madeshay, which Henry I is elsewhere said to have given to Robert Foliot to hold by the service of attesting the summonses made by the serjeant of Hemyock on the arrival of the king's justices. It had escheated to the crown by 1195 – Reichel S2 p. 39 – but shortly afterwards both Hemyock and Madford were among the lands of Robert Foliot which his grandchildren paid 80 marks to have divided among them. *PR 1 John* p. 198. One of these was Richard de Hiddon, who c. 1212 was said to be holding Madeshay by serjeanty – *Red Book of the Exchequer* Vol. II ed. H. Hall (*RS* 1896) pp. 452–3 – and who clearly acquired Hemyock hundred with it. In 1249 the hundred was said to be held by John de Hidon and to be worth 10s. *per annum*, JUST/1/176 m35. Perhaps Henry I's original grant had stipulated

that Madford was to be held of Richard de Redvers, hence the mistake by the jurors in 1238 in attributing the original grant of manor and hundred to Richard de Redvers I, who was sometimes erroneously styled earl.

91   The jurors present that the men of Culmstock used to give 3s. to sheriff's aid but have now withdrawn it, by what warrant it is not known. The jurors are in mercy for concealing that case. Let it be discussed.
   The dean and chapter of Exeter cathedral held the manor and church of Culmstock, Pole, *Collections* p. 204, *PQW* p. 169.

UFFCULME HUNDRED ANSWERS BY SIX JURORS

92   A girl was drowned in 'Forde' water. Her grandmother Gunilda, who first found her, comes and is not suspected. The jurors are in mercy for not presenting the girl's name.
   Uffculme was described as a hundred in the kalendars of 1238, 1244 and 1249, and in the text of this eyre and that of 1249, JUST/1/176 m35; in the text of 1244, on the other hand, it was described as a manor – JUST/1/175 m40 – and in the kalendar of 1281/82 it was described as a vill, though in the text it ranked as a hundred, JUST/1/186 mm40, 46d. It never had more than six jurors. It ranked as a hundred in the 1080s, no doubt as a result of its long tenure by the highly privileged abbey of Glastonbury – *Devonshire Studies*, p. 60 – and clearly kept something of that status thereafter, when it passed, with Bampton hundred, to the Paynels, see nos. 102, 160 below.

93   Gillian wife of Robert Grigku appealed Luke Serviens de Uffeculum of wounding and beating her husband Robert. She does not make suit, so she and her pledges, Richard le Loverde and Walter Wishutkedune, are in mercy. Luke, the appellee, does not come, and he was attached by Thomas de Tetteburne and Robert de Blakeford. Later Robert de Blakeforde came and made fine for himself, Thomas and Luke for 20s., himself as pledge.

(m 28d)
94   Walter Niger complains that Peter the miller and his brother William came to his house wanting more of his ale than he would sell them, and because he would not sell it them they threatened to burn his house, and they broke his house. Peter and William come, and as this happened in Hayridge hundred let them come with that hundred. Later they came with that hundred, and Walter does not make suit as he appealed them in the county court, so he and his pledges, Henry de Bodlai and Roger le Porter, are in mercy. The jurors testify that Peter and William broke Walter's doors as he complains, so let them be taken into custody. Later Walter made fine for 6s. 8d., pledge Richard de Prestcote, and Peter and William came and made fine for 10s., pledges Roger de Godeleghe and William de Foggeshille.

95   Unknown criminals burgled the house of Richard the forester and later met Richard and Adam de Quercu and killed them. No Englishry so Murder fine.

96   William Blundus was killed by a mare. Misadventure. Value of the mare 4s., the sheriff etc.

97   William Ruggehulle, attached for the death of Mabel, wife of Hugh

de Laheie, comes and denies all. Likewise William's brother Stephen, attached for the same, comes, and they both deny all and put themselves on the country. The jurors, with the jurors of Hemyock, Hayridge, Bampton and Halberton, testify that in truth William struck her on the arm with a pickaxe, but she did not die of that wound but of another infirmity, as she was pregnant and had a fever (*morbus callidus*), as a result of which she miscarried her child and died. So William and Stephen are quit in perpetuity.

98   Walter de Fromtone fled to Uffculme church, where he admitted to being a thief and abjured the realm. He was in no tithing, being a vagrant thief, and he had no chattels.

99   Walter son of Walrand appealed William de Raggeshille, Gilbert de Galbere, William de Senewelle and Erlemund Smithenecote that on the Wednesday next before the feast of St. Michael eight years ago (25 September 1230) they came to Sowell Farm, which he had in his keeping through Jordan Lambrit his nephew, and knocked down Jordan's house; and when he fled in fear they took from the house, from William's belongings, a hauberk, a blanket, two linen sheets, a lance, a bow, a sheaf of arrows, twelve nets for catching hares and an iron fork, and that they did this evilly and in felony, in breach of the king's peace, he offers etc., as the court decides. William de Foggeshille and all the other appellees come and ask to be allowed that he appeals them of felony and especially of knocking down a house in his keeping through the said Jordan, and also says they all took the hauberk and the other things, specifying who took what, and says moreover that when they came with many others he fled at once, and so he does not speak from his own sight or hearing, nor does he give the value of the things taken. So it is decided that the appeal is null, but for the maintenance of the king's peace let the country inquire into the case. The jurors testify that Luke Serviens de Uffculum took an iron fork, a bow and several arrows and carried them off, but no hauberk or anything else. But those appealed took nothing, so they are all quit and let William be taken into custody. Later William Walerant came and made fine for one mark, pledges Richard Walerant and Robert de Bradefelde.

> An appellor had to be able to speak from his own experience. Walter's appeal was quashed because, since he had admitted to having fled from the house, he could not claim to have seen or heard the events he described.

100   William de Senewille appealed William son of Walrand that with others he came to his house at Sowell Farm and breaking his chapel door took two loaves and an altar-cloth worth 2s., and then went out and knocked his wife down, and that he did this in felony. The appeal is null, so let the country inquire into the case. The jurors testify that he is not guilty, so he is quit and let William be taken into custody. Later he came and made fine for 6s. 8d., pledges Herlewin and Rannulf de Smithenecote.

> This appears to be the earliest surviving reference to a private chapel or oratory of the sort which became commonplace in Devon in the fourteenth and fifteenth centuries, the size of parishes and the frequent impassibility of paths and highways making them highly desirable, even essential, adjuncts to the private dwellings of the devout well-to-do. Hoskins *Devon* pp 227-8.

101 Walter Lambrit appealed William de Senewelle of breach of the king's peace and felony. He does not come, so he and his pledges, Richard Walrande and Adam de Bantone, are in mercy.

102 The jurors present that half of Uffculme manor, which Alice de Mohun holds, used to contribute 2s. 6d. to sheriff's aid but has now withdrawn it, by what warrant it is not known. Let this be discussed.
> Alice de Mohun owed her interest in Uffculme to her second husband William Paynel, hereditary lord of Bampton hundred, which had gone with Uffculme since the reign of William I. Sanders, *Baronies* pp. 122–3. The order that she be given livery of her dower from William Paynel's lands was issued on 27 February 1228, *CCR 1227-1231* p. 24.

HAYRIDGE HUNDRED ANSWERS BY TWELVE JURORS

103 John the chaplain of Cherltone, arrested for striking a woman called Clarica so that she fell on her son, injuring him fatally, comes, and the jury testifies that he is guilty. Whereupon the bishop of Exeter's official comes and claims him, to do justice on him in Court Christian, and he is handed over to him. Cheriton tithing is in mercy for not presenting this case to the County Court and for default. Later it was testified that John has chattels, grain worth 32s., sheep worth 7s. 6d. and a horse worth 5s., and that he had three furlongs of land in Cheriton, which are to be taken into the king's hand.
> Hayridge hundred was known as Sulfretona (Silverton) in 1086, when it was held by the king *DB* pp. 10–11. Henry II gave it to the earls of Devon, Reichel in *TDA* 42(1910) pp. 215, 229–30. In 1238 it was held by Baldwin III who, being still a minor in wardship, did not appear at the eyre, but who in 1239 was litigating in the Bench to recover suits to this hundred *CRR* XVI nos. 1023, 1035. In 1249 it was valued at 40s. *per annum*. JUST/1/176 m37. Silverton itself had come to be held of the earls by the Vautorts, by the service of acting as beadle for the hundred, *Cal. Inq. PMI* no. 63. The meeting place for the hundred was consequently moved to Whorridge, from which the hundred took its new name, BL Add MS 49359 ff. 52v–53.

104 Roger the clerk of Talletone and John Ruffus, arrested for the death of William Hoeles, come, and Roger is a clerk, but neither is suspected, so they are quit. Adam Whitepruvost made himself scarce for the same but he is not suspected, so he may return if he wishes, but because he did not come he and his pledges, Roger de Langeforde and William de Clist, are in mercy. No Englishry was presented on William, so Murder fine. Later it was testified that Adam had other pledges besides Roger and William, namely Henry de la Leghe, John le Blund, Richard de la Pole, Nicholas le White, Robert Riketrache, Philip de Mora, Jordan Assa, Richeman de Lamore, Thomas Chace and William Ruffus, who are all in mercy as he did not come.

105 Richard de la Pole appealed Roger the clerk of burgling his house, but he does not come, so he and his pledges, Jordan Assa and Nicholas le White, are in mercy. Roger comes, and the jurors testify that he is not guilty, so he is quit.

106 A mound was dug into near Broadhembury hill. No-one is suspected. Payhembury tithing is in mercy for neither presenting this case to the County Court nor coming before the justices.

107 William de Vernun and Robert de Cerde appealed John the parson of Hambire, Philip de Sidebire, William de Wideberghe, Herbert the clerk, Godfrey Gelli, Robert son of Wlmar, Rannulf Chagchefrenchis, Denise de Caneleswrthi, Robert le White, Richard Authman, Geoffrey de Molend', Robert son of Ralph, Roger son of John, Ralph Pepering and Philip de Cumbe of arresting them, detaining them, taking from them their belts with their knives and horns, and carrying off the grain from two acres of land. Herbert does not come, so he and his pledges, Geoffrey Coffin and Richard Giffard, are in mercy. Robert Wlmar, who was attached by Richard Armiger and Hugh de la Ya, Robert son of Ralph, who was attached by Richard Armiger and John de Molend', and Philip de Cumbe, who was attached by Reginald Rokebare and William de Fonte, do not come, so they are all in mercy. All the other appellees come, except Denise, who was not found, and the jurors testify that they have made an agreement, so let them all be taken into custody. William de Vernun and Robert de Cerde, the appellors, do not come, so they and their pledges, Ralph Tale and Ralph Stur for William and Luke de Culum for Robert, are in mercy. Later John the parson came and made fine for himself and all the appellees who came for 40s., pledges John de Cherltone, John Tibbaud, John de Tril, Hugh de la Ya and Richard de Cherltone.

108 Ralph Pipering, who appealed Walter Rugge of breach of the king's peace and premeditated assault, comes but does not make suit, so he and his pledges, Rannulf Chaggefrenchisse and William Modi, are in mercy. The appellee comes, and the jurors testify that they have made an agreement, so they are in mercy. Later Walter came and made fine for 6s. 8d., pledge Thomas de Orreweie. Later Ralph came and made fine for 10s., pledges Nicholas son of William and Rannulf Kacherel.

109 John Billes de Plimtre was found drowned in the river Culm. Misadventure. The jurors are in mercy for presenting no first finder.

110 Jolenta daughter of Adam the smith was found drowned in the river Exe. William Kinesman, who first found her, does not come, so he and his pledges, Robert the miller and Robert Blundus, are in mercy. Misadventure. No-one is suspected.

111 Roger Crocker killed Richard Wisar and fled, so let him be exacted and outlawed. He was living in Netherexe tithing, which is in mercy, and had chattels 25s., that tithing etc. Roger had other chattels in his keeping which were not his, so the sheriff is ordered to let their owners have them, if they can properly show them to be theirs. Richard de Crues took part of the chattels without their being viewed by coroner or sheriff, so let him be taken into custody. Later he came and made fine for two marks, pledges—.

> In 1242 Richard de Crues held one knight's fee in Netherexe of the honour of Barnstaple, *Fees* p. 773. At the 1244 eyre Roger Crocker's brother Simon was accused, but acquitted, of harbouring his brother Roger, an outlaw, JUST/1/175 m40.

112 The jurors testify that William Portman sold wine belonging to Roger son of Henry de Exon' contrary to the assize at Bradnich, so he is in mercy.

The assize of wine of 7 February 1237 had laid down that a sester (four gallons) of white wine from France should not cost more than 8d., or a sester of red wine more than 10d., *CCR 1234–1237* p. 522. That Roger was also amerced for selling wine in breach of the assize in Honiton and Tiverton (nos. 36, 138) suggests that he sold wine both wholesale and retail. This does not seem to have been unusual. At the 1249 eyre Martin Rof, a former mayor of Exeter, was amerced for similar infringements in Tiverton vill, Bradninch manor and Bampton hundred, JUST/1/176 mm36, 37.

113   Thomas son of Torond was killed by a horse and harrow. No-one is suspected. Price of the horse and harrow 2s., the sheriff etc. Bickleigh tithing is in mercy for not having the 2s. before the justices.

(m 29)
114   Bartholomew de Uphexe and Roger Cal were outlawed for the death of Thomas de Ferrariis at the suit of Serlo de Bikebire. Roger Cal was living in Thorverton tithing, which is in mercy, and Bartholomew was in the mainpast of Henry de Tracy, who is in mercy for not producing him. They had no chattels. Serlo appealed Walter de la Rodeweie of the death, and they both come now, but Serlo does not make suit against him, so he and his pledges, Henry de Hyne and Richard de Clive, are in mercy. The jurors testify that Walter is not guilty, so he is quit, and let Serlo be taken into custody. Later Serlo came and made fine for 6s. 8d., pledges Guy le Bret and Hugh de Loges.

For more about this case see no. 494 below.

115   Richard son of Baldwin fatally wounded Richard Cole and was outlawed at the suit of his victim's sister Margery. No-one else is suspected. He was Cadeleigh tithing, which is in mercy, and had chattels 11s. 10d., that tithing etc.

116   Roger de la Hecche's house was burgled. Robert de Alleforde, charged with receiving the goods stolen, comes and is not suspected, so he is quit. The jurors testify that Roger imputed that crime to Robert so as to have some of his chattels, so let him be taken into custody. Later he made fine for 6s. 8d., pledge Robert Cors.

117   Roger le Goiz and Stephen de Ruglestdone, charged with theft, come, deny all and put themselves on the country. The jurors testify that they are not guilty, so they are quit.

118   Robert de Mannor, who found one Alice de Mortest dead, does not come. He was attached by Paganus de Buwele and Walter Ivo, who are in mercy. No-one is suspected. Misadventure.

119   Walter Molle charged (*imposuit*) William Peverel and others with breaking his lord's park (*perchum*). The jurors testify that they are not guilty, so let Walter be taken into custody.

120   Helen daughter of Richard Barlet, who appealed Richard the clerk of rape, does not come. She was attached by John de Alre, who is in mercy, and her other pledge has died.

121   William Herm fled to Kentisbeare church, where he admitted to theft and abjured the realm before the coroner (*per visum coronatoris*). He was in Stockland tithing in Dorset, which is in mercy.

Stockland, now in Axminster hundred, was until 1832 a detached part of Dorset, *PND* p. 647 n.1.

122   Walter son of Thomas de Bulalre was struck dead by a horse. Price of the horse 3s., the sheriff etc.

123   Bradninch was a royal escheat. Henry de Trubleville holds it by King Henry's gift, and it is worth £30.

> A presentment under article 7 "of the king's escheats, what they are and who holds them". An escheat was landed property which had passed into the king's hands either through the holder's forfeiture for treason or felony or because of the failure of heirs on the part of a tenant-in-chief. The honour of Bradninch had been forfeited by William de Tracy, one of Becket's murderers, but Richard I gave it to William's nephew, Hugh de Curterne. At John's accession Henry de Tracy, William's son, offered 1000 marks for his inheritance, but had lost his lands by 1202, when Henry fitz Count successfully offered 1200 marks for them, holding them until his death in 1222 – *PR 4 John* p. 252, S. Painter, *The Reign of King John* (Baltimore 1966) pp. 38–9, Sanders, *Baronies* pp. 20–1. The following year Bradninch manor was granted to Henry de Trublevill for his maintenance in the king's service during pleasure, *CPR 1216–1225* p. 374; possession of the honour was probably implicit in the grant of the manor, since Henry was holding both by March 1226, *Rot. Lit. Claus.* II p. 105. The king's service included two spells as seneschal of Gascony, 1227–32 – *CPR 1225–1232* pp. 149, 502–503 – and 1234–7 – *CPR 1232–1247* pp. 47, 195 – and the leadership of a force of English knights assisting Frederick II at the siege of Brescia in 1238 – Matthew Paris *Chronica Majora* Vol. III ed. H. R. Luard (*RS* 1876) p. 491. His service in Gascony ran him heavily into debt – *CPR 1232–1247* p. 49 – and this may be why in 1233 he granted Bradninch manor to Bernard Berenger, burgess of Pons, to hold for ten years, though in fact Bernard could not obtain possession until Lent 1238, since Gilbert Gruscy, Henry's bailiff, continued to receive the issues. *CPR 1232–1247* p. 83; *CCR 1237–1242* p. 130; JUST/1/174 m23d. Henry was dead by 26 December 1239, *CCR 1237–1242* p. 163.

124   Of defaults they say that Roger Everard, John de Cherltone the chaplain, Henry de la Lane and Albreda de Boterelle did not come before the justices on the first day, so they are in mercy.

> Roger Everard had a free tenement in Bowerwood, imperilled in 1238 by a dyke raised there by the abbot of Dunkeswell, JUST/1/174 m8. No. 103 above explains the absence of John de Cheritone; he may have been cleared in Court Christian, since in 1242/43 John and Richard de Cheritone were said to be holding one eighth of a fee in Cheriton, *Fees* p. 782.
> Henry de la Lane defaulted again in 1244, JUST/1/175 m40d. Albreda de Boterelle had land worth 100s. in Plymtree in 1219, *Fees* p. 264.

125   The jury testified that William de Pissewelle sold an ox belonging to his son Richard to Rannulf de Smithennecote. Rannulf sold it to Robert le Norreis, who afterwards sold it to Richard Walrande. And later, at the instigation of Thomas de Orreweie, who claimed William's son Richard as his villein and for that reason wanted to have his chattels, so that he had taken those chattels and delivered them into William de Pissewelle's keeping, William came and appealed Richard Walrand of stealing the ox. So let Thomas be taken into custody and let Richard have his ox. William, together with John who also appealed Richard, is in mercy, let them be taken into custody. Later Thomas came and made fine for himself, William and John for 100s., pledges William Peverel, Hugh de Bodlai and William de Widdewrthi.

> In 1242 Thomas de Orreweie was said to hold half a fee in Otway and half a fee in Pirzwell, both in Kentisbeare parish in Hayridge hundred, of Philip de Columbers and the honour of Bradninch respectively, *Fees* pp. 782, 792. Presumably Thomas persuaded William de Pissewelle to accuse Richard Walrand of stealing William's son's ox so that either Richard would voluntarily surrender it or so that, on his conviction, it would be returned to its original owner, at which point Thomas could take it as that owner's lord.

126   Daniel de Karsewelle's house was burgled, and Daniel was attached by Robert and Thurstan Prat to be before the justices, but he does not come, so they are in mercy.

127 Richard le Fatte de Branes, who appealed Roger Wronke, Ralph Croppe, Richard de Westicote, Gilbert de Blagchewrthi and John of the same of breach of the king's peace and wounding, does not come, so he and his pledges, Roger de Kinbercnolle and Edwin le Fatte, are in mercy. The jurors testify that they wounded Richard, so let them all be taken into custody. Later Roger and Ralph came and made fine for one mark, pledges Herbert de Merley and Ralph le Rus, Richard de Westicote came and made fine for 10s., pledge Robert de Hammes, and Gilbert and John came and made fine for one mark, pledges Walter de Blagcheswrthi and Robert de Hammes.

BRADNINCH BURGH ANSWERS BY TWELVE JURORS

128 The jurors present that John le Fatte lives in Bradninch vill, where he eats well, drinks well and dresses himself well, but they do not know where his money comes from (*nesciunt unde provenit quod habet*). Asked if they suspect him of anything, they say no, so they are in mercy for presenting this case falsely.

> At the 1244 eyre John, who had made himself scarce, was put in exigent as a suspected stealer of pigs, JUST/1/175 m40d. The grounds of suspicion, as presented here, are strikingly similar to those which might, in Bracton's opinion, justify a presumption of having found treasure – "because he has more than usual in the way of food and richer apparel than before" – Bracton *De Legibus* Vol. II p. 344 f. 122.

129 Alice de Hundehille, who appealed John de Kari and Gilbert de Cloktone of robbery and breach of the king's peace, comes now and makes suit against them. The appellees do not come, and they were not attached as they are travelling merchants. The jurors testify that they are not guilty, so they are quit, and let Alice be taken into custody. Her amercement is pardoned because she is poor.

> Bradninch acquired burgh status through a charter from Earl Reginald of Cornwall between 1141 and 1175. In 1208 its privileges were augmented by King John, who conferred on it all the liberties and free customs enjoyed by Exeter, together with a market and fair – either of which may have been attended by the merchants appealed here. Hoskins *Devon* p. 342.

TIVERTON HUNDRED ANSWERS BY TWELVE JURORS

130 Robert de la Hokederis was found drowned in the river Otter with his horse. Misadventure. Value of the horse's hide 6d., the sheriff etc.

> Tiverton, held by the king in 1086, was in 1106 granted by Henry I to Richard de Redvers, in whose family it descended thereafter. Reichel S1 p. 12. That nobody answered for it, as for Hayridge (no. 103), in 1238 must have been because Baldwin III de Redvers was then a minor, though others of his hundreds were claimed on his behalf later in the eyre (nos. 518, 532, 543 below). In 1245 Tiverton and Hayridge hundreds together were valued at 60s. C132/3 no. 10(4); in 1249 Tiverton hundred alone was valued at £5 *per annum*, but in 1274/5 at only one mark, JUST/1/176 m36; *RH* p. 83.

131 Adam son of William de Luccumbe struck Roger son of William with his fist, killing him instantly, and fled, so let him be exacted and outlawed. He was living in Craze Loman tithing, which is in mercy, and he had no chattels . No-one else is suspected. No Englishry so Murder fine.

132   Alice de Callewdele appealed Miles de Callewdele that on the Monday next before the feast of St. John the Baptist in the twenty-first year (22 June 1237) he came to her courtyard and took from it her flax and vegetables, and that he did this evilly and in felony.
Miles comes, denies robbery and all, and says that in truth he was in Ireland for a year, during which she made an enclosure on his land and planted her vegetables there. And when he returned he broke down the enclosure and took away, by day, and as from his own land, whatever he found there. She cannot deny this, so let her be taken into custody, while Miles is quit. Alice is poor, so nothing.
> This appeal must have been connected with the action for dower which Alice had prosecuted against Miles in 1231, claiming a third part of Bulworthy vill, and which was still in progress in 1238, *CRR* XIV no. 1777; JUST/1/174 m8.

133   Alice's tenant Rose appeals Miles that on the eighth day before the feast of St. Luke in the twenty-first year (10 October, 1237) he beat and ill-treated her, taking from her 3s. and a silver brooch, and that he did this evilly and in felony.
Miles comes, denies all and puts himself on the country, and the jurors testify that he took nothing from her, but that he beat her as she says, so let him be taken into custody, while Rose is in mercy for her false appeal. She is very poor, so nothing. Later Miles came and made fine for 6s. 8d., pledge Robert de Biggeleghe.

(m 29d)
134   Wimar, wife to Algar de Cimiterio, fell from a mare and died at once. Misadventure. Value of the mare 4s., the sheriff etc.

135   William the chaplain of Twivertone drowned by falling from a horse into the river Exe. Misadventure. Value of the horse 2s., the sheriff etc. The twelve jurors are in mercy for not presenting the value of the horse.

136   Nicholas Trove was outlawed for the death of Clarica, mother to Roger Viel, at Roger's suit. He was living outside tithing in Tiverton vill, which is in mercy, and had chattels 2d., that vill etc.

137   Gilbert le Batur stood on a hayrick with an iron fork in his hand, and by misadventure the fork fell on the head of Michael son of Hugh, so that he died three days later. Gilbert fled, and because the justices cannot show him mercy without the King (*cum eo facere misericordiam sine domino rege*), let him be exacted and outlawed. He was in the mainpast of Robert de Bunewelle, who is in mercy, and who made fine for 6s. 8d., pledge Robert Cors.
> No pardon for this death has been found.

138   Roger son of Henry de Exon' is in mercy for selling wine contrary to the assize in Tiverton.

139   Robert Squirel, charged with theft, was arrested and imprisoned at Exeter and later released to pledges, Matthew son of William Butte and Matthew Squirel his father. He does not come, so they are in mercy. The jurors testify that he is a thief, so let him be exacted and outlawed. He was in 'Morele Lanceleve' tithing, which is in mercy, and he had no chattels.

Tiverton

140   Four men drowned by falling from a boat into the river Exe. Misadventure. Value of the boat 6d., the sheriff etc. Later Robert Doilard comes and appeals William Bauzant of the death of his sister Beatrice, whom he wickedly drowned in that river. Likewise Goda, wife of Henry Seward, appeals him of drowning her husband, and Matilda Ruffa appeals him of drowning her son Robert. The jurors of Tiverton hundred and burgh, with four neighbouring vills, say he is not guilty, so he is quit.
>William Bauzant may have been a ferryman whom the appellors believed to have been culpably negligent in the performance of his duties.

TIVERTON BURGH ANSWERS BY TWELVE JURORS

141   The jurors of this burgh present nothing that was not presented in Tiverton hundred.
>Tiverton burgh may have been founded by William de Vernun, fifth earl of Devon, between 1193 and 1217. Burgage rents there are recorded in 1224, *English Medieval Boroughs* p. 99. In 1245 the total annual value of the burgh was estimated at £5 4s. 11d. – C132/3 no. 10(4).

BAMPTON HUNDRED ANSWERS BY TWELVE JURORS

142   William de Leghe, one of the jurors, is in mercy for not coming before the justices with his fellows to answer for their *veredictum*.

143   William Gernun was drowned by falling into the river Exe from a mare and was never found afterwards. Misadventure. No-one is suspected. Value of the mare 2s., the sheriff etc.

144   William de Tunnebrige de Bantone killed Reginald, the parson of Hockford Water's servant, and fled, so let him be exacted and outlawed. He was living in Bampton vill, which is in mercy.

145   Humphrey le Bonde's house was burgled and one Jordan, son of William de Reftone, suspected of the burgulary, was arrested and imprisoned at Exeter when Rannulf de Cerne was sheriff, but it is not known what became of him. So let Rannulf answer for him tomorrow. He does not come, so to judgment on him. Later it was testified that when Jordan was arrested he was in possession of shoes which he was said to have stolen, and for which he vouched to warranty Richard Cule, who was attached by Richard de la Pitte and John Frie. They are in mercy for not producing him. Richard is not suspected, so he may return if he wishes. Later William Peverel came and made fine for Richard's pledges for 10s., the same William as pledge.
>For Rannulf de Cerne see no. 50 above. Voucher to warranty was a process whereby a man could establish that he had come honestly by allegedly stolen goods, by vouching – calling on – the vendor to warrant, to testify, that he had made the sale to him. If three or four successive owners of a chattel had warranted their successors as its owners, the case against the original suspect could no longer be sustained, though proceedings might then begin against one of its intermediate holders. See below nos. 300, 535. It was not a process without incidental dangers. At the 1281/82 eyre the Roborough jurors told how William de Mungomery, vouched to warranty for a sheep by

John Tayleboys, had responded by striking John dead with an axe, JUST/1/186 m19d. See Pollock and Maitland Vol. II pp. 163–4.

146   Matilda wife of Richard de Hanagker, Richard's sons Richard and Robert and Adam his nephew appealed Thomas son of Humphrey of wounding Richard their father. Richard and Robert come now but do not make suit, so they and their pledges, Robert de la Pitte and Oliver de Hollecumbe, are in mercy. Thomas comes, and the jurors say they have made no agreement and he is not guilty, so he is quit and let the others be taken into custody. Later Ralph son of Bernard came and made fine for all the appellors and their pledges for two marks, pledges Jordan son of Roges and William Malherbe.

147   Adam Cuffe and James de Laleghe appealed Richard the miller, Iwein de Remstorre, Iwein Bedel, William Sprot, Godfrey de Warthemore, William son of Alfred, Roger de Brunnescote and Iwein le Bleu of breach of the king's peace. The two appellors and all the appellees come, but the appellors do not make suit, so they and their pledges, Thomas de Vitriaco and Richard Vassallus, are in mercy. Later James came and made fine for himself and his pledges for 10s., pledge William de Widewrthe. Later Adam Cuffe came and made fine for himself and his pledges for one mark, pledge William de Claville. Later Jordan son of Roges came and made fine for all the appellees for 40s., pledges Ralph son of Bernard and William Russel de Holecumbe.

> In 1242 Jordan son of Roges held one fee in Holcombe Rogus – which took its suffix from his father – of the honour of Okehampton, *Fees* p. 786.

148   Eda de Cuddemore's house was burgled, it is not known by whom. No-one is suspected. Eda, attached by Philip de Cuddemore and the tithingman of Cudmore, does not come, so she and her pledges are in mercy.

149   Adam de Cleiangre fell from a tree and died instantly. This happened on the Templars' land. No Englishry so Murder fine.

> In 1086 Clayhanger was part of William de Mohun's honour of Dunster; it subsequently passed to Robert de Perepont, who gave it to the Knights Templars, D. & S. Lysons, *Magna Britannia* Vol. VI Part II (London 1822) p. 112; Dugdale, *Monasticon*, Vol. VI Part II p. 838.

150   Alexander le Maszacrer de Bantone was found dead in Bampton wood, on Bampton vill's land. It is not known who killed him. No Englishry so Murder fine. The jurors are in mercy for not presenting the finder's name.

151   Richard de Cutholvestone was crushed to death when a wall fell on him. Misadventure. Cornwood vill is in mercy for burying him without a coroner's view.

152   Ralph Welifed, Richard Alpenie and Wakeman, outlawed for the death of Hugh de la Crofte, were living in Bampton, which is in mercy. They had no chattels.

153   Walter le Pale and Adam the goldsmith fled to Bampton church, where they admitted to being thieves and abjured the realm before the coroner. They were wandering thieves and were not in tithings.

Bampton 33

154 Cristina de la Fenne's house was burgled. William de la Hirne is suspected of this and other thefts, so let him be exacted and outlawed. He was living on the Templars' land at Clayhanger, which is in mercy.

155 Alice daughter of Rengot appealed John Cumin of rape. She does not come, so she and her pledge, Ralph la Hone, are in mercy. Her other pledge has died.

156 Thomas de Stanlinche, suspected of theft, has made himself scarce, so let him be exacted and outlawed. He had chattels worth 4d., Stallenge Thorne vill etc.

157 William Sonbucke fled to Bampton church where he admitted having harboured thieves and abjured the realm before the coroner. He had chattels worth 12d., Bampton vill etc.

158 The jurors present that John de Hoxtone sold wine contrary to the assize in Bampton, so he is in mercy.

159 Of defaults they say that Herbert son of Matthew, Gervase de Patetone and Simon de Depeforde did not come before the justices on the first day, so they are in mercy. Later is was testified that Gervase and Simon had set out for Santiago over a month before the summons to the justices' eyre.

>   For Herbert son of Matthew see no. 160 below.
>   Gervase de Patetone held one fee in Petton, though of which honour was uncertain, *Fees* p. 797.
>   Simon de Depeforde was a juror for Bampton in 1244 and 1249, JUST/1/175 m35; JUST/1/176 m46.

160 Herbert son of Matthew, asked by what warrant he holds Bampton hundred, says the hundred is held by William son of William son of Painel, whom he has in his custody by the king's gift. And William is twelve years old.

>   Bampton was the seat of the barony which William I gave to Walter of Douai in exchange for Ermington before 1086, Reichel S6 p. 320. It passed with Walter's granddaughter Juliana to Fulk Paynel, great-grandfather of the William Paynel mentioned here. Sanders, *Baronies* p. 5. Its descent in the Paynel family was not, however, smooth or uninterrupted. Fulk's grandson, Fulk II, proffered 1000 marks for Bampton in 1180 – *PR 26 Henry II* p. 94 – but had fled by 1186, when Bampton and Uffculme were being administered by William Brewer. *PR 32 Henry II* p. 203. In 1200, however, Fulk Paynel once more proffered 1000 marks for his honour and was successful, though in the process he had to bribe William Brewer with the manor of Bridgwater in Somerset, *PR 1 John* p. 197, Painter, *Reign of King John* pp. 73–4. Fulk's son and heir William died in 1228, on 18 November of which year the wardship and marriage of his heir, another William, were granted to Herbert son of Matthew – C60/28 m13 – lord of Coleridge hundred and of seven fees in Devon – no. 682 below, *Fees* p. 432. Herbert still held the hundred in 1244 JUST/1/175 m40d. In 1249 it was valued at one mark *per annum* JUST/1/176 m36.

161 The jurors present that the abbot of Torre has withdrawn his manor of Donningstone from making suit to the Hundred Court. Asked for how long that manor has not made suit, they say for thirty years.

>   Donningstone manor was given by William Brewer to Henry de fferendon, who before 1220 gave it to Torre abbey; "the land of Donningstone" was given to Torre by William Brewer the younger between 1224 and 1232. D. Seymour, *Torre Abbey* (Exeter 1977) pp. 148–9. In 1244 the Cliston jurors, for presenting a withdrawal of suit from that hundred, were said to have made "a foolish presentment", since the hundred was not in the king's hand – JUST/1/175 m38d. In 1238 the king may have been regarded as having an interest in a withdrawal of suit from Bampton, not ordinarily a royal hundred, because its holder was a minor whose custody was in the king's gift.

(m 30)
HALBERTON HUNDRED ANSWERS BY TWELVE JURORS

162   Hugh de la Were was found dead in Willand manor. No Englishry so Murder fine.

163   Denise de Bidennebotine complains that Geoffrey Chubbe, Alexander de Prustetone, Walter Keling and one Osbert took her grain by night. Geoffrey and the others come. And because this case does not belong to the pleas of the crown, but would rather be covered by a plea of novel disseisin (*loquela ista non spectat ad placita corone sed potius iaceret ibi breve nove disseisine*), it is decided that Denise is in mercy and the others are quit. She is poor, so nothing.

164   Roger Cogan was outlawed for the death of Walter de Essheforde by the suit of Walter's widow Denise. His chattels were worth 34d., Ayshford tithing etc., and he was living in Ayshford tithing, which is in mercy. John Cogan, charged with that death, comes, denies all and puts himself on the country. The jurors testify that he is not guilty, so he is quit.

165   A Holcombe man was burgled. The jurors are in mercy for not giving his name.

166   Theobald de Englescheville holds Oburnford, which is an escheat to the king, by grant from the same. It is from the earl of Gloucester's fief and is worth £10.

> Oburnford was one of the manors held by Luke son of John, a Norman who forfeited in 1204, *Rot. Lit. Claus.* I p. 5. In 1218 it was given to Henry de Ponte Audomar, along with Luke's other lands in Devon. *Rot. Lit. Claus.* I p. 472, *PR 2 Henry III* p. 86. Henry III gave it to Theobald de Engleschevill, a soldier and courtier, probably at the same time as he gave him the manor of Highweek, also held successively by Luke son of John and Henry de Ponte Audomar, in 1230, *CPR 1225–1232* p. 400, *CCR 1227–1231* p. 345, *Fees* p. 612 (see nos. 720, 722 below). In 1241 he was said to hold the manor for one fee by the service of acting as bailiff in Halberton hundred, Reichel S2 p. 56. Oburnford was valued at 112s. unstocked and £10 stocked in 1204, at £6. 15s. in 1244, £10 in 1249 and £8 in 1281/82; *Rot. Norm.* p. 130, JUST/1/175 m41; JUST/1/176 m36; JUST/1/186 m41d.

167   Of defaults they say that William de Bosco the younger and Robert de Chandes did not come before the justices on the first day, so they are in mercy.

> William de Bosco's father, also William, in 1242 held one fee in Halberton of the honour of Gloucester, *Fees* p. 799. See below no. 168.

168   William Peverel and William de Bosco, asked what warrant they have for Halberton hundred, come. William de Bosco proffers a charter from king Henry the king's grandfather testifying that he has granted and confirmed to William de Bosco £10 of land in Halberton which earl William of Gloucester gave to the same William for his service, with all his liberties, customs and appurtenances in waters, mills, hundreds, ways and paths. And William Peverel comes and proffers a charter from William son of Gregory testifying that he, with the assent of Olive his wife and of his heirs, has granted and given to Hugh Peverel, his father, the other half of that hundred which pertained to them. And he says that Gregory had a royal charter, but he shows no other warrant.

> In 1086 Halberton was held by the king, having been previously held by queen Matilda. Henry I gave it to his illegitimate son Robert of Gloucester, whose son William divided

it into two halves between William de Bosco and Gregory de Turri, so creating the manors of Halberton Boys and Halberton Abbot, rated at half a knight's fee each. In 1238 the hundred was still held jointly, but by 1241 the de Boscos appear to have acquired the overlordship of Halberton Abbot, Reichel S2 pp. 54–5. In 1274/75 the hundred was said to be held by William de Bosco – *RH* p. 71 – but in 1281/82 William de Bosco and Hugh Peverel were described as joint holders. Hugh tried to induce William to admit to having superior right over the entire hundred, but William said that his great-grandfather, Ralph de Bosco, had only held the whole hundred because William son of Gregory had made him a life-grant of his own half, with reversion to himself, which the charter proffered by William Peverel in 1238 might be construed as confirming. In the end, however, William warranted Hugh and claimed ancient tenure for both halves. *PQW* pp. 171–2; JUST/1/186 m41d. In 1249 the hundred was valued at 6s. 8d., *per annum*, JUST/1/176 m36.

CLISTON HUNDRED ANSWERS BY TWELVE JURORS

169   One Gilbert was found dead on 'Pistone' heath. No Englishry so Murder fine. Gilbert Crakie, John de Tonebire and John de Clist are in mercy for trying to present Englishry falsely before the justices. Later Walter de Bathon' the sheriff came and made fine for them for 10s., pledges William de la Berghe and Geoffrey de Wiche.

170   Robert de Grenesclinge and Robert Gulle appealed Ralph Demichevaler of burning Joel de Grenesclinge's grange. They did not come, so they and Joel de Grenesclinge, who mainprised that they would prosecute their appeal, are in mercy. Ralph comes, and the jurors say that they have made no agreement and that he is not guilty, so he is quit. It was testified that they made the appeal on Joel's advice, so he is in mercy.

  Joel de Grenesclinge, who by 1252 had made himself scarce as a suspected felon (not mentioned in 1244 or 1249), held half a ferling at Butterleigh in Cliston hundred, *Fees* p. 1263. At this eyre he was found to have disseised Ralph de la Cumbe of one ferling in Butterleigh, JUST/1/174 m9d.

171   William de Hollewille and his brother Walter were outlawed for the death of William de la Furse at the suit of his wife Emma. They were living in Holwell tithing, which is in mercy, and had chattels worth 6s. 8d., the same tithing etc.

172   Humphrey Mansel and John de Mora, attached for burning the house of Mabel de Mora, who has died, come, deny all and put themselves on the country. The jurors testify that they are not guilty, so they are quit.

173   Robert de Curtenei has newly put up a tumbrel in Whimple vill, by what warrant is not known. Let this be discussed.

  In 1281/82 a jury upheld Hugh de Courtenay's claim to have view of frankpledge, amends of the assizes of bread and ale, gallows, tumbrel, pillory and pleas of blood shed and hue raised, in Whimple and other vills from time immemorial, as pertaining to his barony of Okehampton, *PQW* p. 171.

174   John de Culum, charged with the death of Sara daughter of William Grameire of Cornwall, comes, bringing her alive and well. The jurors testify that it is the same Sara, so John is quit.

  Homicide, and theft where the thief was arrested in possession of stolen goods, were the principal irrepleviable offences, that is, those charged with them could only be released to pledges by means of a writ of bail. *Wiltshire Crown Pleas 1249* pp. 46–51; see also no. 203 below. Such a writ had secured the release of John de Culum. As long ago as March 1229 the king had instructed that since the sheriff had found Sara to be alive, John, in prison for her death, could be released to the bail of twelve men willing to guarantee his appearance before the justices at their next session, *CCR 1227–1231* p. 158.

175 Norman de Uptone and Isaac de Litfare, charged with theft, come, deny all, and put themselves on the country. The jurors testify that they are not guilty, so they are quit.

176 The jurors testify that Isabel countess of Oxford holds this hundred in dower. It is the inheritance of Reginald de Valle Torta, so if he wishes let him show by what warrant he has it.

> Broad Clyst, the hundred-manor of Cliston, was held by the king in 1086, DB pp. 76–7. Subsequently it was granted first to Juhel de Totnes – who was said to have been expelled on the death of William I, Oliver *Monasticon* p. 241 – and then to Roger de Nunant, in both cases as part of the honour of Totnes. The honour descended in the de Nunant family until 1205, when it was claimed by William de Braose as a descendant of Juhel. William's position as John's then favourite made his claims irresistible, he was acknowledged as overlord and the honour was partitioned. Sanders, *Baronies* pp. 89–90; Painter, *Reign of King John* pp. 41–2, 45–6. Henry's powers of resistance must have been sapped by his substantial indebtedness to Jews, and he sold his share of the honour of Totnes – the honour of Harberton – to Roger de Valle Torta, lord of Trematon in Cornwall. Broad Clyst, however, must have remained in Henry's possession, for when he died in 1207 it passed first to the king, as property of the Jews, and then to Henry's widow Isabel de Bulebec, with whom, as her dower, it went to Robert de Vere, earl of Oxford, who died before October 1221. In 1228 Roger de Nunant, Henry's brother, completed the sale of the de Nunant lands to Reginald, son of Roger de Valle Torta, and it must have been in return for this that Reginald made over to Roger "the whole manor of Clyston in its entirety together with the hundred" to be held of himself – Reichel S7 pp. 368–9 and in *TDA* 43(1911) p. 204 n. 41; *Cornwall FFI* no. 240. The grant was to take effect on Isabel's death, which did not happen until 1245, *Complete Peerage* Vol. X pp. 210–13. In 1249 it was presented that the hundred was worth one mark *per annum* and that Guy de Nunant "holds the hundred in fee and is its bailiff", JUST/1/176 m36d.

BUDLEIGH HUNDRED ANSWERS BY TWELVE JURORS

177 From Budleigh hundred, except for liberties, as fine for Murder, 100s.

178 Alice de Lapforde appealed Adam de Chiritone of the death of her sister Katherine. She does not come, so she and her pledges, William de Lapforde, William de la Hole and Edward de Buchwrthi, are in mercy, let her be arrested. Adam does not come, and he was attached by Durandus the clerk's son, his brother Jordan, Walter the smith of Chiritone and Richard Buthel, who are all in mercy. The jurors testify that he is not guilty, nor have they made an agreement, so he is quit.

179 Alexander de Aulescumbe killed Walter de la Hille and fled, so let him be exacted and outlawed. He was living in Rockbeare tithing, which is in mercy, and had chattels worth 4s., the same tithing etc.

180 Baldwin de Cumbe hanged himself in his home. Felony *de se*. No-one is suspected. He had no chattels.

181 William Coc, charged with theft, comes, denies all and puts himself on the country. The jurors testify that he is not guilty, so he is quit.

182 Stephen de Raddone is in mercy for foolish speaking, let him be

taken into custody. Later he came and made fine for 6s. 8d., pledges Baldwin and Roland de Raddone.

183 Adam de Chiltone appealed Jacob the Jew of Exeter of stealing a horse, and later took 16s. from him to withdraw, so he is in mercy. It is testified that he lives in Witheridge hundred.

184 William de Uppedone killed Walter Rolland de Pimecote and fled, so let him be exacted and outlawed. Walter's wife Amice aided and abetted William, so let her be exacted and waivered. William was in Raddon tithing, which is in mercy, and they had no chattels.
> Women who committed felony and fled were waivered rather than outlawed – in practical terms the two statuses were identical. See note on no. 524 below.

185 Walter Murda burgled Stephen de Uppedone's house and fled to Raddon church. It is not known whether he abjured the realm or not, so let him be exacted and outlawed. He had no chattels. East Raddon vill is in mercy for not pursuing him.
> It is surprising that the coroners' rolls were apparently not consulted to discover whether an abjuration had taken place or not. Possibly this case had been the responsibility of one of the two coroners whose deaths led to a royal order that replacements be elected in the County Court in 1233. *CCR 1231–1234* p. 231.

186 John the miller of La Shote was outlawed for the death of Richard Barat at the suit of Richard's wife Avice. He was living in Shute tithing, which is in mercy, and he had no chattels.

187 Julian de Ferleghe pledged Robert the chaplain of Bouleghe that he would stand to the County Court's decision. And before the day of the County Court came, Thomas de la Wile, then sheriff, arrested and imprisoned Julian, and took 40s. from him before he could leave prison, so he is in mercy. Later he came and gave Julian satisfaction for those 40s.
> Thomas de la Wile, who accounted at the exchequer for Thomas de Cirencestre at Easter 1231 and answered for Peter de Rivaux – sheriff of Devon, as of every other English county, during his months in power in 1232 – at this eyre, was probably undersheriff to both men. A small landowner in Devon and Dorset – JUST/1/174 mm6, 44 – he was probably, like Rannulf de Cerne (no. 50 above), a professional administrator – in 1233 he was warden of the Devon stannaries, C60/32 m2. – nor was he well spoken of in 1238. See also nos. 188, 265, 409 below.

188 A mound was dug into at 'Rueberghe'. Thomas de la Wile, then sheriff, took 6s. 8d. from Gittisham tithing, so he is in mercy. Gittisham tithing is in mercy for not presenting this case to the County Court.
> Thomas de la Wile's service as undersheriff, dates this case to between April 1231 and Michaelmas 1233, see no. 187.

189 Gittisham tithing was pledge for William de la Pitte, charged with theft, who later fled. Rannulf de Cerne, then sheriff, took 100s. for his flight, so to judgment on him. Rannulf is present, and says that he was given to understand that he had been outlawed in Dorset, and so he entrusted him to the tithing as surety until he could be more fully informed.
> An amercement of 100s. was the usual penalty for this sort of escape from custody – examples can be found in many counties. That there were exchanges of information about criminals between counties, at least between neighbouring ones, is shown by a case from the 1244 Dorset eyre, where a man was said to have been arrested and imprisoned at Ilchester because he had been appealed of homicide in Devon "as

was testified in letters from the sheriff of Devon". JUST/1/201 m5d. The case is reported JUST/1/175 m43, which also shows that the man arrested was later released, since he had been outlawed by 1244.

190   Wymarc de Chevelestone appealed Edward de la Berghe, Richard de Knolla, John Florentin, John le Hopere, John Rof, Roger the shepherd and Ralph de la Berghe of taking and carrying off her grain by night. All the appellees except John Florentin come, and because the appeal is null they are all quit and let her be taken into custody. Let her obtain a writ of novel disseisin if she wishes. She is poor, so nothing.

191   Gregory de Arecumbe fell from a mare into water at Sidford and drowned. Misadventure. Value of the mare 3s., the sheriff etc. Sidbury vill is in mercy for presenting the value of the mare as 2s.

192   Alan the chaplain's horse struck William the clerk dead. Value of the horse 2s., the sheriff etc. The jurors are in mercy for not presenting the value of the horse.

193   Roger Horsant stole two of Matilda de Nottesdone's sheep and fled, so let him be exacted and outlawed. He was living in Sidbury tithing, which is in mercy, and had chattels worth 41s. 4d., Stone tithing etc.

194   Jordan son of Walter the clerk of Chiritone and William de Morleghe, serjeant of Chiritone, stole two firkins of honey worth 4s. from Adam son of Walter, so let them be exacted and outlawed. Jordan had chattels worth 8s., Cheriton tithing etc., and William had none. Later it was testified that William is not guilty, so he may return if he wishes.

(m 30d)
195   A tun of wine washed up at Sidmouth from a wreck at sea. It was valued at a coroner's view at 6s. 8d., 'Sidecume' tithing etc.

196   Thomas Cole fell from a horse into water at Colaton Raleigh and drowned. Misadventure. Value of the horse 2s., the sheriff etc.

197   Two men drowned by falling into the sea from a boat. Misadventure. Value of the boat one mark, the sheriff etc.

198   Gilbert de Lahille is suspected of theft and has fled, so let him be exacted and outlawed. He was in the abbot of Dunkeswell's tithing in Colaton Raleigh, which is in mercy, and had chattels worth 10s., the same tithing etc. The abbot is in mercy for taking the chattels without a coroner's view.

   In 1228 Richard de Crues quitclaimed 368 acres of land in Colaton Raleigh to the abbot of Dunkeswell, whose holding there obviously constituted a tithing, *Devon FFI* no. 152.

199   Robert de Pinnecote, John de la Dune and Baldwin de la Dune, charged with theft, come, deny all and put themselves on the country. The jurors testify that they are not guilty, so they are quit.

200   William Godswein, charged with theft, has made himself scarce and is suspected of stealing sheep, so let him be exacted and outlawed. He was living in Lower Creedy tithing, which is in mercy, and he had chattels worth 8s. 2d., that tithing etc., and one messuage and eight acres of land

Budleigh

in Lower Creedy. Later Robert Peitevin came and made fine for the land for 6s. 8d.

> In 1242 Lower Creedy – recorded as Cridie Peytevyn in 1305 – was held by Robert le Peytevin of the honour of Berry, *Fees* p. 791; *PND* p. 419.
> The free land, that is, land not held by villein tenure, of any man or woman convicted of felony only escheated to its lord after the king had held it for a year and a day, and had at the end of that period wasted it by taking from it everything of potential value, including crops, trees and buildings. It was common for lords, as here, to make a bargain with the crown, whereby they paid the estimated value of the king's year and waste, and a bit extra, in order to avoid such destruction; Bracton, *De Legibus* Vol. II pp. 363–4, ff. 129, 129b.

201 Adam Kempe appealed William de Beuweis of wounding and robbery, and he comes now and makes suit against him. William does not come, and he was attached by Philip de Saltertone, Roger Smalprut, Alan de Saltertone and Richard Turnehand, who are in mercy. And since William (sic) showed a dangerous wound in the head, the sheriff is told that if Adam gives security for making suit, then he should have him exacted and outlawed according to the custom of the realm.

202 John de Alsedone was drowned in the sea. Misadventure. Bradham tithing is in mercy for not presenting this case in the County Court.

203 William de Porta, arrested for the death of Osanna, wife of William de Bosco, comes, denies all and puts himself on the country. William de Bosco appeals William de Porta that on the Wednesday next before the feast of St. Kalixtus in the nineteenth year (10 October 1235) he came to his home and with a sword struck him on the head, making a great wound, and gave him another wound on the right shoulder, and later in the same year, on the Sunday next before the feast of All Saints (28 October) he came again to his home, with three others, broke his door, gave him a great wound in the chest with an axe and burgled his house. And he puts himself on the country for it, and if this is not enough he offers to prove by his body as etc. William de Porta comes and cannot deny that he wounded him as he says, but he denies burgling his house and the death of his wife, and puts himself on the country as aforesaid. And since William de Bosco's appeal is null for putting William de Porta to law, let the country inquire. The jurors testify that he is not guilty of the death and burglary, so he is quit and let William de Bosco be taken into custody. But since William de Porta admitted wounding William de Bosco as aforesaid, let him be taken into custody. William de Bosco has nothing. Later William de Porta came and made fine for 10s., pledge the prior of Otterton.

> A man or woman arrested on an appeal of homicide had, to secure release, to obtain first a writ *de odio et atya*, ordering an inquest into the trustworthiness of the charge, then, if the inquest found that the appeal had been maliciously made, the defendant could apply for a writ of bail securing his or her release to pledges – see no. 174 above. In January 1235 the king notified the sheriff of Devon that William de Porta could be released to bail as an inquest had found that he had been maliciously appealed, *CCR 1234–1237* p. 37. The wound he was said to have given William de Bosco seems explanation enough for the latter's ill-will. The nineteenth year of the appeal is probably an error for the eighteenth – since Henry III's regnal year began on 28 October, it would have been easy to make such a mistake.

204 Ralph de Potteslake appealed Henry Pertehaie of breach of the king's peace and wounding. He does not come, so he and his pledges,

Walter de Munnirun and William de Cumbe de Wdebire, are in mercy. Henry comes, and the jurors testify that they have made no agreement, so he is quit.

205   Adam Grendel is in mercy for trespass.

206   Eight men were drowned in the sea at Ottermouth. Budleigh vill is in mercy for not presenting this case in the County Court.

207   Benedict Bunta was drowned by falling from a boat into the sea at Ottermouth. Value of the boat 3s., the sheriff etc.

208   A ship's luff was washed up at Littleham. The men of Littleham are in mercy for valuing it at 2s., without a coroner's view, let them answer for the 2s.

209   Men of Withycombe and Bradham found an anchor in Ottermouth harbour. They are in mercy for not presenting this to the County Court. Value of the anchor 12d., those men etc.

210   Richard Kipping drowned in water between Topsham and Lympstone. His brother John, who first found him, and was attached by Walter and Angmerus de Cumbe, does not come, so he and his pledges are in mercy.

211   William de Grindel fell from a mare into the river Exe at Clyst bridge and drowned. Value of the mare 2s., the sheriff etc. Misadventure.

212   Hugh de Cockeville was found killed on Bishop's Clyst manor. Richard son of William, who first found him, does not come, so he and his pledges, William Kempe and Richard le Sumeter, are in mercy. Later Richard comes, and as he is under age nothing from his pledges. Later it was testified that William the baker of Exon' killed him and fled, so let him be exacted and outlawed. He was living in Exeter city, which is in mercy for not producing him.

213   William Kempe's house was burgled. Camekinna daughter of Urcellus the Jew was charged with this and has been imprisoned at Exeter.

> Nothing further was said of Camekinna at this eyre, her case having been doubtless reserved, as was customary, for the next session of justices for the Jews at Exeter. Her father may have been the Ursellus of Exeter, a Jew, said in 1239 to have fled for a felony elsewhere defined as coin-clipping. He had held land worth 15s. in Hele, pledge for money advanced by him to Sir William son of Richard, *CCR 1237–1242* p. 163; *Cal. Inq. Misc.* I no. 81. See also Risdon, *Survey of Devon* p. 236.

214   Thomas, Ralph de Sicca Villa's miller, fatally wounded Raymond the chaplain and fled, so let him be exacted and outlawed. He was living in Bishop's Clyst tithing, which is is mercy, and he had chattels worth 7s., that tithing etc.

> In 1242 Ralph de Sicca Villa, with the prior of St. James, Exeter, held one fee in Bishops Clyst and Creely Barton of the honour of Barnstaple, *Fees* p. 763. In some thirteenth century records Bishop's Clyst appears as Clist Sechevill; Ralph de Sicca Villa sold it to the bishop of Exeter before 1267 to raise money to pay off his debts to the Jews, *PND* p. 587; *CPR 1266–1272* p. 34.

215   Venn Ottery is a royal serjeanty and John de Furneals holds it, paying £4. 4s. 8d. yearly.

A presentment under article 8, "of the king's serjeanties . . ." Serjeanty was the name given to a heterogeneous collection of free tenures, broadly characterised by the performance of non-military services in return for land. By the early thirteenth century such tenures were beginning, as here, to be commuted for money payments – A. L. Poole, *Obligations of Society in the XII and XIII Centuries* (Oxford 1946) pp. 57–76. Other examples are nos. 217, 511, 595 below.
In 1212 Venn Ottery was held by Philip de Fornell', an annual payment of £4. 4s. 8d. being there said to be the service for which Henry I had given it to his ancestors. In 1242 Philip's son John was said to be holding it in socage, *Fees* pp. 95, 763. John was given livery of Venn Ottery in March 1235, *Rot. Fin.* I. p. 275.

216 Hugh, one of the abbot of Dunkeswell's men, was crushed to death in a marl pit. Robert le Blake, who was then with him, does not come, and he was attached by Walter the reeve of Havekerlonde and Richard de Laberghe, so they are all in mercy.

Hawkerland is in the parish of Colaton Raleigh, where in 1242 the abbot of Dunkeswell was joint holder of two thirds of a knight's fee. *Fees* p. 762.

217 Bicton is a royal serjeanty, and Ralph Balistarius holds it by the serjeanty of guarding Exeter gaol.

Exeter gaol was given by Henry I to the ancestor of the John Janitor who held it, together with the lands in Bicton which he held by the service of keeping the gaol, in 1212. John's brother and heir William had forfeited for felony by 1226, when the gaol was granted to Ralph le Petit, or the Norman, followed by the lands in 1227. Ralph was also, as here, known as Balistarius, hence his family name of Arblaster. R. B. Pugh, *Imprisonment in Medieval England* (Cambridge 1968) pp. 145–6. The custody of the gaol also entitled its holder to the custody of all beasts taken in distraint for debts to the king, and so, no doubt, to any payments made for their subsequent release, JUST/1/175 m33.
In 1237 Ralph Balistarius confirmed to Mont St. Michel a grant of twenty acres made to that abbey by John Janitor "from that serjeanty which John held from the King of England", DRO TD 42 f. 47.

218 Budleigh hundred is a royal serjeanty. Robert de Hokesham holds it, paying the king 40s. yearly, and it is worth six marks. And the office of beadle of the hundred is hereditary to Morin son of Robert Morin.

Budleigh was held by the king in 1086, *DB* pp. 12–13. In 1212 Robert de Hokesham was said to be holding the hundred for 40s. yearly "to make up the farm of the county of Devon by gift of King Henry I to his ancestors", *Fees* pp. 95–6. Some time after 1281, however, a memorandum added to the Hundred Rolls – Reichel in *TDA* 35(1903) pp. 305–6 – recorded that the hundred had remained in the king's hand until the reign of John, who gave it to William Brewer to hold at will, and that William gave it to Robert de Hokesham for an annual rent of 40s. This seems unlikely to be true – Budleigh was not, for instance, included among the royal demesnes tallaged in 1168 *PR 14 Henry II* pp. 129–33 – but subsequent events show that the de Hokeshams were not secure in their possession, and it may be that John had dispossessed Robert in William Brewer's favour, in the process converting a hereditary tenure into a tenure at will. Robert was described as holding the hundred at farm from the king in 1244 – JUST/1/175 m39 – and it certainly descended to his son William, since the latter made fine for "his hundred's" trespass in 1249, when the hundred was said to be worth five marks *per annum*, JUST/1/176 m35d. By 1274/75, however, it was in the king's hand as royal demesne – *RH* p. 66 – and the subsequent efforts of Emma de Hokesham, acting in her son's name, to secure its return as held in socage, failed, on the grounds that the king disposed of it at will. For the beadlery see no. 220 below.

219 The jurors present that the abbot of Dunkeswell has newly put up gallows, by what warrant is not known, so let this be discussed.

In 1281/82 the abbot of Dunkeswell claimed to have gallows in Colaton Raleigh by a charter from King John. *PQW* p. 171.
Probably a presentment under article 26, "of new customs", which was used to present a wide range of alleged innovations. Other examples may be nos. 173, 266, 580.

220 The jurors present that when King John gave the land of Bradham to St. Nicholas's church in Exeter he kept in his hand one furlong of land

and one messuage to make a beadlery for the hundred, so that distraints taken within the hundred should be brought to that land until redeemed.

> John's charter, dated 13 July 1204, is printed Oliver, *Monasticon* p. 118. In 1212 Robert son of Robert Morin was described as "the lord king's man of Bradham" – BL Vit. D IX ff. 48–49 – and at about the same time as holding by the serjeanty of making summonses and distraints in Budleigh hundred, *Red Book of the Exchequer* Vol. II pp. 452–3. Before the creation of the beadlery, the tenants of the manor seem to have taken turns to act as beadle. *PQW* p. 170. In 1249 the beadlery was held by Maysent de Hulle, whose descendant, Geoffrey de la Hulle, held it in 1281/82 for acting as beadle "in the eastern part of the hundred", while Ralph de Wylington held a beadlery in its western part, identical with the half carucate in "Langel" held by Richard de la Weye in 1249 by the serjeanty of making summonses and attachments in the parts south of the Exe – early evidence for the separation of East and West Budleigh. JUST/1/176 m35d; *PQW* pp. 167, 170; JUST/1/186 m39.

221 Of defaults they say that Peter son of Ogier, Ralph de Willintone, John de Locumbe, Adam de Braileghe, Augustine de Pouhahille, the archdeacon of Cornwall, Gilbert de La Forde, the abbot of Sherborne, William de Barri, William Gernun, William de Coundeham, Ralph de Sicca Villa, John de Furnelle, Wymund de Raleghe and John de Wdetune did not come on the first day, so they are in mercy.

> In 1244 Baldwin de Raddon quitclaimed to Peter son of Ogier the church of Raddon – perhaps West Raddon, in Budleigh hundred, *Devon FFI* no. 387. Peter defaulted again in 1244 and 1249, JUST/1/175 m39; JUST/1/176 m35d. He also had lands in Cornwall and Oxfordshire, which may account for his repeated absences, *Cornwall FFI* nos. 7, 137.
> Ralph de Willintone was mesne lord of Gittisham, held of the honour of Gloucester *Fees* p. 762. He also defaulted in 1249, JUST/1/176 m35d. Adam de Braileghe appears below as the abbot of Tavistock's steward, no 255.
> Augustine de Poughille in 1242 held Poughill in free socage of Katherine de Monte Acuto, of the barony of Cheselborough, *Fees* p. 763. He defaulted again in 1244, JUST/1/175 m39.
> John Rof was archdeacon of Cornwall in 1238, DRO ED/M/45.
> Gilbert de la Forde was a Budleigh juror in 1249 JUST/1/176 m46. He may have been connected with the Henry de la Forde who in 1242 held one eighth of a fee at Ford Farm of the honour of Okehampton, *Fees* p. 785. The abbot of Sherborne held Littleham in frankalmoin from the king, *Fees* p. 764.
> William de Coundeham may have been connected with the Richard de Coundeham who witnessed a grant by Baldwin son of Gerold of land at "Langelonde", near the road from Harpford, in Budleigh hundred, to Exeter, BL Add. MS. 28649 f. 204v.
> For Ralph de Sicca Villa see no. 214 above.
> For John de Furnelle see no. 215 above.
> In 1234 Wymund de Raleghe, with the abbot of Dunkeswell and Ralph Springan, held one fee in Colaton Raleigh, in Margaret de Affert's portion of the fees of William Brewer, *Fees* p. 399.
> John de Locumbe also defaulted in 1249, when he was said to have lands in 'Stokeleg' – either Stockleigh English or Stockleigh Pomeroy – in what would later be West Budleigh hundred, JUST/1/176 mm14d, 35d.

222 The jurors present that the abbot of Torre has made a great purpresture on the great road which lies next to the land at Greendale, between the bridges at Clyst and Harpford.

> A presentment under article 9, "of purprestures". The abbot had probably enclosed, or even ploughed up, a section of the royal road leading from Exeter towards the Axe valley and south Dorset. It is possible that it was by a wide interpretation of this article that juries were able to bring to the attention of the justices other encroachments on the king, notably withdrawals of suits (161, 268, 721) or of the king's monetary dues (66, 91, 279) and the hearing of pleas of vee de naam (417, 547).
> Greendale – two virgates in the manor of Woodbury – was given to Torre abbey by William Brewer in his foundation charter. The manor had been held by the Albamara family, and it was Reginald de Albamara, William Brewer's uncle, who gave Greendale to William, and whose son and grandson confirmed the grant of it to Torre. Seymour, *Torre Abbey* pp. 82, 133, 138–40.

223   Henry de la Stokke, who is also known as Henry de la Wardrobe, arrested for arson and homicide in Devon, comes, denies all and puts himself on the country. A full inquest cannot be made into this at present, so he is sent to Exeter gaol.
   Nothing further is said about Henry de la Stokke.

224   Alice (Reginald *deleted*) de Mohun, asked by what warrant she holds Axminster hundred, comes and proffers a charter of King John which testifies that he has given and granted and by his charter confirmed to William Briuwerr and his heirs the manor of Axminster in Devon, with all its immunities and appurtenances in Axminster hundred. Whence he says that he is son and heir to Alice de Mohun, who is one of William's heirs.
   The clerk originally wrote Reginald, then deleted his name and substituted Alice's but failed either to correct the gender of the pronouns or to erase the last sentence, which shows Reginald as acting on his mother's behalf – since Alice was named as a defaulter from Axminster's pleas, and answered by an attorney when vouched to warranty during the civil pleas, she probably did not attend the eyre – no. 28 above, JUST/1/174 m14. Axminster was held by the king in 1086 – *DB* pp. 14–15 – and continued to be royal demesne until 1204, when John granted the manor, but not the hundred, to William Brewer, to be held in feefarm for £24 yearly, *Rot. Ch.* p. 139, *PR 7 John* pp. 19–20. In 1215, however, William received the manor, together with the hundred and the right to an annual fair, to be held, along with other lands elsewhere, for the service of three knights' fees, *Rot. Ch.* pp. 217–18. In 1233 Axminster was included in Alice de Mohun's share of the lands of William Brewer, *CCR 1231–1234* p. 228. From her it passed to Reginald de Mohun, her son by her first marriage, who in 1246 gave it to his foundation of Newenham abbey, Oliver *Monasticon* p. 362. In 1249 the hundred was valued at 50s. *per annum*, JUST/1/176 m34.

225   Richard Chartre gives 20s. for releasing Thomas Cayli from prison until Lifton hundred, pledges Touleus de Bosco, Philip de Culleforde, Richard de Yalde Dune and Luke de Wunestone.
   There is no further mention of Thomas Cayli among these pleas.

(m 31)
BLACK TORRINGTON HUNDRED ANSWERS BY TWELVE JURORS

226   Richard Passemer and Angerus de Wile, two jurors, are in mercy for not coming before the justices with their fellows to answer for their *veredictum*. Later each was amerced of 6s. 8d.

227   Avelina wife of Geoffrey Sprot was burnt in her home. Misadventure. Henford vill is in mercy for not presenting this case in the County Court.

228   The twelve jurors are heavily in mercy for a great trespass.

229   Richard Passawand appealed John Boscher and Alice his wife of breach of the king's peace and wounding, and John de Blaketoritone the vicar of aiding and abetting them. Richard has died. John and Alice come, and the jurors testify that they beat and wounded him as appealed, so they are in mercy. They made fine for one mark, pledges Joel de Curforde and Richard de la Clive. John the vicar does not come, so he and his pledges, Adam Parvus de Bleketoritone, Henry Yerle of the same, Richard Gode and Richard Hail, are in mercy.

230 Matilda wife of William de Oiham and William her husband appealed Elias Cancellarius, Roger Kernun and Alexander de Dodecote of breach of the king's peace and wounding. William and Matilda do not come, so they and their pledges, Jordan Espus and Martin de Limescote, are in mercy. Roger and Alexander have died. Elias comes, and the jurors testify that he gave him a wound on the shoulder and that they have made an agreement, so he is in mercy. He made fine for one mark, pledges William de Aubenun and Richard Passemer.

231 Rannulf Almer's house was burgled, it is not known by whom. Sampford vill is in mercy for not pursuing.

232 Stephen Wainarde de Samforde, Rannulf Dokeman, Walter Winnemer and Alan Belling were outlawed for the death of Godfrey de la Leghe at the suit of his son William. They were living in Sampford, which is in mercy. He was found dead in Lifton hundred, so inquire there about Englishry. Stephen had chattels worth 10s., Walter 2s., Sampford vill etc. The other two had no chattels.
> Nothing is said of Godfrey de la Leghe among the Lifton pleas.

233 William de Lithegri the smith killed Roger Cidie and fled, and was outlawed at the suit of his mother Matilda. He killed him in Okehampton vill, which is in mercy for not pursuing him. Inquire about his chattels in Lifton hundred. He had chattels worth 18d., the same vill etc.

234 Ralph de la Holle the smith appealed Richard de Brendeswrthe and his brother John of wounding Richard his son. Ralph and his son Richard have died. Richard de Brendeswrthi and John come, and the jurors testify that John gave Richard a wound, so he is in mercy. He made fine for 10s., pledges William de Aubenun and Richard de Brenneswrthi. They say also that Richard is not guilty, so he is quit.

235 Martin son of John de Stanforde was crushed to death by a mill wheel. Misadventure. Value of the wheel 12d., the sheriff etc.

236 Henry de la Dune killed Roger the ploughman with a fork and fled, so let him be exacted and outlawed. He was living in Clawton tithing, which is in mercy. Robert de la Dune, Henry's brother, who was with him when he struck him, is not suspected, so he is quit. Henry had no chattels.

237 Richard Batalie was crushed to death by a wall. Misadventure. The jurors are in mercy for presenting that his name was William.

238 Walter de Mora was found dead at Bridgerule. Thomas his son, who first found him, comes. No-one is suspected. No Englishry, so Murder fine.

239 Walter de Wlrinlande died suddenly while eating at the house of Walter de Tetcote and Maisenta his wife. They were attached but do not come, so they and their pledges, Richard de Bollelande and Stephen le Wite, are in mercy.

240 Jordan de Stanforde found a groom drowned at Stowford. He does not come, so he and his pledges, Roger de Wintone and William de Stanforde, are in mercy.

Black Torrington

241 Amice daughter of Richard de Spina found a mound dug into. She was attached for this by Hatherleigh tithing, which is in mercy as she does not come.

242 Sara wife of Joel de Paseforde wounded herself with a knife and died eight days later. Felony *de se*. No-one is suspected.

243 Adam the forester was outlawed for the death of Ralph de Pettesho at the suit of Everwin his brother. He was in the mainpast of the abbot of Tavistock, who is in mercy for not producing him, and he had no chattels.
  For more about this case see below no. 265.

244 Seilda widow of Jordan de Kilward hanged herself. No-one is suspected. Felony *de se*. Her chattels 14s., Werrington manor etc.

245 William Priune drowned in Werrington water by falling from a horse. Misadventure. Value of the horse 3s., the sheriff etc.

246 Roger Chagthe, attached by Holsworthy tithing because of the burglary of his home, does not come, so he is in mercy. Holsworthy tithing is in mercy for not pursuing.

247 John de Backemore appealed Richard le Franceis of breach of the king's peace and wounding. He does not come and he had no pledges, so nothing. Richard, also attached, does not come, so he and is pledges, Alric de Hele and Gilbert Pirho, are in mercy.

248 Robert de Cottelee appealed Walter Burnel and Osbert le Hornblowere of wounding and mayhem. Since this case belongs to Shebbear hundred, where the appellees come from, it is to be held over until the appearance of that hundred.
  This appeal is not found among the Shebbear pleas.

249 Roger de Cnolle, attached for biting Joel de Chagkesti's finger, does not come, so he and his pledges, Richard de Curigge, Richard son of Bloiou, Henry le Bischop and William Bischop, are in mercy.

250 Hamelin de Beuford fled to Halwill church where he admitted to theft and abjured the realm by coroner's view. He was in Beaford tithing, which is in mercy, and he had chattels worth 2s., Northlew tithing etc. Later it was testified that Hamelin was arrested by Walter and Roger sons of Gunild de Mora and escaped from them, so they are in mercy. Halwill vill is in mercy for not arresting him when he fled to the church.

251 Robert de Eggebeare, who appealed Robert le Grete of felony, came and withdrew, so he and his pledges, Richard and Philip de Egkebere, are in mercy. Robert le Grete came, and it was testified that they have made an agreement, so let them be taken into custody. Later they come and make fine for themselves and their pledges for 10s., as they are poor, pledges Richard Cole and Adam de Bradeleghe.

252 Robert de la Dune appealed Simon Timme, John Longus and Roger Canuel, Adam the canon's men, and Geoffrey, the parson of Lew's brother, that in felony they beat and ill-treated him and took a knife, a belt and 2s. in cash from him. The appellees come, and the jurors testify that

they are not guilty, so they are quit. Robert de la Dune is in mercy, let him be taken into custody. Later he came and made fine for 6s. 8d., pledges Peter le Franceis and Walter de Goriwis.

253 Richard son of Roger de Diretone died by falling from a horse. Misadventure. Value of the horse 5s., the sheriff etc. Holsworthy tithing is in mercy for not presenting the value of the horse.

254 William Longus le Bedel killed William Perer and fled, and was outlawed at the suit of Matilda wife of William Longus (*sic*). He was in Honeychurch tithing, which is in mercy, and had chattels worth 45s., the same tithing etc. He had one messuage in Hatherleigh, from which the king's year and waste raised 5s., Walter de Bathon' the sheriff etc. Later the abbot came and made fine for one mark for the year and waste from that messuage and from the messuage that Luke Paihard held.

(m 31d)
255 Luke Paiard, who abjured the realm before Jordan Oliver and his fellows, had a messuage in Hatherleigh from which the king had 8d. yearly and the abbot of Tavistock 4d. The abbot is in mercy for enfeoffing a man without warrant. Hatherleigh vill is in mercy for concealing that before those justices. Adam de Braleghe, the abbot's steward, is in mercy because he falsely accused the coroners of meddling with the valuation of that messuage. The king's year and waste from that messuage raised 4s. 6d., Hatherleigh vill etc. Later the abbot of Tavistock came and made fine for having the king's year and waste as appears above, under the case of William Longus.

> Jordan Oliver's gaol delivery was held early in 1238, C66/48m 11d. Luke Paiard abjured the realm at it for forging the king's seal, no. 622 below. His chattels were valued at 32s. 10d. E372/83 m10. Had he been able to attend the eyre, Luke would also have been appealed of homicide – the killing of Walter de Hatherl' for which he had been released to bail in 1231, *CCR 1231–1234* p. 1 – and of breach of the king's peace, no. 623 below.

256 Walter de Mellebire's house was burgled by unknown criminals. Melbury vill is in mercy for not pursuing as it should have done.

257 Walter de Cranebire and his wife Sybil appealed Vielus Trutte of beating them, Walter Gydie of abetting the deed and Nicholas de Tullesho of ordering it. They have not come, so they and their pledges, Robert le Gikur and Walter de Cuthminecote, are in mercy. Vielus and the others come, and the jurors testify that they have made an agreement, so they are all in mercy. Vielus made fine for 6s. 8d., pledge Richard Baustan, Nicholas de Tullesho for 6s. 8d., pledges Richard Passemer and Richard de Kari, William for 6s. 8d., pledge Richard de Tullesho. Later Walter came and made fine for one mark, pledge Jolanus de Correforde.

258 Cristiana de Middelcote, who found a mound dug into, does not come, so she and her pledge, Middlecott tithing, are in mercy.

259 Agnes de Holecumbe appealed Richard de Cumbe, his brother Angmerus, Richard Heile, Henry de Croft, Adam le Fowhe and Ogerus de Foxhille of coming to her house by night and breaking her door and windows, in breach of the king's peace. All the appellees except Richard

Heile come, deny all and put themselves on the country. The jurors testify that all of them except Henry are guilty, so let them be taken into custody, and that Richard Heile was the ringleader, so he is heavily in mercy. She is in mercy for a false appeal, let her be taken into custody. Later it was testified that Richard Heile was attached by Osbert de Bromdone, Philip de Foxole and Roger de Foxole. Later it was testified that Agnes is poor, so nothing. Later Richard and the other appellees came and made fine for two marks, pledges Herbert de Cumbe, Gilbert de Langeforde, Peter le Franceis and Walter de Goriwis.

260 Alice de Lawrthe appealed Robert de Withefelde, Maurice de Colunescote, John Bagghe, Theobald de Colunescote, Osbert of the same and Richemannus of the same that on the Saturday next before the feast of St. Michael they came to her when she was on her own land with her own oxen and ill-treated and beat her. All the appellees come, and as the appeal is null, let the country inquire. The jurors testify that Robert and the others chased Alice's oxen after her, so that she fell and was shamefully hurt by the oxen running over her, so let them be taken into custody. Later Robert and the others came and made fine for 20s., pledges Hugh son of William and Hugh de Loges. The same Alice appealed Geoffrey and Lawrence de Colunescote of the same. They did not come. Geoffrey was attached by Reginald de Putteford and Geoffrey de Whitefelde, and Lawrence had the same pledges. They are all in mercy.

261 Walter de Westecote appealed Henry Crik that when he had delivered his animals to him to be guarded and then asked for them back, Henry, wanting to keep Walter's animals by fraud, told his own wife to pretend to love Walter and seduce him into sleeping with her, so that thus he could get Walter's animals by deceit. And on the night of St. John the Baptist's day Henry told Walter to come to his house to guard it while he went to a fair, and he came there. And Henry, lurking in his home when Walter was asleep in bed in Walter's chamber, came with his followers, took him, bound him, put him under a vat and kept him there until he had quitclaimed to him all the animals he had entrusted to his keeping, and he put his brand (*signum*) on them and drove them into the fields. And on this he puts himself on the country.
Henry comes, denies all and puts himself on the country. The jurors testify that all Walter says is true, so let Henry be taken into custody. It was testified that Walter recovered his animals through the sheriff. Later Henry came and made fine for one mark, pledges Richard de Brendeswrthi and Geoffrey de Langeforde.

> This fair was almost certainly that of Bradworthy, granted to Richard de Langeford in 1234, and until 1236 held on the vigil, day and morrow of the feast of the Beheading of St. John the Baptist – thereafter it was held on the vigil, day and morrow of the feast of the Holy Trinity, *CCR 1231-1234* p. 465; *CCR 1234-1237* p. 382.
> This action shows particularly vividly how an appeal, from which all formalities had been omitted, could be used simply to bring a case before the king's justices, apparently for purposes of revenge, since the appellor had already recovered his livestock. Without much doubt Henry coerced Walter into surrendering his livestock by threatening to castrate him, a mutilation which in 1248 Henry III in person declared that wronged husbands were entitled to inflict upon the adulterous lovers of their wives, Matthew Paris, *Chronica Majora* Vol. V ed. H. R. Luard (*RS* 1880) p. 35. Examples of this actually being done include JUST/1/229 m14d; JUST/1/202 m27d; JUST/1/1078 m39d.

262 Richard, a beggar, was found dead in Werrington manor. Misadventure. Werrington tithing is in mercy for not presenting this case to the County Court.

263 Henry Purdeu, Walter de Kari, Henry de Mimminglan, Robert Serviens de Tettecote, Robert Longus and William Page, men of Thomas Corbet, who appealed John the Welshman, Thomas de Chiddingcote, Richard Carbonel, Roger de Dirhille, John Anglicus, Richard de Curigge, Richard de la Forde, William de la Pomerei and William de Blakedone, men of Herbert son of Matthew, of breach of the king's peace, come, as do all the appellees. They made fine for trespass for 100s., pledges William de Pomerei, Herbert de Merlei, Henry de Valle Torta and William de Briwere. And William le Kyn, who appealed William de Blakedone, does not come, so he and his pledges, William de Bovi and Osbert de Bromdone, are in mercy.

> Two of the appellors take their names from Tetcott and Membland, both of them manors among those which at this eyre William Pipard admitted to having handed over to Thomas Corbet, together with the custody of his own son and heir JUST/1/174 m17. But there is no discernible reason why Corbet's men should have quarrelled with the men of Herbert son of Matthew, who had no known interest in the hundred.

264 Idonea de Buketone drowned by falling from a horse into the river Torridge. Misadventure. Value of the horse 20s., the sheriff etc.

265 The jurors present that when John was abbot at Tavistock he arrested two of his men at his hundred court at Werrington, took them to Tavistock and imprisoned them there. Later twelve men came from the hundred to bail the two men, and the abbot at once arrested them and imprisoned them with the others. On the morrow the whole hundred went to Tavistock to bail all the men arrested and in prison, and as they approached the vill the abbot sent his men from Tavistock against the men of the hundred, and quarrelling and fighting having broken out between them, one Rannulf de Pentesho was killed. Adam the forester was outlawed for his death at the suit of Rannulf's brother Everwin. Be it known that Thomas de la Wile, then sheriff, took six marks from the abbot's men because of Rannulf's death.

> Before the Conquest Werrington had been in Stratton hundred in Cornwall. Between 1066 and 1068 countess Gytha gave it to Tavistock, but the abbey was deprived of it in 1086 because it had not held it on the day king Edward was alive and dead and could show no charter from William I. The sheriff of Devon then administered it as part of the royal demesne in Devon, and when in 1096 the abbey secured Werrington's return from William Rufus, it continued, for the convenience of the abbot, to be treated as part of Devon, *Devonshire Studies* pp. 19–39; Finberg, *Tavistock Abbey* pp. 6–7, 10–12, *RRA-NI* no. 378. Manors whose lords had acquired royal powers of jurisdiction over their tenants were often loosely described as hundreds in Devon deeds and charters – Finberg, *Tavistock Abbey* pp. 211–12. Thus in 1244 the abbot of Ford litigated to compel John de Colum's suit to his "hundred" court at Thorncombe, for which in 1281/82 he claimed to have amends of the assizes of bread and ale, view of frankpledge and gallows. *Devon FFI* no. 384; JUST/1/175 m12d; *PQW* p. 168. Werrington may, however, have always had a genuine measure of administrative autonomy, conferred by distance and the status of its lord. Before 1163 Henry II addressed a writ to "the whole hundred of Werrington" ordering it to render services and dues to the abbot of Tavistock, and a writ of Hamelin son of Richard, lord of Black Torrington hundred, regulating dealings between his hundred and Werrington, granted that the latter should have "all their liberties which pertain to the hundred-manor of Black Torrington which they used to have of old ...", DRO W1258/D67/1; W1258/D65/1.

266 The jurors present that whereas one man should make suit to Black

Black Torrington

Torrington hundred court for all the men of Wonford, Henry de Beumund and Jolanus de Curreforde, serjeants of the hundred, distrain all the men of Wonford to make suit to the hundred court, and take money from them because of this. And the same two serjeants do the same to the men of Chilsworthy, and took 8s. 2d. from them.

> This is Wonford in Thornbury, not the hundred of that name. In 1242 it was held by Alexander de Heremanesdon for half a fee of the honour of Plympton, Reichel S5 p. 212.

267 Walter de Faklefelde, charged with theft, has made himself scarce. The jurors testify that he is a thief, so let him be exacted and outlawed. He had no chattels. It is testified by the twelve that his brother Roger harboured him, so let him be arrested. Later Roger de Falklefelde comes, denies all, and puts himself on the country. The jurors say he is guilty, so he is hanged. He had chattels worth 40s. 8d., Cookbury tithing etc.

268 The jurors present that Bradworthy manor made suit to the County Court before William Briuwer was sheriff, but the suit has been withdrawn since his time, fifty years ago.

> In 1238 the manor of Bradworthy was held by Richard de Langeford, but it had formerly been held by William Brewer, to whom it was given by Henry de la Pomerai in 1198. *Devon FFI* nos. 8, 366. William was sheriff of Devon from 1179 to 1189, in 1200 and from 1202 to 1209.

(m 32)
269 Of defaults they say that Roger de Langeforde, Richard de Langeforde, Bridgerule vill, Milton Damarel vill, Lashbrook vill, Richard son of John, Robert de Bona Villa, Geoffrey de Dunhevid, Roger de Selewrthe, William de Scottewrthe, Walter de la Dune, Nicholas de Blakedone, Henry de Howisdone, John de la Fenne, Robert de Wike, John de Dunnislande, Elias de Trempole, Highampton vill, William de Bisinham, Hugh de Withulake, Stephen de Widebrok, Baldwin de Belestane, Drogo de Teitone, Roger Fliu, Martin le Blake, Ivo de Uppecote, Bartholomew de Melebire, Adam de la Fenne and Henry de la Fenne did not come before the justices on the first day, so they are in mercy.

> Roger and Richard de Langeforde were father and son; the latter held the manor of Bradworthy – *CCR 1231-1234* p. 465 – but both were litigating for land there in 1235, *Rot. Fin.* I p. 290. Richard was a Black Torrington juror in 1244 and 1249, JUST/1/175 m36; JUST/1/176 m46d.
> Richard son of John held one fortieth of a fee in Fernhill in 1242 of the honour of Totnes, *Fees* p. 775.
> Robert de Bona Villa in 1237 brought an assize for land in 'Halwull', probably Halwill in this hundred, C66/48 m11d.
> Geoffrey de Dunhevid, with William Avenell, held two fees in Ashwater in 1242 of the honour of Barnstaple, *Fees* p. 772. His absence was due to his having gone on pilgrimage to Santiago di Compostella, JUST/1/174 m14.
> John de Dunnislande in 1228 sold Kimworthy and Newland, held in his wife's right, to Roger de Parco; in the same year he received two messuages in Ashwater from Hamelin de Waunford, Reichel S5 pp. 210, 227.
> Baldwin de Belstane's heirs in 1242 held half a fee in Belstone of the honour of Okehampton, *Fees* p. 784.
> Drogo de Teitone in 1242 held one twentieth of a fee in Willey, of the honour of Okehampton, *Fees* p. 784; DRO ED/M/10.
> The numerous unidentifiable defaulters were probably typical of those small freeholders then engaged in bringing under the plough the remoter and less profitable parts of Devon – like Black Torrington hundred, on the Culm Measures Belt, described as "characterised by infertile, cold, heavy and wet soils", *Domesday Geography* p. 292.

The four vills that defaulted presumably each failed to send four men and the reeve to the eyre.

270 They say that Lady Joan de la Briuwere is in the king's gift, and her land in this hundred is worth 60s.

Joan was the widow of William Brewer the younger, who died in 1233. Her dower, assigned to her in the following year, included Hamsworthy, a parcel of the manor of Pancrasweek, in Black Torrington hundred, *Fees* p. 397; Reichel S5 p. 233.

271 Of escheats they say that Black Torrington was a royal escheat, worth £13, and Roger de la Zuche's heir holds it by gift from the king. And that Chilsworthy was a royal escheat, worth 30s., and Richard de Boketone holds it by gift from king John. And likewise that Culsworthy was a royal escheat, worth 6s. yearly, and William de Sicca Villa holds it.

Black Torrington manor became separated from the hundred late in the twelfth century. Both had been given by Henry I (with Kingsnympton manor, no. 388 below) to an ancestor of Joel de Meduana, who forfeited in 1189, J. E. A. Jolliffe, *Angevin Kingship* (2nd. Edn., London 1963) p. 129, *PR 1 Richard I* p. 136. In 1212 it was held by Geoffrey de Luscy – *Fees* p. 97 – but by 1228 it had reverted to the crown, for in that year Henry III gave it to Roger la Zuche – *CChR 1226–1257* p. 66 – who still held it in 1237 – *Fees* p. 613 – but who died shortly afterwards, since in 1238 his son and heir Alan had not yet made fine with the king for having livery of his father's lands – no. 280 below. In 1249 Alan was said to hold the manor by the serjeanty of keeping the hundred – JUST/1/176 m42d – in 1274/75 his son William by the serjeanty of distraining for the king's debts throughout the hundred, *RH* p. 64.

The first holder of Chilsworthy was named in 1281/82 as William de Arderne, who held in chief of the crown for homage and fealty, JUST/1/186 m6. It later passed to Robert de Sancto Dionisio, a Norman, who held it of the honour of Marshwood – Reichel in *TDA* 37 (1905) p. 430 n. 23, *Fees* p. 613 – but by 1207 the sheriff was accounting for its issues – *PR 9 John* p. 185 – and John subsequently gave it to Richard de Burton. Henry III confirmed Richard in his occupancy, at first during pleasure, later, in 1233, for life, *Rot. Lit. Claus.* I p. 411, *CPR 1232–1247* p. 20. By 1249 it had come to be held by William le Sauser, JUST/1/176 m42d.

The history of Culsworthy is extremely obscure. Held in 1086 by Coluin, an English thane – Reichel S5 p. 225 – in 1242/43 it was held by Maurice de Coltesuurth for one sixteenth of a fee, *Fees* p. 797. The latter source has Maurice holding of Ralph de Sicca Villa, but in 1249 the Black Torrington jurors said that, like Chilsworthy, Culsworthy had been held by Robert de Sancto Dionisio, who gave it to Maurice de Culteswurth, who gave it to Ralph de Sicca Villa, and that Gervase de Horton now held it by the king's (unrecorded) gift, and that it was worth 3s. per annum, JUST/1/176 m42d. These statements conflict with each other and with the presentment of 1238, but a civil plea from 1249, in which Gervase de Horton claimed that one Henry son of Maurice had held half a ferling in Culsworthy of himself by military service, and made no mention of any Sicca Villa subtenant, goes some way towards confirming the presentment of 1249, JUST/1/176 m7.

272 Pentri Cunel and Geoffrey the taverner are in mercy for selling wine contrary to the assize.

273 Henry de Bello Monte, asked by what warrant he holds Black Torrington hundred, says through Richard de Wangeforde, who is in his custody. And he proffers a charter from Joel de Meduana, son of Geoffrey de Meduana, testifying that he has given and granted to Richard son of Espus de Wangeforde, ancestor to the Richard who is in his custody, the Outhundred of Black Torrington for one silver mark yearly. And he also proffers a charter from King John, testifying that he has granted and by his charter confirmed to Thomas, son and heir to Richard Espus, and his heirs, the Outhundred of Black Torrington, to be held by hereditary right from the heirs of Joel and Walter de Meduana. He also proffers a charter

from Walter, by which he gave and granted to Richard son of Espus and his heirs the Outhundred of Black Torrington, to be held from himself and his heirs, paying one silver mark yearly for it.

> Black Torrington was held by the crown in 1086, *DB* pp. 52–3. Henry I gave manor and hundred to the ancestors of Joel de Meduana in exchange for Gorron and Ambrieres in Normandy – *Fees* p. 97 – and Joel, some time before 1189, granted the hundred (together with lands in Wonford, Northcott and Whiteleigh) to Richard son of Espus, in whose family, known as de Wanford, it descended thereafter – Queens 152 f. 133, *Rot. Ch.* p. 71, Reichel S5 p. 208. Joel specified that for these grants he and his heirs should receive each year one mark for the hundred and 22s. for the other lands, and in 1249 Alan la Zuche, who then held the manor, was duly receiving one mark yearly from Richard de Wanford, JUST/1/176 m42d. In 1238 the great-grandson of Richard son of Espus, another Richard, was a minor, his custody disputed between Henry de Bello Monte and Henry Beaupeil, but the dispute was settled when Henry de Bello Monte made over to the heir all his father Hamelin's lands, with the hundred, though reserving his own wife's dower in those lands, JUST/1/174 m12. In 1249 the hundred was being farmed for twelve marks *per annum*, JUST/1/176 m42d. For the manor see no. 271 above.

NORTH MOLTON HUNDRED ANSWERS BY SIX JURORS

274 Herbert Gale, Robert de Leghe and their fellows, who appealed William Megge, Jordan de Axewrthi and their fellows of breach of the king's peace, come. Likewise William Megge and all the other appellees come, and they all made fine for trespass for five marks, pledges Thomas de Aggalf, Jordan de Pullan, Herbert de Mershe, Archibald de Cruce and Archibald de Pillande.

275 A beggar called Edith was found dead in North Molton fields. The jurors are in mercy for presenting that she was found elsewhere.

276 Robert de Witafeld struck Andrew de Brimmeswrthi on the head with a stick so that he died soon afterwards. Robert fled, and was outlawed at the suit of Andrew's brother Roger. No-one else is suspected. He was living in Whitefield tithing, which is in mercy, and had no chattels.

277 David Mody was outlawed for the death of James de Britteleghe at the suit of James's wife Heloise. He was in Warkleigh tithing, which is in mercy, and he had no chattels.

278 Roger son of Geoffrey le Ridere killed Richard le White with a hatchet and fled, so let him be exacted and outlawed. Adam Bregge, charged with the same death, likewise fled, and it was testified that he is guilty, so let him be exacted and outlawed. They were not in tithing as they were vagrant ruffians, so nothing. They had no chattels. No Englishry, so Murder fine.

279 Walter de Baton' the sheriff says that North Molton manor used to give one mark to the sheriff's aid until Jordan Lespus was bailiff, when it was withdrawn, so let the country inquire. The jurors testify that North Molton manor should make suit to the County Court, and if it does not make that suit it pays the sheriff one mark, as the sheriff says.

> Judging by his name Jordan Lespus was a member of the family which by 1238 held Black Torrington hundred (no. 273), whose chief lord, Alan la Zuche, also held North Molton hundred. It is not known when Jordan was bailiff to North Molton. He was

dead by 1244, having also been at some time steward to the abbot of Tavistock, JUST/1/175 m31d, DRO D66/1. For sheriff's aid see no. 66. Cases like this help explain how the annual value of sheriff's aid in Devon, once £40, had fallen by 1237 to only £21, E368/12 m2.

280   The jurors present that North Molton hundred is in the king's hand because Alan de la Zuche has not made fine with the king for having his land.

> Held by the king in 1086 – DB pp. 38–9 – North Molton was said in 1212 to have been given by Henry I to the ancestors of Roger la Zuche, *Fees* p. 99. It had been forfeited in 1204 because of Roger's support for the French king – *Rot. Norm.* p. 130 – but was obviously recovered later. When Alan de la Zuche received livery of his father's lands is not recorded, but it is likely to have been before Easter 1239, when he was given licence to pay off his father's debts to the crown at 45 marks *per annum*, E159/17 m7. Although a hundred in 1086 – Reichel S9 p. 527 – North Molton's hundredal status was uncertain; it answered as a manor in 1244, a hundred in 1249 and a half-hundred in 1281/82, JUST/1/175 m46d; JUST/1/176 m43d; JUST/1/186 m14d. It was valued at only 2s. *per annum* in 1249, and was subsequently absorbed into South Molton hundred, *PND* p. 335.
>
> Roger la Zuche was sheriff of Devon from November 1228 to April 1231. As well as being lord of Kingsnympton and Black Torrington (271, 338), he also had lands in Norfolk, Cambridgeshire, Shropshire, Hampshire and Leicestershire, *CPR 1216–1225* pp. 37, 64, 87; *CCR 1227–1231* pp. 347–48; *Fees* p. 147. This may help explain why the administration of the county seems largely to have fallen into the hands of his clerk Rannulf de Cerne (see no. 50 above).

SOUTH MOLTON HUNDRED ANSWERS BY TWELVE JURORS

281   Thomas de Erneburne, one of the jurors, is in mercy for not coming before the justices with his fellows to answer for their *veredictum*. He is amerced of one silver mark.

282   Denise daughter of Fulk appealed William Traty that he came to her, took her against her will, and handed her over to Gilbert de Turberville, who detained her for a whole night. The jurors testify that William is not guilty. Let her be taken into custody. It is testified that she is poor, so nothing.

283   Walter de Thirletone was found dead on Exmoor. No Englishry, so Murder fine. The twelve jurors are in mercy for presenting no finder. Anstey Moyne vill is in mercy for not presenting this case to the County Court. Gilbert de Turberville, who holds the hundred, is in mercy for having the corpse buried without a coroner's view.

284   Rannulf de la Pille appealed Henry de Akeleghe, Patrick the reeve, Osbert de la Hille, Richard, the man of Henry de Akeleghe, and Ralph Cnit of breach of the king's peace. He does not come, so he and his pledges, William de la Weie and Geoffrey de Estleghe, are in mercy. Henry and the other appellees come, and the jurors say that they have made no agreement, so they are quit.

285   Sara de Grendone drowned by falling from her horse into Blackpool water. Misadventure. Value of the horse 30d., the sheriff etc.

286   A beggar was found dead on Tawton hill. No Englishry, so Murder fine on Bishop's Tawton vill, which does not participate with the hundred.

> Exemptions from the Murder fine only covered fines levied on the whole hundred; if a

death incurring such a fine occurred in an exempt manor, that manor would have to pay the whole fine itself, *Wiltshire Crown Pleas 1249* p. 62.

287 Elias the huntsman and John de Nortfuc drowned by falling from a little boat (*nacella*) between Tawstock and Tawton. Misadventure. Value of the boat 6d., the sheriff etc.

288 Adam de la Bere drowned by falling from a boat between Tawstock and Tawton. Misadventure. Value of the boat 8d., the sheriff etc.

289 Thomas de Elledone fled to 'Subrigge' church, where he admitted to theft and abjured the realm before the coroner.

290 William Russel and Richard de Stafford were outlawed for wounding Nicholas de Westcote at Nicholas's suit. They had chattels worth 8s. 4d., Stowford tithing etc.

(m 32d)
291 Richard the clerk of South Molton killed Roger Necke. The men of South Molton arrested him, but he later escaped from them and fled to South Molton church, where he abjured the realm. Since he escaped thus from South Molton vill, it is in mercy. He had chattels worth 12s., the same vill etc. The vill is in mercy for concealing those chattels. Geoffrey Gambon, who was then sergeant, is likewise in mercy. Roger's wife Agnes, whom Hugh de Hille appeals of the death, comes before the justices in neither chains nor irons, so to judgment on Walter de Bathon' the sheriff, as she was appealed of homicide. Agnes puts herself on the country, and the jurors testify that she is not guilty, so she is quit. Let Hugh de la Hille be taken into custody for his false appeal. Later he made fine for one mark, pledges Robert Furlang, Robert son of Hugh de la Hille and Alfred Hirdman.

> For all that Bracton believed that suspects should not be brought into court with their hands tied, though their legs might be shackled to prevent excapes – *De Legibus* Vol. II p. 385 f. 137 – it is clear from this and other cases that suspected killers were normally produced in irons. At the 1272 Shropshire eyre two suspects paid not to come into court in fetters, and at a Warwick gaol delivery in 1300 the sheriff of Leicestershire was put in mercy for bringing a suspected killer into court without irons. JUST/1/736 mm37d, 43; JUST/3/99 m7.

292 Margaret daughter of William de la Wheie appealed Arnold the deacon of Soumoutone of rape, in that he took her virginity on the Tuesday next before the feast of St. James the apostle. Arnold comes, and he is a clerk. The jurors say that he did not rape her as she says, because he had been sleeping with her for a long time previously, and then when he wanted to do so again, she refused, and he took her by force and lay with her. Whereupon the bishop of Exeter's official came and claimed him, to do justice on him in Court Christian.

293 Walter son of Richard Burri killed Walter de Anesti and fled, so let him be exacted and outlawed. He was living on the land in Somerset of the prior of Dulverton, who is in mercy.

> The prior of Dulverton was clearly the prior of Barlinch, a small Augustinian house near Dulverton in Somerset with interests in Mariansleigh and Morebath in Devon – the latter near both to South Molton and Dulverton, *PQW* p. 167, JUST/1/186 m14.

294 Of defaults they say that Gilbert de Turberville, John de Dunes-

lande, William de Wlurintone, William de Turberville, Drogo de Teintone and Roger le Moyne did not come on the first day.

> Gilbert de Turbervill was lord of the hundred, see no. 295.
> William de Wlurintone held land in 'Molton' in 1238, JUST/1/174 m13.
> Drogo de Teintone held land in Accott in Swimbridge parish, *Devon FFI* no. 433.
> Roger le Moyne held half a fee in Frodeton and Westecot, of which the latter "certainly is in the hundred of South Molton", *Devon FFI* no. 639 and note.

295 Gilbert de Turberville, who holds this hundred, does not come before the justices to show by what warrant he holds it, so let the hundred be taken into the king's hand.

> Held by the king in 1086, South Molton became part of the honour of Gloucester, possibly, like Winkleigh (no. 397 below), through the marriage of Robert fitz Hamon's daughter to Earl Robert of Gloucester – Pain de Turberville, Gilbert's ancestor, accompanied Robert fitz Hamon to the conquest of Glamorgan, and became lord of Coety there, Reichel S3 p. 77; R. N. Worth, 'Early Days in South Molton', in *TDA* 26 (1894) p. 129; T. B. Pugh (ed.), *Glamorgan County History Vol. III: The Middle Ages* (Cardiff 1971) pp. 22–3. Gilbert later recovered the manor, but soon gave it to Nicholas son of Martin in exchange for the latter's manor of 'Treguz' in Glamorgan, *PQW* p. 172, a move probably prompted by a war against the Welsh in which Gilbert was engaged in 1242, Pugh, op. cit. p. 50. The exchange had taken place by 1246, when Nicholas son of Martin was granted a weekly market and annual fair for his manor of South Molton, *CChR 1226–1257* p. 307. In 1249 the hundred was valued at one mark *per annum*, JUST/1/176 m43d.
> Links between Devon and South Wales were numerous in the Middle Ages. See also no. 611 below.

SOUTH MOLTON BURGH ANSWERS BY TWELVE JURORS

296 Matthew de Saterleghe appealed William Cusin of wounding him four times on the head and in the eye with a knife. William comes, and he is a clerk. The jurors testify that he is guilty. The bishop of Exeter's official came and claimed him, to do justice on him in Court Christian.

> In a charter of, or just before, 1238, since it was witnessed by four of the 1238 jurors for South Molton burgh, Gilbert de Turberville confirmed the burgesses of South Molton in the privileges granted them by his father, grandfather and great-grandfather, suggesting a foundation date of about 1150. He also conferred on them "all the good and free customs which the burgesses of Barnstaple have and hold in their town" – see no. 331 below. R. N. Worth, 'Early Days in South Molton', in *TDA* 26 (1894) pp. 126–8.

297 Walter the miller was drowned under the wheel of South Molton mill. No Englishry, so Murder fine.

298 Roger de Carlescote sold cloths contrary to the assize in South Molton, so he is in mercy.

> A presentment under article 11, "of measures...". Magna Carta c. 35 had laid down that all cloth was to be woven to a single width, that of two ells within the selvedges. Roger de Carlescote had doubtless produced cloth of insufficient width, perhaps exacerbating his offence by stretching it to try to bring it up to the legal width. W. S. McKechnie, *Magna Carta* (2nd Edn., Glasgow 1914) pp. 356–8.

MOLLAND MANOR ANSWERS BY SIX JURORS

299 Ralph de Rugberghe struck himself with a knife, so that he died three weeks later. Misadventure. No-one is suspected. The jurors are in mercy for concealing the name of his mother who was then in the house with him.

Molland

300 One of Thomas Tulion's cows was stolen, and it was later found in Witheridge hundred, skinned, at the house of Roger Mody, who vouched to warranty Simon Godinge who has fled. Inquire more fully in Witheridge. It was testified that Simon is guilty of stealing that cow, so let him be exacted and outlawed. He was living in Molland, which is in mercy, and he had chattels worth 15s., Molland vill etc. Roger is suspected. Later it was testified that Roger Modi was arrested and taken to the County Court, where he was handed over to the men of Witheridge manor, from whom he escaped. And they say that Rannulf de Cerne, then sheriff, took 100s. for the escape, so to judgment on him. He had chattels worth 5s., for which Robert de Hamme and his wife Custance are to answer, Custance having taken them when she was a widow. She is in mercy for taking them without a coroner's view. Robert Mercator, then serjeant, is in mercy because he took no trouble (*apposuit nullam diligenciam*) over inquiring into the chattels. Likewise 'Sprweie' tithing is in mercy for not presenting that to the coroner.

For voucher to warranty see no. 145 above. Robert Mercator was serjeant of Witheridge hundred, see no. 391 below. Rannulf de Cerne was under-sheriff to Roger la Zuche, so these events must have occurred before April 1231. In 1086 Molland was a royal manor, with three hundreds, Braunton, North Molton and Bampton, annexed to it, Reichel S9 p. 527. Soon afterwards it came into the possession of Robert de Romillei, and then passed, with Robert's daughter Cecily, to William le Meschin, lord of Copeland in Cumberland. William's great-grandson, William la Zuche, *alias* William de Belmeis, was said in 1212 to have sold the manor to William de Botreaux, in whose family it descended thereafter. W. Farrer, *Honors and Knights' Fees* Vol. I (London 1923) pp. 129–31. Molland was occasionally described as a hundred, as in the 1238 kalendar, but when in 1281/82 William de Botereaus was challenged as to his tenure of Molland hundred, his response was that "he does not hold any hundred of Molland, but he says Molland is a free manor..."*PQW* p. 179. For the free manors see note on no. 37 above.

BRAUNTON HUNDRED ANSWERS BY TWELVE JURORS

301 Brother Hugh, a monk of Cleeve, proffers a charter of the present king Henry's, which testifies that he has granted and confirmed to the abbot and convent of Cleeve his manor of Braunton in Devon, with the forinsec hundred and other appurtenances, to be held of the king and his heirs by the abbot and his successors for ever at fee farm, paying £22 for it at the exchequer by his own hand.

Braunton was held by the king in 1086, *DB* pp. 6–9, and appears to have remained royal demesne throughout the twelfth century. In 1201 Robert de Seccheville paid 100 marks "to have whatever the king has in Braunton manor, hereditarily, except the out-hundred and except the land which Odo de Carrio holds in the same vill..." and five years later he paid 50 marks and a palfrey to have Odo's lands as well, *PR 3 John* p. 222, *PR 8 John* p. 143. All this, however, does not appear to have amounted to more than a third, at most a half, of the manor – *RH* p. 65, *CRR* XIII no. 697 – while the hundred remained in the king's hand, until in 1229 Henry III gave it to the abbot of Cleeve in Somerset, who was to hold it at feefarm for £22 *per annum*, C60/28 m7, *CCR 1227–1231* p. 211. By 1249 it was valued at £30 *per annum*, JUST/1/176 m43.

302 Geoffrey son of Richard de Hacche was crushed to death by a mill wheel. Misadventure. Value of the wheel 2s., the sheriff etc. The jurors are in mercy for presenting the value of the wheel as 6d. and presenting no finder.

303 Leonard the miller died by falling from a cart. Misadventure. No-one is suspected. No Englishry, so Murder fine.

304 William son of Walter Longus drowned by falling into the sea from his horse. No-one is suspected. Misadventure. Value of the horse 2s., the sheriff etc.

305 An unknown man was found drowned in water below Hampton vill. No Englishry, so Murder fine.

306 A girl called Mariota was struck dead by a foal of her father's. Misadventure. Value of the foal 6d., the sheriff etc.

307 William Coppe was crushed to death by wood which fell on him. No-one is suspected. Misadventure. Value of the wood 4d., the sheriff etc.

308 Walter Golde appeals Geoffrey le Yein, Robert Peccha, Richard Gascon, William le White and Hugh Badde of shamefully treating and badly beating him. He does not specify who gave him which blow or what wound, so it is decided that the appeal is null. Because it is not known on whom justice is to be done, all the appellees are quit. Let Walter be taken into custody. Later Walter came and made fine for 10s., pledges Richard de Whitefelde and Eustace the marshal.

309 Adam de Howintone appealed Geoffrey le Yein and his sons Richard and Godfrey of breach of the king's peace and wounding. He neither comes nor makes suit against them, so he and his pledges, John de Howitone and William de Howitone, are in mercy. John is dead, and William has been outlawed, as below, so nothing.

310 Adam de Howitone, Roger of the same, Theobold son of John de Bramtone and William de Howitone killed Godfrey Longus and fled. They were outlawed at the suit of his wife Agnes. And Gunnilda and Beatrice de Howitone, charged with that death, were likewise waivered at Agnes's suit. The deed was done in Braunton vill, which is in mercy for not arresting them. They had chattels worth 62s. 1d., the abbot of Cleeve's men in Braunton etc.

311 Adam Temple is in mercy for lying before the justices.

(m 33)
312 Richard de Doddescote killed Colin Carbonel and fled, so let him be exacted and outlawed. He was in Buckland tithing, which is in mercy. Later it was testified that he fled to Ham church, where he admitted the death and abjured the realm. He had chattels worth 24s 4d., Buckland 'Brai' tithing etc.

313 Rengold de Bery, his son William, Richard the cobbler, John his father of the same, Stephen son of Simon of the same, Robert Shanke and Richard Blake of the same made themselves scarce on the arrival of the justices because they found a coffer in which they found treasure, so it is said. So Berrynarbor tithing, in which they lived, is in mercy for their flight. Richard had chattels worth 20s. and Rengold 17s., Berrynarbor vill etc. The others had no chattels. William de la Weie, then sergeant, is in

mercy for not attaching those men. Berrynarbor vill is in mercy for not presenting this to the coroner. Later Rengold came and made fine for his chattels for two marks, pledges Henry de Abieco and Hugh de Chageforde. Be it known that Rengold is not suspected of having been at that finding.

314 Thomas de Lustcote, who brought a plaint against Thomas de Blakeforde in the *Curia Regis* for breach of the kings's peace, found pledges for prosecuting, Jordan de Durewrthi and another who has died. He neither comes nor makes suit against him, so he and his pledge are in mercy. Later Thomas came and made fine for himself and his pledge for 20s., pledges Archibald de Pilland and Adam de Mottehou.

There is no record of this action in any of the surviving Curia Regis rolls.

315 Walter Lupus appealed Henry son of Henry of breach of the king's peace and wounding. They both come, but he does not make suit against him, so he is in mercy. The jurors testify that they have made an agreement, so they are in mercy. Walter came and made fine for two marks, pledge Alan de Alleswrthi. Later Henry came and made fine for one mark, pledge William de Raleghe the elder.

316 Walter Russel and his son Richard killed Roger de Trempestane and fled, so let them be exacted and outlawed. Later it was testified that they were outlawed at the suit of Adam de Morthow. They were in Bradwell tithing, which is in mercy, and he had chattels worth 5s., that tithing etc. Trimstone tithing is in mercy for not arresting those criminals.

317 An unknown woman was found killed at Pilton, outside the cemetery towards the spring. It is not known who killed her. Later the sheriff testified that she came from Plympton, so inquire more fully there. Later the Plympton jurors come and testify that one Henry le Ambleur – they do not know where he comes from – was sleeping with Eva, the wife of Ralph de Chows, and took her with him, together with a son of Eva's, and they firmly believe that Eva was the woman found killed there, and they say this because the woman found killed was found in the same clothes that Eva used to wear. And they do not suspect anyone besides Henry of her death.

318 Robert son of Smale killed Richard Ketel at Upcott and fled, so let him be exacted and outlawed. No Englishry, so Murder fine. He was in Charles tithing, which is in mercy.

319 Roger le Batur killed Andrew de Hole, and a married woman called Emelota, in his home at Pilland and fled, so let him be exacted and outlawed. He was harboured at Hole, which is a member of the prior of Barnstaple's estate at Pilland, outside tithing, so it is in mercy.

Pilland was one of the properties given to Barnstaple priory, a daughter-house of St-Martin-des-Champs, Paris, by its founder Joel of Totnes in the early twelfth century, Oliver, *Monasticon*, p. 198.

320 Robert de Hingledene appeals Morinus the reeve, Adam de Vallibus, servant to Godfrey Kalliou, Martin the miller's son, Hamelin de Bokelande and Richard the miller's son of beating him. All the appellees come, and as Robert does not appeal them now as he did in the County

Court, he and his pledges are in mercy. The jurors testify that they have made an agreement, so let them all be taken into custody. Later Robert came and made fine for himself and his pledges for 10s., pledge William de Raleghe the elder. Later Morinus and the other appellees come and make fine for 20s., pledges William de Raleghe the younger, Robert Challiou and Godfrey Challiou. And Adam le Smale, whom Robert appealed of the same, does not come, and he was attached by Robert and Godfrey Challiou, who are in mercy.

321 William Bulloc and William Prat drowned in the sea from a boat. Misadventure. Value of the boat 2s., the sheriff etc.

322 Robert the Irishman stole a tunic from a colleague and fled to Ilfracombe church, where he admitted to the theft and abjured the realm before the coroner. Ilfracombe vill is in mercy for not presenting that case to the County Court.

323 Henry Pinzun, charged with homicide before Robert de Lexintone and his fellows, made himself scarce. Later he returned with a royal writ to the County Court in which, so it is said, it was recorded that he makes fine with the king so that, if he should find pledges for his standing to right if anyone should wish to make suit against him, he should have peace. Whereupon Rannulf de Cerne, then sheriff, came and admitted that he had this writ, but he has lost it. The County testifies to the same. So let this be discussed.

Henry Pinzun paid five marks to be released to bail in April 1230, C60/29 m5, *CCR 1227–1231* p. 337.

324 ' Of defaults they say that Philip de Bello Monte, the abbot of Cleeve, William de Columbers, William son of Maurice, Stephen le Poer, Nicholas de Ferrariis and Nicholas Avenel did not come on the first day.

Philip de Bello Monte held one fee in Ashford of the honour of Okehampton, *Fees* p. 784.
The abbot of Cleeve was lord of the hundred, see no. 301 above.
In 1242/43 the heirs of William de Columbers, with Ralph Morin, held two thirds of a fee in West Down of the honour of Barnstaple, *Fees* p. 782.
William son of Maurice held one fee in Hagginton of the barony of Dartington *Fees* p. 782. He defaulted again in 1244, JUST/1/175 m48.
Stephen le Poer held one fee in Churchill, East Down, of the barony of Dartington, *Fees* p. 782.
Nicholas de Ferrariis, with Robert de Incledene, held one fee in Incledon of the honour of Barnstaple, *Fees* p. 771.

325 The jurors present that Rannulf de Cerne, when sheriff, arrested Walter le Knit and imprisoned him on the appeal of John le Steinur, an approver who died in prison at Exeter. And as soon as the approver was dead, Rannulf took five marks from Walter and released him to pledges. Water now comes, denies all and puts himself on the country, so inquire more fully in Shirwell where he was living. Coming about this, Rannulf admitted taking the five marks, as aforesaid, and he answers for them at the King's exchequer, so he says. So let this be discussed. Later Walter comes and gives one mark to be under pledges until the entry of Shirwell hundred. It is received by pledge of William de Raleghe the elder and William de Raleghe the younger. Later the twelve jurors of Shirwell come and testify that he is not guilty, so he is quit.

326 Robert de la Dene, charged with stealing four lambs, is suspected, so let him be exacted and outlawed. He was the son of the priest of 'Dene' and was harboured there outside tithing, so it is in mercy. He had no chattels. Robert was previously attached by Ralph de Arigge and Baldwin de Bramtone, who are in mercy as he did not come.

327 Walter de Dureville hanged himself in Plympton vill. Felony *de se*. He had chattels worth 58s. 8d., Petronilla his wife etc., by pledge of Walter Knit and Robert de Chevenhancre. He had a house at Plympton, inquire more fully there. Later the Plympton jurors come and say that he had other chattels besides the above, worth 7s., Plympton vill etc. And he had a house and curtilage, from which the year and waste was worth 3s., Reginald the smith etc.

328 A monk of Dunkeswell, the keeper of the fulling mill at Dunkeswell, was crushed to death by the mill wheel. Misadventure. Value of the wheel 2s., the sheriff etc. This case was not presented to the County Court, so the abbot of Dunkeswell is in mercy.

> This is one of the earliest references to a fulling-mill in Devon, the first so far found being to one at Tiverton in 1226, E372/70 m15d. For cloth-making in Devon see also no. 579 below.

329 From Theophania, widow of Lawrence the tailor, twenty marks as fine for trespass, pledges William Boschet, Sampson Peivre, Baldwin Childe, William Busse, John Strang and Richard Strang.

> See nos. 754 and 756 below.

330 Beatrice wife of John Richeman gives five marks to be remanded until the entry of Exeter city, pledges William Coleman, Walter le Granger, John de Okestone, Walter de Okestone, Walter de Moltone and Payn le Maszacrer.

> See nos. 753 and 755 below.

(m 33d)
BARNSTAPLE BURGH ANSWERS BY TWELVE JURORS

331 Richard the roofer fell on his axe and was wounded so that he died at once. No Englishry, so Murder fine.

> The most important town in north Devon, Barnstaple had a mint in the tenth century and in 1086 was described as a royal burgh with forty-nine burgesses, *DB* pp. 2–5, Hoskins, *Devon* pp. 327–30. Its status thereafter has been irreparably confused for posterity by the fact of its allegedly royal charters having been forged in the fifteenth century – S. Reynolds, 'The Forged Charters of Barnstaple', in *EHR* 84 (1969) pp. 699–720 – but in 1218/19 it was described as a free burgh, and as such as one where no judicial combat could take place – JUST/1/180 m2d – while whatever authentic privileges it did enjoy were regarded as worth granting to South Molton, see no. 296 above.

332 Ralph Cluter pulled Emma Gule from the step of an upper room. She fell onto stones, receiving two wounds on the forehead, so that she died seven weeks later. The jurors testify that she died from that, and Ralph has fled, so let him be exacted and outlawed. He was living in Barnstaple, which is in mercy, and had chattels worth 12d., that vill etc. The vill is in mercy again for not presenting the value of the chattels to the

coroner. He also had a house, from which the year and waste was worth 2s., William de Raleghe the elder etc.

333 Ralph the smith poured a bowl full of hot water onto a three-year-old boy, flaying him and killing him instantly, so let him be exacted and outlawed. He was in tithing at Horwood in Fremington hundred, which is in mercy. Inquire about his chattels in Fremington hundred. Later it was testified by the twelve jurors of Fremington that his chattels were worth 33s. 4d., Horwood tithing etc.

334 The jurors present that Richard Spigurnel de Bernestapel and Jordan Kagchefrenkis de Exon' sold wine contrary to the assize in Barnstaple, so they are in mercy.

335 Likewise the jurors present that Adam de Culeghe and Roger Coc sold cloths contrary to the assize in Barnstaple, so they are in mercy.

SHIRWELL HUNDRED ANSWERS BY TWELVE JURORS

336 Robert Gandre and Walter le Hethen, suspected of theft, come, deny all and put themselves on the country. The jurors testify that they are not guilty, so they are quit.

337 Gilbert the miller of Wellangre was struck dead by a mill wheel. Misadventure. Value of the wheel 8d., the sheriff etc.

338 Roger Cosse was found dead on Exmoor. No-one is suspected. Englishry is presented, so nothing. Misadventure.

339 Amicus de Chaudecumbe was found dead on Exmoor. No Englishry so Murder fine.

340 William son of Maurice was crushed to death by a beam. Misadventure. Value of the beam 6d., the sheriff etc.

341 The jurors are in mercy for a false presentment.

342 Of defaults they say that Philip de Beumund, Rannulf de Wellintone and the abbot of Cleeve did not come on the first day.

Philip de Beumund was lord of the hundred, see no. 343 below.
Rannulf de Wellintone held a quarter of a fee in Stoke Rivers of the honour of Plympton, *Fees* p. 787.

343 Philip de Beumund, asked by what warrant he holds Shirwell hundred, comes and says he has no warrant except ancient tenure from the conquest of the kingdom.

Shirwell was held in 1086 by Robert de Beaumont of Baldwin the sheriff, and descended in Robert's family thereafter, Reichel S8 p. 478. In 1249 it was valued at one mark *per annum*, JUST/1/176 m43. The fact that Philip de Beaumont did not attend the first day of the eyre (no. 342 above) but came later to claim his hundred suggests that the forthcoming inquest into hundreds was not publicised when the eyre was first announced, and that holders of hundreds were given comparatively little notice – see Introduction p. xxv.

Fremington

FREMINGTON HUNDRED ANSWERS BY TWELVE JURORS

344   Richard Severe, who found Roger the chaplain drowned, does not come, so he and his pledges, Richard de Bradenesche and Richard de Hertescote, are in mercy. No Englishry, so Murder fine.

345   William de Laweie, who appealed Henry son of Reginald and others of his household of breach of the king's peace, came and withdrew. He made fine for himself and his pledges, Robert de Whitesleghe and John de Winnescote, for one mark.

346   Rannulf de Allescote hanged himself in his home. Felony *de se*. He had chattels worth 5s., Alscott tithing etc. The twelve jurors are in mercy for presenting that case falsely.

347   William and Adam de Foresta de Dene, servants of Gervase son of Henry, killed Gervase and fled, so let them be exacted and outlawed. They had no chattels and were not in tithing, but were in Gervase's mainpast.

348   Scolastica wife of Christian de la Hole, attached for the death of Richard son of Christian, comes, denies the death and puts herself on the country. The jurors testify that she is not guilty.

349   Henry Biwlf fled to Fremington church, where he admitted to theft and abjured the realm before the coroner. He had no chattels.

350   Henry the miller of Coterhalre was crushed to death by the mill wheel. Misadventure. Value of the wheel 12d., the sheriff etc.

351   From five hides found near Torrington wood 12d., the same vill etc.

352   Avice de Toritone was in the king's gift and is married to Nicholas de Boleville through the lord king.

> Avice de Toritone was the widow of William de Toriton, lord of the barony of Great Torrington, who died some time before February 1224, *Rot. Fin.* I p. 111. The manor of Great Torrington in Fremington hundred was part of her dower, *Rot. Lit. Claus.* I p. 589. She had married Nicholas de Boleville by November 1229, *CPR 1225–1232* p. 314.

353   Henry de Traci, asked by what warrant he holds Fremington hundred, comes and says that he has no warrant except ancient tenure from the conquest of the kingdom.

> Fremington was held by bishop Geoffrey of Coutances in 1086, and passed to his nephew and heir Robert de Mowbray, on whose forfeiture in 1095 it was resumed by the crown. Henry I gave it to Joel of Totnes, whose honour of Barnstaple was subsequently divided among his de Braose and de Tracy descendants, Fremington falling within the latter's share. The fall of William de Braose during John's reign, however, enabled Henry de Tracy to reunite the whole honour in 1213, Reichel S8 p. 506. In 1249 Fremington hundred was valued at one mark *per annum*, JUST/1/176 m44d.

354   Boniface de Hunishauwe and Walter Culuerd, charged with theft, fled and are suspected, so let them be exacted and outlawed. They were harboured in Huntshaw manor, which is in mercy. Boniface had chattels worth 8s., Walter had chattels worth 2s., the same manor etc.

355   Simon de Bosco, charged with harbouring thieves, comes, denies all and puts himself on the country. The jurors testify that he is not guilty, so he is quit.

(m 34)
TORRINGTON BURGH ANSWERS BY TWELVE JURORS

356   Geoffrey son of Rannulf fell over Torrington bridge and died three days later. No-one is suspected. The jurors are in mercy for not presenting the finder's name.

> Great Torrington may have been granted burghal status by William III baron of Torrington, who was said to have given common pasture at Torrington to the burgage holders, some time in the twelfth century, H. P. R. Finberg, 'The Boroughs of Devon', in *DCNQ* 24 (1950–51) p. 205. In the kalendar of the 1249 eyre it is listed as Cheping Toriton, i.e. with a market, JUST/1/176 m47.

357   John de Bido, a thief from Cornwall, arrested for theft at Torrington, escaped and fled to Torrington church, where he admitted to theft and abjured the realm. Torrington vill paid the king 100s. for the escape. He had no chattels as he was a vagrant thief.

358   William Calvus died by falling from a ladder. Misadventure. Value of the ladder 2d., the sheriff etc.

359   The jurors present that John le Saliur de Toritone sold wine contrary to the assize in the same vill, so he is in mercy.

HARTLAND HUNDRED ANSWERS BY TWELVE JURORS

360   Thomas de Blakedone killed Richard, canon and priest of Hartland, and fled, so let him be exacted and outlawed. He was not in tithing as he was a free man. Later it was testified that he was in Culm Davy tithing, which is in mercy. He had no chattels. The twelve jurors are in mercy for lying, later they made fine for that and many other trespasses for 100s.

> There had been a college of secular canons at Hartland before 1066, but in about 1169 these were replaced by Austin canons, possibly from Nutley in Buckinghamshire, living according to the rule of Arrouaise. The new house succeeded to all the property of the old one. Chope, *Hartland* pp. 54–6.

361   Theobald de Rostfelde was found dead at 'Rostfelde'. No-one is suspected. No Englishry, so Murder fine.

362   Henry Wotri killed Philip de Milleforde and was outlawed for the death at the suit of Philip's wife Matilda. No-one else is suspected. He was in Milford tithing, which is in mercy, and he had chattels worth 15s. 10d., the same tithing etc.

363   William de Dinant the miller was crushed to death by the mill wheel of the same. Misadventure. Value of the wheel 18d., the sheriff etc.

364   Gunilda de Hemmeforde, who appealed John Teobald, Roger de la Dune and Reginald the reeve of Fernhille of beating Henry her husband, does not come, so she and her pledges, John de Doddecote and Robert de Henneforde, are in mercy. John and the others come, and the jurors testify that they came to Henry's house, forcibly drove him from it and beat him, so they are all in mercy. And the jurors testify that Henry is not maimed by the beating but lies in his bed feloniously, thereby to injure the appellees. Later John comes and makes fine for one mark, pledge Roger

Giffard. Later Roger de la Dune and Reginald came and made fine for 10s., pledges John Teubaud and Roger de Dirhille.

365   Of the king's serjeanties they say that Geoffrey Dinant holds Hartland hundred and finds one hundredor to make attachments which belong to the king, and he makes suit to the County Court, and it is worth one mark yearly. The same Geoffrey, asked by what warrant he holds the hundred, comes and shows nothing except ancient tenure from the conquest of the kingdom, so let this be discussed.

> Hartland was a royal estate in the ninth century – Finberg, *Early Charters* no. 16 – and was still held by the king in 1086, *DB* p. 42. It was probably Henry I who gave it to the Breton family of de Dinant, in which it descended thereafter, Chope, *Hartland* p. 26, Reichel in TDA 34 (1902) pp. 721–2. In 1249 the hundred was valued at 10s. *per annum*, JUST/1/176 m43d.

366   Stephen de Almerstone, one of the twelve jurors, is in mercy for foolish speaking.

367   Stephen de Hewrthi, charged with harbouring burglars and thieves, comes, denies all and puts himself on the country. The jurors testify that he is not guilty, so he is quit.

WITHERIDGE HUNDRED ANSWERS BY TWELVE JURORS

368   Robert Purdeu killed Thomas de la More and fled, so let him be exacted and outlawed. No-one else is suspected. He was in Puddington tithing, which is in mercy, and he had chattels worth 6s. 1d., the same tithing etc.

369   A woman called Emma de Karmetone fled to Puddington church, where she admitted to theft and abjured the realm. Later she was arrested, imprisoned at Exeter and hanged before justices for gaol delivery.

370   Ralph Coppe appealed John Swein, reeve of Branes, and Theobald, sergeant of Branes, of breach of the king's peace. He comes, but John and Theobald do not come, so they and their pledges are in mercy. Robert le Frere and William de Stancume were John's pledges, Roger son of Baldwin de Stancume and Richard le White were Theobald's.

371   Robert de Sicca Villa de Strochille appeals Walter Losmer, Ralph de Hapse, John the Welshman, Roger de Hortone and Robert the huntsman that on the feast of St. Hilary in the seventeenth year (13 January 1233) they seized him at 'Lesmere', took him to Oakford and imprisoned him there, and he offers to prove this by his body or in some other way, as the court shall decide, and he puts himself on the country. Walter and the other appellees come, and as the appeal is null, let the country inquire. The jurors testify that Walter and the others took and imprisoned him as aforesaid, so let them all be taken into custody. Robert de Sicca Villa and his pledges are in mercy as he did not make suit as he appealed them in the County Court. Later Robert the huntsman and John the Welshman came and made fine for 6s. 8d., pledge John Lanceleve. Later Ralph de Lapse came and made fine for Robert de Sicca Villa's

amercement for 6s. 8d., pledge Robert Mercator. Later the same Ralph and Walter came and made fine for one mark, pledges Hugh le Poer and Robert de Sideham.

372 Michael de Hecfertheswrthi was burnt in his house. Misadventure. No-one is suspected. The jurors are in mercy for concealing the name of his wife Joan, who was in the house with him then and escaped.

373 Miles de Calwdeleghe appealed Roger de Acastre, Elias de Blagewrthi, his brother Gilbert, John of the same, Gervase de Lestane and William de la Pole of wounding and robbery. Miles comes but does not make suit, so he and his pledges, Roger de Middelcote and Walter de Bullewrthi, are in mercy. Roger and the other appellees come, and they have made an agreement, so let them all be taken into custody. The same appealed of the same Walter de Brademede, Adam de Coleforde, Richard Pode, Roger Pode and Robert the man of Roger de Acastre, and none of them come. Roger de Acastre mainprised to produce them all, so he is in mercy, his pledges William de Wlurintone and Robert de Sydeham. Later Elias de Blakewrthi and four of his fellow appellees come and make fine for two marks, pledges Roger de Acastre and Robert de Sideham. Gervase de Lestane is poor. Later Miles came and made fine for 10s., pledges Roger le G... and Walter de Mocforde.

> This appeal seems likely to have arisen from a quarrel between neighbours, since Miles de Calwdeleghe had land in Bulworthy, in Rackenford parish – *CCR 1231–1234* p. 315 – while Roger de Acastre held North Coombe in the adjoining parish of Templeton – see no. 390 below.

374 Walter de Blagewrthi, who appealed Miles de Calwodelege and Luke the clerk, who is now a chaplain, comes, and the others likewise, and they have made an agreement, so they are all in mercy. Likewise Walter's pledges, Elias de Blagewrthi and Walter de la Hille, are in mercy as he does not make suit against them. Henry Culling and Sampson Culling are pledges for Luke's amercement.

375 Edward Bigge de Badeleghe was found dead in Bishop's Nympton fields. No Englishry so Murder fine.

376 Richard de la Heie drowned by falling from a horse into the river Nymet. Misadventure. Value of the horse 4s., the sheriff etc.

(m 34d)
377 Roger de Dockewrthi complains that Robert Mercator the sergeant came to his house on St. Brigid's day (1 February) and kicked Margery his wife on her left side so that she died barely six months later. Robert, who is present, denies all and puts himself on the country. The jurors of this hundred, South Molton hundred and South Molton burgh, with the four neighbouring vills, testify that he is not guilty, so he is quit, and let Roger be sent to gaol. Later Roger came and made fine for one mark, pledges Walter de Leghe, Richard de Leghe and William le Brun.

378 Robert Stork killed Stephen the miller and fled, so let him be exacted and outlawed. He was in Drayford tithing, which is in mercy, and had chattels worth 10s., the same tithing etc.

Witheridge

379   Richard son of Godfrey, who found a drowned boy, does not come. He was attached by Ralph Ruffus and Richard le White, who are in mercy. No Englishry so Murder fine.

380   Roger Fuite killed Thomas le Bere and fled, and he was outlawed by the suit of Walter de Farebi, Thomas's brother. He was in Rose Ash tithing, which is in mercy, and had chattels worth 4s., the same tithing etc.

381   Auwenilda daughter of Hawise appeals Henry Huvestrong of burgling her mother's house and strangling her, and she offers to prove this against him as the court shall decide. Henry comes, denies all and puts himself on the country. The jurors testify that he is guilty, so he is hanged. He had no chattels.

382   Richard le Kampere, charged with the same death, comes, denies all and puts himself on the country. The jurors testify that he is not guilty, so he is quit.

383   Hugh le Cat hanged himself in 'Callebrige' wood. Felony *de se*. He had chattels worth 2s., Drayford tithing etc.

384   Richard Hogastre and Walter le Blake de Nimetone quarrelled as they came from a tavern, so that they killed each other. No-one else is suspected. Richard had chattels worth 3s., Cadbury Barton tithing etc. Walter had chattels worth 12d., 'Nimetone' tithing etc.

    'Nimetone' seems most likely to be Kingsnympton, which is considerably closer to Cadbury Barton than either Bishop's Nympton or George Nympton.

385   Simon, park-keeper to Alexander de Crues, appealed Thomas de Santone of breaking Alexander's park and driving his beasts from it. Simon does not come, so he and his pledges, Richard de Capella and Alfred de Bosco, are in mercy. The jurors testify that Thomas, with Thomas le Pulein who comes and Henry son of Emma and Stephen le Claver who do not come, broke his park and took his beasts as said, and moreover they have all made an agreement with Alexander and Simon, so they are all in mercy. Let Alexander and Thomas Pulein, who have come, be taken into custody. The other appellees did not come, as they were not attached. Later Henry de Raleghe came and mainprised to produce Thomas de Santone tomorrow. Later Alexander Crues came and made fine for 20s., pledge Ralph Ruffus. Later William de Raleghe the elder came and mainprised to produce Henry son of Emma and Stephen le Claver next Tuesday.

    Alexander de Crues's park was probably at Cruwys Morchard, where in 1242/43 his heirs held one fee of the honour of Bradninch, *Fees* p. 758.

386   Alan the Welshman was outlawed for the rape of Mabel daughter of Simon de Uppadone by Mabel's suit. He was in the mainpast of William Peverel, who is in mercy. The jurors testify that Simon de Uppedone arrested Alan and led him towards Exeter with Cruwys Morchard tithing and Robert Coterel, then serjeant, and he escaped from them, so they are all in mercy, let them answer for the escape. Simon, who appealed Robert Coterel of that escape, does not make suit, so he and his pledges, Robert

de Mora the elder and the other Robert de Mora, the younger, his neighbour, are in mercy.

387 Richard Knotte, attached by Thomas de Bradeleghe and Thomas Sagke on the indictment of Roger Brune's widow Edith for the death of her husband Roger, does not come, so he and his pledges are in mercy. Be it known that Richard de Northecote, John de Anerigge and Robert de Sideham are pledges for Richard with the others, so they are all in mercy. The jurors testify that he is not guilty, so he is quit.

388 Margery widow of Roger Fitzpayne is in the king's gift. Kingsnympton was an escheat to the king from Normans' lands, and William de la Zuche holds it by gift from Roger de la Zuche, who holds it by grant from the king.

> Roger Fitzpayne was dead by October 1237, when order was given that Margery be assigned her dower, *CCR 1234–1237* p. 504. In December of that year she was granted custody of all Roger's lands until the latter's heir's coming-of-age, in return for 100 marks *per annum*, *CCR 1237–1242* pp. 14–15. They included a half and a tenth of a fee in Witheridge itself, *Fees* p. 758.
> Kingsnympton had been held by Joel de Meduana (see no. 271 above). In 1249 it was presented that king John gave it to Roger la Zuche – JUST/1/176 m44d – a grant which Henry III made permanent in 1228, *CChR 1226–1257* p. 66.

389 Emma de Karmetone was imprisoned at Bishopsnympton and escaped. The sheriff says that the bishop's steward made fine with him for the escape, and for a groom of the bishop's arrested because he secretly took grain from one of his lord's granges to his lord's beasts, all for 60s.

> Probably a presentment under article 32, "of escaped thieves".

390 Alfred le Yolde was arrested at North Coombe by Roger de Acastre's men, and he escaped from them and from Warbrightsleigh Barton tithing, so let them answer for the escape. Rannulf de Cerne, the then sheriff, well admitted that the king has pardoned Roger de Acastre for the escape, but the barons of the exchequer demanded payment from Rannulf for the escape, and he paid them. The jurors testify that he is a thief, so let him be exacted and outlawed. His chattels were worth 5s., Roger de Acastre etc. He is in mercy for taking them on his own authority.

> In 1236 Roger de Acastre was said to be holding Warbrightsleigh Barton and half 'Cumbe', the latter being identifiable as North Coombe in Templeton parish, *Fees* p. 612 and Index p. 162. Roger had been tutor to Richard of Cornwall, N. Denholm-Young, *Richard of Cornwall* (Oxford 1947) pp. 3–5.

391 Robert Mercator acknowledged that he holds Witheridge hundred from Robert son of Roger, who is in the king's custody. Whereupon Robert son of Terrus, who was steward to Roger Fitzpayne, Robert's father, comes and says that Roger had no warrant except ancient tenure.

> Witheridge was held by the king in 1086, *DB* pp. 44–5. Its descent thereafter is wholly obscure. In 1242/43 Roger Fitzpayne's heir was said to be holding a half and a tenth of a fee in Witheridge, through a mesne, of the honour of Plympton, so it is possible that it had once been held by the earls of Devon, *Fees* p. 758. In 1281/82 Roger la Marchaunde, who must have been a descendant of the Robert Mercator holding the hundred in 1238, claimed to hold it by gift of Robert Fitzpayne for two marks yearly – *PQW* p. 166 – this sum being also its estimated annual value in 1249, JUST/1/176 m44d.

WINKLEIGH HUNDRED ANSWERS BY TWELVE JURORS

392 Alan, the priest of Winkleigh's son, killed his brother John. This case was finished before gaol delivery justices. No Englishry, so Murder fine. Later it was testified that John died by misadventure when he fell on his own knife. Winkleigh vill is in mercy for not having the knife before the justices.

393 Henry Ballard killed Edward Yuli and fled, so let him be exacted and outlawed. He was in Loosebear tithing, which is in mercy, and he had chattels worth 5s. 4d., the same tithing etc. Inquire more fully in Wonford hundred. Later Wonford hundred comes and knows nothing about the chattels other than what has been already said.

394 Richard Burdun was found dead in Hollocombe vill, which is in mercy for not presenting this case to the County Court. Likewise Henry Gurande, chief serjeant, is in mercy for the same. No Englishry, so Murder fine.

395 Richard Niger, who appealed William Doggefel of wounding and breach of the king's peace, comes but does not make suit, so he and his pledges, Michael de Sucote and Roger the smith, are in mercy. As it was testified that they have made an agreement through Thomas de Uppecote, William's father, who was imprisoned for this, Thomas is in mercy. He made fine for 6s. 8d., pledge Robert de Bonon'. The same appealed Roger de Langemede, Geoffrey son of Nicholas de la Yalelande, Thomas de Langemede and Stephen le Prestre of the same. He does not make suit, so he and his pledges are in mercy as above. The jurors testify that they have made an agreement, so they are likewise all in mercy. The appellees do not come, so Robert le Copiner, who mainprised to have them before the justices, is in mercy. Later it was testified that Richard Niger is poor because he has paid out all he had on the healing of his wounds.

396 The jurors present that Reginald le Steimur and John de Hakestone sold wine contrary to the assize in Birch, so they are in mercy.

397 Henry Gurand, asked by what warrant he holds Winkleigh hundred, comes and says that he has no warrant except ancient tenure, and that his ancestors were enfeoffed from the earldom of Gloucester.

> Winkleigh was held by the king in 1086, having been held by Earl Brictric before the Conquest, *DB* pp. 84–7. William Rufus gave Brictric's lands to Robert fitz Hamon, whose eldest daughter Mabel married earl Robert of Gloucester and on whom Henry I bestowed her father's lands in Devon, Reichel in *TDA* 29 (1897) pp. 246, 255. Earl William of Gloucester succeeded his father Robert as lord of Winkleigh, but gave it to Philip de Caheines, probably before 1166, BL Vit. D. IX f. 54. Philip's descendants held it thereafter – since a William de Kaygnes was lord of Winkleigh some time before 1238, D & C MS 3672 f. 141, and a Roger de Keynges held it in 1274/75, *RH* p. 87, it is overwhelmingly probable that Henry Gurand, in spite of his name, was a member of this family.

(m 35)
SOUTH TAWTON HUNDRED ANSWERS BY TWELVE JURORS

398 John Burnel, one of the twelve jurors, does not come before the justices with his fellows to answer for their *veredictum*, so he is in mercy. Later he was amerced of one mark by his fellows.

399 Richard the chaplain of Giddeleghe was found dead on the highway to Gidleigh. No Englishry, so Murder fine.

400 Richard de Creuberghe appealed Walter son of Drogo de Esse of breach of the king's peace and wounding. He comes and says nothing by which the appeal might stand (*quare appellum ibi iaceat*). Walter comes, and the jurors testify that Walter is guilty and that they have made an agreement, so let them both be taken into custody. Later Walter came and made fine for 6s. 8d., pledges his father Drogo and John de Atherigescote.

401 Ralph de Creuberghe appealed Thomas de Wnstone of wounding and breach of the king's peace. Thomas, who was attached by Aenol de Wnstone, Luke de Wnstone, his brother Ralph and John Binorthedone, does not come, so they are all in mercy. Ralph comes and has no wounds whereby there could be a duel between them, so let the other party be arrested. Later Thomas came, and the jurors say he is not guilty, so let Ralph be taken into custody for a false appeal. He made fine for 6s. 8d., pledge Tollacus de Bosco.

402 William Halger was found dead in Wonford hundred. Misadventure. The twelve jurors are in mercy for not presenting the finder's name.

403 The jurors present that one day, when Hugh le Criur, then forester, and his fellows were at a party at South Zeal, after the meal Hugh ordered his fellows to go their bailiwicks and guard them faithfully, because he had been given to understand that a woman had been robbed in the forest. A forester named Geoffrey Rugeleon then stood up and in their presence admitted that he had robbed the woman, taking 5s. from her, and ravishing her virginity, whereupon Hugh told Geoffrey that he must find him good pledges for his coming to the County Court, because he admitted that before himself, who was a royal sergeant, and others. Geoffrey then went away to look for pledges, and Hugh at once ordered certain of his sergeants, David the Welshman, a forester, and Eliot, likewise a Welshman, either to guard him safely or to take sound pledges from him. David came to Geoffrey and asked for a pledge from him, and Geoffrey, who had drawn his knife, struck David in the stomach, so that he fell, and fled at once. Eliot followed him, as did David when he could get up, and David struck Geoffrey on the head with a stick as he fled, so that he fell, and Eliot struck him a fatal blow with a knife, and then fled. David was found with a knife in his hand almost dead, and was arrested and imprisoned at Exeter. And because he was not charged with the death, Thomas de la Wile, then sheriff, released him to pledges to be before the justices, to Robert Croppe, Walter de la Grave of Somerset, Alan son of Richard de Acforde, Spherus de Clerkestone, Robert de Stevenhalle, Robert de Horsam, Osbert Dumel and William de Mewy. He

does not come, so they are all in mercy. Afterwards by judgment (*de consilio*) of the court, because it was established that Geofrey had, on his own confession, done felony to the woman, robbing and raping her, it was decided that David and Elias have committed no offence, so they may return if they wish.

> South Zeal is on the northern edge of Dartmoor, and these vividly reported events probably all took place within the bounds of Dartmoor forest, which had remained under forest law after 1204. Except in the New Forest, pleas of the crown arising within the forest were usually, as here, reserved for the common pleas eyre – C. R. Young, *The Royal Forests of Medieval England* (Leicester 1979) pp. 92–4. The reference to Thomas de la Wile (see no. 187 above) probably dates this case to 1231 or 1232.

404 William de Lewe appealed Richard son of Semerus of wounding him on the head, and Semerus his father of aiding and abetting. He says nothing relevant to the appeal, so let the country inquire. William the appellor and the appellees come. The jurors say that they have made no agreement nor are they guilty, so the appellees are quit, let William be taken into custody. Later he made fine for 6s. 8d., pledge Alfred de Coleberghe.

405 Wimarc daughter of Hamelin de Attrescote appealed William son of Richard de Wike of rape. She comes and makes suit. William does not come, and he was attached by Richard de Wike, Richard de Trualai, Reginald de la Sele and Jocelin de Bosco, who are all in mercy. Later it was testified that William was outlawed for homicide, as appears in the roll of Wonford hundred. The same William, before he was outlawed, appealed of felony a man named Springe, who was outlawed at William's suit. Likewise he appealed one Walter Springe, who fled to church and abjured the realm before the coroner. Walter Springe and the other man named Springe were in the mainpast of Richard de Toney, parson of Tawton, who is in mercy. Cocktree vill is in mercy for not arresting them.

406 Nicholas the smith appealed William le Shireve, Humphrey le Shireve, David Canne, Roger Canne and Richard de Charterei, who has died. William Shireve and all the other appellees come, and the jurors testify that they are not guilty, so they are quit.

407 Ansel de Hocsenham and William de Wike, outlawed for the death of Alan de Chirchetone at the suit of John son of Golde, were in South Tawton tithing, which is in mercy. Ansel had chattels worth 3s., the same tithing etc. William had no chattels. Inquire more fully in Wonford hundred.

408 Richard Brocger made himself scarce for burglary, with which he was charged. The jurors testify that he is not guilty, so he may return if he wishes, but as he fled his chattels, worth 4s., are confiscated, South Tawton tithing etc., and the same South Tawton tithing is in mercy for his flight.

409 Thomas de la Wile, when sheriff, accused Thomas Tail of having some of the chattels of Robert Moinel who was hanged, and Thomas admitted having 4s. from his chattels, which Thomas de la Wile took from him, so let him answer. And later, because of this admission, Thomas de

la Wile took 44s. from Thomas Tail, so to judgment on him. Likewise Gilbert de Manebi took 20s. from him for the same reason.

> Gilbert de Manebi also appears as a subordinate of the sheriff Robert de Vallibus, no. 550 below. In 1243 he was recorded as in debt to Jacob the Jew, which may help account for his apparent rapacity here, E372/87 m9.

410 Alfred de Colebere, Ralph Tony's sergeant, asked by what warrant his lord holds South Tawton hundred, says he has no other warrant, so he believes, besides ancient tenure.

> South Tawton – which in 1244 and 1249 was only described as a manor, being subsequently absorbed by Wonford hundred – was given by Henry I to his illegitimate daughter Constance, wife of Roscelin *vicomte* of Maine. It appears to have been in the king's hand early in the reign of Henry II – *PR 3 Henry II* p. 74 – but subsequently passed to Constance's son, Richard de Beaumont, whose daughter Constance married Roger de Tony, father of the holder of 1238, *Fees* p. 98, *Rot. Ch.* pp. 20–1, Reichel in *TDA* 44 (1912) pp. 346–8. In 1249 the jurors of South Tawton manor presented that Ralph de Tony's son Roger was a minor, with lands in that hundred (presumably Wonford) worth £37 *per annum*, JUST/1/176 m41d.

CREDITON HUNDRED ANSWERS BY TWELVE JURORS

411 William Barat de Chiritone died by falling from his horse. Misadventure. Value of the horse 2s., the sheriff etc.

412 Agnes de Sakiatone, attached on the indictment of a thief hanged at Chulmleigh, does not come, so she and her pledges, Osbert de la Leghe, Edward de la Bidene, Richard de la Crosse, William Levele, Osbert de Cumbe and Richard de Cumbe, are in mercy The jurors testify that she is not guilty, so she is quit.
Hawise de Raulestone, attached for the same, comes. The jurors testify that she is not guilty, so she is quit.

> The gallows at Chulmleigh will have been those of Robert de Curtenay, *PQW* p. 171, JUST/1/186 m14.

413 Richard Fuel and his wife Gillian appealed Robert Morgan of burglary. He comes and makes suit against him. Robert comes, denies all and puts himself on the country. The jurors say he is not guilty, so he is quit, let the other party be taken into custody. He is poor, so nothing.

414 Osbert de Bosco killed Hugh de Morcet and was hanged for his death before gaol delivery justices. No-one else is suspected. He had chattels worth 28s. 6d., Rawstone tithing etc.

415 Alexander son of William Burel fell from his horse and drowned in the river Yeo. Misadventure. Value of the horse 2s., the sheriff etc.

416 Luke de Brommelrigge made himself scarce and is suspected of stealing cows and sheep, so let him be exacted and outlawed. He had chattels worth 9s., Doddridge tithing etc., and he had a ferling and a half of land and one messuage. Later Master Peter Wymund came and made fine for having his chattels and for the king's year and waste for one mark, pledge Rannulf de la Were.

> Peter Wymund was parson of Whitestone in Wonford hundred – *CRR* XV no. 177 – and a warden of St. John's hospital in Exeter – DRO ECA Book 53a f. 27. No other evidence has been noticed for his owning property in Doddridge.

Crediton

417 The jurors present that the bishop of Exeter's bailiffs at Crediton plead pleas of vee de naam in the bishop's court. The bishop comes and says he has always been in seisin of holding such pleas since the king gave that manor of Crediton to God and the church of St. Peter at Exeter for the death of a bishop of Exeter who was killed at that manor in the meadows outside the vill. So let this be discussed.

> Vee de naam was the name given to the action which arose when goods taken in distraint were not returned to their owner after the latter had offered security – gage and pledge – for his appearance in court. It was an action which could be pleaded in the County Court without a royal writ, but the closeness to robbery made it a jurisdiction very rarely granted to private individuals. T. F. T. Plucknett, *Legislation of Edward I* (Oxford 1949) pp. 57–9; Cam, *Hundred Rolls* p. 210; Pollock and Maitland Vol. II p. 577. The bishop's account of the origin of his franchise is highly dubious. Episcopal connections with Crediton began in 739, with the grant by king Aethelheard of Wessex to Forthhere, bishop of Sherborne, of twenty hides at Crediton, Finberg, *Early Charters* no. 2. The subdivision of the see of Sherborne in 909 led to the establishment of a bishopric at Crediton itself, whose first occupant, Eadulf, received a grant of immunity from Athelstan in 933 – Finberg, *Early Charters*, no. 20. It may have been this charter with which Bishop Brewer in 1238 hoped to justify his franchise of vee de naam, though since the latter originated in the reforms of Henry II – H.Cam, *Law-finders and Law-makers in Medieval England* (London 1962) p. 35 – such a claim would certainly have been anachronistic, as indeed was the reference to the bishop of Exeter, an office unknown before 1050. William of Malmesbury – *De Gestis Pontificum*, ed. N. E. S. A. Hamilton (*RS* 1870) p. 178 – describes the violent death of a west-country bishop in the early tenth century, but if such an event took place it is most unlikely to have resulted in the sort of grant represented here, and it is noteworthy that neither in 1274/75 nor in 1281/82 was the story of 1238 repeated, the bishop's claim to Crediton manor being justified by reference to ancient tenure only, *RH* p. 69, *PQW* p. 175. The hundred was certainly regarded as an appurtenance of the manor, so the bishop's claim to the former was subsumed in his claim to the latter. In 1249 Crediton hundred was valued at two marks *per annum*, JUST/1/176 m45.

(m 35d)

418 Adam de Sakiatone made himself scarce and is suspected of stealing oxen and cows, so let him be exacted and outlawed. He had chattels worth 42s., John de Dunneslande etc., by pledge of William Trenchard and William de Ralege the younger. He also had one messuage and four ferlings of land, and the same John gives 24s. 8d. for having the king's year and waste from them, pledges William Trenchard and William de Raleghe the younger.

419 Of defaults they say that William Tosard, Thomas de Teteburne, John Barlet, Richard de la Leghe and William de Cumbe did not come on the first day, and likewise that Hugh de Sancto Vasto did not come.

> William Tosard held half a fee in Colebrooke manor, Devon *FFI* no. 367. He defaulted again in 1244 and 1249, JUST/1/175 m49; JUST/1/176 m45.
> Thomas de Teteburne held one fee in Yeo, on land formerly William Brewer's, *Fees* p. 399.
> John Barlet, with his wife Agatha, held two-thirds of a fee in Crediton, JUST/1/174 m18d.
> Hugh de Sancto Vasto in 1241 acknowledged Colebrooke manor to be the right of Walter of Bath, "as that which Walter has by his gift", *Devon FFI* no. 367.

420 John le Blake de Sumertone Regis, arrested for stealing a tunic and imprisoned at Crediton, escaped from there, fled to church and abjured the realm. To judgment for the escape. He was not in tithing and had no chattels as he was a vagrant thief.

421 Osbert Horn and Robert de la Bergh made themselves scarce.

Osbert is suspected of stealing cows, Robert of harbouring thieves, so let them be exacted and outlawed. Osbert had chattels worth 2s., Smallbrook vill etc. That vill is in mercy for not producing him. Robert had chattels worth 9s., Rannulf de la Were etc., and he was in Henstill tithing, which is in mercy.

422 The jurors present that Robert le Taverner and Philip le Palmer sold wine contrary to the assize at Crediton. Because the jurors wished to conceal that, they are all in mercy.

CREDITON BURGH ANSWERS BY SIX JURORS

423 These jurors present nothing that was not presented in Crediton hundred.

> Crediton burgh may have originated in the bishop of Exeter's payment, on 25 January 1231, of five marks for a royal charter granting a market and fair at his manor of Crediton – C60/30 m7. It was certainly a recent foundation in 1238, since a civil plea that year alleged disseisin of the plaintiff's "free tenement in the new burgh of Crediton", JUST/1/174 m8.

SHEBBEAR HUNDRED ANSWERS BY TWELVE JURORS

424 The jurors are in mercy for a foolish presentment.

425 Walter Hurlefod fell from a mare and drowned in the river Torridge. Misadventure. Value of the mare 2s., the sheriff etc.

426 William Finamur was crushed to death by the branch of a tree. Misadventure. Value of the branch 4d., the sheriff etc.

427 Reginald Balle is suspected of stealing pigs and has fled, so let him be exacted and outlawed. He was in the abbot of Dunkeswell's tithing in Buckland, which is in mercy, and he had no chattels.

> This Buckland was Buckland Brewer, where Dunkeswell had property at the Dissolution – Oliver, *Monasticon* p. 400. It took its suffix from William Brewer, who held half the manor in 1219 – *PND* p. 88 – but subsequently gave it to Ford abbey, which by 1227 had, under William 's directions, made it over to Dunkeswell, Reichel S10 p. 572, Dugdale, *Monasticon* Vol. V p. 679. Perhaps it is not surprising that in 1281/82 the abbot of Dunkeswell claimed to hold Buckland Brewer manor by gift and grant of William Brewer, JUST/1/186 m3d.

428 An unknown man was found killed and stripped (*exscaturizatus*). It was said that one William Byalla, who fled to church, admitted that he had killed him, so it is said, and abjured the realm there. No Englishry, so Murder fine. William had no chattels. Little Yarnscombe vill is in mercy for not presenting that case to the County Court.

429 Gilbert de Galleshoure appealed Walter de Tuddecote, John de Vielestone, Gilbert of the same, Ralph of the same, Walter de la Thrudogge, Robert of the same, Roger de Akewrthi, William Coffin de Aliuntone and Roger Laweles of taking him in his bed and badly beating him. Gilbert comes now and does not make suit against them as he appealed them, so he and his pledges, Robert de Hallewlle, Reginald de

Hankeforde and Walter de Tuddecote, are in mercy. All the appellees come, and as Gilbert's appeal is null, it is decided that the country inquire. The jurors testify that except for William Coffin and Roger Laweles they have made an agreement, so let them all be taken into custody.

> This case, and the two following it, must be connected with the action of novel disseisin which Gilbert brought at the 1238 eyre over land in North Galsworthy against Huard de Bikkeleg and Hugh the baker, an action which led to Huard de Bikkeleg, convicted of disseisin, paying 40s. to have a jury of 24 to attaint the twelve jurors who had found against him, that is, reverse their verdict as perjured or ill-founded, JUST/1/174 m7. Whether this was done is not recorded, but it was certainly not the end of the matter, for in 1244 Gilbert was litigating against William de Bikeleg, presumably Huard's son, and against Walter Gervase and his wife, this time for land in South Galsworthy – JUST/1/175 m20d – and again in 1249 against Walter Gerveys, William de Bikeleg and three others for land in Galsworthy – JUST/1/176 m9. Since in 1238 the jurors thought it necessary to declare that "Gilbert is a free man and holds freely", while in 1249 William de Bikeleg actually claimed Gilbert as his villein, though the jurors upheld the latter's denial, all this litigation, civil and criminal, probably stemmed from a lord's wish to bring a neighbouring small-holder under control.

430   Robert de Bulkewrthi appealed Walter Gervasius, William son of Huward, Walter Cole, Walter Trudogge, John de Vielestone, Thomas son of Ailmer, Roger Gove, Gilbert Ruffus, Thomas de Silkelande, Ralph de Thorne and Roger Ristivel of breach of the king's peace. Robert comes and does not make suit against them as he appealed them, so he and his pledges, Thomas de Hortone and Lawrence le Flemeng, are in mercy. All the appellees come, and the jurors say that they have made an agreement, so let them all be taken into custody.
The same appealed Huward the baker and Warin de Twichene of the same. They do not come. Huward de Bikelege and Walter Gervasius, together with Walter de Burne, Isaac de Bikeleghe, Richard de Bourne, Walter de Huphille de Bikeleghe, William de Monte, Alfred de la Toune de Bikeleghe, William King and Osbert de la Toune, mainprised to produce them, so they are all in mercy. Later Robert de Bulkewrthi came and made fine for himself and his pledges for 100s., pledges Huward de Bikeleghe and Herbert de Pinu.

431   Huward the baker son of Geoffrey le Pestur appealed Gilbert de Gallesoure and Walter son of Elias de Hesewelle, Richard Busse and others whom he could not name. Huward does not come, so he and his pledges, Henry de la Hethe and Hugh de Bukedone, are in mercy. The appellees come, and they have not made an agreement, so they are quit. Later Walter Gervasius and Huward de Bikeleghe came and made fine for Gilbert de Gallesoure the appellor and his pledges, for the others whom Gilbert appealed, for all the men whom Robert de Bulkewrthi appealed, except Walter Gervasius, and for Huward the baker the appellor and those that he appealed, for five marks, pledges Walter Gervasius and Huward de Bikeleghe.

432   A boat which washed up at Abbotsham from a wreck at sea was worth 12d., the same tithing etc.

433   Rannulf de la Forde appealed John de Dunneslande, Hugh son of William, Robert de Whiteslade, his son Geoffrey, Walter de Horestane, Lawrence de Colviscote, Roger le Shorte, Osbert le Singhere, Drogo de

Colnescote and Richard de Colnescote that on the vigil of the blessed apostle Matthew in the fifteenth year (20 September 1231) they came by night to his fold and took from it five oxen, two cows, six wethers and five goats.

John de Dumeslande appeals the same that on the same night they took from the fold of his man William, who has died, an ox and a mare.

Geminianus de Forda appeals the same that on the same night they took from his fold a horse and two sheep.

Dewicus de la Forde appeals the same that on the same night they beat him and took from him a bow and a quiver of arrows.

Richard de Smetheam appeals the same that on the same night they took from him a mare, a foal and an ox.

Rannulf de Smetheham appeals the same that on the same night they took from him a mare, and that they did this evilly and in felony. And that this is true he puts himself on the country. All the appellors and appellees come, and as the appeal is null let the country inquire. The jurors testify that Hugh son of William and the other appellees took those beasts for the service which John owed the same for the land which he holds from the same, on the orders of the king and likewise by judgment of the County Court. So the appellees are quit, let Rannulf de la Forde, John and the others be taken into custody. Later Rannulf de la Forde and the other appellees came and made fine for 40s., pledges Alan de Alleswrthi and Robert de Blakeforde.

> In 1228 Roger de Hele sued against John de Dunneslande for one virgate of land in West Ford and Smytham, both in Little Torrington parish in Shebbear hundred. The case ended with a concord, whereby John and his heirs would hold the land from Roger de Hele and his wife Emma during Emma's lifetime, and after her death from Robert de London and his heirs, *CRR* XIII no. 1044, *Devon FFI* no. 251. The confused syntax of the plea roll leaves it obscure as to who was distraining John de Dunneslande to do what.

434 A boat washed up at 'Taumowe' together with two drowned men. Misadventure. Value of the boat 16s., the sheriff etc.

435 William de Fedefenne's groom William was killed by an ox which drew a plough over him, so that he was fatally injured by the ploughshare. Misadventure. Value of the ox and plough 4s., the sheriff etc.

(m 36)
436 An unknown man was found dead in a pit in Frithelstock. It is not known who killed him. No Englishry, so Murder fine.

437 A girl named Joan was killed by a mill wheel at Merton. Misadventure. Value of the wheel 6d., the sheriff etc. Merton vill is in mercy for not presenting that case to the County Court.

438 William le Lungmuner was outlawed for the death of Sarah, wife of Robert de Hundetorre, at Robert's suit. He was in Merton tithing, which is in mercy, and he had chattels worth 8s 3d., the same tithing etc.

439 Martin le Bedel drowned with his horse in the river Torridge. Misadventure. Value of the horse's hide 6d., the sheriff etc.

Shebbear

440   Robert le White drowned with a horse in the river Torridge. No-one is suspected. Misadventure. Value of the horse's hide 4d., the sheriff etc.

441   William de la Wdelande, outlawed for forcibly raping Matilda, daughter of Robert the Welshman, was later arrested and hanged at Exeter before Jordan Oliver and his fellow gaol delivery justices. He had chattels worth 8s., Twigbear tithing etc.
> Jordan Oliver was the principal justice at deliveries of Exeter gaol ordered for 1 December 1235, 4 June 1237 and 14 January 1238 – C66/46 m14d; C66/47 m9d; C66/48 m11d. There is nothing to indicate at which of these William was hanged.

442   Rosamund daughter of Hugh was crushed to death by Iddesleigh mill wheel. Misadventure. Value of the wheel 18d., the sheriff etc.

443   Walter de Quercu appealed Walter de Tukebere, who has died, of beating his wife. He does not come, so he and his pledges, Richard de la Clive and William de la Sele, are in mercy.

444   John son of Peter de Merland threw a stone, and Ralph son of William running under it, the stone struck him on the head so that he died. He fled to church, acknowledged the deed and abjured the realm. He was in Little Marland tithing, which is in mercy, and he had no chattels.

445   Henry de Benforde killed Hugh de Benford, and was arrested and hanged at Exeter before William de Raleghe and his fellows. He had chattels worth 10s., Beaford tithing etc.

446   William de Benford drowned by falling from a boat. Misadventure. Value of the boat 6d., the sheriff etc. Beaford tithing is in mercy for not presenting the value of the boat to the coroner.

447   Richard Totedai and Robert de Cumbe, charged with the death of an unknown man, come, deny all and put themselves on the country. The jurors testify they are not guilty, so they are quit.

448   Matilda Claper complains that Walter Lupus, on the Wednesday next after the feast of St. Mary in the twenty-first year, came to her on the king's demesne at Shebbear, took her and her daughter Gillota, led them to the house of Adam in the same vill, kept them in chains there all that night and next day took them to Kentisbury, where he kept them in chains for three days and then made them, under guard, reap the crops on his land for the whole autumn, and then allowed them to go away, and would not pay them anything for their remuneration.
Walter comes, denies imprisoning and unjustly taking them and all. He says that in truth Matilda's father was his father's villein, with all his brood (*sequela*), and that when his father died he remained in wardship. Meanwhile Matilda's father died, and his children then left Walter's land, and later he came and took her as his serf and fugitive. She says she is free. And because Walter admitted that he arrested her as a villein, and she is free, he is in mercy. Later he came and made fine for 20s., pledges Ralph de Esshe and Hugh son of William.
> William Lupus held one fee at Kentisbury of the honour of Okehampton, *Fees* p. 784.

449 Roger de Alnicote, arrested for the death of a man, comes and is not suspected, so he is quit.

450 William Tredeluve and Maisanta de Parva Toritone, charged with associating with William Pipping who was hanged for theft, come, deny all and put themselves on the country. The jurors testify that they are not guilty, so they are quit.

451 Richard de Anri appealed Walter the sergeant of Leghe Monachorum of breach of the king's peace and felony. He does not come, so he and his pledges, John de Curreforde and Richard de la Clive, are in mercy. Walter comes, and they have made no agreement, so he is quit.
'Leghe Monachorum' was Monkleigh, held by Montacute priory in Somerset, Risdon, *Survey of Devon* p. 276.

452 Be it remembered that Shebbear hundred is in the king's hand. Walter de Bathon' the sheriff is its keeper appointed by the king.
Shebbear was held by the king in 1086 – *DB* p. 55 – and continued to be so thereafter, the only Devon hundred to remain in royal hands.

BIDEFORD BURGH ANSWERS BY SIX JURORS

453 Henry de Whitestane was drowned at Northam. The jurors are in mercy for not presenting the finder's name.

454 Bideford Burgh is in mercy for placing on its jury two men attached for crown pleas.
There is no discernible mention of any of the Bideford jurors named in the kalendar among those attached elsewhere – the William le Turnur, schepman of Shorham, of no. 750 below, seems unlikely to be identical with the William le Turnur who was one of the Bideford jurors. It is probable, therefore, that the two attachments were removed from the jury at an early stage and two others elected to replace them before the kalendar was enrolled.
Bideford, a royal manor in 1086 – *DB* pp. 80–1 – was given by William Rufus to Richard de Grenville, whose descendant, another Richard, founded the burgh between 1204 and 1217, Hoskins, *Devon* p. 336, *English Medieval Boroughs* p. 87. For the foundation charter see R. Granville, *The History of the Granville Family* (Exeter 1895) p. 33.

455 John Batte was drowned by falling into the sea from a boat. Misadventure. Value of the boat 2s., the sheriff etc.

456 John le Bulle fell from a horse into the sea and drowned. Misadventure. Value of the horse 2s., the sheriff etc.

(m 36d)
NORTH TAWTON HUNDRED ANSWERS BY TWELVE JURORS

457 A woman named Dulcia, arrested and imprisoned at Tawton out of suspicion, has now escaped, so to judgment for the escape. Later came Joel de Valle Torta who gave satisfaction (*pacavit*) for the escape, but he does not know to which sheriff.

458 A mound was dug into at Umberleigh. The jurors are in mercy for not presenting the finder's name.

459   John Stilbe killed Augustine le Gidie and fled, so let him be exacted and outlawed. He was in Lapford tithing, which is in mercy, and he had no chattels.

460   Gervase the miller was crushed to death by the wheel of Eggesford mill. Misadventure. Value of the wheel 12d., the sheriff etc.

461   Gilbert Trusti was outlawed for the death of Gilbert Kelli at the suit of his wife Ascelina. He was in Riddlecombe tithing, which is in mercy, and he had chattels worth 12s. 5d., the same tithing etc.

462   William de la Hoke's house was burnt. Elias son of Cristmana and William de Huttenesleghe were attached for this by Richard Serle, and the other pledge has died.

463   An unknown man was found dead in the river Torridge. No Englishry, so Murder fine. Robert Winter, who first found him, is in mercy for a false presentment. He made fine for 6s. 8d., pledge Walter de Capella.

464   Reginald de Wrai killed Robert Hereward and fled, so let him be exacted and outlawed. No-one else is suspected. He was in Chawleigh tithing, which is in mercy, and he had chattels worth 34s. 8d., the sheriff etc., as he received them.

465   Wymarc de Leiham, who found Scolastica daughter of Bracy drowned, does not come. She was attached by Reginald Baghil and Edward Baghil, who are in mercy.

466   Philip de Kaillewei killed Anketill de Dugheltone. Philip came and brought letters patent from the king attesting that he has pardoned him Anketill's death as long as he stands to right if anyone wishes to proceed against him. He also proffers letters close from the king, directed to the justices, saying that Philip may have peace for the death, if he stands etc. By virtue of their office the justices had it proclaimed that anyone wishing to proceed against him for it should come, and no-one comes. So he is quit of it in perpetuity.

> Philip's pardon, "on condition of his making peace with Anketil's kin and standing trial if anyone proceeds against him", was issued on 8 May 1235, *CPR 1232–1247* p. 104. At the 1272 Shropshire eyre solemn proclamation was made from Prime to Nones that anyone wishing to prosecute a pardoned killer should come forward, and only when no-one did so did his pardon apparently take irreversible effect, JUST/1/736 m28.

467   Roger Knavenmaistre appealed Thomas de Chene that on the Thursday next before the feast of the Assumption of the Blessed Virgin he came to him, wounded him and took from him a horse and a tunic. The appeal is null, so let the country inquire. The jurors testify that Roger entered Thomas's garden and left his horse in Thomas's corn, where Thomas found it, took it to his home and impounded it. And later he came to his garden, found Roger there and beat and wounded him, so he is in mercy. And because Thomas offered him his horse and tunic under security, which he refused, and because he appealed him of robbery, Roger is in mercy. Later Roger made fine for 6s. 8d., pledge Roger de Bulkewrthi. Later Thomas came and made fine for 6s. 8d., pledge Robert de Champeus.

This appeal, a sort of vee de naam in reverse (see no. 417 above), shows how easily distraint could shade into robbery. Every freeholder had the right, exercised by Thomas here, to impound livestock *damage feasant* on his tenement, Plucknett, *Legislation of Edward I*, p. 57 n. 1. But when Thomas had gone on to offer to return the horse against security, probably for damages, Roger had refused to take it, so as to give himself grounds for an action of robbery.

468   Robert son of William the huntsman was crushed to death by the wheel of Ashley mill. Misadventure. Value of the wheel 12d., the sheriff etc.

469   Pain the miller fell from a wall and died three days later. Misadventure. Ashreigney vill is in mercy for not presenting this case to the County Court.

470   Unknown thieves came by day to the house of Roger Cole, beat him and took his goods, and also carried off his horse to Ashley wood, where they left it. Later it was testified that Richard son of Edward de Churbeare and his brother Robert, charged with that deed, have made themselves scarce, and they are suspected, so let them be exacted and outlawed. Richard was not in tithing as he was a clerk. Robert was in Cherubeer tithing, which is in mercy, and had chattels worth 48s., that tithing etc.

471   Roger de la Pole, Philip de la Pole, Simon de la Pole, Jordan le Hore, Roger son of Walter de Hille and Richard Blanchart were charged with breaking Herbert son of Matthew's park. The jurors testify that they crossed the ditch of the park and took his hinds, so let them be arrested.
   A presentment under article 29, "of poachers in parks and fishponds". See also no. 474 below.

472   Robert de la Slade found a false gallon, it was believed, in the possession of Alexander de Tautone, which Richard the taverner at length acknowledged as his. Later Richard came before the justices bringing the gallon, and it was established before them that the gallon is false, so let him be sent to gaol. Later he came and made fine for 20s., pledges Walter de Wike, Robert de Wikedone, William de Tauwe and Reginald de Lasele.

473   William de Molis appeals Robert de la Slade and Geoffrey de Greneslade that on the Saturday before the feast of the Purification of the Blessed Mary in the eighteenth year (28 January 1234) they killed William de Molis, son of Henry de Molis, with a knife, evilly and in felony, and he offers to prove this by his body as the court shall decide. Robert and Geoffrey come and deny all word for word, and because William does not speak of his sight or hearing, it is decided that the appeal is null and that William be taken into custody for a false appeal. Let the country inquire, and let Robert and Geoffrey be taken into custody until the inquest comes. He also appealed Walter Bruning of the same death, and he does not come, so it was ordered that his lands and all his chattels be taken into the king's hand. And Hugh the taverner, attached for the same, comes and likewise puts himself on the country.
The jurors of North Tawton, South Tawton, Winkleigh, Wonford and Crediton hundreds, with the vills of Spreyton, Throwleigh and Hittisleigh, say that Robert de la Slade and Geoffrey de Greneslade are guilty,

so they are hanged, and that Hugh the taverner is not guilty, so he is quit. They also testify that Walter Bruning is guilty, so let him be exacted and outlawed. Robert had chattels at Churchstanton worth 64s., the sheriff and Churchstanton vill each to answer for 32s. He had a messuage there, from which the king's year and waste was worth 7s., Gundreda de Tudeham etc. pledge her son John. He had chattels at Tawton worth £9 17s. 1d., the sheriff etc. He had one messuage and one carucate of land with appurtenances, for the king's year and waste from which Joel de Valle Torta gave 64s.

> In 1251/52 it was presented that Slade in North Tawton manor had come into the king's hand through the hanging of Robert de Seleda on Friday after the feast of SS Peter and Paul 21 Henry III, *Fees* pp. 1263–4. Assuming that 21 is a scribal error for 22, and that the rest of the date is correct Robert was hanged on 2 July 1238, and proceedings were well up with, even ahead of, the timetable (see Introduction). Robert also had land in Crocker's Hele in Shebbear hundred – JUST/1/176 m2d – while during the 1238 eyre he surrendered land in North Tawton and withdrew from an action for land in Newinton, JUST/1/174 mm14d, 15. On 10 August 1238 the king granted the chattels of Robert de Slad and Geoffrey de Greneslad to William Chubbe, *CCR 1237–1242* p. 86.

474 Gilbert le Brun was outlawed for the death of Ralph le Bret at the suit of Thomas de Marisco, his wife Imeina and Ralph's wife Gillian. He was in the mainpast of Herbert son of Matthew, who is in mercy, and he had no chattels.
The said Thomas, Imeina and Gillian appeal John the clerk, sergeant of Chittlehampton, Richard le Flentur, Martin le Kaioler de Lideforde, Robert le Hurt and William son of Henry de Hocforde of the same death. They come, deny all and put themselves on the country. The jurors testify that Ralph le Bret was arrested in Herbert's park and taken to Lydford, where he was imprisoned but escaped. Later Ralph came to Burrington, and because he had escaped from prison Gilbert came there and struck him with an arrow so that he died. Be it known that Ralph's wife Gillian makes suit for her husband's death against nobody except Gilbert. The jurors testify that they are not guilty because they did not come intending to kill Ralph (*animo interficiendi*), but only to arrest him, as he had broken out of Lydford gaol, so they are quit.

> Order was given on 25 March 1238 that John the Clerk and other appellees could be released to bail, since Gilbert Brun, appealed of the death of Ralph le Bret, had now been outlawed for the deed, *CCR 1237–1242* p. 37. Custody of Lydford castle and Dartmoor forest was committed to Herbert son of Matthew on 24 March 1234, *CPR 1232–1247* p. 42. His park has not been identified.

475 Gundreda de Tudeham puts her son John in her place against Henry de Corne and others for a plea of novel disseisin.

> This action does not appear to have taken place; in the only civil plea noticed as involving Gundreda de Tudeham, she appears as one of thirteen defendants sued by Adam Mante for land in Stanton in Stanborough hundred, JUST/1/174 m4.

(m 37)
476 From Robert de Bulkewrthi, as fine for several trespasses, for novel disseisin, crown pleas and other things, 100 marks, pledges Herbert de Pinu, Guy de Brian, Roger Giffard, Ralph de Alba Mora, Alan de Alleswrthi, Jordan de Esse, Henry de Mertone, Hugh de Chaggeforde, Sir Robert de Putiforde, William de Widdewrthi, Walter Giffarde and William de Alwintone.

Robert de Bulkewrthi appears three times among the civil pleas, but he was not charged with novel disseisin and was not convicted of any offence, JUST/1/174 mm9d, 14d, 22. His substantial fine was almost certainly connected with his involvement in the quarrel between Gilbert de Galleshoure and Huward de Bikeleg (nos. 429–31 above), obscure though that involvement was – he had half a fee at Bulkworthy, barely a mile from Galsworthy, *Fees* p. 797. Of his total fine of £71. 13s. 4d., he paid £20. 10s. in 1239; thereafter he was allowed to pay £14. 6s. 8d. yearly, and for the next three years did so, the last £8. 3s. 4d. being paid off in 1243.

477   Of defaults they say that Ralph de Welitone, Gaudinus de Blancmuster, Thomas de Sidelinche, Adam le Gai, William Trenchard, Henry son of Reginald, Robert de Curtenay, Engeram de Cuilli, Gilbert de Umfranville, Ralph de Sicca Villa, Walter de Nimet, Robert Burnel, Henry Walensis and Warin de Penpol did come on the first day etc.

Ralph de Welitone held Umberleigh in the right of his wife Joan de Campo Arnulfi, Risdon, *Survey of Devon* pp. 316–17.
Gaudinus de Blancmuster had land in High Bickington, Deptford and Umberleigh, from 1244 held of him by Nicholas de Vaus, *Devon FFI* no. 418.
Adam le Gai had land at Hook in Ashreigny parish, *Cornwall FFI* no. 249.
Robert de Curtenay held the manors of Chawleigh and Dolton, JUST/1/186 m7d, *Devon FFI* no. 279.
Gilbert de Umfranville had married Sibyl, one of the five sisters of Matthew de Toriton and as such a coheiress to the barony of Torrington, Sanders, *English Baronies* pp. 48–9. Her share included Lapford in North Tawton hundred, *Cal. Inq. P.M.* I no. 798.
Ralph de Sicca Villa held one fee in Coldridge of the honour of Barnstaple, *Fees* p. 773.
Walter de Nimet held one fee in Nymet Rowland, Rashleigh Barton and Cherubeer of the honour of Okehampton, *Fees* p. 783. He defaulted again in 1249, JUST/1/176 m45.
Robert Burnel held one fee in Crooke of the honour of Plympton, *Fees* p. 787.
Henry Walensis defaulted again in 1249, JUST/1/176 m45.
Warin de Penpol had lands in Cornwall, hence no doubt his failure to attend the Devon eyre, *Cornwall FFI* nos. 27, 95.

478   Nicholas the miller appealed John son of Richard the carpenter that, with others, he hindered him from pursuing Geoffrey the miller who wounded Thomas the miller, in breach of the king's peace. Nicholas does not come, so he and his pledges, John le Parmenter – the other pledge has died – are in mercy. John comes, and he is guilty, so let him be taken into custody. And John the tailor appealed Reginald de Bere of the same. John does not come, so he etc., namely John de Holecrucke, and the other has died. Reginald comes, and he is guilty, so let him be taken into custody. And John de Holecrucke appeals William Makerel of the same. John does not come, so he and his pledges, Nicholas the miller and Geoffrey Archebaud, are in mercy. William comes, and he is guilty, so let him be taken into custody. And Geoffrey Archebaud appeals Reginald de la Bere of the same. He does not come, so he and his pledges, Nicholas the miller and John the tailor, are in mercy. And Reginald comes, and he is guilty, so as before he is in mercy. Later William Makerel and Reginald de la Bere came and made fine for two marks, pledge Robert le Copiner. Later John son of Richard Carpenter came and made fine for one mark, pledges Robert the smith of Moutone, John de Brai, Richard Carpentar, John's father, and Robert the taverner of Moutone.

479   Joel de Valle Torta, asked by what warrant he holds North Tawton hundred, came and admitted that he has no warrant besides ancient tenure and old enfeoffment.

North Tawton was held by the king in 1086, *DB* pp. 40–1. The manor, and presumably the hundred with it, came to be held by Robert Foliot, doubtless the same man who held Hemyock hundred by gift of Henry I (no. 90 above), but by 1181 it had passed into the possession of Joel de Valle Torta, an ancestor of the holder in 1238, BL Vit. D. IX ff. 37–38. In 1249 it was valued at six marks *per annum*, JUST/1/176 m45.

WONFORD HUNDRED ANSWERS BY TWELVE JURORS

480   Jordan de Derewrthi complains that Thomas Finamur and Jordan son of Beatrice came to his home by night, broke his doors and badly beat him. Thomas and Jordan come, and the jurors testify that they beat him, giving him bloodless wounds, so let them be taken into custody. Later they came and made fine for 20s., pledges Richard de Teingne and Jordan de Cabewelle.

481   Stokeinteignhead tithing is in mercy for not pursuing after the hue was raised.

482   A mound was found dug into at 'Bourigge.' The jurors are in mercy for presenting no finder. 'Bergh' and Combeinteignhead tithings are in mercy for not presenting this case to the County Court.

483   A pipe of wine washed up at 'Peggenesse.' 'Peggenesse' vill is in mercy for not presenting this to the County Court. Later Stephen de Acumbe came and made fine for his vill for 20s., Stephen pledge. The jurors testify that Guy de Peggenesse, Alice de Peggenesse, Ralph de Peggenesse and Stephen, sergeant of the hundred, took that pipe and drank the wine, and they testify that they have all died.

484   Bagtor vill is in mercy for a foolish presentment. William de Baggetore is likewise in mercy for the same, pledges Robert de la Heie and Thomas de Swinespathe.

485   An unknown man was found dead in Alphington. No Englishry so Murder fine.

486   Osbert the smith killed Richard son of Walter and fled, so let him be exacted and outlawed. He was in 'Heie cancellarii Exon' tithing, which is in mercy, and he had no chattels.

> In 1244 the Wonford jurors presented an accidental death on the road outside 'Stokes', and 'Stokes Cancellarii' vill was put in mercy for burying the corpse without a coroner's view, JUST/1/175 m45d. This was almost certainly Stoke Canon, granted to St. Mary's monastery at Exeter by Athelstan and later becoming the property of the dean and chapter of Exeter cathedral, Finberg, *Early Charters*, no. 22, *H.M.C. Various Collections* Vol. IV pp. 25–6. It is probable that 'Heie' was a small appendage of Stoke Canon, and that the chancellor of the cathedral was farming this manor from the chapter at this time – a suggestion I owe to Mrs. Audrey Erskine.

487   John Watta, who was hanged at Exeter, had chattels worth 3s. 3d. Walter de Bathon', then sheriff, is to answer as he received them.

488   Walter Luvetrot was found drowned in the river Exe. No Englishry, so Murder fine. This was on the land of 'La Heie cancellarii Exon' which does not share in Murder fines with the hundred.

489   William Knit and his servant Richard killed Robert Bolle and fled. They were outlawed at the suit of Robert's brother John Bolle. They were

in the king's manor of Kenton, which is in mercy, and they had no chattels. No-one else is suspected of the death.

490   Agnes de Swetlache, who found her daughter drowned, does not come. She was not attached, nor was this case presented, so 'La Heie' vill is in mercy.

491   Roger the cobbler of Exon' killed Reginald the clerk and fled through the middle of Exeter city to Cowick Barton church, where he abjured the realm. He was living in Exeter city, which is in mercy for neither arresting nor producing him.

492   Walter Leuwin, who appealed Richard Longus, Jordan Du Wate and others who have died of wounding and breach of the king's peace, comes and makes suit. Richard and Jordan do not come. Richard was not attached as he was not found. Jordan was attached by Christopher de Smalelake and Richard de Stoddone, who are in mercy. The jurors testify that they are guilty of that wounding and have not made an agreement, so it is decided that if Walter wants to make suit against them and find pledges for making suit against them in the County Court, they may be exacted and outlawed at his suit, according to the custom of the realm, if they will not stand to right.

493   Henry Wlf and Walter de Colum beat Walter the miller so that he died three days later. They have fled, so let them be exacted and outlawed. Henry was living in Poltimore vill, and Walter was in the mainpast of John de Colum, so these are in mercy. Henry had chattels worth 12d., Poltimore vill etc.

> John de Colum is not recorded as owning land in Poltimore, but since he twice witnessed settlements of disputes over property there – Queens 152 f. 48v – it is likely that he did have some landed interest in that manor.

494   Because a full inquiry could not be made in Hayridge hundred into the death of Thomas de Ferrariis, it was decided that a full inquiry should be made in this hundred. The jurors of this hundred testify that Bartholomew de Uperexe, Henry de Tracy's sergeant, Roger Cal, Walter de la Redewei, John son of William de Were, John Herding, Richard son of Richard Herding, Roppe, Henry de Tracy's ploughman, Henry Atteweie and Walter Atteweie left Up Exe manor to take a distraint on Richard Lespek's land. And Thomas would not allow them the writ of distraint, so that they quarrelled, and Bartholomew killed him and fled to Thorverton church. And he freely left it in the presence of Ralph de la Holte, Nicholas de Ashille, Roger de Lestane, Robert Harding, Nicholas the reeve of Thorvertone, William Niger and Henry de la Heithe, who are in mercy for not arresting him. Later Bartholomew went to Henry de Tracy's house, from which he had first come, and was there for three days, with Henry's knowledge. And Henry de Beumond, Henry's steward, came to the church immediately after Bartholomew left it, and he saw Thomas's corpse, and went to Up Exe, and wittingly harboured Bartholomew for three days in his lord's household, and did not arrest him. So let him be arrested. The jurors testify that Bartholomew and Roger Cal alone are guilty of that death, and they have been outlawed. So the others charged with the death are quit. Later Henry de Tracy came

and made fine for himself, Henry de Beumond his steward, Henry de la Heithe and Ralph de la Holte, as appears in another part of this roll.

In 1242/43 Richard le Espek's heir held half a fee in Brampford Speke of Henry de Tracy's honour of Barnstaple, while Henry himself held half a fee in demesne in Up Exe, *Fees* p. 773. Thorverton, Brampford Speke and Up Exe are all within a few miles of each other. See also no. 114 above. Henry de Tracy's fine was the substantial one of 400 marks. Having paid £50 of it in 1239, he was allowed to pay the rest of it at the rate of 50 marks (£33 6s. 8d.) *per annum*, and he duly paid this sum for each of the next six years, clearing the last £17. 13s. 4d. in 1247.

(m 37d)

495 An unknown man was found dead at Topsham. No-one is suspected. Topsham vill is in mercy for not presenting the finder.

496 Ralph son of Ralph de Whitestane appealed Ralph Binadder and Alfred Prat of breach of the king's peace and wounding, but he says nothing to justify a duel between them. Ralph and Alfred come, and the jurors testify that they have made no agreement, and that they wounded him as he says, so let them be taken into custody. Let Ralph the appellor be likewise taken into custody for a false appeal. Later Alfred came and made fine for 6s. 8d., pledge Ralph de Albemarl. Later Ralph Binarder came and made fine for 6s. 8d., pledge Matthew de Alleforde. Nothing from Ralph the appellor, because he is poor.

497 Hugh de la Tune was killed by falling from his horse. Misadventure. Value of the horse 2s. 6d., the sheriff etc.

498 Edmund Treipas was outlawed for wounding Luke de Colrebrigge at Luke's suit. He was in 'Hyde Sancti Petri' tithing, which is in mercy, and he had no chattels.

499 Walter de la Leghe killed Richard de la Leghe and fled, so let him be exacted and outlawed. He was in Throwleigh tithing, which is in mercy, and he had chattels worth 15s., the same tithing etc.

500 Reginald Rugge appealed Richard Ailwinus, servant of the prior of St. James, that on the morrow of the feast of St. Peter *ad Vincula* he came to him and struck him with an arrow on the shin and with a knife on the shoulder, and he offers to prove this as the court shall decide. The appeal is null, so he is in mercy. Richard comes, and the jurors testify that he wounded him as he says, so let him be sent to gaol. Later Richard came and made fine for 6s. 8d., pledge the prior of St. James. Later it was testified that Reginald is poor, so nothing.

The priory of St. James was a small Cluniac house to the south-east of Exeter in Wonford hundred, which lay round the city. It had landed property at Topsham, Alphington and Cotley, and the church of St. James in Heavitree, all in that hundred, Oliver, *Monasticon* p. 192, Pole, *Collections* p. 234, JUST/1/174 mm10, 17.

501 A mound was dug into at Spreyton. Spreyton tithing is in mercy for not presenting this to the County Court.

502 Robert Slote was outlawed for the death of Brian de Whitestane at the suit of Brian's wife Mariota. He was in Whitestone tithing, which is in mercy, and he had no chattels.

503 Walter de Tiwescumbe appealed Luke, servant of the lady of

Tedbufn, that with his followers, on the Thursday next before the feast of the Assumption of the Blessed Virgin in the nineteenth year (9 August 1235), he came to him and badly beat him. The appeal is null, so he is in mercy for a false appeal. Luke comes, and the jurors testify that he beat him, so let him be taken into custody. Later Walter came and made fine for one mark, pledge Martin de Fhisacre. Later Luke came and made fine for 6s. 8d., pledge Jolanus de Curiforde.

504 William King's house was burgled. He was attached by Hugh de la Lake de Whitestane and Walter de Tyuwescumbe, who are in mercy as he does not come.

505 Walter le Bai was outlawed for the death of Ralph the miller at the suit of Ralph's wife Agnes. No-one else is suspected. He was in Cheriton Bishop tithing, which is in mercy, and he had chattels worth 10s., the sheriff etc.

506 Sarah de Coleghe, attached by Thomas de Uppecote and Robert de Uppecote because she found a woman's corpse, does not come, so they are all in mercy. No-one is suspected.

507 Henry son of Robert de Uppecote was attached by Thomas de Uppecote and Robert de Uppecote, as he found a trench. He does not come, so they are all in mercy. No-one is suspected.

508 A little wine washed up in a cask at Maidencombe. Value of the wine 4s., the same tithing etc.

509 Henry Tirel is in mercy for trespass. He made fine for 6s. 8d., pledge Peter de Albemarl.

510 Margery, widow of Roger Fitzpayne, holds the land of Stokeinteignhead and is in the king's gift. The vill is worth £8.

> Margery would have been holding Stokeinteignhead as a result of her bargain with the king in 1237, see no. 388 above. Since in 1242/43 the heir of Roger Fitzpayne was said to be holding half a fee in Stokeinteignhead with Higher and Lower Gabwell of the honour of Plympton – *Fees* p. 788 – Margery was probably dead by then.

511 Robert de Droscumbe holds the land of Drascombe in serjeanty, by the service of a bow and three arrows when the king comes to hunt on Dartmoor. The land is worth one mark.

> In 1212 the serjeanty was said to have originated in a grant by William I to the ancestors of Richard de Droscumbe, who then held it, *Fees* p. 96. In 1244 the land was valued at 9s. *per annum*, JUST/1/175 m45d. By 1281/82 its annual value had risen to 15s., though the serjeanty itself, now held by Walter de Bromhull, had been commuted for a money payment of 5s. *per annum*, JUST/1/186 m36d.

512 Robert de Blakeforde holds Dunsford and Rewe, with Avicia daughter of Philip Chacebeof, by gift from William Bruiwer, who had them by gift from king John. Dunsford is worth eight marks, Rewe 60s.

> Dunsford and Rewe had been held by William Bacon and Gilbert de Vilers respectively, Normans who had forfeited in 1204, *Rot. Norm.* p. 130, *Fees* p. 612. Nothing in the latter source is said about William Brewer, rather the lands are said to have been given by John to Robert de Secheville, and this is confirmed by the Fine Rolls, which record Robert as paying fifteen marks and palfrey for them in 1204, *Rot. Ob. Fin.* p. 217. Robert's heir was his nephew Philip Chacebeof, who in 1218 paid twenty marks and a palfrey for livery of his uncle's lands – *Rot. Fin.* I p. 7 – and whose daughter and heiress married Robert de Blakeforde.

513 Matilda, widow of Robert de Vallibus, holds Pinhoe, which is worth £15. She is in the king's custody.

> The family of Robert de Vallibus, or Vaux, is better known for its connections with the north of England than with Devon – its members were lords of Gilsland in Cumberland from the mid-twelfth century. But they also had a long-standing connection with the de Redvers earls of Devon –.G. W. S. Barrow, *The Anglo-Norman Era in Scottish History* (Oxford 1980) p. 196. Robert was an experienced soldier and may have owed his appointment as sheriff of Devon at Michaelmas 1233 to military considerations, since in November 1233 Henry de Tracy, in a measure probably related to the revolt in Ireland of Richard Marshal, some of whose supporters had lands in Devon – *CCR 1231–1234* pp. 330, 354, 356 – was instructed "to keep the sea-shore of the county of Devon against the incursions of evil-doers and the king's enemies" – *CPR 1232–1247* p. 33. Robert was replaced on 15 January 1234; he was dead by November 1236, when his widow secured Pinhoe as part of her dower – *Devon FFI* no. 734 – and may have died in office.

514 From William Kye, 10s. for a false claim, pledge Alan de Alleswrthi.

515 The land of Shilstone was a royal escheat, and Baldwin de Rivers holds it. John Bretenche, who is present, says that Baldwin's father made fine with king John for having freely all escheats from his land, both from Normans' lands and others. And Baldwin holds it because of this grant.

> Shilstone escheated to the crown through the forfeiture of Hugh de Saucey, hanged for felony probably in 1212, *Rot. Lit. Claus.* I p. 148. In 1213 earl William of Devon gave three palfreys for having seisin of Hugh's lands, in Shilstone as elsewhere, but there is no suggestion that this bargain had any wider application, of the sort described here, *Rot. Ob. Fin.* p. 486.

516 Of defaults they say that Thomas de Blakeforde and Drogo de Teintone did not come on the first day etc.

> Thomas de Blakeforde held half a fee in Cowley of the honour of Barnstaple, *Fees* p. 773. Drogo de Teintone gave his name to Drewsteignton, to which in 1244 he acknowledged the right of Richard son of Drogo, probably his son, *Devon FFI* no. 390.

517 Bartholomew de Bromhame, charged with the death of Heulina de Affintone, comes, denies all and puts himself on the country. The jurors testify that he is not guilty, so he is quit.

518 John Bretesche, asked by what warrant Baldwin de Rivers holds Wonford hundred, comes and says he holds the hundred by old enfeoffment and ancient tenure, and he has no other warrant, so he says.

> Wonford was held by the king in 1086, *DB* pp. 38–39. In 1130 Godfrey, clerk of Baldwin de Redvers, was accounting for £8. 6s. 8d. "that he may hold the land of Wonford at farm", *PR 31 Henry I* p. 154. Presumably he was acting on his lord's behalf, or at least with his lord's consent, for Wonford was certainly one of the hundreds which came into the possession of the earls of Devon and remained in their hands. In 1249 it was valued at five marks, in 1274/75 at £5, *per annum*, JUST/1/176 m41d, *RH* p. 86.

519 Thomas de Horreweie and Adam de la Bere, arrested for the death of William de Senewille and burning the house of Daniel the fisherman, come, deny all and put themselves on the country. The jurors testify that they are not guilty, so they are quit. They say that Beatrice, wife of Thomas de Seinthille, burnt that house with her husband's consent, so let her be waivered. They also say that William died a natural death and that no-one is guilty of it. Thomas had half a ferling of land by gift from Daniel's wife Matilda and another half furlong from Matilda's sister Cenota. The year and waste from each of the half ferlings was worth 9s. 8d. Later it was testified by Hayridge and Hemyock hundreds that Thomas died before he was convicted, so let his outlawry be stayed and let his land remain with his heirs. And as it is testified that Daniel holds half a

ferling of land of which Thomas de Seinthille was seised on the day he set out for the Holy Land, if his heir now wishes to claim it that land may revert to him.

<small>A ferling was a variable measure of arable land, which could represent anything from 15 to 32 acres, Finberg, *Tavistock Abbey* p. 39 and n, 1.</small>

(m 38)
ROBOROUGH HUNDRED ANSWERS BY TWELVE JURORS

520   Walter Longus de Tavi Sancti Petri, who appealed Robert Foliot, William Durand, Reginald de Uphille the reeve and Walter le Babeler of breach of the king's peace, comes but does not want to make suit against them, so he and his pledges, Martin de Baketorre and Jordan de Haregrave, are in mercy. Robert and all the others come, and the jurors testify that they have made no agreement, so they are quit.
The same appealed Roger le Haveker, who does not come. He was attached by Geoffrey the smith and Robert de Horsam, so they are all in mercy. Later Walter Longus came and made fine for himself and his pledges for 10s., pledges William Durand and Walter Cule.

521   Walter Eggulf appealed Stephen Russel of the death of his aunt Alice. He does not speak of his own sight, so the appeal is null. Stephen comes, denies all, and puts himself on the country. It was ordered that he should be taken into custody until tomorrow, so that a fuller inquiry can be made. Later the jurors come and testify that he is not guilty, so he is quit, let Walter be taken into custody, he is sent to gaol. Later Walter came and made fine for 6s. 8d., pledge Richard de Langeford.

522   Odo de Exe was found dead at his home at Whitchurch. No-one is suspected. No Englishry, so Murder fine.

523   Edward le Calve killed Gilbert Bret, and he was arrested and imprisoned at Launceston. Later Edward came and put himself on the country. The jurors testify that he is guilty, so he is hanged. He had no chattels.

524   Sibyl de Ebforde appealed Geoffrey de Marisco and Roger le Avernaz that on the day of the blessed Mary Magdalene (22 July) they came with weapons to her home, broke her doors, entered her chamber, broke her coffer and took 60s. 1½d., and badly beat her with drawn swords, and they did this evilly and in robbery. And that this is true she puts herself on the country. She appealed Humphrey de Limbire, his clerk Reginald and his groom William of the same, and they do not come. Humphrey was attached by Alexander de Heneremerdone and Roger de Kaddewrthi, Reginald the clerk by Robert Eustache and Robert de Harestane, and William by Richard de Fenton and Robert de Horsam, so they are all in mercy.
The jurors testify that Geoffrey de Marisco and all the appellees are not guilty, so they are all quit. And William de Ebforde, Sibyl's husband, who was present, is sent to gaol for a false appeal. Later the prior of Plympton came and made fine for Humphrey and his pledges for one mark, pledge

the prior. Later William de Ebbeforde came and made fine for 10s., pledge Colin Bastarde.

> It may seem strange that William de Ebforde should have been sent to gaol when his wife's appeal failed, but thirteenth century law, which declared unequivocally of women that "their position is inferior to that of men" – Bracton, *De Legibus* Vol. II p. 31 f. 5 – made husbands responsible for much of their wives' behaviour, so much so that when at the 1244 Devon eyre a woman was convicted of hitting a man on the head with a stone it was her husband who was taken into custody, JUST/1/175 m49d. That women were not outlawed, but were instead waivered, reduced to the status of abandoned livestock, probably stems from ancient ideas of male lordship, even ownership, Pollock and Maitland Vol. II p. 482 n.2. Such notions at least had the advantage for wives that their inability to disobey their husbands could provide a valid defence if they were arraigned on charges of felony committed in their husbands' company – a Norfolk woman, of whom it was said that "she did no crime without an order from her lord", thus went quit when her husband was hanged, JUST/1/564 m3. Other examples include JUST/1/1109 m10, JUST/1/614B m44d, JUST/1/872 m33d.

525   Isabel de Westone, who appealed Joel de Stanhuse of breach of the king's peace, neither comes nor makes suit against him. She was attached by William the smith of Westone, who is in mercy. Joel comes, and the jurors testify that they have made no agreement, and that he is not guilty, so he is quit.

526   Noreis de Boclande drowned by falling into the sea from a boat. Misadventure. Value of the boat 1½d., the sheriff etc. Bere Ferrers vill is in mercy for valuing the boat without the coroner.

527   Hamelin de Havecumbe appeals Germanus de Bikecumbe and Roger Kempe that, with Roger de Ferrariis who has died, and with others they came by night and broke the doors of his house and his chamber door, carried off all the tools in his house and the corn from his grange, and took away three pigs, and they did this evilly and in robbery, and he offers to prove this by his body as the court shall decide etc. And because Hamelin neither specifies a day nor sets a value on the things taken, it is decided that the appeal is null and that the country should inquire. Germanus and Roger come, and the jurors testify that they are not guilty, so they are quit, let Hamelin be sent to gaol. For they say that Hamelin was Roger's reeve and his villein, and because he would not be his reeve as he used to be, he wanted to distrain him for this as his villein. And for that reason they came to his house, not with the intention of robbing him, (*non animo ipsum robandi*) as is said. Later Hamelin came and made fine for 6s. 8d., pledge Robert de Cappeleghe.

> Roger de Ferrariis may have been related to the William de Ferers who in 1242/43 held 1¼ fees in Bere Ferrers and Leigh, both in Roborough hundred, *Fees* p. 796.
> The question of intent was as relevant in cases of theft as it was for homicide – without the *animus furandi*, according to Bracton, using a phrase paralleled here, theft was not committeed, *De Legibus* Vol. II p. 425 f. 150b. For goods taken *non animo furandi* see JUST/1/614B m48d. Consequently insanity could extenuate what would otherwise have been capital larceny, *Somersetshire Pleas* no. 272, and so perhaps could drunkenness, JUST/1/614B m41, *Miscellanea Vol. II* ed. K. E. Bayley (Surtees Society Vol. 127, 1916) no. 352.

528   Robert Sparke appealed Amadas de Wike and Walter de Wike that, on the Saturday next before the feast of the nativity of the blessed Mary in the thirteenth year (1 September 1229) they came to his house, broke his doors, seized him, badly beat him, took 10s. 6d. from him, carried away his horse, worth two marks, bound him and bore him off with them to

Killigorrick in Cornwall, where they imprisoned him and kept him in chains. And that this is so he puts himself on the country. Amadas and Walter come and deny all etc., and likewise put themselves on the country. The jurors testify that Amadas and Walter, with Odo de Tindel and others who have died, took Robert in his house at Cudlipptown and bore him off from there, against his will, to Cornwall, and took from him his horse and money, but they do not know how much money. And they did all this to disseise him of his tenement, and not out of felony. So it is decided that they be sent to gaol. Later Amadas came and made fine for 40s., pledges Ralph Gurdet and Roger de Caddewrthi. Later Walter came and made fine for 40s., pledges Geoffrey de Curitone, Michael le Archediakene, Amadas de Wike and Walter Fulke.

> This appeal is related to the action of novel disseisin which Robert Sparke brought against eight men, including Odo de Tyndel and Michael le Archediakene, and which terminated with the conviction of six of them of disseising him of land in Cudlipptown, JUST/1/174 m7.

529   Matilda de Hiddestone appealed Hugh de la Kage of rape. She does not come, and she found no pledge except her oath. Hugh comes, and the jurors testify that they have made no agreement, nor is he guilty, so he is quit. Let Matilda be arrested.

530   William the miller was crushed to death by the wheel of a mill in Walkhampton. Misadventure. Value of the wheel 12d., the sheriff etc.

531   Margery the weaver has been waivered for the death of Ralph le Pil at the suit of Germanus de Bikecumbe, and her son Richard was outlawed for the same at the same suit. They were living in Buckland manor, which is in mercy. Beatrice (*sic*) had chattels worth 6d., the same manor etc.

532   Baldwin de Rivers holds this hundred by ancient tenure, and he has no other warrant.

> Roborough hundred – originally named from the manor of Walkhampton, held by the king in 1086, *DB* pp. 26–9 – was given by Henry I to Richard de Redvers, in whose family it descended until Isabella de Fortibus, the last of the line, gave it to her mother Amicia, who in turn gave it to her own foundation of Buckland abbey, Reichel S3 p. 117. In 1249 it was valued at 20s. *per annum*, JUST/1/176 m37d.

533   John le Chen, charged with robbery and theft, comes, denies all and puts himself on the country. Nicholas le Chen, his brother, charged with the same, comes and is a clerk. The bishop of Exeter's official, who is present, claims him as a clerk, to do justice on him in Court Christian, and he was handed over to him. Later the same John came, renounced the country, admitted being a thief, became an approver and appealed many unknown men. So by judgment of the court he was hanged.

(m 38d)
PLYMPTON HUNDRED ANSWERS BY TWELVE JURORS

534   An unknown man was found dead on William de Bikeforde's land. No Englishry, so Murder fine.

535   Maurice de Puddehelle was arrested with sheep stolen from the fold of Henry de Langhewis, for which Alice de Langhewis and her son Ralph

made suit against him. Maurice came, and said that if anyone had stolen those sheep it was Henry de Langhewis, who had sold them to him in the presence of Roger the Welshman, who was then present. And Henry came, denied stealing those sheep, and gave 20s. to have the country. The country came, and said that he had stolen those sheep, and he was then hanged by judgment of Plympton court, which was then in the hand of the earl of Gloucester, in whose custody Baldwin de Rivers, who is now lord of this hundred, then was, and Reginald del Hause was then constable. So to judgment on the court. Be it known that Henry's wife Alice appealed Ralph de Culiforde that the judgment was made through him, as he hated Henry because of Alfred de Lodretone, Henry's nephew, whom he killed. Alice does not come, and she had no pledges save her oath. Ralph comes, denies all and puts himself on the country. The jurors testify that he is not guilty, so he is quit, but they say that Ralph de Northemore killed Alfred and was outlawed for that death.

> For the process of voucher to warranty see no. 145 above.
> Gilbert de Clare, earl of Gloucester, paid 2000 marks in 1226 to marry his eldest daughter to the young Baldwin de Redvers, and to have in his custody £200 worth of the land which had been earl William of Devon's until Baldwin's coming of age, *CPR 1225–1232* p. 87. Gilbert died in 1230, however, and in August 1233 custody of Baldwin's lands, until his coming of age, was granted to Richard of Cornwall, *CCR 1231–1234* p. 252. These events therefore probably took place between 1228 and 1230, and Alfred de Lodretone may well have been killed before the former date.

536 Cecilia daughter of Robert de Pridias, who appealed Hugh de la Kage of rape, has died. Hugh comes, denies all and puts himself on the country. The jurors testify that he is not guilty, so he is quit.

537 Richard son of Hodierna de Brixtone, who appealed Walter de Winstone of breach of the king's peace and wounding, comes and does not make suit. He was attached by Richard Mauri, who is in mercy. Later he came and made fine for himself and his pledge for 6s. 8d., pledges Roger le King and Godfrey the Welshman.

538 Maurice the swineherd was scalded to death in a cistern full of hot water. Misadventure. Value of the cistern 4s., the sheriff etc. The jurors are in mercy for a false presentment.

539 From Wembury tithing, 4s. for a tunic and a net which washed up at Wembury from a wreck at sea.

540 Thomas Edrig de Plimtone is in mercy for trespass.

541 A boy named John was scalded to death in a bowl. Misadventure. Value of the bowl 4d., the sheriff etc.

542 John the priest's son killed Robert son of Edith and fled, so let him be exacted and outlawed. He was not in tithing, and he had no chattels. No-one else is suspected. William le Geg was attached for the death by Ailward Sampson his father, Robert Lewinus, Richard Ailwarde and Richard Brian; Edward le Peitevin by John the smith and Ralph le Parmenter; Roger Cok by John Paz de Teignemue and Ralph le Parmenter; Wymund Brice by Osbert the cobbler and Richard le Bretun; Osbert Crespin by Walter de Scopelake, Geoffrey le Sopere, Richard Forst and Robert Pecum; Richard Tolla by Walter de Cokford and Seward

Slug; Robert Wiking by Henry Blowa and Richard Cointerel. They did not come, so they are all in mercy. The jurors testify that they are not guilty, so they are all quit.

> On 26 May 1238 the justices were ordered to inquire whether John the priest's son, imprisoned at Exeter for homicide, had escaped from Exeter gaol with the connivance of Ralph Balistarius, its keeper. *CCR 1237–1242* p. 56. If such an inquest was held, its findings have not survived.

543   Baldwin de Rivers holds this hundred by ancient tenure.

> Plympton was held by the king in 1086, *DB* pp. 24–5. Henry I gave it to Richard de Redvers, and it gave its name to his honour, Sanders, *Baronies* pp. 137–8. Thereafter it was held by the earls of Devon. The hundred was valued at 26s. 8d. *per annum* in 1245, and at 20s. in 1249 – C132/3 no. 10(2), JUST/1/176 m38.

THE FREE MANOR OF PLIMLAND ANSWERS WITH THE HUNDRED BY SIX JURORS

544   William le Pele was found dead at 'Plimland'. No-one is suspected. No Englishry, so Murder fine.

545   A groom named Ralph died by falling from a horse. Misadventure. Value of the horse 2s., the sheriff etc.

546   Margery de la Cumbe, arrested for burgling a house, comes. The jurors testify that she is not guilty, so she is quit.

547   The jurors present that Plympton hundred pleads pleas of vee de naam. Asked by what warrant, they say that they have never known it otherwise, and they say they do this by ancient tenure, so let this be discussed.

> For vee de naam see no. 417 above.
> The identity of Plimland is obscure. No such place is mentioned in Domesday Book, but it was mentioned as among the demesnes of the earls of Devon in 1178 and 1197 – *PR 24 Henry II* p. 18, *PR 8 Richard I* p. 209 – and as a tithing in 1256, E372/101 m4d. To John Hooker, in the sixteenth century, it appears to have been identical with Plympton – Reichel S6 p. 276 – and from the fact that Plimland manor and Plympton hundred had the same twelve jurors in 1238, and that in 1249 it was the hundred jurors who presented what the manor jurors presented in 1238, that pleas of vee de naam were held at Plympton – JUST/1/176 m38 – it seems reasonable to deduce that Plimland was the original, and possibly very ancient, hundredal manor, in 1238 still just retaining its separate identity; this was the last recorded occasion on which it was represented by its own jury.

PLYMPTON BURGH ANSWERS BY TWELVE JURORS

548   Richard Luxi killed Ralph le Vere and fled, so let him be exacted and outlawed. He was living in Plympton vill, which is in mercy, and he had no chattels.

> Plympton burgh was founded by William de Vernon, earl of Devon, in about 1194 – burgesses are mentioned there in 1195, *English Medieval Boroughs* p. 97. In 1245 the burgh was farmed for £24. 2s. 2d., C132/3 no. 10 (2).

549   Roger de Pencuit was outlawed for the death of Elias le Bedel at the suit of Elias's wife Helen. He was living in Plympton vill, which is in mercy, and he had no chattels. The jurors present that this happened at night, and the coroners say by day, so all the jurors are in mercy.

550 Edelina wife of Stephen the carpenter appealed Reginald Balaam of breach of the king's peace and wounding. She comes and makes suit, but Reginald does not come, nor was he attached. Her wound was inspected and seen to be deadly (*visa est plaga eius que mortalis fuit*), so she was ordered to find pledges and to make suit afresh against him until he should stand to right or be outlawed according to the custom of the realm. It was testified that Reginald was arrested for the same and imprisoned at Exeter when Robert de Vallibus, who has died, was sheriff. Gilbert de Manneby, who was then under him, released him from prison, and as he does not come to answer for his period of office, he is in mercy. The sheriff was ordered to arrest Reginald if he can be found.

551 Esgher de Cokforde was outlawed for the death of Richard son of Odo at the suit of Richard's brother Geoffrey. He was living in Kenton manor, which is in mercy, and he had chattels worth 2s., the same tithing etc.

552 Henry le Taliur, Roger de Walwrthi and Robert Redebert, arrested on the indictment of an approver who has been hanged, come and are not suspected, so they are all quit.

553 Rannulf le Potter de Cornubia is suspected of stealing oxen and sheep, so let him be exacted and outlawed. He had no chattels.

554 The jurors present that Gocius de Vado, Humphrey de Dunitone, William the smith and Robert de Ekewrthi have sold wine contrary to the assize, so they are in mercy.

555 Nicholas son of Eustace the smith, his wife Gillian and Alice the weaver from Cornwall, arrested for theft, come. Alice was arrested for stealing two pairs of shoes, which Richard Servant claims as his stolen chattels. The jurors testified that they are his, so let him have them, and let her have an ear cut off (*absciditur eius auricula*). Nicholas and his wife Gillian put themselves on the country, and since a full inquest cannot be held into this at present, let them be taken into custody until there can. Later they came, and the jurors testify that they are not guilty, so they are quit.

(m 39)
ERMINGTON HUNDRED ANSWERS BY TWELVE JURORS

556 Walter de Mimminglande, one of the jurors, does not come with his fellows before the justices to answer for their *veredictum*, so he is in mercy, and his land is taken into the king's hand.

> Walter de Mimminglande held half a fee in Membland in Ermington hundred of the honour of Totnes, *Fees*, p. 770.

557 William de Luvetone and David the tailor appealed Reginald de Bradeford of breach of the king's peace and wounding, and Thomas the miller of aiding and abetting. William and David come, and still make suit against them, but Reginald and Thomas do not come, so they and their pledges are in mercy. Reginald's pledges were Richard le White and

Roger Palmerus de Mannhevid, Thomas's Richard Inthecumbe and Adam le Bel de Mannhevid. And as they did not come and they wounded them, the sheriff is ordered to arrest them, while if William and David find pledges to make suit against them, they are to be outlawed according to the custom of the realm if they will not stand to right. John Lullepate, whom they appealed of the same, was outlawed at the suit of William and David. He was in Holbeton tithing, which is in mercy, and he had no chattels.

558 Edelota Anven complains that Thomas de Iadecumbe badly beat her, cut off her hair (*tresciam*) and took 5s. from her. Thomas comes, denies all and puts himself on the country. The jurors testify that he is not guilty, so he is quit, and let Edelota be taken into custody. She is poor, so nothing.

559 Three casks washed up in Bigbury tithing from a wreck at sea. Two were completely empty, the third contained a little wine valued at 5s., Bigbury tithing etc.

560 Michael son of William de Vado killed his sister Alice and fled to Holbeton church, where he admitted to that death and abjured the realm. He was in Flete and Battisborough tithing, which is in mercy, and he had chattels worth 3s. 6d., Flete tithing etc.

561 Andrew de Crenecumbe appealed Nicholas de la Fenne and Stephen de Coudeforde of breach of the king's peace and wounding, and that they did this he puts himself on the country. Nicholas and Stephen come, and as his appeal is null, let the country inquire. The jurors testify that they are guilty, so let them be sent to gaol, and Andrew is in mercy for a false appeal. Later Nicholas came and made fine for himself, Stephen and Andrew the appellor for two marks, pledges Richard de Porta, William de Bosco and Adam de Bosco.

562 Walter Cusin was found drowned by falling from a boat between Membland and Newton Ferrers tithings. Misadventure. Value of the boat 5s., the sheriff etc. Those tithings are in mercy for not presenting this case to the County Court.

563 Walter the cobbler was found dead in his home. No-one is suspected. No Englishry, so Murder fine.

564 Osbert de Niwetone drowned by falling from his horse into the river 'Pusling'. Misadventure. Value of the horse 2s., the sheriff etc.

565 William son of Gervase was found dead on Cornwood heath. No Englishry, so Murder fine.

566 John Giffard appealed William de la Pomerai, together with Ralph Ruffus who abetted the same, of breach of the king's peace and robbery. He does not come, and he was not attached save by his oath, so let him be arrested. William comes, but Ralph Ruffus does not, so he and his pledges, William de Omnibus Sanctis, Richard le Bastard, Peter le Calve and Walter le Calve, are in mercy. The jurors testify that they are not guilty, so they are quit.

Ermington

567 William de Wike appealed William son of Roger de Baucumbe, William son of Isolda and his brother Denis of beating him and breaking his shin, evilly and in felony, and he offers to prove this by his body as the court shall decide. As the appeal is null, it is decided that the country should inquire. The jurors testify that when they were playing together – – –

568 Ivo son of Angot is in mercy for a false appeal against Reginald Ruffus, as are his pledges, Godus de Redmore and the other has died, because he does not make suit against him as he appealed him in the County Court. Likewise Richard de Wrford is in mercy for a false appeal against Alfred de la Ya, as are his pledges, Ralph de Buretone and Gervase de Bureforde. Likewise Michael de la Torre is in mercy for a false appeal against Roger Longus, as are his pledges, Alfred de Clegland and Nicholas de Medwelle. Later Ivo came and made fine for himself, his fellows and their pledges for four marks, pledges David de Holecumbe, Gervase de Strode, Reginald de Baucumbe and Gilbert de Addestone.

569 Andrew de Wodelond is in mercy for a false appeal against Geoffrey son of William and certain others, as are his pledges, Nicholas de la Forde and Roger de la Wodelande, because he does not make suit against them. Later Andrew came and made fine for 20s., pledges William de la Pomerai and David de Holecumbe.

570 Richard de Dunneswelle, who appealed Richard Ode de Loddebroc, comes and does not make suit against him, so he and his pledge, Gilbert de Bosco, are in mercy.

571 Roger le Gui was outlawed at the suit of Walter Calvus for wounds which he gave him, as he says. The same Walter appealed Walter de Horiflode and Peter son of Godfrey of abetting. They come, and the jurors testify that they are not guilty, so they are quit, let Walter Calvus be taken into custody for a false appeal. He is poor, so nothing.

572 Robert son of Joce de Torre, who was appealed of wounding by Agnes daughter of Geoffrey, who has died, does not come, so he and his pledges, Ailward de Orchertone and Roger de la Leghe, are in mercy.

573 Osbert Whaitemel was crushed to death by a mill wheel. Misadventure. Value of the wheel 18d., the sheriff etc.

574 William son of Angod appeals Walter, servant of the nuns of Polsloe, Robert Crobe, William Drake, William Goiz, Ralph son of Swanekil, John Osmund, Roger Osmund and William son of Belicot of wounding and breach of the king's peace. Walter and all the appellees come. And because William does not name any of the appellees specifically, nor say which of them wounded him, it is decided that the appeal is null, let him be taken into custody for a false appeal.
The same appeals Robert the cobbler of the same. He does not come, so he and his pledges, Ralph de la Furse and Godfrey de Luvestone, are in mercy. Ivo son of Angot appeals all the aforesaid of the same, and specifically John Osmund of wounding him on the head, William son of Belicot of giving him another wound, Walter the servant of giving him

another wound, and all the appellees of beating him. They all come. The same Walter, the servant of the nuns, appeals Ivo son of Angot and his brother William of beating and wounding him. And all those named above on either side come. The jurors testify that they have all made an agreement, so they are all in mercy. Likewise the pledges of Ivo son of Angot, Gervase de Strode and Simon de Langebrok, because he did not prosecute his appeal as he made it in the County Court. Similarly Walter's pledges, William Brun and Roger Shanke, are in mercy for the same. Later Walter the servant came and made fine for himself and his pledges for 10s., pledges Geoffrey de Cottemore de Toteneis and Geoffrey son of Sara de Toteneis.

By 1291 the nuns of Polsloe had land at Heathfield in Ermington hundred, Dugdale, *Monasticon* vol. IV p. 427.

575 Simon de Langebrok, who appealed Robert the smith of Houboutone, Richard Wartha, Ralph Underhille, Ralph Whiteside, William le Goiz, Godfrey de Houboutone, Ralph son of Swanekilda and Philip son of Gilbert the smith of breach of the king's peace, does not come, so he and his pledges, Robert Spinbec; who has died, and another who has also died, are in mercy. All the appellees come, and the jurors testify that they have made an agreement, so let them be taken into custody. The same appealed Robert the cobbler of the same. He does not come, so he and his pledges, Robert de Levestone and Godfrey de Levestone, are in mercy. Later Thomas de Blakeforde came and made fine for Robert Crobe and all the other appellees, except Walter the servant, for four marks, because they are poor, pledges Thomas himself and Geoffrey de Pridias. Be it known that Ivo and William Angod, who appealed these men, made fine for themselves within that four mark fine which Ivo made for his false appeal against Reginald Ruffus, as appears above in this roll.

576 Henry the chaplain, the fuller's son, and his brother Richard Redeman were outlawed at the suit of Richard de Porta for wounding him. They had no chattels.

577 Serlo de Bikebire, charged with homicide in wartime, comes, denies all and puts himself on the country. The jurors testify that he killed him in the time of the great war, so he is quit.

This great war was presumably the civil war at the end of John's reign. There were obscure manoeuvres in the south-west in 1215, when a revolt against the king was suppressed, apparently without any fighting – Painter, *The Reign of King John* pp. 307–10 – while in 1216 the lords of Torrington and Barnstaple were in arms against John – J. J. Alexander, 'Early Barons of Torrington and Barnstaple', in *TDA* 73 (1941) pp. 162–3. But the loyalty of the earl of Devon, of Henry fitz Count and of Robert de Courtenay, lord of Okehampton, kept Devon safe for John, and the number of Devon rebels licensed to return to the king's allegiance in 1217 was very small, Painter, op. cit. p. 359, *Rot. Lit. Claus.* I pp. 300–337 *passim*. If Serlo de Bikebire had any connection with the William de Bykebyr whose heir in 1242/43 held a fee in Great Englebourne of the honour of Okehampton – *Fees* p. 786 – he may well have been active on the king's side.

578 Richard de la Dune, charged with theft, comes, denies all and puts himself on the country. The jurors testify that he is not guilty, so he is quit. Ugborough vill is in mercy for not presenting this case.

(m 39d)
MODBURY BURGH

579 Henry the wool carder of Mobire killed Benedict le Combere on the advice of Benedict's wife Agnes, so let Henry be exacted and outlawed and Agnes be exacted and waivered. They were living in Modbury, which is in mercy for not producing them, and they had no chattels.

> This eyre provides what appears to be the earliest reference to a burgh at Modbury. It was probably founded by a member of the Vautort family, who by 1238 held the manor directly from the king, *Fees* p. 770.
> The importance of cloth-making to Devon's economic life is indicated by the presence of no. 24 among the articles of the tourn – Appendix II (b). This case suggests that Modbury was one of those smaller towns whose cloth-manufacture expanded during the thirteenth century as a result of the development and spread of the fulling-mill (see no. 328 above). See also Hoskins, *Devon* pp. 124–5; J. Youings, 'Monastic Wool Sales', in *DCNQ* 30 (1965–7) pp. 70–2.

580 The jurors present that Hugh Peverel takes 2d. from each cart that comes onto his land at 'Berforde' to take peat or to have pasturage. And because it is testified that the soil (*fundus*) of that land is his, he is told that he can certainly do this, but that he may not take anything for the right of way (*occasione itineris*). So he is quit.

> Probably at issue here were rights of use of and access to the waste, the scrub, wood and moor land which lay outside the cultivated fields of Devon villages and hamlets, and which villagers used to pasture their flocks and herds on and as sources of peat and firewood. Cultivation of the waste was often controlled by lords of manors like Hugh Peverel, who was thus lawfully able to exact money when peat or hay was taken from his land at 'Berforde'. But it was important that villagers should have unimpeded access to waste, including those parts of it not under direct seigneurial control; perhaps Peverel had been trying to prevent the men of Modbury (which owed suit to his manor and hundred of Ermington until he himself remitted it at about this time, Bodl. Wood E. 11 p. 85) from going elsewhere for peat and hay, by taking money from them whenever they crossed his land. See Finberg, *Tavistock Abbey* pp. 32–4.

581 The same Hugh Peverel made fine for trespass for two hundred marks, pledges Reginald de Alla Mara, Joel de Valle Torta, Philip de Beumond, Durand son of Richard, Herbert de Pinu, Roger de Langeford, Richard de Langeford, William de la Pomerai, Geoffrey Copphin, Martin de Fishacre, Hamelin de Deudone, Michael de Spicwik, William Trenchard, Richard Baustan, Warin son of Joel, Nicholas de Blakedone and Huward de Bikeleghe.
The same, asked by what warrant he holds this hundred, says he has no warrant except ancient tenure, so let this be discussed.

> For Hugh Peverel's fine see no. 583 below.
> Ermington and Aveton Giffard, having been given to Walter of Douai after 1066, had by 1086 passed to the king, who gave Bampton (no. 160 above) to Walter in exchange, *DB* pp. 34–35. The history of the hundred thereafter has been somewhat obscured by the accident of there having been two important Peverel families in medieval Devon, both apparently owing their fortunes to grants from Matilda Peverel, sister of William Peverel of Essex, herself the beneficiary of grants from Henry I. Peverel of Sampford received Sampford Peverell, Aller and Kerswell – *Fees* p. 96 – while Peverel of Ermington came to hold Ermington, Kingston and Kilbury – *RH* p. 69. The two families may have been related, but their armorial bearings were totally different, Risdon, *Survey of Devon* p. 185. Ermington hundred was valued at £2. 13s. 4d. *per annum* in 1249, and at 40s. *per annum* in 1274/75, JUST/1/176 m39, *RH* p. 69.

582 John de Haredone is suspected of theft, so let him be exacted and outlawed. He had chattels worth 10s., Ugborough tithing etc.

583 Hugh Peverel, charged with the death of a cook called Alfred, comes

and denies all. The juries of Coleridge, Haytor, Ermington and Stanborough, with twenty four other knights of the county, testify that he is not guilty, so he is quit.

> According to the Pipe Roll, Hugh Peverel's fine was for having an inquest, a statement which the size and composition of his trial jury renders wholly credible, E372/83 m10. He paid £40 in 1239, and was then allowed to pay off the rest at forty marks yearly; he paid this sum for each of the next three years, and was cleared of the last twenty marks in 1243.

STANBOROUGH HUNDRED ANSWERS BY TWELVE JURORS

584 Michael de Warwik, who appealed Roger Prigke and his brothers Robert and Richard of breach of the king's peace and beating him, does not come or make suit, so he and his pledges, Richard Mei and Robert de la Torre de Teing Canonicorum, are in mercy. Roger and the others came, so they are *sine die*.

585 Alina daughter of Erneburne, who appealed Benedict the clerk of rape, comes but does not make suit. She had no pledge except her oath, so let her be taken into custody. Benedict comes, and the jurors testify that they have made no agreement, so he is quit. Alina is poor, so nothing.

586 Vincent, the prior of Plympton's servant, fell from his horse into the river Avon and drowned. Misadventure. Value of the horse 4s., the sheriff etc.

587 Alina de la Ya appeals William de Bretteville that, with Stephen the clerk, Rannulf de Falewille, Jordan de Hode, Eliot de Dertinctone and Geoffrey de Hathelande, he came to the house of Gilbert de Herding, where she then was, beat her badly and struck her on the jaw with a sword, breaking one of her teeth; and they took her son Robert, bound him and led him to the gallows, where they threatened to hang him. And they did this evilly and in felony. And that this is so she puts herself on the country. William de Bretteville and all the appellees come, except for Stephen the clerk, who was attached by Roger Hilemer and Walter Tug, so they are in mercy. The appeal is null, so let the country inquire. Later Robert comes and appeals William de Bretteville and all the others named, that they took him, beat him badly, led him to the gallows and threatened to hang him. And that this is so he likewise puts himself on the country. The jurors testify that they are not guilty, so they are quit as regards Alina, let her be taken into custody for a false appeal. But they say that they all beat Robert, but they did not take him to the gallows as he said. So they are all in mercy, let Robert be taken into custody for a false appeal. Later William de Bretteville came and made fine for himself, all the appellees and Alina and Robert the appellors for 20s., pledges Henry de Altaribus and William de Sancto Stephano.

> William de Bretteville may have been related to the coroner Guy de Bretteville, who had lands in the south of Stanborough hundred, *Fees* p. 766. William himself, however, had property in Totnes – H. R. Watkin, *The History of Totnes Priory and Medieval Town* Vol. I (Torquay 1914) pp. 99–100 – a fact which, taken with the place-names identifying others involved in this case, make it likely that these events took place in the north of the hundred, and that the gallows involved with either at Diptford, Dean Prior or Rattery, held by Nicholas de Molis, the prior of Plympton and the abbot of St. Dogmells respectively, JUST/1/186 m24.

588 Alexander de Beialdeleghe was outlawed for the death of William de Shiredone at the suit of William's brother Oliver. He was in Skerraton tithing, which is in mercy, and he had no chattels.

589 Robert de Benleghe is heavily in mercy for a false appeal against Walter son of William and others. He is sent to gaol.

590 Gunilda de Leghe, who appealed Martin de Ponte of forcibly raping her daughter Agnes, does not come, and she had no pledge except her oath. Martin comes. They have made no agreement, nor is he guilty, so he is quit.

> Such an appeal by proxy is unusual, though no. 364 above provides another example; in theory an appellor must prosecute on the basis of his or her own experience, cf. no. 99 above. It is possible, however, that Agnes was a minor, which might have made her unable to prosecute in person – Bracton, *De Legibus* Vol. II p. 399 f. 141b – though this did not prevent appeals of rape, or attempted rape, being brought elsewhere by women who had been under age at the time of the alleged assaults – JUST/1/778 m50, JUST/1/328 m6.

591 An unknown man was found dead in 'Stoneforde'. No Englishry, so Murder fine.

592 Walter Godwin de Ethfelde is in mercy for the trespass which he did to Richard son of Rannulf. Later he came and made fine for 6s. 8d., pledges Philip Girard and William the tailor of Mobire.

593 Vincent de Boltebire, who appealed Martin son of Richard Wimund of breach of the king's peace, does not come, and he was attached by Robert de Burleghe and Robert de Baketone, so they are all in mercy. Martin comes, and the jurors testify that they have made an agreement, so let him be taken into custody. Later Martin came and made fine for one mark, pledge William de Morleghe.

594 A boy named Henry was scalded when a piglet knocked a pot full of vegetables onto him. Value of the piglet 4d., the sheriff etc. As the jurors present neither the first finder nor the value of the bowl, they are all in mercy.

595 Skerraton is a royal serjeanty, and Master Walter de Shiredone holds it by the service of providing three arrows when the king comes to Dartmoor to hunt. And he holds one carucate of land in demesne and has revenues of twelve shillings and two pounds of wax.

> Skerraton was given to Walter le Deveneis, or Walter de Novingtone, who was Hubert de Burgh's doctor, in January 1229, *CCR 1227–1231* p. 147. In 1212 it had been held by David de Scyredun, whose ancestors were said to have held it since the Conquest, *Fees* p. 98. In 1228, however, David's son Roger Mirabel was outlawed for felony and his land forfeited to the crown. *CCR 1227–1231* p. 62, *RH* p. 79. Much of that land had previously been alienated; Shapley, held by David de Scyredun in 1212, had been given to his daughter Oresia for her marriage portion, JUST/1/174 m10d, and Walter engaged in a good deal of litigation to recover lost fragments of the serjeanty lands, apparently to little purpose, *CRR* XIII no. 2597, *CRR* XIV nos. 2061, 2112, 2323, *CRR* XV no. 464. In 1249 Skerraton was valued at 40s. *per annum*, JUST/1/176 m39, while by 1281 the serjeanty had been commuted for an annual payment of 3s., JUST/1/186 m24.

596 Diptford is a royal serjeanty, and Nicholas de Molis holds it with the advowson of the church, which is worth £10. The land too is worth £10. He also holds Haytor and Stanborough hundreds by the service of half a

knight's fee. Nicholas neither comes nor shows any warrant, so let this be discussed.

> Diptford was the original hundredal manor, and in 1086 had been held by the king, *DB* pp. 22–23. By 1157 it had been granted to earl Reginald of Cornwall, *PR 3 Henry II* p. 74, while in 1194 Richard I granted it to Reginald's illegitimate son Henry fitz Count, *Ancient Charters* Part I (PRS X 1888) no. 62. Henry having died in 1222, in 1230 it was given by Henry III to Nicholas de Molis, together with the advowson of the church and Haytor hundred, all to be held by the service of half a knight's fee, *CCR 1227–1231* p. 378. In 1249 the manor was valued at £10 *per annum*, the hundred at 40s., JUST/1/176 mm39, 39d. Nicholas's failure to produce his warrant in 1238 was matched by that of his son Roger in 1281/82 – when challenged over the advowson of Diptford, though claiming to have the charter given to his father, he confessed himself unable to lay his hands on it, and had to refer the justices to the Chancery rolls, *PQW* pp. 173–4. No references to Diptford as a serjeanty have been noticed elsewhere. For Haytor see no. 707 below.
>
> Nicholas de Molis was sheriff of Devon between May 1234 and April 1236. Besides being a Devon magnate, he was a man of national consequence as ambassador, soldier and administrator, who was at various times sheriff of Yorkshire and Hampshire, warden of the Channel Islands and seneschal of Gascony, and who carried one of the sceptres at queen Eleanor's coronation in 1236 – *Complete Peerage* Vol. IX pp. 1–4. Unsurprisingly, perhaps, he appears to have left local government largely to his undersheriff, Walter of Bath, in 1236 confessing himself unable to account at the exchequer in his subordinate's absence, E159/14 m13d.

597 Archibald Wasteper and Matthew de Hortone are in mercy for a false appeal against Geoffrey de la Ya. Later they come and make fine for 20s., pledges William Trenchard and William de Praule.

598 Ashwell is a royal escheat and is worth 60s. Theobald de Englescheville holds it, but it is not known by what service.

> When Henry III gave Diptford manor to Nicholas de Molis, he excepted from the grant rents totalling 60s. 1d. from the vills of Horner, Tennaton and Ashwell, all in that manor, which he gave to Theobald de Englescheville, *RH* p. 79. These vills clearly represent the land in Diptford formerly held by Luke son of John, lands which, like Luke's manors of Oburnford and Highweek (nos. 166, 720, 722) also came into Theobald's hands, *Rot. Lit. Claus.* I p. 472.

599 Eva de Breusa is in the king's gift. She holds Loddiswell manor, which is worth £10.

> Eva de Breusa was the fourth daughter of William Marshal. She was widowed in 1230 when her husband, William de Braose, lord of Abergavenny and Builth, was hanged by Llywellyn the Great for adultery with that prince's wife – F. M. Powicke, *The Thirteenth Century* (Oxford 1953) pp. 395–6 – and was given livery of her dower in June of that year, *CCR 1227–1231* pp. 354–5. When the honour of Totnes was divided between William de Braose the elder and Henry de Nunant in 1205 (see no. 176 above), Loddiswell, which was also partitioned, was valued at £10, and William's share of it at £5. 16s. 8d., *Devon FFI* no. 56. Clearly at some point either William or one of his descendants had been able to reunite the manor.

600 West Alvington is a royal escheat from the Normans' lands. Matthew Besile holds it by the king's gift, by what service is not known, and it is worth £10.

> West Alvington escheated to the crown in 1204 on the forfeiture of Oliver de Aubeny, a Norman, *Rot. Norm.* p. 130. In 1228 it was granted to Pain de Chaurces for his maintenance, and in 1232 to Pain's son Adam, at his father's request, *CCR 1227–1231* p. 24, *CCR 1231–1234* p. 18. In 1237, however, it was granted to Matthew Besile, a diplomat and courtier who in 1240 became marshal to the queen's household – *CCR 1237–1242* p. 342 – to be held by him until it should be restored to the rightful heirs, *CChR 1226–1257* p. 231. The only services recorded as owing from it were the payment of 26s. yearly to Nicholas de Molis's manor of Diptford, and the finding for Nicholas of a beadle for his hundred of Stanborough, *Fees* p. 766. In 1249 the manor was valued at sixteen marks *per annum*, JUST/1/176 m39.

Stanborough

601   From a cask of wine washed up at Thurlestone from a wreck at sea, 20s., South Milton tithing etc; from wine likewise washed up at Thurlestone, 10s., the same tithing etc.; from wine likewise washed up there, 2s., Huish tithing etc.; from Diptford tithing for the same, 8d. Richard de la Ya took an empty cask without permission or a coroner's view, and because he did not produce a sack which was likewise found there before the justices, he is in mercy. Later he came and made fine for one mark, pledge Nicholas de la Ya.

602   A Welsh groom named William was killed by a colt. Misadventure. Value of the colt 7s., the sheriff etc. Elias de la Blakehale and William le Norreis are in mercy for valuing it at 4s.

(m 40)
603   Of defaults they say that Nicholas de Molis, the abbot of Caen, Geoffrey de Insula, Odo de Treuerbi, Matthew Besil, Ralph de Albemarle, Baldwin de Waiford, Eva de Breuse, Richard Chamel, Herbert Buzun, William Herizun and Jordan Barnage did not come on the first day.

>   Nicholas de Molis, see no. 596 above.
>   Geoffrey de Insula held a quarter of a fee in Leigh, in Churchstow parish, of the honour of Gloucester, *Fees* p. 765.
>   Odo de Treuerbi married the daughter of the younger son of Robert, baron of Cardinan, and received East Allington with her, Pole, *Collections* pp. 302-3, *Fees* p. 766. He defaulted again in 1249, JUST/1/176 m39.
>   Matthew Besil held West Alvington manor, no. 600 above. He defaulted again in 1249, JUST/1/176 m39.
>   Ralph de Albemarle held one fee in Woodleigh and was mesne lord of Beenleigh, both of the honour of Plympton, *Fees* pp. 765, 766. He defaulted again in 1244, JUST/1/175 m43.
>   Baldwin de Waiford, with the heirs of Ralph le Abbe, held one fee in South Milton of the honour of Plympton, *Fees* p. 766, *Devon FFI* no. 106.
>   Eva de Breusa held the manor of Loddiswell, no. 599 above.
>   Herbert Buzun held land in Sewer, no. 621 below, JUST/1/175 m27.
>   William Herizun held half a fee in Moreleigh of the barony of Dartington, *Fees* p. 765.
>   Jordan Barnage held half a fee in Luscombe of the barony of Dartington, *Fees* p. 765.

THE FREE MANOR OF YEALMPTON ANSWERS BY THREE JURORS

604   The jurors of this manor present nothing that was not presented in Plympton hundred.

>   Yealmpton manor was held by the king in 1086, *DB* pp. 26-27. It was granted by Henry I to the de Mandeville family, in which it descended until Joan de Mandeville married Matthew son of Herbert, and became by him the mother of Herbert son of Matthew, who held the manor in 1238, Sanders, *Baronies* p. 42 n.5.

LIFTON HUNDRED ANSWERS BY TWELVE JURORS

605   Walter le Turnur was killed at Great Haye in Lamerton manor, it is not known by whom. No Englishry, so Murder fine.

606   Pelagia and her daughter Avice appeal Robert de Wdemanneswille of the death of Berenger de Langestone. He comes, denies all and puts

himself on the country. The jurors testify that he is not guilty, so he is quit. Let Pelagia and Avice be taken into custody. They are poor.

607   Robert Trenchard appealed Robert son of Geoffrey Berde, Geoffrey Berde and William Biwlf of breach of the king's peace. Later he came but does not make suit, so he and his pledges, Nicholas Trenchard, Michael de Monte and Henry Baustan, are in mercy. The jurors testify that they have made an agreement, so they are all in mercy.
The same appealed William Ireis, who does not come, so he and his pledges, William de Grenefenne, Ralph de Radershe, Richard de Rudone, Michael de Kingforde and William de Taintone, are in mercy. Later Robert Trenchard came and made fine for 40s., pledges Roger de Brente and Geoffrey de Curitone. Later Robert Berd came and made fine for 6s. 8d., pledge Geoffrey Berd and John de Thornecumbe.

608   William Trenchard appealed Robert Trenchard but came and withdrew, so he and his pledges are in mercy. He came and made fine for one mark, pledges Hugh de Bolay and Hamelin de Deudone.

609   Of prises taken to castles they say that Thomas de Tetteburne took three of Philip de Brente's cows against his will, and he still withholds 16s. from him, so he is in mercy.

> A presentment under no. 25 of the articles of the eyre in its extended form by 1238—it had in effect come to have another article, originally distinct, concerning prises (goods arbitrarily commandeered and taken to castles), tacked onto it, *Surrey Eyre 1235* pp. 92–3. Wardens of royal castles were legally permitted to make such prises in order to maintain their garrisons; Thomas de Tetteburne's offence lay in his failure to make full payment for the cows he had taken within the forty days prescribed by the 1217 reissue of Magna Carta, McKechnie, *Magna Carta* pp. 329–33. The castle in question must have been Lydford.

610   A mound was found dug into in Marytavy tithing, which is in mercy for not presenting this case to the County Court.

611   Ralph Futur appealed Ralph Neirun that he came by night to the house of William de Sancto Stephano, where he took two beds, five silver marks and a palfrey, and likewise abducted William's wife, whom he forcibly carried off to Wales, and he did this evilly and in felony, and that this is so he puts himself on the country. Ralph comes and denies all, and as the appeal is null, let the country inquire. Ralph is in mercy for a false appeal. The jurors testify that Ralph came to William's house and carried clothes away from it, but they do not know how many, and likewise they do not know about the taking of money. And they say Ralph took William's palfrey and carried it off together with his wife to Wales. And they say that Ralph had a seal of William's when he was with him, and he made a deed in William's name and pawned it in the Jewry (*posuit in Judaismo*) for twenty five marks, which William later paid. So it is ordered that he be taken into custody until tomorrow. Later Ralph Futur came and made fine for 6s. 8d., pledge Ralph de Albemarle.

> Ralph Futur's appeal was quashed because the offence it alleged had been committed against someone other than the appellor. It may also have been committed in another hundred, since William de Sancto Stephano had property at Dean Prior in Stanborough, *Fees* p. 764, *Devon FFI* nos. 232, 442, 447.

612   William de la Berghe's house was burgled, and he does not come.

He was attached by Elias de Smethestone and Geoffrey de Tavitone, so they are all in mercy.

613   Agnes daughter of Robert de Medwille appealed Almaric de Sideham that he came to her father's house on Wednesday in the first week of Lent in the twenty-first year (11 March 1237), around the middle of the night, and raped her, lying with her by force and ravishing her virginity, and that he did this evilly and in felony she offers to prove against him as the court shall decide. Almaric comes, denies all and puts himself on the country. The jurors testify that he is not guilty, so he is quit, let Agnes be sent to gaol for a false appeal. She is poor.

614   Alice daughter of Ailward, who has died, appealed Nicholas de Kelly of the death of her sister Emelota. Nicholas de Kelli comes, denies all and puts himself on the country. The jurors testify that he is not guilty, so he is quit. They appealed Richard le Pichelere of the same, and he does not come, nor was he attached as he was not found. The jurors testify that he is not guilty, so he is quit and may return if he wishes.

615   Robert Heriz fell from his horse into the river Carey and drowned. Misadventure. Value of the horse 5s., the sheriff etc. Rannulf de Albemarle, one of the coroners, is in mercy because he was present at the valuation of the horse when it was valued at 2s., and it is now established that it was well worth 5s.

616   Walter de Shaldeford, who appealed Peter de Whitefelde, Thomas de Aureford and Richard de Aureford of breach of the king's peace, does not now make suit as he appealed them. Peter has died. Thomas does not come, and he was not attached as he was not found, but Richard comes. The jurors testify that they have all made an agreement, so they are all in mercy, let Walter and Richard, who are present, be taken into custody. Later Richard de Alreforde came and made fine for 10s., pledge Roger de Parco. Walter is poor.

617   Robert de Lanteprei complains that fifteen years ago Joel de Buketone came to his house, took all his chattels and carried them off to Lydford castle, so that he had to pay Joel five marks before he could have them back. Joel comes and says that he arrested all his chattels and himself because Robert was charged with homicide, as a man whom he had struck was in danger of death, and as soon as he had recovered he gave all his beasts and chattels back to him, and that this is so he puts himself on the country. The jurors testify that Joel did not take his chattels, but that his father William Giffard had the chattels taken as aforesaid, as he was then constable, but they do not know what fine he made with William. So Joel is quit and Robert is in mercy, let him be taken into custody. Later Robert de Lanteprei came and made fine for 6s. 8d., pledge Roger de Dirhille.

At the time of these events Lydford castle was in the custody of William Brewer, who held it between 1216 and 1227 (see no. 637 below). William Giffard, who in 1234 held, with William de la Bruere, one fee, probably in Holbeton in Ermington, of the fees which had been William Brewer's, *Fees* p. 400, was presumably William Brewer's deputy.

The arrest of Robert de Lanteprei was in basic accord with the procedure prescribed by Bracton, *De Legibus* Vol. II pp. 345–6 ff. 122b, 123, where it was laid down that anyone appealed of wounding must, if the wound appeared dangerous, be arrested and imprisoned until it was known whether his victim would recover or not, and that while he was in prison he should be maintained out of his own chattels.

618   Nicholas Passemer appeals John Anglicus, Alan the forester, Richard le Flentur, John the Welshman and William le Pruz that they, with Walter the Welshman, David the Welshman and Gilbert the Welshman, came to him on the feast of St. Bartholomew in the twentieth year (24 August 1236), took him, beat him and ill-treated him, John striking him on the head with a stake and wounding him, and they gave him three other wounds. Then they dragged him into the castle where, having shut the gates, they badly beat him again and later imprisoned him. And that they did this evilly and in felony he offers to prove by his body as the court shall decide.

John and all the appellees except for Walter, David and Gilbert come, and as the appeal is null it is decided that the country should inquire. Walter was attached by Henry de Praule and William de Dunnestone, David by Richard Kene and Roger de Arneberghe, so they are in mercy. Gilbert was not attached, as it was testified that he has been outlawed.

The jurors testify that John Anglicus and Walter le Pruz are not guilty, so they are quit, let Nicholas be taken into custody for his false appeal against them. Alan the forester and all the others named except Richard le Flentur are guilty of wounding and beating, so let all those present be taken into custody, the others who are absent are in mercy. They say that Nicholas was taken to the castle and imprisoned there on the orders of John Anglicus, so let him be taken into custody. Later Nicholas came and made fine for one mark, pledge William de la Pomerai.

   This must have been Lydford castle. The connection of John Anglicus with it is not recorded.

619   William son of Henry de Breulishille hanged himself in Breazle wood. Felony *de se*. He had chattels worth 37s. 8d., of which Bratton tithing is to answer for 27s. 8d., Stowford tithing for 10s.

620   Richard de Cumbe appealed Walter Haie that he, with his sons John and Henry, who were in his mainpast, struck him with a furze fork (*furcha januparia*), evilly and in felony, and he offers to prove this by his body, as a man over age, as the court shall decide. Walter and the others come, deny all and put themselves on the country. The jurors testify that they are guilty, so let them be sent to gaol. Richard is in mercy for a false appeal. Later Richard came and made fine for 6s. 8d., pledges William Trenchard and Herbert de Cumbe.

   Lifton hundred included a good deal of the western end of Dartmoor where, as trees were very scarce, furze was greatly in demand as a fuel, G. M. Spooner and F. S. Russell (eds.), *Worth's Dartmoor* (Newton Abbot 1967) pp. 65–6.

621   Robert de Colestok, Richard Stranga, Thomas le Curteis and Oliver son of Richard Piper appeal Reginald Bloiob, Roger, Peter and Walter de Baketone that on the Thursday next after the feast of St. Hilary nine years ago (18 January 1229) they came to Thurlestone with the men of Thurlestone, South Milton, Galmpton, Huish, Little Bolberry, Great Bolberry and Herbert Buzun's vill of Sewer. And when Robert and the

Lifton

others came through a tempest (*tormentum*) towards Thurlestone with two ships laden with wine, and because of that tempest disembarked from the ships and came to land at Thurlestone, and shortly afterwards the ships were broken up by the tempest, and all the wine in them and all their chattels were thrown to land by the tempest, Reginald and the other appellees, with the men of those vills, then came and broke the heads of the tuns and poured away the wine, and carried off all the chattels in the ships, and their coffers with their money and their other things, and they likewise took their beds with their bed-clothes, whereby they suffered losses to the value of five hundred marks, and they were ready to prove this as the court shall decide. Reginald, Peter and Walter come and ask for judgment on their appeal. And as they do not say in their appeal what loss each of them suffered from the injury done to them, nor who inflicted how much loss on whom, it is decided that the appeal is null and Robert and the others are in mercy, let the country inquire. Later Robert and the other appellors came and made fine for two marks, pledge – – –

The jurors testify that Reginald and the other appellees, together with those vills, had nothing from those wines or chattels against the will of their owners. Indeed they say that if they had anything they had it with their free will. So they are quit, Robert and the other appellors are in mercy.

> This entry is written on a separate piece of parchment which has been sewn onto the foot of m40, which happens to be the wrong place for it, since the events it records took place not in Lifton, an entirely land-locked hundred, but in Stanborough.
> The reference to shipwrecks scattered through this roll show how frequent they were on the coasts of Devon; this and other cases show how profitable they could be to the inhabitants of coastal villages, enthusiastically disregarding the rights of shipowners and king (see no. 26 above). At the 1281/82 eyre the justices heard how tuns of wine valued at £40 had been washed ashore at Saunton and carried off by men from twenty-six neighbouring villages, in some cases coming from several miles inland, JUST/1/186 m12. See also *Cal. Inq. Misc.* I no. 2412.
> This use of the word *tormentum*, meaning a storm or tempest, is highly unusual; clearly related to the Portuguese *tormenta*, it is not found in DuCange or the *Revised Medieval Latin Word-List*.

(m 40d)
622   Margery, wife of Stephen Paiard, appeals Lawrence de Dunkerigge, Wyotus de Grenetone and Alan de La Yoldelande of aiding and abetting Ralph Neirun when Luke Spaiard, who abjured the realm for forging the king's seal, beat her so that she miscarried. Lawrence and the others come and deny all etc. The jurors testify that they are not guilty, so they are quit, let Stephen and his wife Margery be taken into custody. Richard de Veteri Ponte is in mercy for trespass. Later Stephen came and made fine for himself and his wife for one mark, pledge Guy de Bretteville.

> Luke Spaiard had abjured the realm at a gaol delivery held in January 1238, see no. 255 above. Forging the king's seal was treason, and its perpetrators would not, at least in the fourteenth century, be allowed benefit of clergy, J. G. Bellamy, *The Law of Treason in England in the Later Middle Ages* (Cambridge 1970), pp. 5–6, 8, 92. So unusual a procedure in the case of Luke Spaiard is probably best explained by the assumption that he was a clerk, effectively forced into exile for a crime which the justices thought merited a punishment more severe than anything he was likely to suffer at his bishop's hands. At the 1255 Hereford eyre a clerk convicted of counterfeiting royal writs and seals was handed over to the bishop – JUST/1/300c m28 – but a clerk charged at the 1288 Dorset eyre with forging the king's seal and unclaimed by the bishop's representative was remanded to custody until the king could be consulted, "as that felony and crime of forging and counterfeiting the king's seal touches the king. . ." – JUST/1/213 m29d.

623 Sampson de Mora, who appealed Luke Paiard of breach of the king's peace, does not come, so he and his pledges, Stephen de Bateshille and Philip le Franceis, are in mercy. Luke does not come, as he was outlawed as aforesaid.

624 William Atewater, who appealed Lawrence de Dunkerigge of breach of the king's peace, comes but does not make suit, so he and his pledges, William Corbet and Robert de Wlnethecote, are in mercy. Later William came and made fine for himself for 6s. 8d., pledges Stephen Paiard and Walter Pain.

625 An unknown man was found killed on William Trenchard's land. No Englishry, so Murder fine.
> During the 1238 eyre William Trenchard acknowledged the right of Michael son of Godfrey in two ferlings of land in Lewtrenchard (to which he or his family gave their name, *PND* p. 187), Michael to hold the land of him thereafter, *Devon FFI* no. 315.

626 John de Le Orscherd, who has died, appealed William Trenchard and his sons Michael and Robert of beating his wife Christina so that she miscarried. William and the others come, deny all and put themselves on the country. The same appealed William of the death of his wife Christina. He comes, denies all and puts himself on the country as before. The jurors testify that they are not guilty, either of the miscarriage or, in William's case, of the death, so they are quit.
> The release of bail of William Trenchard, appealed of beating Christiana wife of John del Orchard so that she miscarried, was ordered on 19 May 1235, an inquest having found that he had been maliciously appealed, *CCR 1234–1237* p. 93.

627 Benedict de Buttelescumbe in in mercy for a false appeal against Reginald Hulbere, as are his pledges, Richard le Bastard and John de Bitlescumbe. Reginald Hulbere is also in mercy for a false appeal against Benedict, as are his pledges, William Hulbere and Jordan de Waterfalle. Later Reginald Hulbere came and made fine for himself and his pledges for two marks, pledges John de Cardewille and William de Puttokescumbe. Later Benedict came and made fine for himself and his pledges, as they are poor, for 6s. 8d., pledge John de Arkeswrthi.

628 William de Northicote and his pledges are in mercy as he did not prosecute his appeal against Vincent de Estcote and his brother Jordan. His pledges are Belengarius de Lidetone and his own oath.

629 One Botilda was found dead in Sprytown wood. Robert the tithingman of Stafford first found her. The twelve jurors are in mercy for presenting that the bishop of Exeter first found her.

630 William the miller and Elias de Sprei, whom Thomas and Richard, the sons of Clarice, appealed of Clarice's death, come, deny all and put themselves on the country. The jurors testify that they are not guilty, so they are quit. Thomas and Richard, who are under age, did not come, and they had no pledges.

631 William de Molis appealed Richard de Battishille and others of the death of Alan de Lidetone. William does not come, so he and his pledges, Hugh Coffin and Hugh de Molis, are in mercy. Richard comes, denies all and puts himself on the country. Be it known that William David and

Geoffrey le Poter were outlawed for Alan's death at the suit of Alan's widow Margery. Belengarius de Lidetone, who appealed Richard and the others of the death, does not come. His pledges were Roger the cook of Lidetone and another who has died.
The jurors testify that Richard is not guilty, so he is quit. William and Geoffrey were living in Bridestowe manor, which is in mercy. William had chattels worth 5s., the same tithing etc. Geoffrey had no chattels. Rannulf de Albemarle, then coroner, and Richard de Cockewrthi the sergeant are in mercy for not holding an inquest into those chattels. Later it was testified that Rannulf took those 5s. because William was his man, so he is in mercy.

632 Wymarc, wife of John de Craneforde, appeals John de Millentone of beating her so that she miscarried, and that he did this evilly etc., she offers etc., as etc. John comes, denies all and puts himself on the country. The jurors testify that he is not guilty, so he is quit, let John de Craneforde and Wymarc be taken into custody. Later John came and made fine for himself and his wife for 10s., pledges Adam le Brun and Richard le Clerk de Lideforde.

633 Clarice, wife of Drogo de Dikeport, who appealed William Cole of maiming her husband Drogo, comes, and William also comes. The jurors testify that they have made an agreement, so let them be taken into custody. Later William came and made fine for 6s. 8d., pledge Durand son of Richard. Clarice is poor.

634 Roger de Dirhille and Thomas de Holdik, charged with the deaths of two merchants found on Blackdown moor, and Walter son of Ruiwelin and his mother Matilda, charged with harbouring thieves, come, deny all and put themselves on the country. The jurors testify that Roger de Dirhille is not guilty, so he is quit. But they say that Thomas, Walter and Matilda are guilty, so they are hanged. Thomas had chattels worth four marks, Walter and Matilda chattels worth 10s., Lifton manor etc.

635 Thomas le Veg and Reginald Martin de la Heie are suspected of harbouring hanged thieves, so let them be exacted and outlawed. They were in Lamerton tithing, which is in mercy. Thomas had chattels worth 3s., Reginald chattels worth 10s., Lifton manor etc.
Thomas le Veg was attached by Reginald Lambert, Reginald de Charke, William le Slutere, George de Lamberton and Robert Blundus.
Reginald son of Martin was attached by Roger Beupenie, John son of Gunnild, Robert Cardinel de Cheldesangre, Geoffrey iuxta Iter, John de la Forde and John de la Cumbe.

636 Lifton is a royal manor. Amice de Cadigdene holds it by king Richard's gift and it is worth £10. The church is worth ten marks, and the dean of London has it by Amice's gift.

> For Amice de Cadigdene and Lifton manor see no. 639 below.
> The dean of London was Geoffrey de Lucy, dean of St. Paul's, whose receiving Lifton church from Amice de Cadigdene is made less surprising by the fact of that lady's having been his own mother, probably by Godfrey de Lucy, later bishop of Winchester – M. G. Cheney, 'Master Geoffrey de Lucy, an early chancellor of the university of Oxford', in *EHR* 82 (1967) pp. 758–60.

637 Lydford is a royal manor, and it is worth £4. 4s. Herbert son of Matthew holds it at the king's pleasure. Lydford church is worth 40s., and Michael the priest holds it by gift from William Briuwerre.
> Lydford was important as a centre for the administration of the Devon stannaries, A. D. Saunders, 'Lydford Castle', in *Medieval Archaeology* 24 (1980) pp. 127–33. Custody of the castle and of Dartmoor forest were committed to Herbert son of Matthew in March 1234, and doubtless remained in his hands until they were given to Richard of Cornwall in 1239, *CPR 1232–1247* p. 42, Saunders, art. cit. p. 129.
> William Brewer was given custody of Lydford castle in July 1216, and retained it until January 1227, *Rot. Lit. Claus.* I p. 279, *CPR 1225–1232* p. 106. The advowson of St. Petrock's church was the king's, and William may have taken advantage of Henry III's minority to present to the living, though this did not deter Henry from granting the tithe of the hay-crop of Dartmoor to the parson in 1237, *CPR 1232–1247* p. 187. In 1249 the church was valued at five marks *per annum*, JUST/1/176 m38d.

638 Paris de Rogerstone fled to Broadwoodwidger church, where he admitted having committed homicide and abjured the realm. He was in Richard de Veteri Ponte's tithing of Broadwoodwidger, which is in mercy, and he had chattels worth 10s., Lifton manor etc.
> In 1242/43 Richard de Veteri Ponte held 1¾ fees in Broadwoodwidger, Bradaford, Middlecott and Moor, all of the honour of Totnes, *Fees* p. 786.

639 Be it known that Lifton hundred is in the hands of earl Richard.
> A royal estate in the ninth century – Finberg, *Early Charters* no. 16 – Lifton came to be one of the manors traditionally bestowed on the queen as part of her dower, having been held by queen Edith before 1066, *DB* pp. 34–7, and by Matilda, wife of Henry I, and by Eleanor of Aquitaine afterwards, H. P. R. Finberg, *West-Country Historical Studies* (Newton Abbot 1969) pp. 91–2. *RH* p. 74. It was one of the properties which should have formed the dower of Richard I's queen Berengaria of Navarre – T. Rymer (ed.), *Foedera* Vol. I Part I (London 1816) pp. 102–103 – while in 1204 John conferred it on queen Isabella. By this time, however, Eleanor had given it to Amice de Cadigdene (*alias* Agatha de Gatesdene), formerly the fostermother to one of Eleanor's children, possibly John himself – Cheney, art. cit. no. 636 above, p. 760 – while John confirmed the grant in 1199, *Rot. Ch.* pp. 7–8; when John gave Lifton to Isabella it was on the understanding that Amice and her husband William were to hold it for life, with reversion to the queen afterwards, *Rot. Ch.* pp. 213–4. The issue was then complicated by Amice's giving or selling her rights in Lifton to Andrew de Cancellis, and by Henry III's nevertheless conferring it on Richard of Cornwall in 1228, *CCR 1227–31* p. 137, but a settlement was ultimately reached, for in 1242/43 Andrew was recorded as holding Lifton in free socage from earl Richard – *Fees* p. 757 – while he also acted in the king's courts on the earl's behalf during the latter's absence on crusade, *CRR* XVI nos. 1507, 2575. He was succeeded by his son and grandson in his possession of Lifton, which was valued at 40s. *per annum* in 1249 and 100s. in 1281/82, JUST/1/176 m38d, JUST/1/186 m18. On the latter occasion the special status the hundred had come to enjoy, with its own coroner and court sessions matching those of the County Court, was attributed to its tenure by Andrew de Cancellis.

LYDFORD BURGH ANSWERS BY TWELVE JURORS

640 The twelve jurors are in mercy for presenting before the justices a case which does not belong to the crown.

641 The jurors present that the merchants of Lydford used to be quit of tolls throughout all the king's lands, but now Roger de Valle Torta's men at 'Esshe' and Alan de Aldeswrthi's men at Holsworthy take tolls from them, so let this be discussed. And they present that the king's bailiffs at Lydford cannot have the revenues which they used to receive from strangers who were not resident in that vill, to allow them to be in their guild and liberty. And they present that a market was set up at

Okehampton, to the detriment of their market at Lydford, so let this be discussed.

Lydford was a royal burgh in 1086, *DB* pp. 4–5. In the years round 1200 its development was deliberately furthered by the crown, with its market being revived in 1195, Saunders art. cit. no. 637 above p. 127, a process which was taken so far that in 1208 Henry de la Pomeraie, doubtless nervous of the allure its burghal privileges might have for his own tenants, paid five marks "that the men of Lydford should not have a better liberty than the men of Exeter," *PR 9 John* p. 185. These words suggest that Lydford did have the same liberties as Exeter, which included freedom from tolls throughout the realm, G. Oliver, *The History of the City of Exeter* (Exeter 1861) pp. 279–80. Presumably merchants from elsewhere had been willing to pay for membership of Lydford's merchant guild so as to enjoy Lydford's toll exemptions, a privilege which ceased to be worth paying for when tolls were nevertheless levied in neighbouring towns – see S. Reynolds, *An Introduction to the History of English Medieval Towns* (Oxford 1977) pp. 82–3. Okehampton had had a market in 1086, *DB* pp. 378–81; the development complained of was probably associated with Robert de Courtenay's paying to have an annual fair there in 1221, E372/65 m5. Alan de Aldeswrthi had leased Holsworthy for ten years from Patrick de Chaorcis in 1237, and was probably anxious to make the maximum profit out of it, *CPR 1232–1247* p. 193.

(m 41)
OKEHAMPTON BURGH ANSWERS BY TWELVE JURORS

642 Be it known that Okehampton vill is in mercy for the flight of a man who killed another man in that vill, as they did not arrest him, as appears in Black Torrington's roll.

For this case see no 233 above.
Four burgesses and a market were recorded at Okehampton in 1086, *DB* pp. 378–381. The liberties of the burgesses were confirmed *in extenso* by Robert de Courtenay between 1218 and 1222 – S. Fraser, *Reports of the Proceedings before Select Committees of the House of Commons in Cases of Controverted Elections* Vol. I (London 1791) pp. 82–4 – that is, at about the same time as he paid five marks to have an annual fair there on the vigil and day of St. James the apostle, in 1221, E372/65 m5.

643 Of wines sold in breach of the assize, they say that Walter Side has sold wine contrary to the assize, so he is in mercy.

TAVISTOCK HUNDRED AND TAVISTOCK BURGH EACH ANSWER BY TWELVE JURORS

And be it known that they answer together as they could not reasonably answer separately

644 Nicholas Durant, charged with the death of Alice, wife of Ralph de la Wike, comes, denies all and puts himself on the country. The jurors testify that he is not guilty, so he is quit.

645 Thomas de Creubere fled to Tavistock church, where he admitted to theft and abjured the realm. Later he was arrested and imprisoned at Tavistock in the keeping of the tithing, from which he escaped, so it is in mercy. It is testified that Rannulf de Cerne, then sheriff, took 100s. for that escape. He had chattels worth 7s., Hurdwick tithing etc.

646 William de Crundel appealed Bartholomew de Middeltone and Master Richard de Warwik of the death of John Abbas de Tavistok. He

does not come, so he and his pledges, Roger de Burnintone and William de La Weie, are in mercy. Bartholomew and Richard come and are not suspected, so they are quit.

> Abbot John of Tavistock died during the period covered by this eyre, on 13 April 1233, but the Tavistock Annals which record this convey no hint that he died by violence – Bodl. Digby 81 f. 88v – so the name John Abbas is without much doubt a coincidence.

647 Warin Grille was found drowned in the river Tavy. No-one is suspected. No Englishry, so Murder fine, on the hundred.

648 Morwell vill is in mercy for not presenting in the County Court the case of the son of Augustine who drowned in a vat. Wimarc the cobbler's daughter, charged with his death, is not suspected, so she may return if she wishes.

649 William Marsille, on behalf of his mother Beatrice, appealed Roger Dwole, William de Maidenstane, William the baker and William Harevel of breach of the king's peace and felony. Later Beatrice prosecuted her own appeal against them, and she has died. Roger Dwole, William the baker and William Harevel come, and the jurors testify that they are not guilty, so they are quit. William de Maidenstane does not come, and he was not attached. The twelve jurors present that William appealed John Abbas de Tavistok of the same, but the coroners contradict them, so they are all in mercy.

650 Robert de Carselake killed Richard the clerk and fled, so let him be exacted and outlawed. No-one else is suspected. He was not in tithing as he was a free man. He had chattels worth four marks, Milton Abbot tithing etc, and annual rents worth 7s., Alice de Champeus, the lady of Leigh Barton, etc. Robert Kempe and Stephen de Cattebere, who were then present, are not suspected, so they are quit.

> Alice de Champeus was the daughter and heiress of William de Legh, one of Tavistock abbey's knights. That she brought Leigh Barton to her husband, Robert de Champeus, is shown by their jointly granting Leigh Barton chapel to Tavistock abbey, Finberg, *West-Country Historical Studies* p. 99.

651 Belengarius de Liddetone appealed John de Raddone, Augerus de la Wile, Walter the forester of La Lake and Margery de Liddetone of breach of the king's peace and wounding. He does not come, so he and his pledges, Joce de Brente and Roger Godfin, are in mercy. All the appellees except Walter the forester come, and the jurors testify that they have made an agreement, so they are all in mercy. Walter was attached by John de Dunneslande and John le Broc, so they are all in mercy. Later John came and made fine for 10s., pledge Adam de Braleghe. Later Augerus came and made fine for 6s. 8d., pledges Adam de Brayleghe and Maurus de Sidehame. Margery is poor.

652 Walter son of Thurstan fled to Tavistock church, where he admitted to homicide and abjured the realm. He had no chattels, as he was a vagrant thief.

653 Robert le Champiun, who was outlawed, was later arrested at Tavistock by Thomas de la Wyle, who did not know that he was outlawed and took pledges from him, Richard de Rogerstone, Walter and John de

Frankeberghe and Richard le Blund, who are in mercy for not producing him. Thomas made fine for this elsewhere.

654   Two of the servants of the abbot of Tavistock fought together. One struck the other, who fell, and then out of fear fled to church, but when he saw that the other was unhurt he came out of his own accord. Rannulf de Cerne, who was then sheriff, took 100s. from Tavistock vill because of this, so to judgment.

655   Robert de Sulhand, charged with theft, comes, denies all and puts himself on the country. The jurors testify that he is not guilty, so he is quit.

656   Of wines sold in breach of the assize, they say that Joel de Toritone and David son of La Bloie have sold wine contrary to the assize, so they are all in mercy.

657   The abbot of Tavistock holds the forinsec hundred of Tavistock by ancient tenure, that is, from before the conquest and after it, and he has no other warrant.

> Far from predating the Conquest, Tavistock hundred owed its existence to Henry I's charter of 1116, which separated it from Lifton hundred, *RRA-N* II no. 1131. In 1274/75 it was valued at one mark *per annum*, *RH* p. 81. The burgh of Tavistock also originated in a grant from Henry I, who in about 1105 granted the abbey a weekly market in Tavistock, and whose charter of 1116 added a yearly fair, to run from 29 to 31 August. There were burgage tenements in the town by 1185 and a burgh court by 1224, *Devonshire Studies* pp. 172–97.
> Burgh and hundred answered separately in 1244 and thereafter.

KENTON BURGH ANSWERS BY TWELVE JURORS

658   The jurors present that Kenton manor, with its appurtenances, was a royal manor, and earl Richard now holds it by the king's gift, and it is worth £60. The church of the manor, which also used to be in the king's gift, has now been appropriated (*perhendata est*) to Salisbury church by the king's gift.

> Only in 1238 was Kenton described as a burgh; in 1244 and 1249 it was listed as a vill in the kalendar and as a manor in the text, in 1281/82 as a vill in both kalendar and text. A royal manor in 1086 – *DB* pp. 36–7 – Kenton seems usually to have gone with Lifton as part of the queen's dower (see no. 639 above). In itself this probably conferred privileged status, which can only have been enhanced when in 1205 the men of Kenton were able, in return for a payment of 40 marks, to secure the right to hold their vill at farm from the crown for £60 *per annum*, *PR 6 John* p. 88. It was granted to Richard of Cornwall in 1228, *CCR 1227–1231* p. 137.
> The presentment of 1238 to the contrary, Salisbury's tenure of Kenton church was extremely ancient in its origins, going back to the days when there was only one bishop, at Sherborne, for the whole of the west of England, of whose endowment Kenton church formed part. Sherborne continued to hold it after the creation of the see of Crediton, and when the see of Sherborne became that of Sarum/Salisbury, the new bishopric retained this old endowment. Between 1238 and 1244, by an agreement between the bishop of Salisbury and the canons of Exeter, Kenton and West Alvington were transferred to the latter, Reichel in *TDA* 47 (1915) pp. 195–8. The canons did not, however, manage to keep their new possession for long, for it was presented at the 1281/82 eyre that Henry III had given it to earl Richard, JUST/1/186 m31d.

659   Walter de Vuerlande's house was burgled. Walter has died. William le Parmenter and William Leg were attached for the burglary by Richard le Paumer, Almerus the miller, Ralph the miller and other pledges who have died. They are in mercy for not producing them. The jurors testify

that they are not guilty of the burglary, so they are quit and may return if they wish.

660   Reginald Brun killed John le Franceis and was outlawed for the death at the suit of John's wife Gunilda. No-one else is suspected. He was in 'Wicke' tithing, which is in mercy, and had chattels worth 8d., the same tithing etc.

COLERIDGE HUNDRED ANSWERS BY TWELVE JURORS

661   Elias the parson of Charleton's servant was outlawed for the death of Robert Leg at the suit of Martin de Selbirne. He had no chattels. Martin the miller, charged with the same death, fled to Totnes church, where he admitted the death and abjured the realm. He was not in tithing as he was a vagrant, and he had no chattels. Peter de Chirletone, a clerk, charged with the same, comes, denies all and puts himself on the country. The jurors testify that he is not guilty, so he is quit.

662   William son of Nicholas de Fernhille appealed Warin son of William that on the Saturday next after the feast of St. James in the fourteenth year (27 July 1230) he came to him on the king's highway and struck him on the arm with a hatchet. And he appeals Stephen son of Athelard that at the same hour he struck him on the head with a hatchet. And that they did this evilly and in felony he offers to prove as the court shall decide. And he appealed Gervase Gysti, Paul de Abbedosle, William Horn, Iwanus son of Ascelo . . . de Whiteleghe, Edward de Vuingestone, Edward Turnepain and Gilbert de Vuingestone of aiding and abetting, and that they did this evilly etc. he offers to prove by his body. The appeal is null. Warin, Stephen and all the other appellees come and deny all. Later William de Pomerai came and made fine for William the appellor and for Warin and all the other appellees for 40s., pledges William and Richard Baustan.

(m 41d)
663   William de Altaribus and Nicholas Lighe were outlawed for the death of William son of Seilda de Cornewde at the suit of William's wife Cecilia, who comes and appeals Osbert David and Richard Hele of the same death. Osbert and Richard come, deny all and put themselves on the country. The jurors testify that they are not guilty, so they are quit, Cecilia is sent to gaol for a false appeal. William de Altaribus was in Harbourneford, Nicholas in Washbourne, tithing, so they are in mercy. William had no chattels, Nicholas had chattels worth 42d., Washbourne tithing etc.

664   Guy le Taliur fled to Harberton church, where he admitted to having killed a man in Somerset and abjured the realm. He was living in Ashprington, which is in mercy. Harberton vill is in mercy for not presenting this case in the County Court. He had no chattels.

665   Gilbert the miller was outlawed for the death of William the smith of Cornewrthe at the suit of his wife Helen. He was living in Dittisham, which is in mercy, and he had chattels worth 4s. 2d., the same tithing etc.

In another hundred he had one ox, which died before it could be valued. Value of the hide 18d., Alice de Punchardun etc.

666 Walter son of Hugh de Hellewelle was found dead in Dittisham quarry. No-one is suspected. No Englishry, so Murder fine.

667 Peter Hervy was outlawed for the death of Peter le Fair at the suit of Peter's brother Lawrence. He was in Fuge tithing, which is in mercy, and he had chattels worth 30d., the same tithing etc.

668 Robert Stake, who appealed David de Modbire of breach of the king's peace, does not come, so he and his pledges, Richard de Emerigge and Markerus de Stokes, are in mercy. David comes, and the jurors say that they have made no agreement, so he is quit.

669 David de la Forde, who appealed Thomas Wombe, who has died, of the death of Roger de Lukes, does not come, so he and his pledges, John son of Robert de Pikewille and John's father Reginald (*sic*), are in mercy.

670 William the miller killed William the baker and fled, so let him be exacted and outlawed. He was in Dartmouth tithing, which is in mercy, and he had chattels worth 2d., Dartmouth vill etc.

671 Roger the miller burnt his own house together with his wife and three children and fled, so let him be exacted and outlawed. He was in Dartmouth tithing, which is in mercy, and he had no chattels.

672 Robert Costard was crushed to death by an empty cask. Misadventure. Value of the cask 10d., the sheriff etc.

673 Of wines sold in breach of the assize they say that Adam Bobernot, Richard de la Sege, William Graveshevede and Adam de Riddesforde have sold wine contrary to the assize, so they are in mercy.

674 Richard Purdeu fell into the sea from a boat and drowned. Misadventure. Value of the boat 2s., the sheriff etc.

675 Robert Mirifel was crushed to death in his solar by a beam. Misadventure. Value of the beam 1½d., the sheriff etc.

676 Jordan de Praule and Robert Cobbe were outlawed for the death of Matthew son of Hugh at the suit of his brother Stephen. They were living in Herbert son of Matthew's tithing of Prawle, which is in mercy. Jordan had chattels worth 2s., the same tithing etc. Robert had no chattels.

677 Richard Kegh was arrested and imprisoned at Stokenham manor, but has now escaped. Walter de Bathon' the sheriff took 100s. from the manor for that escape. It is testified that he was not seised of anything when he was arrested, but he is suspected of thefts, so let him be exacted and outlawed.

For Stokenham manor see no. 682 below.

678 John de Widewille killed Semannus Codyer and fled, so let him be exacted and outlawed. He was in Stokenham tithing, which is in mercy, and he had no chattels.

679 Six casks of salted wine were washed up at Herbert's manor of Stokenham from a wreck at sea. They were worth 40s., Chillington tithing etc.

680 Richard Barun fell into the sea from a mare and drowned. Misadventure. Value of the mare 2s., the sheriff etc.

681 Peter le Poter was outlawed for the death of Luke de Cumbe at the suit of his wife Selena. He was in Dawlish tithing, which is in mercy, and he had chattels worth 40s., the same tithing etc. William David and Jordan de Carleghe, attached for the same, come and are not suspected, so they are quit.

682 Herbert son of Matthew holds this hundred, but shows no warrant as yet.
> Chillington was the original hundred-manor, held by the king in 1086 – *DB* pp. 46–49 – but given by Henry I to Roger de Nonant. Thereafter the meeting place for the Hundred Court was Coleridge, which gave its name to the hundred. Coleridge was, however, within the manor of Stokenham, and an inquest of 1309 described the hundred as belonging to that manor, which at an unrecorded date was given to one of the ancestors of Herbert son of Matthew, Reichel in *TDA* 43 (1911) pp. 201–205, *Devonshire Studies* pp. 253–5. In 1249 the hundred was valued at two marks *per annum*, JUST/1/176 m40.

TOTNES BURGH ANSWERS BY TWELVE JURORS

683 Thomas the chaplain of Aspringtone killed William Longus and fled, so let him be exacted and outlawed. He had chattels worth 32d., Totnes vill etc.
> It was said in 1305 that "the town of Totnes was a free borough from time beyond memory", *Cal. Inq. Misc.* I no. 1961. In legal terms, at least, this was true, since Totnes had a burgh court in the early eleventh century, while in 1086 there were 95 burgesses inside the burgh and 15 outside it, *English Medieval Boroughs* p. 99. An annual fair was granted in 1130, Hoskins, *Devon* p. 506.

684 Geoffrey Brevel de Totenes appealed Geoffrey de la Ya of breach of the king's peace and wounding, and of breaking a tooth and two ribs of his wife's. He comes and continues to make suit against him. The same appealed Nicholas de Duntestorre, Roger de Assewille and William de Wetecumbe of aiding and abetting him. Geoffrey does not come, and he was attached by William de Whitetone, Robert de Asshecumbe of Exminster hundred, Jordan le Yein and Richard Crespin of Stanborough hundred. It is testified that Geoffrey lies sick of fever (*infirmitate callida*). Nicholas and the other appellees come, and the jurors testify that they have made no agreement. But they say that Geoffrey wounded him and beat him badly, so that he almost died, so he is in mercy. Nicholas and the other appellees were present and thus badly beat him, so let them be taken into custody. Later Nicholas came and made fine for all the appellees for 20s., pledges Richard Crespin and Richard de Cumbe.

685 The jurors say that Nicholas de Ponte, Adam le Methyne, John Killebole, William de Fonte, Richard de Clautone, William Page, Geoffrey de la Stoke, Richard Umfrei, Robert de Clautone, Richard le

Cordewaner, Stephen Hag, Richard Infans and Robert the smith have sold wine contrary to the assize, so they are all in mercy.

HAYTOR HUNDRED ANSWERS BY TWELVE JURORS

686 Richard Galfridus and Elias le Archer were attached to come before the justices because they were with Adam de Bytorre when he died at sea. They do not come, so they and their pledges, Gilbert de Wodewis and Martin the reeve of Brayham for Richard, Hugh le Rus and Robert le Fag for Elias, are in mercy. No-one is suspected of the death.

687 Gilbert Godwin killed John de Torre and fled to Denbury church, where he abjured the realm. He was in Torbryan tithing, which is in mercy, and he had chattels worth one mark, Tor tithing etc. No-one else is suspected.

688 Jordan de Aubenon appealed Rannulf de Anbroke, Walter Bolle, John the miller and Elias le Carver of breach of the king's peace etc. He does not come, so he and his pledges, William de Spina and Walter de Vivario, are in mercy. Rannulf and all the other appellees come, and they have made no agreement, so the appellees are quit. Later Jordan came and made fine for himself and his pledges for one mark, pledges Robert de Wllewelle and James de Vado.

689 Richard de Hamptone and William de Coletone, who have died, appealed Peter de Mukwdes, Michael the man of William de Montana, Walter Pais and Roger Hererman of breach of the king's peace and mayhem. Peter and all the appellees come, and the jurors testify that they have made no agreement, so they are all quit.

(m 42)
690 An unknown pilgrim was found dead under Totnes cliff. No-one is suspected. No Englishry, so Murder fine.

691 John de Ipelpenne, attached for his ill fame (*pro malo retto*) by Gilbert de Ambrok, Roger le Prude, John de Bulleghe (dead), Elias de Wlneburg, Elias le Parmenter, Roger de Dornefelde, William de Forda, Roger son of Rawenilda, his brothers Geoffrey and Gilbert, Richard Snel and William Corne, does not come, so they are all in mercy. The jurors say that he is a lawful man, so he may return if he wishes.

692 Robert Blundus and Geoffrey le Fauchur were outlawed for the death of John the marshal at the suit of his brother Bartholomew. Robert was living in 'Bugkedeleghe', which is in mercy. Ipplepen vill is in mercy for not arresting them. Richard de Bugkedeleghe, Richard Marie and Roger le Havek, attached for the same, come and are not suspected, so they are all quit. Geoffrey le Fauchur was living in Ashburton tithing, which is in mercy. They had no chattels.

693 Michael de Ipelpenne fled to Denbury church, where he admitted to theft and abjured the realm. He was in Ipplepen tithing, which is in mercy, and he had no chattels.

694 Roger de Kente and Daniel, men of Henry le Daneis, who were attached on the appeal of Nicholas le Bate who has died, do not come. They were attached by Hugh de Bollay, Richard de Hundestorre and William le Daneis de Horleghe, so they are all in mercy.
>   Henry le Daneis was dead by February 1234, *Rot. Fin.* I p. 254. In 1242/43 his heirs were holding one fee in Coleton, in Brixham parish, of the bishop of Exeter, *Fees* p. 767.

695 Henry son of Alice killed William le Prute and was arrested by Tormoham tithing, but he escaped from them and fled to Tormoham church, where he abjured the realm, so let them answer for the escape and be in mercy. He was in Tormoham tithing, which is in mercy, and he had chattels worth 3s. 2d., the same tithing etc. No-one else is suspected.

696 William Gotham's house was burgled. The burglars left chattels worth 6d. behind them in their flight, the abbot of Sherborne's tithing of Kerswell etc.
>   Kerswell, or Abbotskerswell, was held in 1086 by Horton abbey, a small Benedictine house in Dorset annexed to Sherborne in the early twelfth century, Dugdale, *Monasticon* Vol. II pp. 511–512. In 1242/43 the abbot of Sherborne was described as holding Kerswell manor in free alms by the king's gift, *Fees* p. 769.

697 Gilbert the palmer died by falling from a horse. Misadventure. The horse likewise died the next day, value of its hide 6d., the sheriff etc.

698 Robert de Chete was found dead in the fields. The twelve jurors are in mercy for presenting no finder. No Englishry, so Murder fine.

699 Alice daughter of Walter was crushed to death by the roof (*tetricum*) of a house which fell on her. Value of the roof 6d., the sheriff etc.

700 A ship was broken up at Brixham, and all the sailors drowned. Five casks of wine were washed up there from the wreck at sea, and they were valued at five marks. Thomas de Cirnestre had three casks, worth three marks, and timber worth twelve shillings from the ship, so let him answer for them. Roger de Caddewrthi had one cask, worth one mark, and timber worth eight shillings, so let him answer for them, Guy de Bretteville and Robert de Virga are his pledges. And Kingskerswell tithing had one cask worth one mark, so let it answer for it. Let Brixham tithing answer for 6s. 8d. from an anchor and the abbot of Torre for 40d. from ship's ropes.
>   Torre abbey had properties at Upton and Kingswear, of which the latter used to be in Brixham parish, while the former still is, Seymour, *Torre Abbey* pp. 213–16, Thomas de Cirencestre held one fee in Woodhuish (also in Brixham parish) of the honour of Cardinan, *Fees* p. 769.

701 Rannulf de Duenebire, charged with theft, comes, denies all and puts himself on the country. The jurors testify that he is not guilty, so he is quit.

702 Philip, servant to Guy de Briane, appealed Martin de Fishacre and Gilbert de Tiuwe of breach of the king's peace etc. He does not come, and he was attached by Jordan de Asshebi and Ailot de Swarteberge, who are in mercy. Martin and Gilbert come, and the jurors testify that they have made no agreement, so they are quit. Later Philip came and made fine for himself and his pledges for one mark, pledges Jordan de Aissebi and Adam de Sewennestone.

703   Robert de Torkeshege, a canon of Torre, died by falling from a horse between Kerswell and Torre. Misadventure. Value of the horse 6s. 8d., the sheriff etc.

704   Nicholas de Stokes, Michael de Blakedone, Richard Rugge de La Penne and Germanus de Pristritone are suspected of theft, so let them all be exacted and outlawed. They were all in Paignton tithing, which is in mercy. Nicholas had chattels worth 18d., Michael 3s. and Richard 7s., the same tithing etc. Germanus had no chattels.

705   Four casks of salted wine were washed up at Paignton. They were valued at two marks, Paignton tithing etc.

706   Part of a mast was washed up at Goodrington. It was worth 3s., the same tithing etc.

707   Kerswell is a royal escheat. Nicholas de Molis holds it by the king's gift, together with Diptford manor and the advowson of the church, by the service of half a knight's fee. It is worth £20 with the hundred. It is testified that he has a charter for the manor but not for the hundred.

> Kerswell, or Kingskerswell, was the hundred-manor for Haytor, and was held by the king in 1086, *DB* pp. 18–19. Like Diptford (no. 596 above), it is recorded as having been granted successively to Earl Reginald, Henry fitz Count and Nicholas de Molis. In 1274/75, however, it was presented that the first lord of Kerswell after the Conquest had been John le Droun, who held it with the hundred by the service of a quarter of a knight's fee, and was succeeded by his son Hamelin de Draiford, who died without issue in Henry II's reign. Henry II then gave manor and hundred to Countess Denise, before John gave them to Henry fitz Count, *RH* pp. 71–72. Since earl Reginald, who held the manor in 1157, died in 1175, and Richard I (not John) gave it to Henry fitz Count in 1194, it is perfectly possible that Henry II gave the manor to Countess Denise – presumably the widow of Earl Richard of Devon who died in 1162 – in the interim. But John le Droun and his son remain mysterious figures; they may have held before Earl Reginald, or they may have been sub-tenants. In 1249 Haytor hundred was valued at 40s. *per annum*, JUST/1/176 m39d.

708   Ipplepen is an escheat from the Normans' lands. Almaricus de Sancto Amando holds it by the king's gift, and it is worth £30.

> The chief lords of Ipplepen manor before 1204 were certainly the important Breton family of de Fougeres, which held Ipplepen in 1086 – *DB* pp. 908–9 and later gave its church to Fougeres abbey, Oliver, *Monasticon* p. 300. A contract of marriage in 1189, however, between Waleran of Meulan and Margaret, daughter of Ralph de Fougeres, led to Ipplepen being temporarily made over to them, in earnest of the reversion of the manor of Bennington in Lincolnshire, then subject to a life tenancy – T. Stapleton (ed.), *Magni Rotuli Scaccarii Normanniae* Vol. II (London 1844) pp. cxcvii – cc – and this must account for the presentments subsequently made that it had been forfeited by one Ralph de Meulent – *Fees* p. 612, *RH* p. 72 – Ralph being probably a kinsman of Waleran, who was dead by then, and the subtenant of this portion of Margaret's dower. When the de Fougeres family forfeited their English lands in 1203, they were given at first to Rannulf of Chester in the right of his second wife Clementia, sister of Geoffrey lord of Fougeres, but his claim was only allowed with the qualification that these lands were "not of just right annexed to his honour" – F. M. Powicke, *The Loss of Normandy* (Manchester 1913) pp. 245 n. 1, 496 – and though Rannulf was confirmed in his possession of Ipplepen in 1221 – *Rot. Lit. Claus.* I p. 481 – by 1230 it had come into the hands of the king, who gave it to Nicholas de Lettres for his maintenance, *CCR 1227–1231* p. 439. Nicholas held in until his death, and in 1235 the king gave it to Almaricus de Sancto Amando, a courtier and man-of-affairs who by 1233 was one of the king's stewards – *CPR 1232–1247* p. 26 – to be held by hereditary right, *CCR 1234–1237* p. 134, *Fees* p. 1262.

709   Of defaults they say that the lord of Berry, Nicholas de Molis, Almaricus de Sancto Amando, the countess of Oxford, Guy de Brione, Nicholas de Blachedene, Hamelin de Daudune, Matthew de Clifdone,

Thomas de Cirnecestre, the abbot of Sherborne, William de Mohun and Torbryan, 'Cumbepunchard' and Loventor vills did not come on the first day etc.

> The lord of Berry was Henry de la Pomerai, whose barony took its name from Berry Pomeroy in this hundred; in 1238 he was an infant, Sanders, *Baronies* pp. 106–7. For Nicholas de Molis see no. 707 above.
> For Almaricus de Sancto Amando see no. 708 above. At the time of the eyre he was probably in Wales, *CPR 1232–1247* p. 235.
> The countess of Oxford held the manor of Brixham in dower, *Cornwall FF1* no. 64.
> Guy de Brione held one fee in Torbryan and Weston, *Fees* p. 768.
> Nicholas de Blachedene had land at Yalberton, JUST/1/175 mm20d, 32.
> Hamelin de Daudune took his name from his own manor of Dewdon (now lost), in the parish of Widdecombe in the Moor, Pole, *Collections*, p. 275.
> Matthew de Clifdone was found in 1238 to have been disseised of land in Natsworthy, JUST/1/174 m10d.
> Thomas de Cirnecestre held one fee in Woodhuish and a quarter of a fee in St. Mary Church, both of the honour of Cardinan, *Fees* pp. 767, 768.
> The abbot of Sherborne held the manor of Abbotskerswell, see no. 696 above.
> William de Mohun held the manor of Tormoham from his mother Alice de Mohun, and she from the earl of Devon, *Fees* p. 769. He defaulted again in 1244, JUST/1/175 m44d.
> The three vills must have defaulted by each failing to send four men and the reeve to the eyre.

710 William Palmer, charged with theft, comes, denies all and puts himself on the country. The jurors testify that he is not guilty, so he is quit.

TEIGNBRIDGE HUNDRED ANSWERS BY TWELVE JURORS

711 Gunilda daughter of Edward, who appealed Adam son of the smith of Cornewille of raping her, does not come, so she and her pledges, Martin de Teintone and Warin de Teintone, are in mercy. Adam comes, and he is not guilty, nor have they made an agreement, so he is quit.

712 A piece of metal was found at Tavy. Tavy tithing is in mercy for not presenting this case to the County Court. The jurors testify that nothing was found there which belonged to the king.

713 Richard de Bredeleghe, charged with stealing a horse, comes, denies all and puts himself on the country. The jurors testify that he is not guilty, so he is quit.

714 A man was found dead in the river Bovey. No-one is suspected. No Englishry, so Murder fine.

715 Joel Giffard, who appealed Richard de Hundetorre and his wife Emma of breach of the king's peace, comes but does not make suit against them, so he and his pledges, William Hagana and Osbert the reeve of Buketone, are in mercy. Richard and Emma come, and the jurors testify that they have made an agreement, so let them all be taken into custody. Later Joel came and made fine for himself and the appellees and his pledges for one mark, pledges Osbert de Creivetorre and Turgis de Hundetorre.

716 Hugh de Ludene, attached by Geoffrey Thethigmanne de Ludene and Alnothus de Ludene because he found a child of his drowned, does not come, so they are all in mercy.

Teignbridge

717   William the miller of Teing killed Osmund de Slade and fled, so let him be exacted and outlawed. He was in Canonteign tithing, which is in mercy, and he had chattels worth 4d., the same tithing etc.

718   Joel the miller made himself scarce for burning a grange and a mill of Roger de Farneswrthi. The jurors testify that he is guilty, so let him be exacted and outlawed. He was living in Manaton, which is in mercy, and he had no chattels.

719   Robert Barat, Eva de Traci's reeve, charged with theft, comes, denies all and puts himself on the country. The jurors testify that he is not guilty, so he is quit.

> Eva de Traci was the widow of Oliver de Tracy, who died in 1210, *PR 12 John* p. 59; Robert Barat was probably reeve of her manor of Bovey Tracy, for which she had obtained a weekly market in 1219, *PR 3 Henry III* p. 23.

(m 42d)
720   Theobald de Englescheville holds half of Teignbridge hundred at the king's pleasure. Richard Burdun, who holds the other half by ancient tenure, comes and says that he has a charter of king Henry the elder for the hundred, but he did not produce the charter in court.

> As this presentment suggests, Teignbridge came to have two hundred-manors, Highweek and Kingsteignton. Of these only the latter was mentioned in 1086 *DB* pp. 12–15 – when it was held by the king. There was a large royal estate at the mouth of the Teign – Hoskins, *Devon* p. 421 – doubtless administered at first from Kingsteignton alone; it looks as if another royal manor developed on the other, western, side of the estuary, from which the king's lands around it came to be administered, and that the two manors eventually became effectively independent of one another. The division between them was probably the line first of the Teign then of the Bovey; it may be significant that whereas Fludda, in Hennock parish east of the Bovey, owed suit to Kingsteignton – Seymour, *Torre Abbey* no. 70 – Ashburton, Manaton and Kendon, west of the Bovey, owed suit to Highweek, see no. 721 below. In 1274/75 Kingsteignton, with half the hundred, was said to have been given to Peter Burdun by Henry II, *RH* p. 81. For Highweek see no. 722 below. In 1249 the hundred was valued at 30s. *per annum*, JUST/1/176 m40d.

721   The jurors present that the men of the bishop's manor of Ashburton, the men of Manaton manor and the men of Kendon manor do not make suit to Teignbridge hundred as they used to do, so let this be discussed.

> Without much doubt this presentment is related to an action among the civil pleas brought by Theobald de Englescheville against Walter de Chiredon, Gervase de Maneton, Robert de Heliun and Jolanus de Bucheton for suits allegedly withdrawn from his hundred – Robert de Heliun claimed to have a tenant in Neadon, whose responsibility it was to make suit for him to the Hundred Court, Jolanus to have a tenement in Bickington, held of the bishop, for which he owed suit three times yearly only, JUST/1/174 m5. Gervase de Maneton may have been identical with the Gervase de Horthon who held half a fee in Manaton of the honour of Berry, *Fees* p. 791; Henry le Daneis had also had land in Manaton, which in 1238 was held by Rogo son of Simon, *Fees* p. 399, *Rot. Fin.* I. p. 254. Roger de Praulle held one fee in Kendon and 'Ernecumb' of the honour of Berry, *Fees* p. 792. Ashburton was an episcopal manor by the early eleventh century, *EHD* I p. 536.
> This presentment came within the cognisance of the eyre because in 1238 Theobald only held Highweek during pleasure; had he held by hereditary right the justices would probably have penalised the jurors for presenting something of no concern to the crown (cf. no. 161 above) – during the civil plea referred to above, the defendants successfully pleaded that they need not answer to Theobald because the hundred was not his, only to be told that "because this plea touches the king, and Theobald can claim nothing for that suit save in the king's name, as the hundred is the king's, it is decided that they should answer to the king for the same suit".

722   Highweek is a royal escheat. Theobald de Englescheville holds it, and it is worth £8.

Early in his reign Henry II confirmed Highweek to "Luke my butler . . . as freely as ever his ancestors held in the time of king Henry my grandfather", Queens 152 f. 162v. Luke's grandson, Luke son of John, forfeited as a Norman in 1204 – *Rot. Norm.* p. 130 – but his wife Eustachia de Curtenay was allowed to hold his Devon lands for £15 *per annum, Rot. Lit. Claus.* I pp. 5, 29, 352, and even after Henry de Ponte Audomar was granted Luke's lands in Diptford, Highweek and Oburnford (see nos. 166, 598 above) for his maintenance in 1221, Eustachia continued to receive 100s. *per annum* from Highweek, *Rot. Lit. Claus.* I p. 472, *Rot. Fin.* I pp. 268–9. In 1230 Highweek was granted to Theobald de Englescheville for his maintenance during pleasure, *CCR 1227–1231* p. 345, and his tenure was made hereditary in 1247, *CChR 1226–1257* p. 322. Subsequently, however, Theobald gave it to Robert Bussell, "my kinsman and foster-son" – Queens 152 f. 162 – whose son Theobald held it in 1281/82, *PQW* p. 165. See also nos. 720, 721 above.

ASHBURTON BURGH ANSWERS BY TWELVE JURORS

723 William Alisandre killed William le Mazacrer and fled, so let him be exacted and outlawed. He was living in Ashburton, which is in mercy for not producing him. He had chattels worth 4d., the same vill etc.

Ashburton, which was held by the bishop of Exeter, acquired a market during the twelfth century, *English Medieval Boroughs* p. 86.

724 A woman was drowned in a vat full of broth. Misadventure. Value of the vat 2s., the sheriff etc.

725 A piglet killed a child. Misadventure. Value of the piglet 3d., the sheriff etc.

726 The jurors present that Joel Kide, Walter le Chapman and John Barat have sold wine contrary to the assize in Ashburton vill, so they are in mercy.

EXMINSTER HUNDRED ANSWERS BY TWELVE JURORS

727 Godrey Calliow, one of the twelve jurors, is in mercy because he did not come with his fellows to answer for their *veredictum*.

728 Roger Iuvenis was outlawed for the death of Swein de Mannhevid at the suit of Swein's wife Edith. He was in Mamhead tithing, which is in mercy, and he had chattels worth 16s., the same tithing etc.

729 Beatrice daughter of William de Muliwhis appealed Peter son of Robert de Exon' of breach of the king's peace and beating her. Peter comes and denies all. The jurors testify that Peter beat her badly and is guilty, so he is in mercy, let him be taken into custody. Later Peter came and made fine for 6s. 8d., pledge William de la Briuwerre. Beatrice is poor.

730 Roger Spileman was arrested for theft and imprisoned at Dawlish, but he escaped and fled to Dawlish church, where he admitted to homicide and abjured the realm. So Dawlish is in mercy. Roger was previously arrested because of his ill fame and released to pledges, namely Robert son of William de Cumbe, William de Nortone, Roger Spileman, Roger's father, William le White and Robert de la Heie de Nortone, who

are in mercy for not producing him. He had chattels worth 6d., Dawlish tithing etc.

731 Two unknown thieves fled to Teignmouth church, where they abjured the realm for theft. Cofton of Dawlish tithing is in mercy for not pursuing them.

732 Adam Algar, who was attached by Adam le Ware and Robert Pecun, does not come, so they are all in mercy.

733 The yard-arm of a ship was washed up below Dawlish vill from a wreck at sea. It was worth 2s., Dawlish tithing etc.

734 Adam Colle was killed by a mast which was washed into his boat (*qui applicuit in quodam batello*) at Teignmouth. No-one is suspected. Misadventure. Value of the mast 6d., the sheriff etc.

735 A cask of salted wine was washed up at Holcombe from a wreck at sea. It was worth 5s., Holcombe tithing etc.

736 An unknown man was found drowned in the sea at Dawlish. Dawlish tithing, which presented to the County Court that he was found on the sea shore, is in mercy for a false presentment.

737 Six men fell from a boat and drowned in Teignmouth harbour. Misadventure. Value of the boat 6s. 8d., the sheriff etc.

738 Peter Cunand, who appealed Hugh de Rileghe, Geoffrey of the same, Geoffrey's son Walter, Bernard de Craccumbe, Roger de Whetistanne, Roger Grivel, John son of Richard de Hewis, Robert de Bodetorre, Robert de Boudone and Stephen brother of Robert de Bodetorr of breach of the king's peace, comes, but he does not make suit against them, so he and his pledges, William Cunand and Peter de Morleghe Peverel, are in mercy. Hugh and all the appellees come, except for Geoffrey de Rileghe, Bernard, Roger de Whetistanne and Roger Grivel. The jurors testify that they have made an agreement, so let them all be taken into custody. Geoffrey de Rileghe was attached by Nicholas de Cresme and John de Hewis, who are in mercy. Bernard, Roger and Roger were not found, so nothing of them. Later Robert de Bodetorre, Robert de Boudone, Stephen de Bodetorre and John son of Richard de Hewis came and made fine for one mark, pledge William de la Pomerai. Peter the appellor is poor. Later Hugh and Walter de Rileghe came and made fine for 10s., pledge Richard de Treminet.

739 The jurors are in mercy for a foolish presentment concerning the prior of St. James and John de Midwinter, and for several trespasses.

740 Walter le Franceis was outlawed by the appeal of Richard de Morkishille because he maimed him. He was in the mainpast of the prior of St. James, who is in mercy.

741 Adam Lithe's son was found dead. No-one is suspected. No Englishry, so Murder fine. Kenn tithing is in mercy for trying to present Englishry falsely.

742   John de la Holeweie and Philip de la Yate, charged with harbouring thieves, come, deny all and put themselves on the country. The jurors testify that they are not guilty, so they are quit.

743   From Richard le Hordere, charged with associating with John de la Berghe, who comes and puts himself on the country, as fine for having an inquest, twenty marks, pledges the twelve jurors of Exminster.

> Richard le Hordere paid £10. 4s. of his fine in 1240 and the rest in 1241. In 1244 he was serjeant of Exminster hundred, JUST/1/175 m35. For John de la Berghe see no. 35 above.

744   William Spileman was outlawed for the death of Baldwin Wikoc at the suit of Baldwin's wife Avice. He was in Kenton tithing, which is in mercy, and he had no chattels.

745   John de la Berghe, an approver hanged at London, had chattels worth 16s. 4d., the sheriff etc. The jurors testify that John de Holeweie owed him 33s., as he admitted before the sheriff, so let him answer for them. The sheriff testifies that he admitted owing him 30s., so let him answer for 30s.

746   Agnes Pigoc, charged with harbouring the same John, comes, denies all and puts herself on the country. The jurors testify that she is guilty, so she is hanged. She had chattels worth 10s., William Travers and William Hog etc.

747   Walter de Bouhille accidently struck himself on the shin with an axe, so that he died. Value of the axe 4d., the sheriff etc.

748   Reginald le Smale, charged with harbouring John, comes, denies all and puts himself on the country. The jurors testify that he is not guilty, so he is quit.

749   William de Dunsidiok and his son Nicholas, hanged on the appeal of one Dureman, an approver, had chattels worth 18s. 4d., which William de Haies, bailiff of Nicholas de Molis took. Let his lord answer for them now.

> It is not clear from this entry whether Nicholas de Molis's bailiff was acting for him in an official capacity. Nicholas is not recorded as owning property in Exminster hundred, but his ancestor Roger de Molis had held the manor of Teign George in 1086, and though by 1238 this had passed to Gerard de Spineto, it is possible that Nicholas had retained some part of it, Reichel in *TDA* 47 (1915) p. 224.

750   William le Turnur, schepman of Shorhame, arrested by Robert de la Slade on suspicion of theft, comes. And as he was not in possession of stolen goods, nor can it be established that he is suspected of anything, as he is a stranger, he is quit.

751   Adam Lida, charged with the death of Osbert Bidel de Hunetone, comes, denies all and puts himself on the country. The jurors testify that he is not guilty, so he is quit.

> Nothing was said about the tenure of Exminster hundred during the eyre, doubtless because its lord, Earl Baldwin, was a minor and so unable to show his warrant. A royal estate in the late ninth century – Finberg, *Early Charters* no. 16 – it was still held by the king in 1086, *DB* pp. 6–7. In 1178, however, it was recorded among the demesnes of Earl Richard of Devon – *PR 24 Henry II* p. 18 – having probably, like so many other hundred-manors in Devon, been given to his grandfather, Richard de Redvers, by Henry I. In 1249 the hundred was valued at two marks *per annum*, JUST/1/176 m41.

(m 43)
CROWN PLEAS OF EXETER CITY

752   From Exeter city, fine before judgment, and for drapers, vintners and measures, £100.

> Exeter, which had a burgh court by the early eleventh century – *English Medieval Boroughs* p. 91 – had by 1238 long been the centre of the county's administration and its ecclesiastical life. Henry II's charter, issued before 1161, acknowledged that the citizens enjoyed the customs of London, presumably those recorded in his own charter of 1155 for the latter city, *EHD II* pp. 946–947; no more than in London did these include the right to hold the city at fee-farm, which was not obtained until 1259, and then only temporarily, *CChR 1257–1300* pp. 24–5. Exeter remained under immediate royal control until December 1228, when Henry III granted it to Richard of Cornwall for his maintenance, *CCR 1227–1231* p. 137. On 5 July 1238 the king ordered that the issues of this eyre from Exeter, Kenton and Lifton hundred be paid directly to earl Richard – *CCR 1237–1242* p. 70 – so the £100 fine was not accounted for at the exchequer. For Exeter's charters see G. Oliver, *The History of the City of Exeter* (Exeter 1861) pp. 279–80.

753   From Beatrice, wife of John Richeman de Exon', for having a jury, 65 marks, pledges Roger son of Henry, John Turberne, Walter la Chowe, Martin Rof, Adam de Rifforde, Walter de Moltone, John de Okestone, Richard Walrande, Philip le Paumer, Walter le Granger, William Boschet, Roger Belebuche and John Hamelin.

754   From Theophania, widow of Lawrence le Taillur, for the same, 20 marks, pledges Sampson Piper, Martin Rof, John Turberne, William Boschet, Baldricus Chil, John Strange, William Busse and Richard Strange.

755   Beatrice, wife of John Richeman, and her maid Edelota, charged with killing an unknown man, come and put themselves on the verdict of the twenty four jurors of Exeter city for good and ill. They say on their oath that they are not guilty, so they are quit.

756   Theophania, Lawrence's widow, charged with the death of Lawrence her husband, comes and puts herself on the verdict of the twenty four jurors for good and ill. They say on oath that she is not guilty, so she is quit.

757   One Nicholas, an unknown tailor, fled to St. Peter's church in Exeter, where he admitted to theft and abjured the realm. He had no chattels, it is not known where he came from.

758   Nicholas de la Penne was drowned while trying to cross the river Exe. His father Ralph, who was then with him, is not suspected, nor is anyone else. Misadventure. The twenty four jurors presented no finder, so to judgment on them.

759   Ralph de Cruke, a stranger, fled to the church of St. Sidefulle, where he admitted to being a thief and abjured the realm. He had no chattels. It was testified that he was living in Crewkerne vill in Somerset, so inquire about him in that county.

760   William de Caditreu, charged with receiving goods burgled from Sir Roger de Acastre by criminals in Dorset, comes, denies burglary and puts himself on the verdict of the twenty four jurors for good and ill. They say on oath that he is not guilty, so he is quit.

761 Gervase Viel, who appealed Richard de Liftone of premeditated assault, came and withdrew, so let him be taken into custody. His pledges have died, so nothing from them. It was testified that they have made an agreement, so they are both in mercy. Richard de Liftone made fine for one mark, pledges William Busse and John de Okestone. Gervase has nothing.

762 Robert le Pestur, wishing to bathe in the river Exe, was accidentally drowned. Sabina his wife, who first found him, has died. Later it was established that he voluntarily drowned himself. Felony *de se*. He had no chattels.

763 Two unknown women named Idonea and Isabella, charged with the theft of two gowns, fled to St. Edmund's church on the bridge over the Exe, where they admitted to theft and abjured the realm. They had no chattels, it is not known where they came from.

764 A stranger named Robert fled to St. John's church, where he admitted to having stolen a gown and a linen sheet and abjured the realm. He had no chattels, nor is it known who he was.

765 Alice daughter of Bela, an eighteen-month-old child, was crushed to death by a cart which Ralph the carter took through Exeter vill. Ralph, arrested for the death, comes, denies all and puts himself on the jurors, who say that he is not guilty of the death, so he is quit. No-one is suspected. Misadventure. Value of the cart and of the horse which drew it, 5s. 3d., W. the sheriff etc.

766 Philip le Furbur, a vagrant, fled to St. Peter's church in Exeter, where he admitted to having stolen a tunic and abjured the realm. He had no chattels.

767 Richard Sulke was crushed by a mill wheel outside the western gate of Exeter as he tried to oil its cogs, so that he died. Henry Croppe the miller, who was then with him in the mill, at once fled to the church of the Blessed Mary inside the western gate, and out of fear stayed there. And as he would not leave, the bailiffs at length made him abjure the realm. The twenty four jurors say on oath that they do not suspect him of that death or anything else. Misadventure. Value of the wheel 8d., the sheriff etc. Since the bailiffs of Exeter made him abjure the realm when he was not guilty of the death, to judgment on the city. Speak with the king, that Henry may have the grace of returning.

> No record has survived of Henry Croppe's receiving a pardon, though gaps in the close and patent rolls at this time make it impossible to say with certainty that none was issued.

768 William de Wodeham complained to the bailiffs of Exeter that his servant, Roger Peche, had taken forty shillings worth of his goods, which were in his custody, and he found pledges for his prosecuting him before the justices. William and Roger now come, but he does not make suit, so he and his pledges are in mercy. His pledges have died. Roger Peche, charged with taking those goods, comes, denies all and puts himself on the verdict of the twenty four jurors for good and ill. They say on oath that he is not guilty, so he is quit.

Exeter City 123

Since both William de Wodeham's pledges were dead by 1238, this action is not likely to have been only recently begun, and it suggests that Exeter city court had a status comparable to that of the County Court for individuals initiating cases to be prosecuted before justices itinerant thereafter.

769   John Home, servant to the Priory of St. Nicholas at Exeter, fell by accident into a vessel full of boiling broth, so that he died. No-one is suspected. Misadventure. Value of the vessel 3d., the sheriff etc.

770   Richard the cobbler of Exon' fled to St. Michael's church at Heavitree, where he admitted to theft and abjured the realm. He had chattels worth 5d., John Bretesche etc. Let him also answer for 3d., from the chattels of John the Cornishman and his son Peter, who abjured the realm for the death of Reginald le Cunte.

Heavitree was in Wonford hundred, so John Bretesche would have answered on behalf of Baldwin de Redvers, that hundred's lord – see no. 518 above.

771   Roger de Eynesham, Robert de Bradwede, Geoffrey de Dunesforde, Thomas Capun from Wiltshire, William Russel, Anthony de Bere, William Ernis from Gloucestershire, Roger son of Andrew the chaplain and Nicholas le Taillor de Boctone, all vagrant thieves, fled to various churches in Exeter, where they admitted to various thefts and abjured the realm. They had no chattels.

772   From Martin Rof, as fine for trespass, four marks.

773   Richard Walerande appeals William de Gatepathe that on the Friday next before Ash Wednesday this year (12 February 1238) he came to his house in Exeter and, in breach of the king's peace, broke a door of the house and entered it. And he barred three doors in that house, and later broke through a wall and entered the solar, where he stayed. Asked if he was then in the house, he says he was not, as he was at mass in St. Nicholas's church, but as soon as he heard of this he came to the bailiffs of the city and showed them that William had entered his house. And that he did this in felony and in breach of the king's peace he offers to prove as the court shall decide, according to the law and custom of the city of Exeter. William comes and asks to be allowed that in his appeal Richard mentioned no robbery, nor does he show wounds. And as Richard does not show that any robbery was committed, and as he shows no wounds, nor has he made suit in proper form, it is decided that his appeal is null. So let Richard be taken into custody, William is quit of the appeal. Later Richard came and made fine for 20s., pledges Peter de Culumstoke and Paulinus le Ireys.

This appeal, and that in no. 774 below, must have been related to the action of novel disseisin which in 1238 William de Gatepathe brought against Richard Walerande and two others for a messuage in Exeter, an action which went against William, JUST/1/174 m43d. At around this time Richard gave to the twenty-four vicars serving Exeter Cathedral a rent of 12d. "in the High Street of Exeter in the eastern part called Wollardislane", BL Add. MS. 52779, and he also had property in All Saints' parish, BL Vit. D. IX f. 79v.

774   The same William de Gatespathe, who is in mercy for a false appeal against the aforesaid Richard, made fine for two marks, pledges John de Babecumbe and William de Gatepathe the sergeant.

775 Baldwin de Raddone appeals Walter la Chowe that, as he, with his wife and household, passed by Walter's home on their way towards Raddon on Monday in Easter week in the fifteenth year (24 March 1231), in breach of the king's peace and in felony he arrested him, imprisoned him in his house and in robbery took from him his palfrey, worth five marks, his sword worth two shillings and his belt and knife worth 12d., and moreover he took his wife and put her in fetters. And that he did this evilly and in felony and in breach of the king's peace, he offers etc. Walter comes, denies arrest, imprisonment, robbery and all etc., and says that because of a trespass which Baldwin did to him that same day, namely for a wound on the head which he gave him, so that he was in danger of death, Baldwin was arrested while fleeing by the hue and cry of the city and taken back to Walter's house until it could be known whether Walter could recover from the wound. And that Baldwin was never arrested by him, nor imprisoned, nor his wife put in fetters, and that he did him no robbery, as he said, he puts himself on the verdict of the twenty four jurors. And they say on oath that Walter neither imprisoned Baldwin nor took his palfrey, sword, belt or knife, as was said. So it is decided that Walter be quit of that appeal, and let Baldwin be taken into custody.

> On 2 April 1231 the sheriff was ordered to go to Walter la Chawe, then mayor of Exeter, allegedly wounded by Baldwin de Raddon, and find out his condition; if Walter was in danger of death Baldwin, who had been previously arrested by the citizens, should be kept in prison, but if he was not then Baldwin could be released to pledges, *CCR 1227–1231* pp. 486, 487–8. During the 1238 eyre Baldwin acknowledged before the justices that he had given Walter all his land in Pennicott (near West Raddon), with the meadow and grove of Pennicott and 1½ ferlings in Upper Pennicott, JUST/1/174 m22d. This could have been the cause of the quarrel, but is just as likely to represent its settlement.

776 Walter la Chowe appealed Baldwin de Raddone that, as he was in the king's peace in his home in Exeter on Monday in Easter week in the aforesaid year, Baldwin came before the door of his house and called to him to come and speak with him. And as he went peacefully to the door of his house, Baldwin with his sword gave him a wound on the head six inches long. And that he did this evilly and in felony and in breach of the king's peace, he offers to prove as a man over age and according to the custom and law of Exeter. And Baldwin comes and gives five marks to have respite, pledges Ralph le Rus, William de la Pumeray and Richard Bazan. Later both came and put themselves in the king's mercy, so let them be taken into custody. Later they came and made fine for 10s., pledges Michael Pollarde and Gervase Tripling.

APPENDIX I: VEREDICTA FOR AXMOUTH AND TIVERTON HUNDREDS

The numbers in brackets are those of the equivalent entries among the crown pleas.

(a) *JUST/1/1593* This is the *veredictum* for Axmouth Prioris hundred of crown pleas since the departure of the justices last itinerant.

1 (39)   Burglars came to the house of Roger de Wathkumbe on the land of 'Dune Sibille', broke the door, bound him and Susan his wife, burgled the house of everything found in it and left. After their departure the hue was raised on the burglars, and the neighbourhood came but found no traces. This happened on the night before the feast of the Circumcision (31 December) and was presented at the next County Court. R. and his wife found pledges to be before the justices, Robert Ailric and Walter Surreva.

2 (40)   A fight began between two men, William Hurnewai de Kuliforde and Richard Curlepais, on the king's highway, and William struck Richard on the head, so that he died eight days later. He called the neighbours together and imputed his death to Richard (sic), and William the criminal fled and was never afterwards seen. This was presented at the next County Court and an appeal was made on it by the deceased's wife Christina. He was viewed by the coroner.

3 (41)   A tun with a little salted wine in it came to land in Axmouth harbour after a storm. It was viewed by the coroner and bailiffs and valued at 3s., the prior etc. Adam del Havene was first finder.

4 (42)   Peter de Bolonge, a servant of the prior's, was killed by a man from Axmouth called Robert de Bendone, who hid him in the sand. This happened one Saturday, in the prior's wood, and as he did not return home he was looked for through the whole hundred till the following Thursday, when he was found on the sea-shore by an Axmouth woman named Joan, with the whole hundred nearby. He was viewed by the coroner. Meanwhile Robert fled with all the goods he had except for a little grain worth 2s. The fugitive was appealed by the dead man's brother Robert and outlawed in the County Court. Philip de Bendone, the fugitive's lord, should answer for the value of the corn as he was then the bailiff of the hundred.

5 (43)   A youth named Philip de Witeforde came by night to the home of Walter the chaplain of Cumba, and a quarrel started between them, so that the priest wounded Philip with a knife, about which an appeal was made in the County Court. Of the priest's chattels a little grain was found, valued by the coroner and bailiffs at 4s., Philip de Cumbe and Henry de Clanemer etc.

6 (44)   A youth from the neighbourhood of Andover, so he said, came to Osbert Hose's house and stole shirts and breeches. When Osbert saw this he ran after him, and when he saw this he fled to Axmouth church, where he was guarded until the coroner came. He acknowledged that theft and other things and abjured the king's land.

7 (45)   Four men from Seaton in Colyton hundred were drowned in the sea outside Axmouth harbour, and three of them and a boat came to land at Axmouth in a great storm. They were viewed by the coroners, who handed them over to the people of Seaton. The boat was valued at 3s. 6d.

8 (46)   William le Flemec does not come before the king's justices, but they believe him to be essoined.

9 (47)   The men of Sidbury pursued four thieves to the home of Nigel de Done, stolen goods and criminals were found there, and judgment was done on them. The said Nigel, because he was father to one of the criminals and because stolen goods and thieves were found in his home, was imprisoned and his wife and two daughters put to pledges. Later Nigel, his wife and the pledges died, but the daughters live and will appear, so they say.

(b) *JUST/1/1591 Veredictum* of Tiverton hundred

1 (130)   ... nedone: Robert de la Hokedris was found drowned in the river Otter with his horse, his sons Gilbert and William first found him.

2   Uplowman: Alice daughter of Goscelin de Lumene was found dead on Loman moor, ... found her.

3   Chettiscombe: the house of Richard de Gyrifenna, who has died, was burgled, and the hue was raised.

4   A great stone was overturned and a ditch made in the great road which runs from Tiverton to Bampton.

5   Coombe and Murley: the hue was raised at Coombe because of a fight between Alan de Banlinch and Geoffrey Copia.

6 (131)   Craze Loman: Adam son of William de Luccumbe and Roger son of William Sturra played together. Adam struck Roger with his fits as he ran towards him, so that Roger fell into a coma. Later he rose, went to water, drank, and died instantly.

7 (132)   West Exe: Alice, widow of Peter de Kalewdeleghe, appealed Miles de Kalewodeleghe.

8 (133)   Rose, the same Alice's tenant, appealed the same Miles.

9   The hue was raised because of a fight between Ralph de Doddelescumbe's men and Robert de Cheor ... hille and his wife over a ...

10 (134)   Tiverton manor: Wimarc, wife of Algar de Cimiterio, set out on a pilgrimage, fell from the mare she rode, and died at once.

11   Nicholas son of Algar was found drowned in the river Exe. Algar first found him.

12 (135)   William the chaplain of Tuvertone was found drowned in the river Exe below Tiverton mill. Edward Leg first found him.

13 (136)   Nicholas Truve killed Claricia mother of Roger Viel. Roger appealed Nicholas and prosecuted the same until he was outlawed.

14 (137)   Gilbert le Batur killed Michael son of Hugh de Binewulle.

15   The house of the lepers of Tiverton was burgled.

16   The house of William Hals de Tidecumbe in the same way.

17   Walrand son of Walter Longus de Bollehame was found drowned in the river Exe. Walter his father first found him.

18   A hue was raised, coming from Cadeleigh towards Tiverton manor and followed to Sellake in Halberton hundred.

19   William de Orweya appealed John Lanceleve.

20 (138)   Wine was sold contrary to the assize at Tiverton.

21 (139)   Robert Scurel was arrested in Tiverton hundred, taken to the County Court and delivered to the gaol.

22 (140)   Henry Seward, Robert son of Matilda Ruche, Beatrice sister of Boillard and Clarica de Witheleghe were drowned in the river Exe.

Notes

Nos. 2 and 5 show that in 1238 Uplowman parish was in Tiverton hundred, though it later became part of Halberton hundred – PND pp. 552–3. No. 15 appears to be the only reference to a leper hospital at Tiverton – it is not mentioned in the early fourteenth century list in bishop Bitton's will: W. H. Hale and H. T. Ellacombe (eds.), *Account . . . of the Executors of Thomas Bishop of Exeter*, Camden Society, New Series Vol. X (1874) p. 28.

APPENDIX II: ARTICLES OF THE EYRE AND OF THE TOURN

(a) ARTICLES OF THE EYRE

No full list of the articles used at the 1238 Devon eyre has survived, that at the foot of the Tiverton *veredictum* being both incomplete and partly illegible. It is used here, but what follows is essentially a fairly free rendering of the articles as listed in two *veredicta* surviving from the 1236 Shropshire eyre – JUST/1/1589 and JUST/1/1599. In both of these the articles are transcribed in abbreviated form; they are therefore filled out where necessary by reference to the lists in H.Cam, *Studies in the Hundred Rolls* (Oxford 1921), Appendix II pp. 92–5, and *Surrey Eyre 1235* pp. 91–4.

1. Of old crown pleas not yet concluded
2. Of new crown pleas arising since the previous eyre
3. Of those who are in the king's mercy and have not been amerced
4. Of minors and maidens who are or should be in the king's custody
5. Of ladies who are or should be in the king's custody
6. Of churches which are or should be in the king's gift
7. Of the king's escheats, what they are and who holds them
8. Of the king's serjeanties, what they are and who holds them
9. Of purprestures (encroachments) made on the king
10. Of those who have taken money from people harbouring strangers in breach of the assize (of the watch, 1233)
11. Of measures, and infringements of the ordinances relating to them
12. Of wine sold in breach of the assize
13. Of treasure trove
14. Of officials who have held pleas of the crown, and what pleas
15. Of officials who have summoned hundred courts to hold inquests and amerced those not answering the summons
16. Of Christian usurers
17. Of the chattels of Frenchmen, Flemings and others of the king's enemies
18. Of the chattels of Jews killed
19. Of forgers and clippers of coins
20. Of mints or exchanges of currency held without licence
21. Of burglars and criminals
22. Of outlaws and fugitives returning without licence
23. Of those over whose lands outlaws have passed without pursuing them
24. Of markets moved from one day to another
25. Of bribes taken that victuals be not commandeered to munition castles
26. Of new customs
27. Of defaults by those summoned to come before the justices on the first day of the eyre and not appearing
28. Of gaols delivered without licence
29. Of poachers in parks and fishponds
30. Of losses caused to, and goods commandeered from, foreigners
31. Of those who do not allow the king's bailiffs to enter their lands to make summonses and distraints
32. Of escaped thieves

33 Of wrecks at sea
34 Of bailiffs who have taken money to remove recognitors (jurors) from assizes

(b) ARTICLES OF THE TOURN
DRO TD42 (Otterton Cartulary, compiled in 1260) f. 72:

These are the articles over which the sheriff has authority by virtue of his office at his tourn once every year:

1 Of old and new pleas of the crown
2 Of the advowson of churches which are or should be in the king's gift
3 Of minors, ladies and girls who are in the king's gift
4 Of purprestures made on the king
5 Of wrecks at sea
6 Of escaped thieves
7 Of hues raised
8 Of men imprisoned, and how they were delivered
9 Of outlaws, if they have returned and those harbouring them
10 Of burglars and those harbouring them
11 Of treasure trove
12 Of those who are not in a tithing and should be
13 Of those who put others out of a tithing without judgment
14 Of wine sold in breach of the assize
15 Of paths obstructed to the detriment of the countryside
16 Of those who resell (*regratoribus*) fish and other things, whereby the countryside is injured.
17 Of hundred bailiffs who hold pleas which do not belong to them
18 Of those who take protection money (*advocaciones*) from others besides their villeins
19 Of poachers in parks and fishponds
20 Of Christian usurers alive or dead, and who have their chattels
21 Of those who having lands worth £15 should be knights and are not
22 Of purveyances made unjustly on others and by whom
23 If all came to the sheriff's tourn as they are wont
24 Of burel worked into grey cloth (*de burlla apposita in grisanco*)
25 Of those who made themselves scarce from the king's justices and later returned, and who harboured them
26 Of those who hold pleas of vee de naam
27 Of broken boundaries and diverted watercourses
28 Of measures of all sorts
29 Of distraints recovered from the king's bailiffs
30 Of the king's watches, how they are kept
31 Of the sheriff's aid in this hundred

APPENDIX III: STATISTICS OF CRIME FROM DEVON EYRES

1238	A	B	C	D	E	F	G	H	I	J
East of Exe	43	9	33	2	2	12	10	9	10	17
North of Cornish Road	47	1	42	4	5	16	14	6	5	10
South of Cornish Road	58	2	43	9	2	17	9	4	9	19
Exeter	3	1		1		3		16		1
Totals	151	13	118	16	9	48	33	35	24	47

1244	A	B	C	D	E	F	G	H	I	J
East of Exe	32	10	22	2		11	3	2	1	12
North of Cornish Road	22	1	12	4	1	9	15	5	9	38
South of Cornish Road	23		22	4	1	18	9	2	5	17
Exeter	3		2			4	1	3	1	
Totals	80	11	56	12	2	42	28	12	16	67

1249	A	B	C	D	E	F	G	H	I	J
East of Exe	26	7	17	4	2	12	7	1	8	30
North of Cornish Road	19		19	1	2	8	15	8	1	29
South of Cornish Road	20	2	18		1	6	13	5	4	34
Exeter	4		2	2		1	1	4		3
Totals	69	9	56	7	5	27	36	18	13	96

1281/82	A	B	C	D	E	F	G	H	I	J
East of Exe	82	18	77	4	7	50	35	6	37	4
North of Cornish Road	152	18	136	11	14	71	36	14	29	6
South of Cornish Road	160	25	160	7	18	80	17	14	37	6
Exeter	7		6	4	1		2	18	8	1
Totals	401	61	379	26	40	201	90	52	111	17

A Maximum total of killings
B Killings by unknown criminals
C Killers outlawed and put in exigent
D Killers who abjured the realm
E Killers hanged, before and at the eyre
F Acquittals of homicide, in court and *in absentia*
G Suspected thieves put in exigent
H Thieves who abjured the realm
I Thieves hanged, before and at the eyre
J Acquittals of theft, in court and *in absentia*

In working out these statistics, Lifton and Wonford have always been included among the hundreds south of the Cornish road, although Lifton was placed among those north of it in 1244, and Wonford east of Exe in 1281/82. The 1281/82 homicide figures do not include three killings dealt with in the gaol delivery of the eyre, as no indication is given as to where they took place.

INDEX OF PERSONS AND PLACES

The numeration of the references in this index has been arranged according to the position in the text of the relevant entries. Those appearing in the Introduction are referred to by Roman numerals, those appearing in the kalendar of juries and in the appendices have been given page references, with the page number preceded by the letter p., while those appearing in the numbered crown pleas have been given the number of the relevant plea or pleas. References to pleas also contain all references to any notes which may accompany them. In addition to the standard use of semi-colons in paragraphed entries, plea references are separated by semi-colons from references to names appearing in the kalendar or appendices. People taking their names from places have been indexed as 'of' or 'de' those places according to whether the relevant place-names have or have not been identified in their modern forms. Such identifications have been made with caution throughout; where personal names are concerned, moreover, modern forms of place-names have been supplied only when those place-names are unequivocally used to show a place of origin, and only in the cases of men and women named in the 1238 crown pleas, not in those of people named in other sources. Where identified, place-names may be assumed to be those of Devon, unless otherwise indicated, where the counties referred to are those in existence until 1974. The opportunity which the compilation of an index presents for such amendments has been used to draw attention to one or two place-names which were either wrongly identified or not identified at all when the text was prepared for publication.

ABBAS, John, of Tavistock, 646, 649
Abbe, Ralph le, 603
Abbedosle, Paul de, 662
Abbots Bickington (Buketone), Idonea of, 264
Abbotsham (Abbudesham), 432
Abbotskerswell, *see* Kerswell
Abieco, Henry de, 313
Acastre, Sir Roger de, 373, 390, 760; Robert his man, 373
Accott, 294
Acforde, Alan son of Richard de, 403
Acumbe, *see* Haccombe
Adam, Richard son of, p. 6
Addiscott (Atherigescote), John of, 400
Addistone (Addestone), Gilbert of, p. 3; 568
Aethelheard, king of Wessex, 417
Affatone, Robert de, p. 5
Affert, Margaret de, 221
Aggalf, Thomas de, 274
Ailmer, Thomas son of, 430
Ailric, Robert, p. 125
Ailward, Alice daughter of, 614; Emelota her sister, 614
Ailwarde, Richard, 542
Ailwinus, Richard, 500
Aissebi (Asshebi), Jordan de, 702
Akeleghe, Henry de, 284; Richard his man, 284
Akewrthi, *see* Eckworthy
Albemarle (Albamara, Alba Mora, Albemarl, Alla Mara), family, 222 Peter de, p. 3; 509; Ralph de 37, 476, 496, 603, 611; Rannulf de, p. 1; 615, 631; Reginald de, 222, 581
Albernon, *see* Aubenun
Alebrigge, Richard de, p. 4
Aldeswrthi, Aleswrthy, *see* Holsworthy

Alexander, William, p. 2
Alfred, William son of, 147
Algar, Adam, 732
Algar, Nicholas son of, p. 127; Algar his father, p. 127
Alice, Henry son of, 695
Alisandre, William, 723
Aliuntone, *see* Alwington
Allacott (Alnicote), Roger of, 449
Alla Mara, *see* Albemarle
Alleforde, Matthew de, 496; Robert de, 116
Aller (Alre), 581
John of, 120
Allerford (Alreforde, Aureford), Richard of, 616; Thomas of, 616
Allescote, *see* Alscott
Alleswrthi, *see* Holsworthy
Allington, East, 603
Almer, Rannulf, 231
Almiston (Almerstone), Stephen of, p. 4; 366
Alnethistone, John de, p.3
Alneto, Luke de, 37; Richard de, p. 6; Roger de, p. 2
Alnicote, *see* Allacott
Alpenie, Richard, 152
Alphington (Aufintone), 485, 500
Alre, *see* Aller
Alreforde, *see* Allerford
Alscott (Allescote, Alwarescote), 346 Rannulf of, 346
Alsedone, John de, 202
Altaribus, Henry de, p. 3; 587; William de, 663
Alvington, West (Alfintone), 600, 603, 658
Alwington (Aliuntone, Alwintone), William of, 476; William Coffin of, 429

Ambleur, Henry le, 317
Ambrieres (dep. Mayenne), France, 273
Ambrook (Ambrok, Anbroke), Gilbert of, 691; Rannulf of, 688
Anderbode, Thomas, 20; Thomas his nephew, 20
Andover (Andevere, Hants), p. 126
Anerie, *see* Annery
Anerigge, John de, 387
Anesti, *see* Anstey
Angerus, Hamelin son of, p. 7
Anglicus, John, 263, 618
Angod, *alias* Angot, Ivo, *alias* Ivo son of, 568, 574, 575; William, *alias* William son of, 24, 574, 575
Annery (Anerie, Anri), Osbert of, p. 7; Richard of, 451
Anstey (Anesti), Walter of, 293
Anstey Moyne (Anesty monachorum), 283
Anven, Edelota, 558
Appelthorn, 33
Aqua, William de, 6
Arblaster, *see* Balistarius
Archebaud, Geoffrey, 478
Archediakene (Archediakne), Michael le, 528
Archer, Elias le, 686
Archiepiscopus, Reginald, p. 5
Arderne, William de, 271
Arecumbe, Gregory de, 191
Argentein, William de, p. 5
Arigge, *see* Horridge
Arkeswrthi, *see* Axworthy
Armiger, Richard, 107
Arneberghe, Roger de, 618
Arrouaise (dep. Somme), France, abbey, 360
Ash, East (Esse), Drogo of, 400; Walter his son, 400
Ashburton (Aspertone, Aspertone Episcopi), 692, 720, 721; burgh, p. 7; 723–6
Ashcombe (Asshecumbe), Robert of, 684
Ashford, 324
Ashille, Nicholas de, 494
Ashley (Asseleghe, Essheleghe), 468, 470
Ashprington (Aspringtone), 664
Thomas the chaplain of, 683
Ashreigney (Esshereingni), 469, 477
Ash Thomas (Eshe), Thomas of, p. 2
Ashwater, 269
Ashwell (Esshewille), 598
Assa, Jordan, 104, 105
Assewille, Roger de, 684
Asshebi, *see* Aissebi
Asshecumbe, *see* Ashcombe
Atewater, William, 624
Athelard, Stephen son of, 662
Athelstan, king, 417, 486
Attestute, Ailmer, p. 8
Atteweie, Henry, 494; Walter, 494
Attrescote, Wimarc daughter of Hamelin de, 405
Aubenun (Albernon), Jordan de, 688; William de, p. 4; 230, 234
Aubeny, Oliver de, 600
Aulescumbe, *see* Awliscombe
Aure, Adam de, p. 1
Aureford, *see* Allerford

Authman, Richard, 107
Avenel, Nicholas, 38, 324
Avenell, William, 269
Avernaz, Roger le, 524
Aveton Giffard, 581
Avon (Avene), river, 586
Awliscombe (Aulescumbe), 80
Alexander of, 179
Axe, river, xiii, 222
Axewrthi, *see* Axworthy
Axminster (Ausemenistre, Axemenistre, Axeministre, Exemenistre), hundred, xxv, p. 1; 1–29, 47, 121, 224; manor, 27, 37, 224
Axmouth (Axemue), hundred, xii, p. 1; 39–47; pp. 125–6
jurors of, 28
Axmouth, prior of, p. 1; 13, 41, 42, 47; p. 125; *see also* Loders, prior of
Axmouth, Joan, a woman of, p. 125
Axworthy (Arkeswrthi, Axewrthi), John of, p. 4; 627; Jordan of, 274
Ayshford (Esshheforde), 164
Walter of, and Denise his widow, 164

BABBACOMBE (BABECUMBE), John of, 774
Babeler, Walter le, 520
Bacbake, John de, p. 3
Baccamoor (Backemore, Backemores), John of, 247; Ralph of, p. 4
Bacon, William, 512
Bacun, Henry, p. 4
Badde, Hugh, 308
Badeleghe, Edward Bigge de, 375
Bagga Tor (Baketorre), Martin of, 520
Baggetore, *see* Bagtor
Bagghe, John, 260
Baghil, Edward, 465; Reginald, 465
Bagton (Baketone), Robert of, 593; Walter of, 621
Bagtor (Baggetore), 484
William of, 484
Bai, Walter le, 505
Baisdone, William de, p. 5
Baker (*pistor*), Hugh, *alias* Huward, the, 429, 430, 431; William the, xxxii, 670; William the (another), 649
Baketone, *see* Bagton
Baketorre, *see* Bagga Tor
Bal, John, 17
Balaam, Reginald, 550
Baldwin the sheriff, 343
Baldwin, Richard son of, 115
Balistarius, *alias* Arblaster, *alias* the Norman, *alias* le Petit, Ralph, 217, 542
Ballard, Henry, 393
Balle, Reginald, 427; Robert le, p. 7
Baltforde, Robert de, p. 3
Bampton (Bantone, Bauntone), hundred, xxiv, p. 2; 92, 97, 102, 112, 142–61, 300, 581; manor, xxiv; vill, xxxvi, 144, 150, 152, 153, 157, 158; p. 126
Adam of, 101; Alexander le Maszacrer of, 150; William de Tunnebridge of, 144
Banlinch, Alan de, p. 126
Bantone, *see* Bampton

Index of Persons and Places   133

Barat, John, 726; Richard, p. 6; Richard (another), and Avice his wife, 186; Robert, 719; William, de Chiritone, 411
Barcombe, 65
Bare, Peter de la, p. 4
Barlet, Helen daughter of Richard, 120; John, and Agatha his wife, 419
Barlinch, prior of, 292.
Barnage, Jordan, 603
Barneville, Roger de, p. 2
Barnstaple (Bernestapel, Bernestapele, Bernestapl), burgh, p. 7; 331–5; burgesses of, 296
Barnstaple, honour of, xxxii, 111, 214, 269, 324, 353, 477, 494, 516; lord of, 577. *See also* Tracy, Henry de
Barnstaple, prior/priory of, 319
Barnstaple, Richard Spigurnel of, 334
Barri, William de, 221
Barset, *see* Basset
Bartholomew, bishop of Exeter, xliv, xlv, xlvi, 58
Barun, Richard, *alias* Richard le, p. 3; 680
Basset (Barset), Gilbert, 71; Thomas, 68, 69, 71
Bastard (Bastarde), Colin, p. 4; 524; Richard le, 566, 627
Batalie, Richard, 237
Bate, Nicholas le, 694
Bateshille, *see* Battishill
Bath (Bathon', Baton'), Walter of, x, xxiii, xxvii, li, p. 1; 169, 254, 279, 291, 452, 487, 596, 677
Batte, John, 455
Battisborough (Batenesberghe), 560
Battishill (Bateshille, Battishille), Richard of, 631; Stephen of, 623
Battishorne (Battesthorne), 38
Batur, Gilbert le, 30; p. 127; Roger le, 319
Baucumbe, *see* Bowcombe
Bausan, Stephen, 71
Baustan, Henry, 607; Richard, 257, 581, 662
Bauzant, William, 140
Bazan, Richard, 776
Beaford (Benford, Benforde, Beuforde), 250, 445, 446
Hamelin of, 250; Henry of, 445; Hugh of, 445; William of, 446
Beatrice, Jordan son of, 480 William son of, 74
Beauchamp, Eudo de, xviii; Robert de, ix, x
Beaumont (Bello Monte, Beumond, Beumund, Byamaunt), Henry de, p. 4, 266, 273, 494; Philip de, p. 5; 324, 342, 343; Richard de, 410; Constance his daughter, 410; Robert de, 343
Beaupeil, Henry, 273
Bec (dep. Eure), France, monks of, xlvi
Becket, St. Thomas, xliv, 123
Bedel, Elias le, and Helen his wife, 549; Iwein, 147; Martin le, 439; William Longus le, 254
Beechcombe (Bitlscumbe, Buttelescumbe), Benedict of, 627; John of, 627
Beenleigh (Benleghe), 603 Robert of, 589

Beialdeleghe, Alexander de, 588
Bel, Adam le, of Mamhead, 557; Walter le, p. 6
Bela, Alice daughter of, 765
Belebuche, Roger, 753
Belestane, *see* Belstone
Belicot, William son of, 574
Bellestane, Walter, p. 6
Belling, Alan, 232
Bello Monte, *see* Beaumont
Belmeis, William de, *alias* Zuche, William la, 300
Belstone (Belestane), 269 Baldwin of, 269
Bendone, *see* Bindon
Benford, Benforde, *see* Beaford
Benleghe, *see* Beenleigh
Bennington (Lincs), 708
Berd (Berde), Geoffrey, 607; Robert his son, 607
Bere, Adam de la, 288; Adam de la (another), 519; Alan de, 50; Anthony de, 771; Reginald de, *alias* Reginald de la, 478; Robert de la, p. 5; Thomas de la, p. 2; Thomas le (another), 380
Bere Ferrers (Ber), 526, 527
Berengaria of Navarre, queen, 639
Berenger, Bernard, 123
'Berforde', 579
'Bergh', 482
Bergh (Berghe), Edward de la, 190; John de, *alias* John de la, 35, 743, 745, 746, 748; Ralph de la, 190; Robert de la, 421; William de la, 169; William (another), 612
Beri, *see* Berrynarbor
Berkhampstead (Herts), honour of, 16
Bernard, Ralph son of, p. 3; 146, 147; Robert son of, 33
Berne, Richard de la, p. 6
Bernestapel, *see* Barnstaple
Bernus, Walter, p. 4
Berry, honour of, 28, 200, 721 lord of, *see* Pomerai, Henry de la
Berrynarbor (Beri, Berry, Bery), 313 Rengold of, 313; William his son, 313; Richard Blake of, 313; Richard the cobbler of, 313; John his father, 313 Robert Shanke of, 313; Stephen son of Simon of, 313
Berry Pomeroy, 709
Bery, *see* Berrynarbor
Besil (Besile), Matthew, 600, 603
Besseheie, Richard de, 29; Emma his daughter, xli, 29
Beta, Richard, 78
Beuforde, *see* Beaford
Beumond, Beumund, *see* Beaumont
Beupenie, Roger, 635
Beuweis, William de, 201
Beville, Robert de, p. 3
Biccadewe, Richard de, p. 5
Bickford Town (Bikeforde), William of, 534
Bickham (Bikecumbe), Germanus of, 527, 531
Bickington (Buketone), 721 Osbert the reeve of, 715
Bickington, High, 477

Bickleigh (Biggeleghe, Bikelee, Bikeleg, Bikelege, Bikeleghe, Bikkeleg), 113 Alfred de la Toune of, 430; Huard, *alias* Huward, of, 429, 430, 431, 476, 581; Isaac of, 430; Robert of, 133; Walter de Huphille of, 430; William of, p. 3; William of (another), 429
Bickton (Boketone, Buketone), 217 Joel of, xlii, 617
Bideford (Bideforde, Bydiforde), burgh, p. 7; 453–6
Bidel, Osbert, of Honiton, 751
Bidene, Edward de la, 412
Bidennebotine, Denise de, 163
Bido, John de, 357
Bigbury (Bikebire, Bykebyr), 559 Serlo of, lii, 114, 577; William of, 577
Bigge, Edward, de Badeleghe, 375
Bikebire, *see* Bigbury
Bikecumbe, *see* Bickham
Bikeforde, *see* Bickford Town
Bikelee, Bikeleg, Bikelege, Bikeleghe, Bikkeleg, *see* Bickleigh
Billes, John, of Plymtree, 109
Bimelee, William de, p. 3
Binadder (Binarder), Ralph, 496
Bindon (Bendene, Bendone, Byendone), 42
 Philip of, p. 125; Robert of, 42; p. 125; Thomas of, p. 1
Bingwell (Binewulle), Michael son of Hugh of, p. 127
Binorthedone, John, 401
Birche, Ogerus de la, p. 5
Bischop, Henry le, 249; William, 249
Biset (Bisetter, Byset), John, p. 1; 64, 68; Alice his wife, 64, 68
Bishop's Clyst (Clist Sicce Ville, Sechevill), 212, 214
Bishop's Tawton (Tautone Episcopi), 286
Bisinham, William de, 269
Bissop, Nicholas, 78
Bisudebrok, Walter, p. 7
Bitlescumbe, *see* Beechcombe
Bitton, Thomas, bishop of Exeter, p. 127
Biwlf, Henry, 349; William, 607
Blachedene, Nicholas de, 709
Blackaton (Blakedone), Michael of, 703
Blackdown hills, xiii
Blackdown (Blakedone), moor, 634
Black Hall (Blakehale), Elias of, 602
Blackpool (Blakepol), water, 285
Blagcheswrthi, Blagchewrthi, *see* Blatchworthy
Blagdon (Blakedone), Nicholas of, 269, 581; Thomas of, 360; William of, 263
Blagewrthi, *see* Blatchworthy
Blake, John le, of Somerton, 420; Martin le, 269; Richard le, of Berrynarbor, 313; Robert le, 216; Walter le, of Kingsnympton, 384
Blakebene, Walter, p. 6
'Blakedone', 51
Blakedone, *see* Blackaton, Blagdon
'Blakedune', 74
Blakeford (Blakeforde), Robert de, 93, 433, 512; Thomas de, 4, 314, 516, 575
Blakehale, *see* Black Hall

Blakelake, John de, p. 2
Blaketoritone, *see* Torrington, Black
Blakewrthi, *see* Blatchworthy
Blanchart, Richard, 471
Blancmuster, Gaudinus de, 477
Blanecumbe, Henry, p. 8
Blannicombe (Blanecumbe), Stephen of, 16; William his son, 16
Blatchworthy (Blagcheswrthi, Blagchewrthi, Blagewrthi, Blakewrthi), Elias of, 373, 374; Gilbert of, 127, 373; John of, 127, 373; Walter of, p. 5; 127, 374
Bleketoritone, *see* Torrington, Black
Bleu, Iwein le, 147
Bloie (Bloye), David son of La, *alias* David le, p. 7; 656
Bloiob, Reginald, 621
Bloiou, Richard son of, 249
Blowa, Henry, 542
Bloye, *see* Bloie
Blund, John le, 104; Richard le, 653
Blundel, William, p. 2
Blundus, Arnold, p. 7; Peter, p. 8; 71; Richard, p. 5; Robert, 110; Robert (another), 635; Robert (another), 692; Walter, p. 7; William, p. 7; William (another), 96
Bobernot, Adam, 673
Boclande, *see* Buckland
Boctone, Nicholas le Taillor de, 771
Bodetorr, Bodetorre, *see* Bottor
Bodlai (Bolay, Bollay), Hugh de, p. 2; 125, 608, 694; Henry de, 94
Bogge, Hugh, 63
Bois, Adam le, p. 6
Bokelande, *see* Buckland
Boketone (Burton), Richard de, 271
Boketone, *see* Bickton
Bolay, *see* Bodlai
Bolberry (Boltebire), Little, Great, 621 Vincent of, 593
Boleville (Bona Villa), Nicholas de, 21, 352; Robert de, 269
Bolham (in Clayhidon), 80
Bolham (Bollehame, in Tiverton), Walter Longus of, p. 127; Walrand his son, p. 127
Bollay, *see* Bodlai
Bolle, Robert, 489; John his brother, 489; Walter, 688
Bollehame, *see* Bolham
Bollelande, Richard de, 239
Bolonge, *see* Bonon'
Bon, Roger le, 87
Bona Villa, *see* Boleville
Bonde, Humphrey le, 145
Bonon', (Bolonge, Bononia), Peter de, 42; p. 125; Robert de p. 6; 395; Robert de (another), 42; p. 125
Bonus Homo, William p. 7
Boscher, John, and Alice his wife, 229
Boschet, William, p. 6; 329, 753, 754
Bosco, Adam de, 561; Alfred de, 385; Gilbert de, 570; Godfrey de, p. 6; Jocelin de, 405; Nicholas de, p. 7; Osbert de, p. 2; Osbert de (another), 414; Philip de, p. 2; Ralph de, 168; Richard de, p. 2; Roscelin de, p. 5;

Bosco—*cont.*
  Serlo de, p. 6; Simon de, p. 4; Simon de (? another), 355; Tholi, *alias* Tollacus, *alias* Touleus de, p. 3; 225, 401; William de, p. 2; 168; William de (? another), and Osanna his wife, 203; William de (another), 561
Boteilerheie, *see* Butterleigh
Botereaus, Boterelle, *see* Botreaux
Botilda, 629
Botreaux (Botereaus, Boterelle), Albreda de, p. 5; 124; William de, 300; William de, (another), 300
Bottor (Bodetorr, Bodetorre), Robert de, 738; Stephen his brother, 738
Boudone, *see* Bowden
Bouhille, Walter de, 747
Bouleghe, *see* Bulleigh Barton
'Bourigge', 482
Bourne, Richard de, 430
Bovey (Bovi), river, 714, 720
Bovey Tracy, xxxiv, 719
Bovi, William de, 263
Bowcombe (Baucumbe), Reginald of, p. 3; 568; William son of Roger, 567
Bowden (Boudone), Robert of, 738
Bowerwood, 124
Bowewode, Walter, p. 8
Bracton (legal text), xii, xxxvi, 26, 128, 291, 527, 617
Bracy, Scolastica daughter of, 465
Bradaford, 638
Bradefelde, *see* Bradfield
Bradeford, *see* Broadaford
Bradele, *see* Bradley
Bradeleghe, *see* Brayley Barton, Broadley
Bradeleghe, Thomas de, 387
Brademede, *see* Broadmede
Brademore, Robert de, p. 5
Bradenesche, *see* Bradninch
Bradfield (Bradefelde), Robert of, 99
Bradford (Shropshire), hundred, x, xi
Bradham (Bradam, Bradeham), 202, 209, 220
Bradley (Bredeleghe, Teignbridge), Richard of, 713
Bradley (Bradele, Tiverton), Thomas of, p. 2
Bradninch (Braaneys, Bradenesche, Branes), burgh, p. 6; 112, 128–9; manor, xlvii, 112, 123
Bradninch, honour of, 123, 385
Bradninch, John Swein, reeve of, 370; Richard of, 344; Richard le Fatte of, 127; Theobald, serjeant of, 370
Bradwede, Robert de, 771
Bradwell (Bradewille), 316
Bradworthy (Brawrthi), xxxiv, 261, 268, 269
Brai, John de, p. 7; 478
Braleghe, Braileghe, *see* Brayley Barton
Bramlee, Bramlege, Thomas de, p. 1; 48
Brampford Speke, 494
Bramtone, *see* Braunton
Branscombe (Brangescumbe, Brantescumbe), 52, 65, 66
Braose (Breusa, Breuse), Eva de, 599, 603; William I de, 176, 353, 599; William II de, 599

Bratton (Brattone), 619
Braundsworthy (Brendeswrthe, Brendeswrthi, Brenneswrthi), Richard of, 234, 261; John his brother, 234
Braunton (Brangtone, Bramtone), hundred, xxv, p. 4; 300, 301–30; manor, 301; vill, 310
  Baldwin of, 326
  Theobald son of John of, 310
Brayham, Martin the reeve of, 686
Brayley Barton (Bradeleghe, Braileghe, Braleghe, Brayleghe), Adam of, 221, 251, 255, 651
Breazle (Breulishille), 619
  William son of Henry of, 619
Bredeleghe, *see* Bradley
Bregge, Adam, 278
Bremridge (Brommelrigge), Luke of, 416
Brendon, xxxiv
Brendon hills, xiii
Brentor (Brente), xxxiv
  Joce of, 651; Philip of, 609; Roger of, p. 4; 607; William of, p. 4
Brescia (prov. Brescia), Italy, 123
Bret, Gilbert, 523; Guy le, lii, p. 4; 114; Ralph le, and Gillian his wife, 474; Thomas le, p. 7
Bretesche (Bretenche), John le, 16, 515, 518, 770
Bretone, Daniel le, p. 5; Thomas le, p. 5; Walter le, p. 5
Bretteville, Guy de, p. 1; 29, 587, 622, 700; William de, 587
Bretun, Richard le, 542
Breulishille, *see* Breazle
Breusa, Breuse, *see* Braose
Brevel, Geoffrey, of Totnes, 684
Brewer (Briuwer, Briuwere, Briuwerr, Briuwerre, Bruiwer), Lady Joan, 37, 270; William I, xxii, 4, 27, 37, 160, 161, 218, 221, 224, 268, 419, 427, 512, 617, 637; William II, xxii, 27, 161, 222, 270; William, bishop of Exeter, xv, xlvi, 417
Brian (Briane, Brione), Guy de, 476, 709; Philip his servant, 702; Richard, 542
Brice, Wymund, 542
Brictric, Earl, 397
Bridestowe (Brittestowe), 631
Bridgerule (Brigge Roald, Bruges), 238, 269
Bridgwater (Somerset), xxii, 160
Brightley Barton (Britteleghe), James of, and Heloise his wife, 277
Brimmeswrthi, Andrew de, 276; Roger his brother, 276
Brione, *see* Brian
Briteristone, William de, p. 4
Britteleghe, *see* Brightley Barton
Briuwer, Briuwere, Briuwerr, Briuwerre, *see* Brewer, Bruere
Briwere, *see* Bruere
Brixham (Brixham), 694, 700, 709
Brixton (Brixtone), Richard son of Hodierna of, 537
Broadaford (Bradeford), Reginald of, 557
Broadley (Bradeleghe), William of, p. 3
Broadhembury (Hambire), 106
Broadmede (Brademede), Walter of, 373

Broadwoodwidger (Brawd, Brawde), 638
Broc, John le, 651
Brocger, Richard, 408
Brode, Walter, 88
Brok, William le, p. 2
Brokere, John le, 26
Bromdone, Osbert de, 259, 263
Bromhille, Gerard de, p. 3
Bromhull, Walter de, 511
Brommelrigge, see Bremridge
Bronescombe, Walter, bishop of Exeter, xxxiv, xlvi
Bruere (Briuwerre, Briwere), William de, *alias* William de la, p. 1; 263, 617, 729
Bruiwer, see Brewer
Brumlege, Thomas de, 33
Brun, Adam, *alias* Adam le, p. 7; 632; Gilbert le, 474; Reginald, 660; William le, 24; William le (? same), 377; William (? same), 574
Brune, Roger, and Edith his widow, 387
Bruning, Walter, 473
Brunnescote, Roger de, 147
Brutham, Gervase de, 19
Bryanston (Dorset), xxxvi
Bucheton, Jolanus de, 720
Buchiwises, see Bucks Mill
Buchwrthi, Edward de, 178
Buckerell (Buckerel), 76, 77
Bucktast, abbey, xlv
Buckinghamshire, xxiii, 360
Buckland (Boclande, Boglande, Bokelande), abbey, 532; manor, 531 Hamelin of, 320; Noreis of, 525
Buckland (Bokelande) 'Brai', 312
Buckland Brewer (Bokelande), 427
Bucks Mill *or* Cross (Buchiwises), Robert of, p. 4
Budde, Elena daughter of Richard, 81; Gorwy, 81
Budleigh (Buddeleghe), hundred, xlix, p. 2; 50, 51, 53, 177–225; vill, 206
Buggepattesheie, Henry de, 22
'Bugkedeleghe', 692
Richard de, 692
Bugkedone, Roger, p. 4
Bukedone, Hugh de, 431
Bukerel, Richard, 77
Buketone, see Bickington, Abbots Bickington, Bickton
Bule, Robert le, p. 7
Bulealler (Bulalre), Walter son of Thomas of, 122
Bulebec, Isabel de, countess of Oxford, p. 2; 176, 709
Bulefen, Walter, p. 6
Buletrug, Richard, 81
Bulkworthy (Bulkewrthi, Bulkewurth, Bulkiwrthe), 476
Robert of, p. 1, 55, 430, 431, 476; Roger of, 467
Bulle, John le, 456
Bulleigh Barton (Bouleghe, Bulleghe), John of, 691; Robert the chaplain of, 187
Bullewrthi, see Bulworthy
Bulloc, William, 321
Bulworthy, (Bullewrthi), 132, 373
Walter of, 373

Bunewelle, Robert de, 137
Bunta, Benedict, 207
Bunz, John le, 17
Burdun (Burdon), Peter, 720; Richard, xxv, p. 3; 720; Richard (another), 394
Burford (Bureforde), Gervase of, 568
Burel, Alexander son of William, 415; Thomas, p. 7
Burelle, Hugh, 57
Buretone, see Burraton
Burgh, Hubert de, 595
Burleigh (Burleghe), Robert of, 593
Burn (Burne), Nicholas of, p. 2
Burne, Walter de, 430
Burnel, John, p. 5; 398; Robert, p. 5; Robert (? another), 477; Walter, 248
Burnintone, Roger de, 646
Burraton (Buretone), Ralph of, 568
Burri, Robert, p. 6; Walter son of Richard, 293
Burrington (Beringtone), 474
Burton, see Boketone
Busse, Richard, 431; William, p. 6; 329, 753, 761
Bussel, Robert, 722; Theobald his son, 722
Butehors, Richard, p. 6
Buthel, Richard, 178
Buthkeshide, Alan de, p. 4
Butland (Buttelonde), Walter of, p. 6
Butler, Luke the, 722
Butor, Roger le, p. 3
Butte, Matthew son of William, 139
Buttelescumbe, see Beechcombe
Buttelonde, see Butland
Butterleigh (Boteilerheie), 170
Walter of, and Wymarcha his wife, 38
Butyn, Ralph, p. 2
Buwele, Paganus de, 118
Buzun, Herbert, 603, 621; Robert, p. 2; William, xlv
Byalla, William, 428
Byamaunt, see Beaumont
Byendone, see Bindon
Bykebyr, see Bigbury
Byset, see Biset
Bytorre, Adam de, 686
Bywood in Dunkeswell, 80

CABEWELLE, see Gabwell
Cadbury Barton (Caddebire), 384
Caddewrthi, see Cadworthy
Caddiford (Cadewrthi), Peter of, p. 6
Cadeheghe, see Cadhay
Cadeleigh (Caddalege, Kadaleghe), 115; p. 127
Cadewrthe, see Cadworthy
Cadewrthi, see Caddiford
Cadewrthy, see Cadworthy
Cadhay (Cadeheghe), William of, p. 2
Cadigdene, Amice de, *alias* Gatesden, Agatha de, p. 4; 636, 639; William her husband, 639
Caditreu, William de, 760
Cadworthy (Caddewrthi, Cadewrthe, Cadewrthy, Kaddewrthi), Roger of, p. 4; 524, 528; Roger of (another), p. 6; Roger of (? another), 700

Caen (dep. Calvados), France, abbot of, 603
Caheines (Kaygnes, Keynges), Philip de, 397; Roger de, 397; William de, 397
Cailli, William, p. 1
Caillo (Challiou), Robert p. 5; 320
Cailloel, William, p. 2
Caillou (Calliow, Challiou, Kalliou), Godfrey, p. 3; 320, 727
Cal, Roger, lii, 114, 494
'Callebrige', 383
Callewdele, see Calverleigh
Calve, Edward le, 523; Peter le, 566; Walter le, 566
Calverleigh (Callewdele, Calwdeleghe, Calwodelege, Kalewdeleghe, Kalewodeleghe), Alice of, 132; p. 126; Rose, her tenant, 133; p. 126 Miles of, 132, 133, 373, 374; p. 126
Calvus, Walter, 571; William, 358
Calwdeleghe, Calwodelege, see Calverleigh
Cambridgeshire, 280
Campo Arnulfi, Joan de, 477
Cancellarius, Elias, 230
Cancellis, Andrew de, 639
Candebec, Ralph de, p. 1
Caneleswrthi, see Colesworthy
Canne, David, 406; Roger, 406
Canon (*canonicus*), Adam the, 252
Canonteign (Teing Canonicorum), 717 Robert de la Torre of, 584
Canuel, Roger, 252
Capella (Cappella), Anketill de, p. 7; Gilbert de, p. 6; Richard de, 385; Robert de, 24; Walter de, 463
Capie (Capy), John, 6
Capiehayes, 6
Cappeleghe, Robert de, 527
Cappella, see Capella
Capun, Thomas, 771
Capy, see Capie
Carbonel, Colin, 312; Richard, 263
Cardewille, see Cardwell
Cardinan, honour of, 65, 700, 709 Robert, baron of, 603
Cardinel, Robert, of Chaddlehanger, 635
Cardwell (Cardewille, Kerdewelle), John of, p. 4; 627
Carey (Kari), river, 615
Carey Barton (Kari), John of, 129; Richard of, 257; Walter of, 263
Carleghe, see Carley
Carlescote, Roger de, 298
Carley (Carleghe), Jordan of, 681
Carpentar, Richard, 478
Carpenter (*carpentarius*), Edelina wife of Stephen the, 550; John son of Richard the, 478
Carpenter, Walter le, p. 2
Carrio, Odo de, 301
Carselake, Robert de, 650
Carter (*carettarius*), Ralph the, 765
Carver, Elias le, 688
Casewolde, Robert, p. 1
Cat, Hugh le, 383
Cattebere, Stephen de, 650
Cayli, Thomas, 225
Cerde, see Chard
Cerne (Cerne, Dorset), Rannulf of, xxii,

Cerne—*cont.*
 p. 1; 50, 86, 145, 187, 189, 280, 300, 323, 325, 390, 645, 654
Cesarisburgo, Richard de, prior of Loders, 47
Chace, Thomas, 104
Chacebeof, Philip, 512; Avicia his daughter, 512
Chaddlehanger (Cheldesangre), Robert Cardinel of, 635
Chagchefrenchis (Chaggefrenchisse), Rannulf, 107, 108
Chagford (Chageford, Chaggeforde, Chakeforde), Hugh of, p. 3; 313, 476
Chaggefrenchisse, see Chagchefrenchis
Chagkesti, Joel de, 249
Chagthe, Roger, 246
Chakeforde, see Chagford
Challacombe (Chaudecumbe), Amicus of, 339
Challiou, see Caillo, Caillou
Chamel, Richard, 603
Champeneis, Robert, p. 5
Champeus, Robert de, p. 5; 467, 650; Alice his wife, 650
Champiun, Robert le, 653
Chandes, Robert de, 167
Channel Islands, 596
Chaorcis (Chaurces), Pain de, 600; Adam his son, 600; Patrick de, 641
Chaplain (*capellanus*), Alan the, 192; Andrew the, Roger son of, 771; Henry the, 576; Raymond the, 214; Roger the, 344
Chapman, Walter le, 726
Chard (Cerde, Somerset), Robert of, 107
Chareter, Thomas le, 85
Charke, Reginald de, 635
Charles (Charles), 318
Charleton (Chirletone), Elias servant of the parson of, 661; Peter of, 661
Charterai, Reginald de, p. 5
Charterei, Richard de, 406
Chartre, Richard, 225
Chastel, William, p. 4
Chaudecumbe, see Challacombe
Chaurces, see Chaorcis
Chawe, see Chowe
Chawleigh (Chavele), 464, 477
Chedeledone, see Cheldon Barton
Cheldesangre, see Chaddlehanger
Cheldon Barton (Chedeledone), Richard of, p. 5
Chelson (Chevelstone), Wymarc of, 190
Chen, John le, 533; Nicholas le, his brother, 533
Chene, Thomas de, 467
Cheor... hille, see Churchill
Cheriton (Cheritone, Cherltone), 103, 124 John of, p. 2; 107; John the chaplain of, 103, 124; Richard of, 107, 124
Cheriton Bishop (Cheritone), 505
Cheriton Fitzpaine (Chiritone), 194 Adam of, 178; Jordan son of Walter the clerk of, 194; Walter the smith of, 178; William de Morleghe, serjeant of, 194
Cherltone, see Cheriton

Cherubeer (Churbeare), 470, 477
   Richard son of Edward of, 470;
   Robert son of Edward of, 470
Cheselborough, barony of, 221
Chester, Rannulf earl of, and Clementia his wife, 708
Chete, Robert de, 698; Ruwelin, p. 6
Chettiscombe (Certecumbe), p. 126
Chevelestone, *see* Chelson
Chevenhancre, Robert de, 327
Chevithorne (Chivethorn), Richard of, p. 2; William of, p. 2
Chiddingcote, Thomas de, 263
Chieurestone, Ralph de, p. 3
Chil (Childe), Baldricus, *alias* Baldwin, 329, 754
Chillington (Chedelingtone), 679, 682
Chilsworthy (Chilleswrth, Chulleswrthe), 266, 271
Chilton (Chiltone), Adam of, 183
Chintellesbere, Geoffrey de, p. 3
Chirchehille, *see* Churchill
Chirchetone, Alan de, 407
'Chirchhamton', xxxiv
Chiredon, Walter de, 721
Chiritone, William Barat de, 411
   see also Cheriton Fitzpaine
Chirletone, *see* Charleton
Chittlehampton (Chitelhamptone), John the clerk, serjeant of, 474
Chivethorn, *see* Chevithorne
Chowe (Chawe), Walter la, p. 6; 753, 775, 776
Chows, Eva wife of Ralph de, 317
Christian, Richard son of, 348
Chubbe, Geoffrey, 163; William, 473
Chulmleigh (Chammeleghe), 412
Churbeare, *see* Cherubeer
Churchill (East Down), 324
Churchill (Loxbeare; Cheor... hille, Chirchehille), Robert of, pp. 2, 126
Churchstanton (Chiristantone), 84, 473
Churchstow, 603
Churston Ferrers, xlv
Cidie, Roger, 233; Matilda his mother, 233
Cimiterio, Wimar, *alias* Wimarc, wife to Algar de, 134; p. 126
Cirencester (Cirencestre, Cirnecestre, Cirnestre, Gloucs), Thomas of, xxii, li, p. 1; 3, 31, 187, 700, 709
Clanemere (Clanemer), Henry de, pp. 1, 125
Claper, Matilda, 448; Gillota her daughter, 448
Clare, Gilbert de, earl of Gloucester, 535
Clarica, 103
Clarice, Thomas son of, 630; Richard son of, 630
Clautone, *see* Clawton
Claver, Stephen le, 385
Claville, William de, p. 2; 147
Clawton (Clautone), 236
   Richard of, p. 6; 685; Robert of, 685
Clayhanger (Cleiangre), 149, 154
   Adam of, 149
Cleeve (Clive, Somerset), abbot/abbey of, p. 4; 301, 310, 324, 342
   brother Hugh of, 301
Clegland, *see* Clickland

Cleiangre, *see* Clayhanger
Clerk (*clericus*), Benedict the 585; Durandus son of the, 178; Herbert the, 107; John the, serjeant of Chittlehampton, 474; Jordan son of the, 178; Jordan son of Walter the, of Cheriton Fitzpaine, 194; Luke the, 374; Peter son of John the, 15; Reginald son of John the, 15; Reginald the, 491; Richard le, of Lydford, 632; Richard the, p. 6; Richard the (another), p. 7; Richard the (another), 120; Richard the (another), 650; Roger the, 105; William the, p. 7; William the (another), 192
Clerkestone, Spherus de, 403
Clickland (Clegland), Alfred of, 568
Clifdone, Matthew de, 709
Clifford (Clifford), John of, p. 4
Clist, John de, 169; William de, 104
Cliston (Clistone), hundred, p. 2; 161, 169–76
Clit, Gerard de, p. 2
Clive, Richard de, lii, 114; Richard de la (? other persons), 229, 443, 451
Cloktone, Gilbert de, 129
Clugnie, Alexander de, p. 4
Cluter, Ralph, 332
Clyst (Clist), 211, 222
Clyst, Broad, 176
Clyt, William de, p. 2
Cnit, Ralph, 284
Cnolle, Adam de la, 33; *see also* Knowle
Cnutstane, *see* Knowstone
Cobba, Henry, p. 3
Cobbaton (Cobetone), Arnold of, p. 7
Cobbe, Robert, 676
Cobbler (*sutor*), Osbert the, 542; Robert the, 574, 575; Walter the, 563; Wimarc daughter of the, 648
Cobe, Hugh, p. 5
Cobern, William, p. 7
Cobetone, *see* Cobbaton
Coc, Roger, p. 7; 335 William, 181
Cocforde, *see* Cofford Farm
Coche, Robert, 17; Henry and Ralph his sons, 17
Cockeville, Hugh de, 212
Cockewrthi, *see* Cokewrthy
Cockington (Cokintone), Roger of, p. 3
Cocktree (Kaketreu), 405
Codyer, Semannus, 678
Coety (Glamorgan), 295
Coffin (Cophin, Copphin), Alice, 44; Rose her daughter, 44
   Geoffrey, p. 1; 107, 581; Hugh, p. 5; 631; William, of Alwington, 429
Cofford Farm (Cocforde, Cokford, Cokforde), Esgher of, 551; Walter of, p. 7; 542; William of, p. 7
Cofton (Coketone de Deulis), 731
Cogan, John, 164; Roger, 164
Cointerel, Richard, 542
Cok, Roger, 542
Cokeman, Robert, p. 7
Cokewrthy (Cockewrthi), Richard de, p. 4; 631
Cokford, Cokforde, *see* Cofford Farm

Index of Persons and Places

Cokintone, *see* Cockington
Colaton Raleigh (Coletone), 196, 198, 219, 221
Colbern, Robert, p. 7
Colcombe, 71
Coldmere, Richard, p. 6
Coldridge, 477
Cole, Richard, 115; Margery his sister, 115
 Richard (another), 251; Roger, 470; Thomas, 196; Walter son of, 16; Walter, 430; William, 633
Colebere, Coleberghe, *see* Collybeer
Colebrooke, xxiii, 419
Colecote, *see* Collacott
Coleford (Coleforde), Adam of, 373
Coleghe, *see* Colley
Coleheia, *see* Colhayes
Coleman, William, 330
Coleridge (Curigge), hundred, p. 3; 160, 583, 661–82
 Richard of, 249; Richard of (? same), 263
Colerole, Luveric de, p. 7
Colestocks (Colestok), Robert of, 621
Colesworthy (Caneleswrthi), Denise of, 107
Coleton (Coletone), 694; William of, 689
Coleville, *see* Colwell Barton
Colhayes (Coleheia), 78
 John of, 78; William of, 78
Collacott (Colecote, Collecote), John of, p. 6; Nicholas of, p. 6
Collaford (Culliforde), Ralph of, 535
Colle, Adam, 734
Collecote, Walter, p. 6; *see also* Collacott
Colley (Coleghe), Sarah of, 505
Collop, Robert, 57
Collybeer (Colebere, Coleberghe), Alfred of, p. 5; 404, 410; John of, p. 5
Colnescote, Drogo de, 433; Richard de, 433
Colrebrigge, Luke de, 498
Colscott (Colunescote), Geoffrey of, 260; Lawrence of, 260; Maurice of, 260; Osbert of, 260; Richemannus of, 260; Theobald of, 260
Coltesuurth, *see* Culsworthy
Coluin, 271
Colum, John de, 265; John de (? same), 493; Walter de, 493
Columbers, Philip de, 125; William de, 324
Colunescote, *see* Colscott
Colviscote, Lawrence de, 433
Colwell Barton (Colevile), William of, p. 1
Coly, river, 69
Colyford (Culiford, Culiforde, Kuliforde), burgh, p. 7; 37, 69–70; manor, 40 Matthew of, p. 7; Odo of, p. 7; William Hurnewai (Ernewei) of, 40; p. 125
Colyton (Culitone, Kulitone), hundred, xxv, p. 1; 48–68; p. 126; church, 63; manor, 68
 Alice of, 62; Walter son of the smith of, 62
Combe Martin, xxxiv
Combe Pyne (Cumba), 44
Combeinteignhead (Cumbe), 482

Combere, Benedict le, and Alice his wife, 579
Cook (*cocus*), Alfred the, xxxii, 583
Cookbury (Cukebire), 267
Coombe (Cumbe), p. 126
Coombe, North (Cumba), 373, 390
Copeland (Cumberland), 300
Copener (Copiner), Robert le, p. 5; 395, 478
Cophin, *see* Coffin
Copia, Geoffrey, p. 126
Copiner, *see* Copener
Coppe, Geoffrey, 26; Ralph, 370; William, 307
Coppeshore, *see* Gobsore
Copphin, *see* Coffin
Corbet, Thomas, 263; William, 624
Corbin, Miles, p. 5; Richard, p. 3
Cordewaner, Richard le, 685; William le, p. 7
Corne, Henry de, 475; William, 691
Cornewde, *see* Cornwood
Cornewille, Adam son of the smith of, 711
Cornewrthe, *see* Cornworthy
Cornishman (*Cornubiens*), John the, 770; Peter his son, 770
Cornu, John le, xlv, xlvi
Cornubia, *see* Cornwall
Cornutus, William, p. 4
Cornwall (Cornubia), ix, xiii, xxxv, 16, 34, 59, 174, 176, 221, 265, 357, 477, 528
 Alice the weaver of, 555; archdeacon of, *see* Rof, John; Rannulf le Potter of, 553; Reginald de Dunstanville, earl of, 129, 596, 707; Richard earl of, xxv, xxvi, xlvii, xlix, 1, 16, 59, 390, 535, 637, 639, 658, 752
Cornwood (Cornewde, Cornewode, Cornwde), 151, 565
 Richard of, p. 2; William son of Seilda of, and Cecilia his wife, 663
Cornworthy (Cornewrthe), William the smith of, and Helen his wife, 665
Correforde, *see* Curreforde
Cors, Robert, 116, 137
Cosse, Roger, 338
Costard, Robert, 672
Cotemore, *see* Cotmore
Coterel, Robert, 386; Roger, p. 3; Sampson, p. 6
Coterhalre, Henry the miller of, 350
Cotleigh (Cottelee, Cottelleghe), 65
 priest of, xliv, 61; Robert of, 248
Cotley, 500
Cotmore (Cotemore, Cottemore), Geoffrey of, p. 6; 574
Coudeford, Stephen de, 561
Coundeham, Richard de, 221; William de, 221
Courtenay (Curtenay, Curtenei, Curterne), Eustachia de, 722; Hugh de, 123; Hugh de (another), 173; Robert de, 28, 173, 412, 477, 577, 641, 642
Coutances (dep. Manche), France, bishop Geoffrey of, 353
Cowick Barton (Cuwik), 491
Cowley, 516
Craccumbe, *see* Crocombe

Crakie, Gilbert, 169
Cranbury (Cranebire), Walter of, and Sybil his wife, 257
Crandford (Craneforde), John of, and Wymarc his wife, 632
Crane, Reginald, p. 6
Cranebire, see Cranbury
Craneforde, see Crandford
Craze Loman (Lumeneclaville, Lumene Claville), 131; p. 126
Creaber (Creuberghe), Ralph of, 401; Richard of, 400
Creacombe (Crenecumbe). Andrew of, 561
Crebor (Creubere), Thomas of, 645
Crediton (Criditone, Critone), bishops of, see Eadulf; see of, 417, 658
Crediton, hundred, p. 6; 411–22, 423, 473; manor, 417, 423
Creedy, Lower (Cridie Peitevin, Peytevyn), 200
Creely Barton, 214
Creivetorre, Osbert de, 715
Crenecumbe, see Creacombe
Cresme, Nicholas de, 738
Crespin, Gilbert, p. 3; Guy, p. 5; Osbert, 542; Richard, p. 3; 684
Crestien, Thomas, p. 7
Creubere, see Crebor
Creuberghe, see Creaber
Crewkerne (Cruke, Somerset), 759 Ralph of, 759
Crik, Henry, 261
Cristmana, Elias son of, 462
Criur, Hugh le, 403
Crobe, Robert, 574, 575
Crock, Martin, p. 7
Crocker, Roger, 111; Simon his brother, 111
Crocombe (Craccumbe), Bernard of, 738
Croft (Crofte), Henry de, 259; Hugh de la, 152
Crooke, 477
Croppe, Henry, 767; Ralph, 127; Robert, 412
Crosse, Richard de la, 412
Crowndale (Crundel), William of, 646
Cruce, Archibald de, p. 5; 274; Walter de, p. 6
Cruch, Reginald, p. 7
Crues, Alexander, alias Alexander de, 385; Simon his park-keeper, 385; Richard de, 111, 198
Cruke, see Crewkerne
Crundel, see Crowndale
Crunttetone, Richard de, 72
Crus, Richard de, p. 4
Cruwys Morchard (Morzetecrues), 385, 386
Cuddemore, see Cudmore
Cude, William, 29
Cudlipptown (Cudelipe), 528
Cudmore (Cuddemore), Eda of, 148; Philip of, 148; tithingman of, 148
Cuffe, Adam, 147
Cuilli, Engeram de, 477
Cule, Richard, 145
Culeghe, Culeleghe, see Culleigh
Culiford, Culiforde, see Collaford, Colyford

Culitone, Geoffrey de, p. 4 see also Colyton
Culleforde, see Culliford
Culleigh (Culeghe, Culeleghe), Adam of, p. 7; 335; William of, p. 4
Culliford (Culleforde), Philip of, 225
Culling, Henry, 374; Sampson, 374
Culm (Culum), river, 109
Culm Davy (Nordcumbe, Northcumbe), 87, 360
Culmstoke (Culmstoke, Culumstoke), 91 Peter of, 773
Culsworthy (Coltesuurth, Culteswrthe, Culteswurth), 271 Maurice of, 271
Culuerd, Walter, 354
Culum, John de, 174; Luke de, 107
Culumstoke, see Culmstoke
Cumbe (Cumba), Angmerus de, 210, 259; Baldwin de, 180; Herbert de, 259; Herbert de (? another), 620; John de la, 635; Luke de, and Selena his wife, 681; Margery de la, 546; Michael de, p. 3; Nicholas de, p. 1; 2; Osbert de, 412; Philip de, 107; Philip de (? another), p. 125; Ralph de la, 170; Richard de, or Richard de la (various persons), pp. 3, 5, 7; 11, 259, 412, 620, 684; Robert de, 447, Robert Mercator de, p. 6; Robert son of William de, 730; Roger de la, p. 8; Thomas de la, 11; Walter de, 210; Walter the chaplain of, 43; p. 125; William de, 419; William de, of Woodbury, 204; William del, p. 2
'Cumbe', 8
'Cumbepunchard', 709
Cumberland, 300, 513
Cumin, John, 155
Cumpaniun, William, p. 6
Cunand, Peter, 738; William, 738
Cunel, Pentri, 272
Cunitone, Peter de, p. 3
Cunte, Reginald le, 770
Curant, see Gurand
Curforde, Curiforde, see Curreforde
Curigge, see Coleridge
Curitone, see Curriton
Curlepeis (Curlepais), Richard, and Cristiana, alias Christina, his wife, 40; p. 125
Curreforde (Correforde, Curforde, Curiforde), Joel, alias Jolanus, de, 229, 257, 266, 503; John de, 451
Curriton (Curitone), Geoffrey of, 528, 607
Curteis, Thomas le, 621
Curtenay, Curtenei, Curterne, see Courtenay
Cusin, Walter, 562; William, 296
Cuthminecote, Walter de, 257
Cutholvestone, Richard de, 151

DAGEVILLE, RICHARD DE, p. 3
Daneis, Henry le, 694, 721; Daniel his man, 694
Richard le, p. 1; William le, de Horleghe, 694

Index of Persons and Places

Daniel, Thomas, p. 3
Dante Alighieri, xv
Darracott (Doddescote), Richard of, 312
Dartington (Dertinctone), barony of, 324, 603
  Eliot of, 587
Dartmoor (Dertemore), xiii, xiv, xxviii, 403, 474, 511, 595, 620, 637
Dartmouth (Dertemue, Dertumue), xxxiv, 670, 671
  Robert of, p. 6
Daudune, *see* Dewdon
David, Osbert, 663; William, 631; William (another), 681
Dawlish (Deulis, Dovelis), 681, 730, 733, 736
Dean (*decanus*), Walter son of the, p. 6
Dean (Foresta de Dene, Gloucs.), Adam of the Forest of, 347; William of the Forest of, 347
Dean Prior, xxxiv, 587, 611
Demichevaler, Ralph, 170
Denbury (Devenebire, Duenebire), 687, 693
  Rannulf of, 701
Dene, Henry de, 50; Robert de la, 326
'Dene', priest of, 326
Dene, *see* Dean
Deneridge (Denrighe), John of, p. 6
Depeforde, *see* Dipford
Deptford, 477
Derewrthi, *see* Derworthy
Derneburne (Erneburne), Thomas, *alias* Thomas de, p. 5; 281
Derrill (Dirhille), Roger of, 263, 264, 617, 634
Derriton (Diretone), Richard son of Roger of, 253
Dertemue, *see* Dartmouth
Derworthy (Derewrthi), Jordan of, 480
Despenser, John le, p. 5
Deudone, *see* Dewdon
Deveneis, William le, p. 2; *see also* Skerraton
Devon, earls of, 103, 391, 513, 518, 543, 547, 577; *see also* Redvers, Vernun
Dewdon (Daudune, Deudone), 709
  Hamelin of, 581, 608, 709
Didworthy (Duddewrth), Alfred of, p. 3
Digerestone, Roger de, 11
Diggaport (Dikeport), Drogo of, and Clarice his wife, 633
Dinant (Dynant), family, 365
  Geoffrey, p. 4; 365; William de, the miller, 363
Dipford (Depeforde), Simon of, 159
Diptford (Depeford), 587, 596, 598, 600, 707, 722
Diretone, *see* Derriton
Dirhille, *see* Derrill
Dittisham (Diddesham), 665, 666
Dockworthy (Dockewrthi), Roger of, and Margery his wife, 377
Doddecote, Dodecote, *see* Dodscott
Doddelescumbe, *see* Doddiscombe
Doddescote, *see* Darracott
Doddiscombe (Doddelescumbe, Dotescumbe), Ralph of, pp. 3, 126
Doddridge (Todderigge), 416

Dodscott (Doddecote, Dodecote), Alexander of, 230; John of, 364
Doget, William, p. 7
Doggefel, William, xli, 395
Doilard (Doillard), Robert, 140; Beatrice his sister, 140; p. 127
Dokeman, Rannulf, 232
Dolton (Dugheltone), 477
  Anketill of, 466
Done, Nigel de, p. 126
Donningstone (Duningestone), 161
Doo, Hugh, p. 3
Dorchester (Dorset), 69
Dornafield (Dornefelde), Roger of, 691
Dorset (Dors', Dorsette), xiii, xxii, xxxvi, xliii, xlv, xlvii, 3, 20, 50, 58, 121, 187, 189, 222, 622, 696, 760
  William of, 19; Painetus his son, 19
Dotescumbe, *see* Doddiscombe
Douai (dep. Nord), France, Walter of, 160, 581; Juliana his granddaughter, 160
Down, East, 324; West, 324
Draiford, Hamelin de, 707
Drake, William, 574
Drascombe (Droscumbe), 511
  Richard of, 511; Robert of, 511
Drayford (Draiforde), 378, 383
Drewsteignton (Teitone, Teintone), Drogo of, 269, 294, 516
Drogo, Richard son of, 516
Droscumbe, *see* Drascombe
Droun, John le, 707
Duddewrth, *see* Didworthy
Duenebire, *see* Denbury
Dugheltone, *see* Dolton
Dulcia, 457
Dulverton (Ulvertone, Somerset), prior of, *see* Barlinch, prior of
Dumel, Osbert, 403
Dumeslande, John de, 433; William his man, 433
Dunchideock (Dunsidiok), William of, 749; Nicholas his son, 749
Dune, Adam de, p. 1; Baldwin de la, 199; Gilbert de, 73; Henry de la, 236; John de la, 199; Ralph de, p. 1; Richard de la, 578; Robert de la, p. 8; Robert de la (another), 236; Robert de la (? another), 252; Roger de la, 364; Walter de la, 269
Dunesforde, *see* Dunsford
'Dunesibille', 'Dune Sibille', 39; p. 125
Duneslande, *see* Dunsland
Dunhevid, Geoffrey de, 269
Duningtone (Dunitone), Humphrey de, p. 6; 554
Dunkerigge, Lawrence de, 622, 624
Dunkeswell (Dunekewelle, Dunekeswelle, Dunkewelle, Dunkewille), 85, 328
  abbey/abbot/monks of, 80, 85, 124, 198, 216, 219, 222, 328, 427
  Hugh, the abbot's man, 216
Dunnestone, William de, 618
Dunneslande, *see* Dunsland
Dunneswelle, *see* Dunwell
Dunnislande, *see* Dunsland
Dunsford (Duneforde, Dunesforde), 512
  Geoffrey of, 771

Dunsidiok, *see* Dunchideock
Dunsland (Duneslande, Dunneslande, Dunnislande), John of, 269, 294, 418, 433, 651
Dunstanvil, Robert de, 68; Walter de, 68
Dunster (Somerset), honour of, 149
Duntestorre, Nicholas de, 684
Dunwell (Dunneswelle), Richard of, 570
Durand, William, 520
Durant, Nicholas, 644
Dureman, an approver, 749
Dureville, Walter de and Petronilla his wife, 327
Durewrthi, Jordan de, 314
Dwole, Roger, 649
Dyer (*tinctor*), Philip the, p. 6
Dynant, *see* Dinant

EADULF, bishop of Crediton, 417
Eastcott (Estcote), Vincent of, 628; Jordan his brother, 628
Eastleigh (Estleghe), Geoffrey of, 284
Easton Barton (Estennestone), Geoffrey of, p. 6
Ebbeforde, Ebforde, *see* Efford
Ebor', *see* York
Eckworthy (Akewrthi, Ekewrthi), Robert of, 55; Roger of, 429
'Eddicumbe', 11
Eddileghe, Adam de, 11
Edgar, Alfred son of, 64
Edith, a beggar, 275
Edith, queen, 639
Edith, Robert son of, 542
Edrig, Thomas, of Plympton, 540
Edward the Confessor, king, 74, 265
Edward, Gunilda daughter of, 711
Efford (Ebbeforde, Ebforde), William of, and Sibyl his wife, 524
Eggbear (Eggebeare, Egkebere), Philip of, 251; Richard of, 251; Robert of, 251
Eggesford (Egkeneforde), 460
Eggulf, Walter, 521; Alice his aunt, 521
Egkebere, *see* Eggbear
Egkeneforde, *see* Eggesford
Ekewrthi, *see* Eckworthy
Eleanor of Aquitaine, queen, 639
Eleanor of Provence, queen, 596
Elledone, Thomas de, 289
Embridge (Emerigge), Richard of, 668
Emelota, a married woman, 319; a thief, 34
Emerigge, *see* Embridge
Emma, Henry son of, 385
Englebourne, Great, 577
Englescheville, Theobald de, p. 3; 166, 598, 720, 721, 722
Ermington (Ermintone), hundred, xxxii, p. 3; 160, 556–78, 580, 581, 583, 617
Erneburne, Alina daughter of, 585; *see also* Derneburne
'Ernecumb', 721
Ernewei, *see* Hurnewai
Ernis, William, 771
Erthi, Robert de, 55
Eshe, *see* Ash Thomas

Espus, *see* Lespus, Wanford
Essche, Edward de, p. 3; Richard de, p. 3
Esse, Jordan de, 476
 see also Ash, East
Essex, 581
'Esshe', 641
Esshe, Ralph de, 448
Essheforde, *see* Ayshford
Estcote, *see* Eastcott
Estennestone, *see* Easton Barton
Estleghe, *see* Eastleigh
Estre, Robert del, p. 2
Eswaie, William de, p. 6
Ethfelde, *see* Heathfield
Ettard, Richard, p. 7
Eustache, Robert, 524
Eveforde, Martin de, p. 1
Everard, Roger, 124
Exe (Exe), river, xii, xxi, xxviii, xxxiii, 37, 110, 135, 140, 143, 211, 220, 488, 758, 762, 763; pp. 127, 130
Exe, Odo de, 522
Exe, West, p. 126
Exeter (Exon'), bishop of, xiii, p. 6; 214, 389, 417, 423, 629, 694, 721, 723; official of, 103, 292, 296, 533
 see also Bartholomew; Bitton, Thomas; Brewer, William; Bronescombe, Walter
Exeter cathedral, St. Peter's church, 417, 757, 766; canons, chapter of, 66, 91, 186, 658; chancellor of, 486; treasurer of, *see* Ralegh, William de; vicars serving, 774
Exeter, city, ix, x, xiii, xv, xix, xx, xxiv, xxviii, xxix, xxxi, xxxiii, xxxvi, xli, 1, p. 6; 50, 51, 69, 129, 139, 145, 212, 213, 220, 222, 325, 330, 369, 386, 441, 445, 487, 491, 500, 542, 550, 641, 752–76; All Saints' parish in, 774; High Street of, 774; 'Wollardislane' in, 774
Exeter, castle, ix; gaol in, 13, 217, 223, 441, 542
Exeter, churches in, St. Edmund's, 763; St. John's, 764; St. Mary's, 767; St. Sidefulle's, 759
Exeter, religious houses in or near; St. James's priory, 214, 500, 739, 740; St. John's hospital, 416; St. Mary's monastery, 486; St. Nicholas's priory, 220, 769, 773
Exeter, Beatrice wife of John Richeman of, 330, 753, 755; Edelota her servant, 755
 Jacob the Jew of, 183; Jordan Kagchefrenkis of, 334; Peter son of Robert of, 729; Richard the cobbler of, 770; Roger the cobbler of, 491; Roger son of Henry of, 36, 112, 138; William the baker of, 212
Exminster (Exemenistre, Exeministre), hundred, p. 3; 684, 727–51; manor, xlviii
Exmoor (Esshemore, Exemor, Exemore), 283, 338, 339
Exon', *see* Exeter
Eynsham (Eynesham, Oxfordshire), Roger of, 771

FADDECOTE, see Vaddicott
Fag, Robert le, 686
Fair, Peter le, 667; Lawrence his brother, 667
Faklefelde, see Vaglefield
Falewille, see Velwell
Falklefelde, see Vaglefield
Farebi, see Veraby
Farewei, see Farway
Farleigh (Ferleghe), Julian of, 187
Farneswrthi, Roger de, 718
Farway (Farewei), 57
 Gilbert of, 33
Farwood (Forwde), 57
 Richard Juvenis of, 57
Fatacott (Fattecote), Geoffrey of, p. 4
Fatte, Edwin le, 127; John le, xxxv, 128; Richard le, of Bradninch, 127
Fattecote, see Fatacott
Fauchur, Geoffrey le, 692
Fauvel, William, p. 4
Fedefenne, William de, 435; William his groom, 435
Fendone, William de, p. 2
Fenne, Adam de la, 269; Cristina de la, 154; Henry de la, 269; John de la, 269; Nicholas de la, 561
Fentone, Richard de, 524
Ferers, William de, 527
Ferleghe, see Farleigh
Fernhill (Fernhille), 269
 Nicholas of, p. 4; Reginald the reeve of, 364; William son of Nicholas of, 662
Ferrariis, Nicholas de, 324; Roger de, xliii, 527; Thomas de, lii, 114, 494
Fferendon, Henry de, 161
Fhisacre, see Fishacre
Fichet, William p. 3
Filleigh (Fileleghe), Nicholas of, p. 4
Finamur, Thomas, 480; William, 426
Fishacre (Fhisacre, Fishacre), Martin of, 503, 581, 702
Fisherman (*piscator*), Daniel the, and Matilda his wife, 519; Cenota her sister, 519
Fitz Count, Henry, 123, 577, 596, 707
Fitz Hamon, Robert, 295, 397; Mabel his daughter, 397
Fitz Pain, Fitz Payne, Robert, p. 1; 32, 391; Roger, 388, 391; Matilda his widow, 388, 510
Fitz William, Adam, ix
Flemeng (Flemec), Lawrence le, p. 3; 430; William le, xxiv, 46, 47; p. 126
Flentur, Richard le, 474, 618
Flete (Flet), 560
Fliu, Roger. 269
Florentin, John, 190
Fludda, 720
Foggeshille, see Foxhill Farm
Foliot, Robert, 90, 479; Robert (another), 520
Fonte, Richard de, p. 6; William de (various persons), p. 7; 107, 685
Ford (Forda), abbey/abbot, xliii, 23, 265, 427

Ford Farm, 221
Ford next Trill, 28
Ford, West, 433
Forde (Forda), David de la, 669; Dewicus de la, 433; Geminianus de, 433; Gilbert de La, 221; Henry de la, 221; John de la, 635; Nicholas de la, 569; Rannulf de la, 433; Richard de la, p. 3; 263; Roger de la, p. 7; William de la, p. 8; William de la (? same), 16; William de (another), 691
'Forde', water, 92
Forester (*forestarius*), Adam the, 243, 265; Alan the, 618; Geoffrey the, 51; Richard the, 95
Fornell', see Furnelle
Forst, Richard, 542
Forthhere, bishop of Sherborne, 417
Fortibus, Isabella de, 532; Amicia her mother, 532
Forwde, see Farwood
Fosseto, Nicholas de, p. 7
Fougeres (dep. Ille-et-Vilaine), France, abbey, 708; family, 708
 Geoffrey, lord of, 708; Margaret daughter of Ralph de, 708
Fowhe, Adam le, 259
Foxhill Farm (Foggeshille), William of, 94, 99
Foxhole (Foxhille, Foxole), Ogerus of, 259; Philip of, 259; Roger of, 259
France. 112
Franceis, John le, and Gunilda his wife, 660; Peter le, p. 2; 252, 259; Peter le (another), p. 3; Philip le, 623; Richard le, 247; Walter le, 740; William le, p. 5
Franckelein, William le, p. 2
Frankaborough (Frankeberghe), John de, 653; Walter of, 653
Frederick II, German emperor, 123
Fremington (Fremigtone, Fremintone, Fremitone), church, 349; hundred, p, 4; 333, 344–55
Frere, Robert le, 370
Freschet, Richard, p. 2
Frie, John, 145
Frithelstock (Frithelakestok), 436
Frodeton, 294
Fromind, Roger, p. 5
Fromtone, Walter, de, 98
Froudetone, William de, p. 5
Fuel, Richard, and Gillian his wife, 413
Fuge (Fuwighe), 667
Fuite, Roger, 380
Fuke, Hugh, 78
Fulco, Walter, p. 7
Fulk, Denise daughter of, 282
Fulke, Walter, p. 7; Walter (? same), 528
Furbur, Philip le, 766
Furel, William, p. 4
Furlang, Robert, 291
Furnelle (Fornell', Furneals), John de, 215, 221; Philip de, 215
Furse, Henry de, 50; Nicholas de la, 38; Ralph de la, 574; William de la, and Emma his wife, 171
Futur, Ralph, 611

GABWELL (CABEWELLE), Higher and Lower, 510
Jordan of, 480
Gai, Adam le, 477
Galbere, Gilbert de, 99
Gale, Herbert, 274
Galfridus, Richard, 686
Galleshoure, Gallesoure, see Galsworthy
Galmpton (Calmetone), 621
Galsworthy (Galleshoure, Gallesoure), 429, 476
Gilbert of, 429, 431, 476
Galsworthy, North, 429
Gambon (Gambun), Geoffrey, alias Geoffrey de, p. 5; 291
Gandre, Robert, 336
Gaoler, Thomas le, 31
Gappah (Gatepathe, Gatespathe), William of, 773, 774; William of, the serjeant, p. 3; 774
Gascon, Richard, 308
Gascony, xiv, 123, 596
Gatcombe (Gatecombe, Godcumbe), 49
Adam of, pp. 5, 7
Gate, Henry de la, p. 1
Gatesdene, Agatha de, alias Cadigdene, Amice de, p. 4; 636, 639; William her husband, 639
Geg, William le, 542
Gelli, Godfrey, 107
Geoffrey, Agnes daughter of, 572
Gernun, William, 143; William (another), 221
Gerold, Baldwin son of, 221
Gervase (Gervasius, Gerveys), Walter, 429, 430, 431
Gervase, William son of, 565
Giddeleghe, see Gidleigh
Gidie, Augustine le, 459
Gidleigh (Giddeleghe), 399
Richard the chaplain of, 399
Giffard (Giffarde), Joel, p. 4; 715; John, 566; Richard, 107; Robert, xxiii, p. 4; Roger, p. 1; 29, 364, 476; Walter 1, p. 4; 476; William, 617
Gikur, Robert le, 257
Gilbert, 169
Gilsland (Cumberland), 513
Girard, Philip, p. 6; 592
'Giseweie', 7
Gittisham (Giddesham), 188, 189, 221
Giuwold, William, 26
Glamorgan, 295
Glanvill (legal text), xxxvii
Glastonbury (Glastinbire, Glaston'), abbey/abbot, xlvi, 26, 28, 92
Glendon (Glindone), William of, p. 6
Gloucester (Gloucestre), honour of, 166, 221, 295, 397, 603
Gilbert de Clare, earl of, 535; Robert earl of, 168, 295, 397; William earl of, 168, 397
Gloucestershire (Glouc'), xxxv, xxxvi
William Ernis from, 771
Gobshore (Coppeshore), William of, p. 8
Godalming (Surrey), hundred, xlix
Godcumbe, see Gatcombe
Goddeleghe, see Goodleigh
Gode, Richard, 229

Godegrom, William, p. 2
Godeleghe, see Goodleigh
Godesaltre, see Goodshelter
Godeswrthi, see Godsworthy
Godfin, Roger, 651
Godfrey, Michael son of, 625; Peter son of, 571; Richard son of, p. 2; 75; Richard son of (another), 379
Goding, John, p. 4; Simon, 300
Godknave, Walter, 62
Godswein, William, 200
Godsworthy (Godeswrthi), Richard of, p. 4
Godwin, Gilbert, 687; Walter, of Heathfield, 592
Goiz, Elias le, p. 3; Roger le, 117; William, 574, 575
Golde, John son of, 407; Walter, 308
Goldsmith (aurifaber), Adam the, 153; John the, p. 6
Goodleigh (Goddeleghe, Godeleghe), Roger of, p. 2; 94
Goodrington (Cudrintone), 706
Goodshelter (Godesaltre), Ralph of, p. 3; William of, 24
Gorhuish (Goriwis), Walter of, 252, 259
Gorron (dep. Mayenne), France, 273
Gotham, 696
Gove, Roger, 430
Graham, Master Thomas de, xxxi
Grameire, Sara daughter of William, 174
Granger, Walter le, p. 6; 330, 753
Grave, Walter de la, of Somerset, 403
Graveshevede, William, 673
Greendale (Grindel, Grondelf), 222
William of, 211
Greendown (Grendone), Sara of, 285
Greenslade (Greneslad, Greneslade), Geoffrey of, 473; Thomas of, p. 6
Greenslinch (Grenesclinge), Joel of, 170; Robert of, 170
Greenway (Greneweie), Philip of, p. 1; 33
Gregory, William son of, and Olive his wife, 168
Greihille, Jocelin de, 22
Greistone, William, p. 7
Grendel, Adam, 205
Grendone, see Greendown
Grenefenne, see Grenoven Wood
Grenesclinge, see Greenslinch
Greneslad, Greneslade, see Greenslade
Grenetone, Wyotus de, 622
Greneweie, see Greenway
Grenoven Wood (Grenefenne), William of, 607
Grenville, Richard de, 454
Grete, Robert le, 251
Grigku, Robert, and Gillian his wife, 93
Grille, Warin, 647
Grindel, see Greendale
Grivel, Roger, 738
Grob, William, p. 6
Grocy, Walter, p. 6
Grucy (Gruscy), Gilbert, alias Gilbert de, p. 2; 123
Gui, Roger le, 571
Gule, Emma, 332
Gulle, Robert, 170
Gunilda, 92

Index of Persons and Places

Gunnild, John son of, 635
Gurand (Gurande, Curant), Henry, p. 5; 394, 397; Walter, p. 7
Gurdac, Ralph, p. 4
Gurdet, Ralph, 528
Gutt, William, 26
Gydie, Osbert le, p. 5; Walter, 257
Gylene, Robert le, p. 7
Gyrifenna, Richard de, p. 126
Gysti, Gervase, 662
Gytha, countess, 265

HACCHE, Geoffrey son of Richard de, 302
Haccombe (Acumbe, Haccumbe), Jordan of, p. 3; Stephen of, p. 3; 483
Haddon Moor, xxxvi
Hafrige, Walter de, p. 7
Hag, Stephen, 685
Hagana, William, 715
Hagginton, 324
Haie, Walter, 620; Henry and John his sons, 620
Haies, William de, 749
Hail, Richard, 229
Hakestone, see Oxton House
Halberton (Haubeton, Haubertone), hundred, xxv, p. 2; 97, 162–8; p. 127
Halberton Abbot, 168
Halberton Boys, 168
Halbiri, see Halsbury
Halebem, see Holbeam
Hale Farm (Hale, Lahale), Ralph of, p. 8; 16
Halger, William, 402
Hallewlle, Robert de, 429
Hals, William, of Tidcombe, p. 127
Halsbury (Halbiri), Baldwin of, p. 4
Halwell (Hellewelle), Walter son of Hugh of, 666
Halwill (Hackewille, Halkewille, ?'Halwull'), 250, 269
Ham (Hamme), 312
Hambire, see Payhembury
Hamelin, John, 753; William, 78, 89
Hamme, Robert de, and Custance his wife, 300
Hammes, Robert de (? same), 127
Hampshire, 280, 596
Hampton (Hamptone, recte Heanton Punchardon), 305
Hamptone, Richard de, 689
Hamsworthy, 270
Hamund, Gilbert, 26
Hanagker, Richard de, 146; Matilda his wife, 146; Richard and Robert his sons, 146; Adam his nephew, 146
Hankford (Hankeforde), Reginald of, 429
Hapse (Lapse), Ralph de, 371
Harberton (Hurbertone), 664; honour of, 176
Harbourneford (Herburforde), 663
Harcombe (d'Harecumbe), Alfred of, p. 3
Harding, Robert, 494
Harecumbe, see Harcombe
Haredon (Haredone). 581
Haregrave, see Harragrove
Hareston (Harestane), 3
Robert of, 524

Harevel, William 649
Harpford, 221, 222
Harpur, Serlo le, p. 4
Harragrove (Haregrave), Jordan of, 520
Harraton (Harwdetone), Rannulf of, p. 6
Hartland (Hertilande), xxx; abbey, xlvi; canons of, xxxi, 360
Richard canon and priest of, 360
Hartland, hundred, p. 4; 360–7
Harwdetone, see Harraton
Hathelande, Geoffrey de, 587
Hatherleigh (Hatherl', Hatherle, Hatherleghe), xxxiv, 241, 254, 255
Walter of, 255
Hauekedon, Mabel de, xi
Hause, Reginald del, 535
Hauville, William de, p. 1
Havecumbe, Hamelin de, xliii, 527
Havek, Roger le, 692
Haveker, Roger le, 520
Havekerlonde, see Hawkerland
Havene, Adam del, p. 125
Hawise, Auwenilda daughter of, 381
Hawkerland (Havekerlonde), 216
Walter the reeve of, 216
Haye, Great (La Heie), 605
Hayridge (Arigge, Harigge), hundred, xxvi, p. 2; 94, 97, 103–27, 130, 494, 519
Haytor (Haitorre, Heytorre), hundred, xxvi, p. 3; 583, 596, 686–710
Heanton Punchardon, see Hampton
Heathfield (Ethfelde), 574
Walter Godwin of, 592
Heavitree (Hevetre), 500, 770
Hecche, Roger de la, 116
Hecfertheswrthi, Michael de, and Joan his wife, 372
'Heie, La', alias 'Heie cancellarii Exon', 486, 488, 490
Heie, Henry de la, p. 2; Reginald Martin de la, 635; Richard de la, 376; Robert de la, 484; Robert de la, de Nortone, 730
Heighe, Hugh de, p. 2
Heile, Richard, 259
Heine, John le, and Matilda his wife, 18
Heithe, Henry de la, 494
Hekewrthi, Robert de, p. 6
Hele, 213
Hele, Crocker's, 473
Hele, Alric de, 247; Maurice de la, p. 2; Richard, 663; Roger de, and Emma his wife, 433
Helion (Heliun), Robert de, p. 1; 48, 49, 721
Helleredune, see Hillerton
Hellewelle, see Halwell
Hemerdon (Henemeredune, Heneremerdone, Heremanesdon), Alexander of, p. 4; 266, 524
Hemmeforde, see Henaford
Hemyock (Hemiok, Hemioke), hundred, p. 1; 38, 75–91, 97, 479, 519; manor, 90; tithing, 80, 83
Henaford (Hemmeforde, Henneforde), Henry of, and Gunilda his wife, 364; Robert of, 364

Henborough (Hindebereghe, Hinteberghe), Peter of, p. 2; 75
Henemeredune, Heneremerdone, see Hemerdon
Henford (Hindeford), 227
Henneforde, see Henaford
Hennock, 720
Henry I, king, 26, 90, 130, 168, 215, 217, 218, 271, 273, 280, 365, 397, 410, 479, 532, 543, 581, 604, 639, 657, 682, 722, 751
Henry II, king, xxv, 67, 68, 103, 168, 265, 410, 417, 707, 720, 722, 752
Henry III, king, xx, xxvi, xxviii, p. 4; 16, 37, 59, 123, 137, 168, 174, 203, 261, 271, 301, 388, 596, 598, 637, 639, 658, 752
Henry, a boy, 594
Henry, Gervase son of, 347; Henry son of, 315; Roger son of, 753
Henstill (Hennesti), 421
Herbert, Matthew son of, 604; Richard, p. 6
Herbiz, Robert, p. 4
Herding, Gilbert de, 587; John, 494; Richard son of Richard, 494
Herefordshire, 622
Heremanesdon, see Hemerdon
Hererman, Roger, 689
Hereward, Robert, 464
Heriz, Robert, 615
Herizun, William, 603
Herm, William, 121
Hertescote, Richard de, 344
Hervy, Peter, 667
Hesewelle, Walter son of Elias de, 431
Hestow (Historre), Adam of, p. 3
Hethe, Henry de la, 431
Hethen, Walter le, 336
Hewis, see Huish
Hewrthi, Stephen de, 367
Heyle, Jordan de, p. 5
Hialestone, William de la, p. 2
Hiddestone, Matilda de, 529
Hidon (Hiddon, Hidone, Hidune, Hydone), John de, 90; Richard de, p. 1; 32, 88, 90; Richard de (another), p. 6
Highampton (Hamptone), 269
Highweek (Teingnewick), 166, 598, 720, 721, 722
Hilemer, Roger, 587
Hille, Hugh de la, 55; Hugh de, alias Hugh de la (? another), 291; Robert his son, 291
  Jordan de la, p. 1; Osbert de la, 284; Ralph de la, 55; Roger son of Walter de, 471; Walter de la, 179; Walter de la (another), 374
Hillerton (Helleredune), Thomas of, p. 5
Hinderebereghe, see Henborough
Hindone, John de, 35; Robert de, 36
Hingledene, see Incledon
Hinteberghe, see Henborough
Hirdman, Alfred, 291
Hirne, William de la, 154
Historre, see Hestow
Hittisleigh (Huttenesleghe), 473; William of, 462

Hocforde, William son of Henry de, 474
Hockford Waters (Hocforde, Hokeforde), John of, p. 2; Reginald servant to the parson of, 144
Hocsenham, Ansel de, 407
Hode, see Hood
Hoeles, William, 104
Hog, Walter, p. 7; William, p. 6; William (? another), 746
Hogastre, Richard, 384
Hoggehulle, Richard de, p. 7
Hoke, Geoffrey de la, p. 4; William de la, 462
Hokederis, Hokedris, see Hookedrise
Hokeforde, see Hockford Waters
Hokestone, see Oxton House
Hokesham, see Huxham
Holbeam (Halebem), William of, p. 3
Holbeton (Houbautone, Houboutone), 557, 560, 617; Godfrey of, 575; Robert the smith of, 575
Holcombe (Hollecumbe), 165
Holcombe (Holecumbe, Hollecumbe, in Exminster), 735
Holcombe Rogus (Holecumbe, Hollecumbe), 147
  Oliver of, 146; William Russel of, 147
Holdik, Thomas de, 634
Holditch (Hollediche), xxiv, 29
Hole (Hole), 319
  Andrew of, 319; Oliver de la, p. 4; Scolastica wife of Christian de la, 348; William de la, 178
Holecrucke, John de, 478
Holecumbe, see Holcombe, Holcombe Rogus, Hollacombe, Hollowcombe
Holeweie, see Holloway Farm
Holewille, see Holwell
Hollacombe (Holecumbe, Hollecumbe, in Black Torrington), Agnes of, 259; Thomas of, p. 4
Hollacombe (Hollecumbe in Crediton), Osbert of, p. 6
Holle, Ralph de la, the smith, 234; Richard his son, 234
Hollecumbe, see Holcombe Rogus, Hollacombe
Holleham, Reginald de, p. 3
Holleweie, Robert de, p. 6
Hollewille, see Holwell
Hollocombe (Holecumbe Wermund), 394
Holloway (Holleweie), road, 11
Holloway Farm (Holeweie), John of, 742, 745
Hollowcombe (Holecumbe), David of, p. 3; 568, 569
Holne, Robert de, p. 4
Holsworthy (Aldeswrthi, Aleswrthy, Alleswrthe, Alleswrthi), xxxv, 246, 253, 641
  Alan of, p. 4; 315, 433, 476, 514, 641
Holte, Ralph de la, 494
Holwell (Holewille, Hollewille), 171
  Walter of, 171; William of, 171
Holy Land, the, 519
Home, John, 769
Hone, Ralph la, 155
Honeychurch (Hunichirche), 254

Honiton (Hunetone, Unetone), burgh, p. 6; 30–6, 37, 112; manor, p. 8; 16, 37–8
  Henry of, p. 7; Hugh le Taliur of, 30; Osbert Bidel of, 751
Hood (Hode), Jordan of, 587
Hook, 477
Hookedrise (Hokederis, Hokedris), Robert of, 130; p. 126; Gilbert and William his sons, p. 126
Hooker, John, 547
Hope, Walter de la, p. 2
Hopere, John le, 190; Robert, p. 6
Hopetrede, Walter, p. 7
Horder (Hordere), Richard le, p. 3; 743
Hore, Jordan le, 471
Horestane, Walter de, 433
Horiflode, Walter de, 571
Horleghe, William le Daneis de, 694
Horn, Osbert, 421; William, 662
Hornblowere, Osbert le, 248
Horner, 598
Horreweie, see Orway Farm
Horridge (Arigge), Ralph of, 326
Horsam, see Horsham
Horsant, Roger, 193
Horsham (Horsam), Robert of, 403, 520, 524
Horthon, see Horton
Horton (Dorset), abbey, 696
Horton (Horthon, Hortone), Gervase de, 271, 721; Matthew de, 597; Robert de, p. 2; Roger de, 371; Thomas of, p. 4; Thomas de (? another), 430
Horwaie, see Orway Farm
Horwood (Horewode), 333
Hose, Osbert, 44; p. 126
Hospitallers, Knights, xlvi
Houbautone, Houboutone, see Holbeton
Houghton (Hugetone, Hugotone), Michael of, p. 3; Richard of, p. 3
Houndtor (Hundestorre, Hundetorre), Richard of, p. 3; 24, 694, 715; Emma his wife, 715; Robert of, and Sarah his wife, 438; Turgis of, 715
Howintone, see Howitone
Howisdone, Henry de, 269
Howitone (Howintone), Adam de, 309, 310; Beatrice de, 310; Gunnilda de, 310; John de, 309; Roger de, 310; William de, 309, 310
Hoxham, see Huxham
Hoxtone, see Oxton
Hubbert, William, 29
Hugetone, see Houghton
Hugh, Matthew and Stephen sons of, 676; Michael son of, 137; p. 127; Rosamund daughter of, 442
Hugotone, see Houghton
Hugun, Robert, 16
Huish (Heiwis, Hewis, Hywis), 601, 621
  John of, 738; John son of Richard of, 738
Hulbere, Reginald, 627; William, 627
Hulle, Geoffrey de la, 220; Maysent de, 220; William de la, p. 8
Humphrey, Richard son of, p. 6; Thomas son of, 146
Hundehille, Alice de, 129

Hundestorre, Hundetorre, see Houndtor
Hunetone, see Honiton
Hunishauwe, see Huntshaw
Hunnesham, see Huntsham
Hunte, Adam, p. 1
Hunteneforde, see Huntford
Huntessor, John de, p. 4
Huntford (Hunteneforde), William of, p. 4
Huntsham (Hunnesham), Robert of, p. 6
Huntshaw (Hunishaue, Hunishauwe), 354
  Boniface of, 354
Huntsman (*venator*), Elias the, 287; John the, 13; Robert the, 371; Robert son of William the, 468
Huphille, Walter de, of Bickleigh, 430
Huppehaie, see Uphay
Hupperiche, Gilbert de, p. 1
Hurdwick (Herwik), 645
Hurlditch (Wrwildic), John of, p. 4
Hurlefod, Walter, 425
Hurnewai (Ernewei), William, of Colyford, 40; p. 125
Hurt, Robert le, 474
Huttenesleghe, see Hittisleigh
Huvestrong, Henry, 381
Huward, William son of, 430
Huxham (Hokesham, Hoxham), Emma of, 218; Robert of, p. 2; 218; William his son, 218
'Hyde Sancti Petri', 498
Hydone, see Hidon
Hyne, Henry de, lii, 114

IADECUMBE, Thomas de, 558
Iae, see Yae
Iddesleigh (Edwisleghe), 442
Idonea, an unknown woman, 763
Iharnecumbe, see Yarnicombe
Ilchester (Somerset), 189
Ilfracombe (Aufrecombe), xxxiv, 322
Incledon (Hingledene, Incledene), 324
  Robert of, 320, 324
Infans, Richard, 685
Insula, Geoffrey de, 603
Inthecumbe, Richard, 557
Ipplepen (Ipelpenne), 692, 693, 708
  John of, 691; Michael of, 693
Ireis, William, 607
Ireland, xiv, 132, 513
Ireys, Paulinus le, *alias* Irishman (*Hiberniensis*), Paul the, p. 6; 773
Irishman (*Hibn'*), Robert the, 322
Isabella of Angouleme, queen, 639
Isabella, an unknown woman, 763
Iseni, Michael de, 25
Isolda, Denis and William sons of, 567
Iter, Geoffrey iuxta, 635
Iuvenis, see Juvenis
Ivaus, Godfrey, p. 4
Ivedon House (Ivedone), Robert of, 24
Ivo, Walter, 118

JANITOR, John, 217; William his brother, 217
Jew, Jacob the, 183, 409; Urcellus (? Ursellus) the, 213; Camekinna his daughter, 213

Joan, a girl, 437
Jocelin, Ralph son of, 89
Joel, Thomas son of, p. 4; Warin son of, 581
John, king, xiv, 13, 69, 129, 176, 218, 219, 220, 224, 271, 273, 388, 512, 515, 577, 639, 707
John, a boy, 541
John, Edward son of p. 7; John son of, 37; Luke son of, 166, 598, 722; Ralph son of, xliii; Richard son of, 269; Roger son of, 107; the priest's son, 542
Jordan, John son of, p. 6
Juvenis (Iuvenis), Matthew, p. 6; Richard, of Farwood, 57; Roger, 727

KACHEREL, Rannulf, 108
Kaddewrthi, *see* Cadworthy
Kagchefrenkis, Jordan, of Exeter, 334
Kage, Hugh de la, xxxviii, 529, 536
Kaillewei, Philip de, 466
Kainges, Philip, p. 7
Kaioler, Martin le, of Lydford, 474
Kalewdeleghe, Kalewodeleghe, *see* Calverleigh
Kalliou, *see* Caillou
Kampere, Richard le, 382
Kari, *see* Carey Barton
Karmetone, Emma de, 369, 389
Karsewelle, *see* Kerswell
Kaygnes, *see* Caheines
Kegh, Richard, 677
Keling, Walter, 163
Kelli, Gilbert, and Ascelina his wife, 461
Kelly (Kelli, Kelly), Nicholas of, 614
Kempe, Adam, 201; Robert, 650; Roger, 527; William, 212, 213
Kendon (Kingdon), 720, 721
Kene, Richard, 618
Keneforde, *see* Kenniford
Kenn (Ken), 741
Kenniford (Keneforde), Osbert of, p. 3
Kente, Roger de, 694
Kentisbeare (Kentelesbeare), 121, 125
Kentisbury (Kentesbire), xliii, 448
Kenton (Kentone), burgh, xxxiv, 1, p. 7; 658–60; manor, 489, 551, 658; tithing, 744
Kerdewelle, *see* Cardwell
Kerl, Alan, 26
Kernun, Roger, 230
Kerselake, Hervey de, p. 2
Kerswell (Karsewelle, in Broadhembury), 581
Daniel of, 126
Kerswell (Carswille, Abbotskerswell), 696, 709
Kerswell (Carsewille, Kingskerswell), 707
Kerswell (Carsewelle, Abbotskerswell, or Kingskerswell), 703
Ketel, Richard, 318
Keynges, *see* Caheines
Kide, Joel, 726
Kilbury, 581
Killebole, John, 685
Killigorick (Kilagoroke, Cornwall), 528
Kilmington (Kelmetone), 21
Kilward, Seilda widow of Jordan de, 244

Kimworthy, 269
Kinbercnolle, Roger de, 127
Kinesman, William, 110
King, the, *see* Henry III
King, Richard le, 537; William, 430; William (another), 504
Kingesforde, *see* Kingsford
Kingford (Kingforde), Michael of, 607
Kingsbridge (Kingbrige), burgh, xxxiv, p. 8
Kingsford (Kingesforde), Philip of, p. 2
Kingskerswell (Carswelle Regis), 700, *see also* Kerswell
Kingsnympton (Nimetone), 271, 280, 384, 388
Walter le Blake of, 384
Kingsteignton (Teintone), 720
Martin of, 711; Warin of, 711
Kingston, 581
Kingswear, 700
Kipping, Richard, 210; John his brother, 210
Knavenmaistre, Roger, 467
Knightshayne (Knitteheie), 12
Knightstone (Knittestone), Alfred of, p. 3; Daniel of, p. 3
Knit, Walter, *alias* Walter le, 325, 327; William, 489; Richard his servant, 489
Knittestone, *see* Knightstone
Knostan, *see* Knowstone
Knotte, Richard, 387
Knowle (Cnolle, Knolla), Richard of, 190; Roger of, 249
Knowstone (Cnutstane, Knostan, Knustone), Everard of, p. 5; William of, pp. 5, 7
Kuliforde, *see* Colyford
Kyde, Joel, p. 7
Kye, William, 514
Kyn, William le, 263

LABERGHE, Richard de, 216
Laforde, Henry de, p. 1
Lahale, *see* Hale Farm
Laheie, Mabel wife of Hugh de, 97
Lahille, Gilbert de, 198; William de, 17
Lake, Hugh de la, of Whitestone, 504; Walter the forester of La, 651
Laleghe, James de, 147
Lamasne, Roger de, p. 6
Lambert, Reginald, 635
Lamberton, *see* Lamerton
Lambrit, Jordan, 99; Walter, 101
Lamer, Ailmer de, p. 7
Lamerton (Lamberton, Lambetone, Lamertone), 605, 635
George of, 635
Lamore, Richeman de, 104
Lanceleve, John, 371; p. 127
Lane, Henry de la, 124
Laneweie, Absolon de, 53
Langaford (Langeforde), Geoffrey of, 261; Gilbert of, 261
Langage (Langhewis), Henry of, and Alice his wife, 535; Ralph her son, 535
Langdon (Langgedone), William of, p. 3
Langebrok, *see* Longbrook

Langeford, Langeforde, *see* Langaford, Langford
'Langel', 220
Langeleghe, Richard de, p. 7
'Langelonde', 221
Langemede, *see* Langmead
Langestone, *see* Langstone
Langford (Langeford, Langeforde), Richard of, 65, 78, 261, 268, 269, 521, 581; Roger of, 104, 269, 581
Langfurlang, *see* Long Furlong
Langgedone, *see* Langdon
Langhewis, *see* Langage
Langmead (Landemede), Roger of, 395; Stephen le Prestre of, 395; Thomas of, 395
Langstone (Langestone), Berenger of, 606
Languil, William, p. 6
Lanpreie, Simon, p. 2
Lanteprei, Robert de, xlii, 617
Lapford (Lapforde, Lappeforde), 459, 477
Alice of, 178; Katherine her sister, 178; William of, 178
Lapse, *see* Hapse
Lasele, *see* Zeal, South
Lashbrook (Lechebroke), 269
Launceston (Lanstevetone, Cornwall), 523
Laweie, William de, 345
Laweles, Roger, 429
Lawike, John de, p. 4
Lawrthe, Alice de, 260
Lea Barton (Leghe), William of, p. 2; 142
Leg, Edward, p. 127; Robert, 661; William, 659
Legh (Leghe), Geoffrey de, p. 4; Geoffrey de (another), 81; Godfrey de la, 232; William his son, 232
Gunilda de, 590; Agnes her daughter, 590
Hamelin de, p. 4; Henry de la, 104; John de, p. 1; Osbert de la, 412; Richard de, 377; Richard de la (another), 419; Richard de la (another), 499; Robert de, 274; Roger de la, 572; Walter de, 377; Walter de la (another), 499; William de (various persons), pp. 1, 4(2), 6; 650
see also Lea Barton
Leghe Monachorum, *see* Monkleigh
Leicestershire, xlviii, 280
Leicestre, John, p. 7; Reginald, p. 7
Leie, Robert de, p. 2
Leigh (Bere Ferrers), 527
Leigh (Churchstow), 603
Leigh Barton (Leghe), 650
Leiham, Wymarc de, 465
Lesbocke, Benedict de, p. 1
'Lesmere', 371
Lespek (le Espek), Richard, 494
Lespus (Espus), Jordan, 230, 279
Lestane, Gervase de, 373; Roger de, 494
Lettress, Nicholas de, 708
Leuwin, Walter, 492
Levele, Richard, 412
Leveneurda, Walensis, 24, 25
Levestone, *see* Luson
Lew (Liu), Geoffrey brother of the parson of, 252

Lewdon (Ludene), Alnothus of, 716; Geoffrey Thethigmanne of, 716; Hugh of, 716
Lewe, William de, 404
Lewinus, Robert, 542
Lewtrenchard, 625
Lexhayne, 71
Lexintone, Robert de, 323
Lida, Adam, 751
Liddaton Green (Liddetone, Lidetone), Alan of, and Margery his wife, 631; Belengarius of, 628, 631, 651; Margery of, 651; Roger the cook of, 631
Lideforde, *see* Lydford
Lideman, Richard, p. 8
Lidetone, *see* Liddaton Green
Lifrere, Robert, p. 6
Lifton (Liftone), hundred, xxi, 1, pp. 1, 4; 225, 232, 233, 605–39, 657, 658; p. 130; manor, 634, 635, 636, 638 Richard of, 761
Lighe, Nicholas, 663
Limbire, *see* Lymbury
Limscott (Limescote), Martin of, 230
Lincolnshire, 708
Lineham, Linham, *see* Lyneham
Litleman, Richard, 17
Litfare, Isaac de, 175
Lithe, Adam, 741
Lithebi, Adam, p. 6
Lithegri, William de, the smith, 233
Littlecombe Barn (Littelcombe, Littelcumbe), Miles of, 54; Robert his son, 54
Rannulf of, 54
Littleham (Litelham), 208, 221
Llywellyn the Great, prince of Aberffraw, 599
Lobb (Loppa), Philip of, p. 5
Locumbe, John de, 221
Loddebroc, *see* Ludbrook
Loddiswell (Lodeswelle), 599
Loders (Dorset), prior/priory, 13, 46, 47
see also Axmouth, prior of
Lodretone, *see* Lotherton
Loges, Hugh de, lii, 114, 260
Logeshore, *see* Loxhore
Lokinge, Gilbert de, p. 8
Loman (Lumene), p. 126
London (London'), 35, 745, 752
dean of, *see* Lucy, Geoffrey de; Robert of, 433
Longbrook (Langebrok), Simon of, 574, 575
Long Furlong (Langfurlang), Joel of, p. 4
Longus, Gilbert, p. 2; Godfrey, and Agnes his wife, 310; John, p. 2; John (another), 252; Richard, 492; Robert, 263; Roger, 568; Walter, of Bolham, p. 127; Walrand his son, p. 127; Walter, of Petertavy, 520; William, 683; William, le Bedel, 254; William son of Walter, 304
Loosebear (Losbere), 393
Loppa, *see* Lobb
Losmer, Walter, 371
Lotherton (Lodretone), Alfred of, 535
Loventor (Luvenetorre), 709

Loverde, Richard le, 93
Lowis, William, p. 7
Loxhore, (Logeshore), Humphrey of, p. 5
Lubalde, Robert de, p. 7
Luccumbe, Adam son of William de, 131; p. 126
Lucy, Geoffrey de, dean of St. Paul's 636; Godfrey de, bishop of Winchester, 636
Ludbrook (Loddebroc, Luddebrok), Richard Ode of, 570; Stephen of, p. 3
Ludene, see Lewdon
Lug, Nicholas, p. 5
Lukes, Roger de, 669
Lullepate, John, 557
Lumene, see Uplowman
Luneput, see Luppitt
Lungmuner, William le, 438
Luppitt (Luneput, Luvepit), 15, 18 Andrew of, p. 1
Lupus, Walter, xliii, 315, 448; William, p. 3
Luscombe, 603
Luscott (Lustcote), Thomas of, 314
Luscy, Geoffrey de, 271
Luson (Levestone, Luvestone), Godfrey of, 574, 575; Robert of, 575
Lustcote, see Luscott
Luunge, William, 17
Luvese, see Ovis
Luvestone, see Luson
Luvet, Philip, p. 5
Luvetone, William de, 557
Luvetrot, Walter, 488
Luxi, Richard, 548
Lydford (Liddeford, Lideford, Lideforde, Lidforde), burgh, p. 7; 640–1; castle, 474, 609, 617, 637; manor, 637; St. Petrock's church, 637
Martin le Kaioler of, 474; Richard le Clerk of, 632
Lymbury (Limbire), Humphrey of, p. 2; 524; Reginald his clerk, 524; William his groom, 524
Lyme Regis (Lim, Dorset), 26
Lympstone (Levenestone), 210
Lyneham (Lineham, Linham), Bartholomew of, p. 7; Walter of, p. 4

MADESHAY, alias Madford, 90
Maidencombe (Maidencumbe), 508
Maidenstane, William de, 649
Maine, Roscelin vicomte of, and Constance his wife, 410
Makerel, William, 44; William (another), 478
Malherbe, William, p. 2; 146
Mallestone, see Malston
Malmesbury (Wiltshire), William of, 417
Malston (Mallestone), Hugh of, p. 3
Mamhead (Mannhevid), 728
Adam le Bel of, 557; Roger Palmerus of, 557; Swein of, and Edith his wife, 728
Manaton (Manetone, Parva Mannetone), 719, 720, 721
Manbire, see Membury
Mandevill, Geoffrey de, 46

Mandeville, family, 604
Joan de, 604
Manebi (Manneby), Gilbert de, 409, 550
Maneton, Gervase de, 721
Manileghe (Manley), William of, p. 2
Manneby, see Manebi
Mannhevid, see Mamhead
Mannor, Robert de, 118
Mansel, Humphrey, 172
Mante, Adam, 475
Marchand (Marchaunde, Mercator), Robert le, xxxii, p. 5; 300, 371, 391; Roger la, 391
Mareis, Robert, p. 6; 36
Mariansleigh, 293
Marie, Richard, 692
Mariota, 306
Marisco, Geoffrey de, 524; Thomas de, and Imeina his wife, 474; William de, p. 2
Marland, Little (Merland Pighie), 444
Marland, Peters (Merland), John son of Peter of, 444
Marlecumbe, see Merlcombe
Marsh (Mersa, Mershe), Herbert of, p. 5; 274
Marshal, Richard, earl of Pembroke, xxii, 513; William, earl of Pembroke, 599
Marshal (marescallus, marscallus), Bartholomew the, p. 7; Eustace the, 308; John the, 692; Bartholomew his brother, 692
Philip the, p. 1; Ralph the, p. 7; Roger the, 78
Marshall Farm (Morkishille), Richard of, 740
Marshwood (Dorset), honour of, 271
Marsille, William, 649; Beatrice his mother, 649
Martin, Nicholas son of, 295
Marwood (Merewde), Eustace of, p. 5
Marytavy (Tavi), 610
Maszacrer (Mazacrer), Alexander le, of Bampton, 150; Payn le, 330; William, 723
Matecumbe, see Metcombe
Matilda, queen, 639
Matthew, Herbert son of, pp. 2, 3; 159, 160, 263, 471, 474, 604, 637, 676, 679, 682
Mauri, Richard, 537
Maurice, Henry son of, 271; William son of, 324; William son of (another), 340
Mazacrer, see Maszacrer
Mazun, Joel le, p. 7
Meadwell (Medwelle, Medwille), Agnes daughter of Robert of, xxxviii, 613; Nicholas of, 568
Meavy (Mewy), Richard of, p. 4; William of, 403
Meduana, Geoffrey de, 273; Joel de, 271, 273; Walter de, 273
Medwelle, Medwille, see Meadwell
Megge, William, 274
Mei, Richard, 584
Melbury (Melebire, Mellebire), 256
Bartholomew of, 269; Walter of, 256
Meldon (Meledone), Alan of, p. 6

Index of Persons and Places

Melebire, *see* Melbury
Meledone, *see* Meldon
Mellebire, *see* Melbury
Membland (Mimminglan, Mimmiglande, Minminlande), 263, 556, 562
  Henry of, 263; Walter of, p. 3; 556
Membury (Manbire, Mebire, Menbire), 6, 20, 23
  Richard of, p. 1
Membury, East (Est Menbire), 5
Mercator, Robert, de Cumbe, p. 6
  see also Marchand
Merchant (*mercator*), William the, 19
Merewde, *see* Marwood
Merland, *see* Marland, Peters
Merlcombe (Marlecumbe), Mabel of, 89
Merlei, Merley, *see* Murley
Merton (Mertone), 437, 438
  Henry of, p. 4; 476
Meschin, William le, 300
Metal-founder (*fundator*), Adam the, 80; Walter the, 80
Metcombe (Matecumbe), Cristina of, 83
Methyne, Adam le, 685
Meulan (Meulent), Ralph de, 708; Waleran of, 708
Mewy, *see* Meavy
Middletone, *see* Milton Abbot
Middlecot (Middelcote, Black Torrington), 258
  Cristiana of, 258
Middlecott (Middelcote, Rackenford), Roger of, 373
Middlecott (Virginstow, Lifton), 638
Middilhille, *see* Middlehills Farm
Middilkote, Reginald de, p. 7
Middlehills Farm (Middilhille), Ralph of, p. 8
Midwinter (Midwinter), James of, 739
Milemead (Milmed), Angerus of, p. 4
Miles, Robert, p. 4
Milford (Milleforde), 362
  Philip of, and Matilda his wife, 362
Millaton House (Millentone), John of, 632
Miller (*molendinarius*), Adam the, 16; Almerus the, 659; Geoffrey the, 478; Gervase the, 460; Gilbert the, 665; Henry son of Ralph the, 64; Joel the, 718; John the, 688; Leonard the, 303; Martin the, 661; Martin son of the, 320; Nicholas the, 478; Pain the, 469; Peter the, 94; Walter his brother, 94 Ralph the, and Agnes his wife, 505 Ralph the (another), 659; Richard the, 147; Richard son of the, 320; Robert the, 110; Roger the, 58; Roger the (another), 671; Stephen the, 378; Thomas the, 478; Thomas the (another), 557; Walter the, 22; Walter the (another), 297; Walter the (another), 493; William the, xxxii, 670; William the (another), 530; William the (another), 630
Milmead, *see* Milemead
Milton, South (Middelton), 601, 603, 621
Milton Abbot (Middeltone), 650
  Bartholomew of, 646
Milton Damarel (Middeltone), 269

Mimminglan, Mimminglande, *see* Membland
Minet, William de, p. 5
Minminlande, *see* Membland
Mirabel, Roger, 595
Mirifel, Robert, 675
Mobire, *see* Modbury
Mocforde, *see* Muckford
Modbury (Mobire, Modbire), burgh, p. 6; 579–83
  David of, 668; Henry the wool carder (*carpissor lane*) of, 579; William the tailor of, 592
Modecumbe, *see* Mothecombe
Modi (Mody) David, 277; Roger, 300; William, 108
Mohun (Moun), Alice de, pp. 1, 2; 4, 13, 27, 28, 224, 709; John de, 4; Reginald de, senior, 27; Reginald de, *junior*, 4, 224; William de, 149; William de (another), 709
Moinel, Robert, 409
Mokeforde, *see* Muckford
Molend' (Molendino), Geoffrey de, 107; John de, 107; Robert de, p. 5; William de, p. 2
Molins, John de, p. 6
Molis, Henry de, 473; William his son, 473
  Hugh de, 631; Nicholas de, xxiii, xxvi, pp. 1, 3; 587, 596, 598, 600, 603, 707, 709, 749; Roger his son, 596; Roger de, 749; William de, 473, 631
Molland (Molande, Molland, Mothlande, Moulande), hundred or manor, x, xiii, pp. 5, 7; 37, 299–300; vill, 300
  Richard of, p. 5
Molland, West (West Mollande, Westmorlande), Robert of, pp. 5, 7
Molle, Walter, 119
'Molton', (Moltone, Moutone – Molton, North or South), 294
  Jocelin of, p. 7; Robert the smith of, 478; Robert the taverner of, 478; Walter of, p. 6; 330, 753
Molton, North (Normotone, Normoutone), burgh, p. 7; hundred, x, xxv, pp. 5, 7; 274–80, 300; manor, 66, 279
Molton, South (Soumoutone, Sumotone, Sumoutone, Sutmoltone), burgh, x, p. 7; 296–8, 331, 377; hundred, xxv, xxvi, p. 5; 280, 281–95, 377; manor, 295; vill, 291
  Arnold the deacon of, xlv, 292; Richard the clerk of, 291
Monkleigh (Leghe Monachorum), Walter the serjeant of, 689
Montacute (Somerset), priory, 451
Montana, Michael the man of William de, 689
Monte, Jordan de, p. 7; Michael de, 607; William de, 430
Monte Acuto, Katherine de, 221
Montebourg (dep. Manche), France, abbey, 47
Monte Sorello, Ralph de, 28
Mont. St. Michel (dep. Manche), France, abbey, 13, 217
Moor, 638

Moorstone Barton (Moristone, Morstone), Roger of, p. 2; Roger of (? same), p. 2
Mora (More), Geoffrey de, *alias* Geoffrey de la, pp. 5, 7; John de, 172; Mabel de, 172; Philip de, 104; Ralph de, p. 8; Robert de, *senior*, 386; Robert de, *junior*, 386; Roger son of Gunild de, 250; Sampson de, 623; Thomas de la, 368; Walter de, 238; Thomas his son, 238
Walter son of Gunild de, 250
Morba, *see* Morebath
Morcellis, Robert de, p. 3
Morchard Bishop (Morcet), Hugh of, 414
Morcok, Matthew, 17
Morcumbe, Peter de, p. 3
More, *see* Mora
Morebath, (Morba), 293
Hugh of, p. 2
Morel, Osbert, 89; Walter, 89
'Morele Lanceleve', 139
Moreleigh (Morle), 603
William of, p. 3
Morgan, Robert, 413
Morin, Morin son of Robert, 218; Ralph, 324; Robert son of Robert, 220
Moristone, *see* Moorstone Barton
Morkishille, *see* Marshall Farm
Morle, *see* Moreleigh
Morleghe, William de, serjeant of Cheriton Fitzpaine, 194
Morleghe Peverel, Peter de, 738
Morley (Morleghe), William of, 593
Morstone, *see* Moorstone Barton
Mortain (dep. Manche), France, count Robert of, 37
Mortest, Alice de, 118
Morthoe (Morthow, Mottehou), Adam of, 314, 316
Morwell (Morwille), 648
Mothecombe (Modecumbe), William of, p. 3
Mottehou, *see* Morthoe
Moun, William, p. 2
see also Mohun
Moutone, *see* 'Molton'
Mowbray, Robert de, 353
Mowlish (Mulehiwis, Muliwhis), Beatrice daughter of William of, 729; Robert of, p. 3
Moyne, Roger le, 294
Muckford (Mocforde, Mokeforde), Richard of, p. 6; Walter of, 373
Mukwdes, Peter de, 689
Mulehiwis, Muliwhis, *see* Mowlish
Mungomery, William de, 145
Munnirun, Walter de, 204
Muntorie, Ralph de, p. 1
Murda, Walter, 185
Murley (Merlei, Merley, Morleghe), p. 126
Herbert of, 127, 263
Mus, *alias* le Veutrer, Richard le, 24
Musbury, 28

Natcott (Notecote), Robert of, p. 4
Natsworthy, 709

Neadon, 721
Necke, Roger, and Agnes his wife, 291
Nectan, Saint, xxx
Neirun, Ralph, 611, 622
Netherexe (Nitherexe), 111
Netherton (Nithertone), 59
Newenham, abbey/abbot, xx, 4, 58, 224
New Forest (Hants), 403
Newinton, 473
Newland, 269
Newton Ferrers (Niwetone), 562
Osbert of, 564
Newton Poppleford, xxxiv
Niger, Richard, xli, 395; Robert, the smith, p. 6; Walter, p. 6; Walter (another), 94; William, 494
Nimet, *see* Nymet Rowland
'Nimetone', *see* Kingsnympton
Niwecumbe, William, 86
Niwetone, *see* Newton Ferrers
Nonant, *see* Nunant
Norfolk, xxxiii, 13, 280, 524
Norman, *see* Balistarius
Normandy, 47
Norreis, Robert le, 125; Thomas le, p. 2; William, p. 3; William le (? same), 602
Nortfuc, John de, 287
Northam (Norham), 453
Northcote (Northcote, Axminster), 16
Alice the widow of, 16; Ralph, Robert and Roger her sons, 16; Robert of, p. 8
Northcote (Northecote, Witheridge), Richard of, 387
Northcote (Northcote or Northcott Barton, North Tawton), Geoffrey de, p. 5
Northcott, 273
Northdown (Northdone), Osbert of, 24
Northemore, Ralph de, 535
Northicote, William de, 628
Northleigh (Northlee), 57
Northlew (Liutoritone), 250
Norton (Nortone), Deodatus of, p. 6
Nortone, Robert de la Heie de, 730; William de, 730
Norwelle, Vincent de, p. 5
Notecote, *see* Natcott
Nottiston (Nottesdone), Matilda of, 193
Novingtone, *see* Skerraton
Nunant (Nonant), Guy de, 176; Henry de, 176, 599; Roger I de, 176, 682; Roger II de, 176
Nutcombe (Nutcumbe), Nicholas of, p. 2
Nutley (Nutleghe), Roger of, p. 4
Nutley (Bucks), 360
Nymet (Nimet), river, 376
Nymet Rowland (Nimet), 477
Walter of, 477
Nympton, Bishop's (Nimetone Episcopi), 375, 384, 389
Nympton, George, 384

Oakford (Acforde), 371
Oburnford (Woberneforde), 161, 598, 722
Ode, Richard, of Ludbrook, 570

Index of Persons and Places

Odo, Richard son of, 551; Geoffrey his brother, 551
Offwell (Ofwelle, Offewelle), 58, 60
  Stephen of, p. 1
Ogbear (Ogbere), Roger of, p. 4
Ogier, Peter son of, 221
Oiham, William de, and Matilda his wife, 230
Okehampton (Hokemantone, Okemantone), burgh/vill, xxxiv, xlvi, p. 6; 641, 642–3
  barony/honour of, 28, 147, 173, 221, 269, 324, 448, 477, 577
Okestone, see Oxton House
Oliver, Jordan, ix, 255, 441
Omnibus Sanctis, William de, p. 3; 566
Orchard (Orscherd), John del, alias John de Le, and Christiana, alias Christina, his wife, 626
Orcheton (Orchertone), Ailward of, 572
Orreweie, see Orway Farm
Orscherd, see Orchard
Orway Farm (Horreweie, Horwaie, Orreweie, Orweya), 125; Thomas of, p. 2; 108, 125, 519; William of, p. 127
Oryvalle, see Rivaux
Osbert, 163
Osmer, Ralph, p. 4
Osmund, John, 574; Roger, 33; Roger (another), 574
Oteri Sancte Marie, see Ottery St. Mary
Oteritone, see Otterton
Otter (Oteri, Otery, Otri), river, 72, 73, 130; p. 126
Otterford (Oteryford), 84
Ottermouth (Otermue), 206, 207, 209
Otterton (Oteritone), prior/priory, xliii, 13, 203
Otterton (Oteritone), Tholomeus of, p. 2
Ottery St. Mary (Oteri Sancte Marie, Sancte Marie Otery), hundred or manor, xiii, xxxiv, p. 2; 37, 72–4
  William of, 8
Ovis (Luvese), Thomas of, p. 5
Oxford, Isabel de Bulebec countess of, p. 2; 176, 709
  Robert de Vere, earl of, 176
Oxfordshire, 16, 221
Oxton House (Hakestone, Hokestone, Hoxtone, Okestone), John of, p. 6; 158, 330, 396, 753, 761; Richard of, p. 7; Walter of, 330
Oysel, Roger, p. 4

PAGE, Thomas, p. 6; 37; William, 263; William (another), 685
Paiard (Paihard, Spaiard), Luke, 254, 255, 622, 623; Stephen, 622, 624; Margery his wife, 622
Paignton (Penitone), 704, 705
Pain, Nicholas, and Ascelota his wife, 58; Walter, 624; William, p. 1
Painel, see Paynel
Pais, Walter, 689
Pale, Walter le, 153
Palmer (Palmerus), Elias, and Cecilia his wife, 9; Gilbert the, 697; Philip le,

Palmer—cont.
  422; Roger, of Mamhead, 557; William, 710
Pancrasweek, 270
Parc, Roger le, p. 4
Parco, Roger de, 269
  Roger de (? same), 616
Paris, France, 319
Parmenter, Elias le, 691; John le, 478; Ralph le, 542; William le, 659
Parvus, Adam, of Black Torrington, 229
Passaford (Paseforde), Sara wife of Joel of, 242
Passawand, Richard, 229
Passemer, Nicholas, 618; Richard, p. 4; 226, 230, 257; Walter, p. 2
Patetone, see Petton
Paumer, Philip le, p. 6; 753; Richard le, p. 6; Richard le (another), 659; Robert le, p. 2; Thomas le, p. 2
Payhembury (Hambire, Paiembire), 106
  John the parson of, 107
Paynel (Painel), family, 92; Fulk I, 160; Fulk II, 160; William, I, 27, 102, 160; William son of William son of, alias William II, 160
Paz, John, p. 3; John de (another), p. 7; John, of Teignmouth, 542
Peccha, Robert, 308
Peche, Roger, 768
Pecum, Robert, 542
Pecun, Robert (? same), 732
'Peggenesse', 483
  Alice de, 483; Guy de, 483; Ralph de, 483
Peitevin (Peytevin), Edward le, 542; John le, p. 6; Robert, alias Robert le, p. 2; 200
Peivre, Sampson, 329
Pelagia, 606; Avice her daughter, 606
Pele, William le, 544
Pelecoke, David, p. 1
Pencuit, Roger de, 549
Penne, Nicholas de la, 758; Ralph his father, 758; Ralph de la (another), 15; Alice his daughter, 15
  Richard Rugge de la, 704
Pennicott (Pimecote, Pinnecote), 775
  Robert of, 199; Walter Rolland of, and Amice his wife, 184
Penpol, Warin de, 477
Pentesho, see Pettesho
Pepering, see Pipering
Perepont, Robert de, 149
Perer, William, and Matilda his wife, 254
Perrer, Philip, p. 4
Pertehaie, Henry, 204
Perville, Walter de, p. 1
Pessy, John de, 16
Pestur, Geoffrey le, 431; Robert le, xxxvi, 762; Sabina his wife, 762
Peter, Robert son of, 33; Roger, 621
Petertavy (Tavi Sancti Petri), Walter Longus of, 520
Pethill (Puddehelle), Maurice of, 535
Petit, see Balistarius
Pettesho (Pentesho), Ralph, alias Rannulf de, 243, 265; Everwin his brother, 243, 265

Petton (Patetone), 159
  Gervase of, 159
Peverel of Ermington, family, 581
  Hugh, xxxii, 1, p. 3; 580, 581, 583
Peverel of Essex, William, 581; Matilda his sister, 581
Peverel of Sampford, family, 581
  Hugh, 168; William, p. 2; 37, 119, 125, 145, 386
Pichelere, Richard le, 614
Pickwell (Pidekeswelle), Robert of, p. 5
Pig, Roger le, p. 5
Pigace, Alan, 9
Pigoc, Agnes, 746
Pikewille, John son of Robert de, 669; Reginald or Robert de, 669
Pil, Ralph le, 531
Pilefen, see Pilliven
Pilketin, William de, p. 2
Pilland (Pilland, Pillande), 319
  Archibald of, 274, 314
Pille, Rannulf de la, 284
Pilliven (Pilefen), Peter of, p. 7
Pilton (Piltone), 317
Pimecote, see Pennicott
Pincerna, Walter, 78; William, 78
Pinhochet, John, 33
Pinhoe (Pinho), 513
Pinnecote, see Pennicott
Pinu, Herbert de, *alias* Herbert le, 32, 37, 430, 476, 581; Simon his son, xxxii, 32, 37; Ralph de, p. 5
Pinzun, Henry, 323
Pipard, William, 263
Piper, Oliver son of Richard, 621; Sampson, 754
Pipering (Pepering), Ralph, 107, 108
Pipping, William 450
Pirho, Gilbert, 247
Pirzwell (Pissewelle), 125
  William of, 125; Richard his son, 125
'Pistone', 169
Pitford, Great (Putiforde), Sir Robert of, 476
Pitte, Richard de la, p. 2; 145; Robert de la, 146; William de la, 189
Pittescombe (Puttokescumbe), William of, 627
'Plimlande', manor, p. 8; 37, 544–7
Plimtone, see Plympton
Plimtre, see Plymtree
Ploughman (*carucarius*), Roger the, 236
Plympton (Plimtone), burgh or vill, p 6; 327, 547, 548–55; honour of, 6, 57, 266, 342, 391, 477, 510, 603; manor, 30
Plympton, prior/priory, xxxiv, 524, 587
  Vincent servant of, 586
Plympton, Thomas Edrig of, 540
Plymtree (Plimtre), 124
  John Billes of, 109
Pode, Richard, 373; Roger, 373
Poer (Poher, Pohier), Hugh le, 371; Roger le, p. 2; Stephen le, 324; William le, xxi
Poke, Robert, p. 1
Pole, Anthony de la, p. 2; Philip de la, 471; Richard de la, 104; Roger de la, 471; Simon de la, 471; William de la, 373

Poleham, see Pulham
Pollarde, Michael, 776
Polsloe (Polleslowe, Polslou), prioress/nuns of, 67, 68, 574
  Walter servant of, 574
Poltimore (Pultimor), 493
  Bartholomew of, p. 3
Pomerai (Pomeraie, Pomerei, Pumeray), Geoffrey de la, 28; Henry de la, 268, 641; Henry de la (another), 709; William de, *alias* William de la (various persons), 263, 566, 569, 581, 618, 662, 738, 776
Pons (dep. Charente-Maritime), France, 123
Ponte, Martin de, 590; Nicholas de, 685; William de, p. 6
Ponte Audomar, Henry de, 166, 722
Porta, Richard de, p. 5; Richard de (another), 561; Richard de (? same), 576; William de, 203
Porteman (Portman), William, p. 6; 112
Porter, Roger le, 94
Portmore (Portmora), Wermund of, p. 6
Postlake (Potteslake), Ralph of, 204
Poter (Pottere), Geoffrey le, p. 6; Geoffrey le (another), 631; Osbert le, p. 7; Peter le, 681
Potteslake, see Postlake
Poughill (Pouhahille), 221; Augustine of, 221
Poyt, Roger, p. 7
Prat, Alfred, 496; Robert, 126; Thurstan, 126; William, 321
Prawle (Praule, Praulle), 676; Henry of, 618; Jordan of, 676; Roger of, 721; William of, p. 3; 25, 597
Prescott (Prestcote), John of, p. 1; Richard of, p. 2; 94
Prestre, Stephen le, of Langmead, 395
Pridias, Cecilia daughter of Robert de, 536; Geoffrey de, p. 3; 575; Roger de, xxvii
Priest (*sacerdos*), Michael the, 637
Prige, John, p. 7
Prigke, Roger, 584; Richard and Robert his brothers, 584
Pristritone, Germanus de, 704
Priune, William, 245
Prude, Roger le, 691
Pruston Barton (Prustetone), Alexander of, 163
Prute, William le, 695
Pruz, William le, 618
Puddehelle, see Pethill
Pudding, Richard, p. 2
Puddington (Potingtone, Putitone), 368, 369
Pulein, Nicholas, p. 7; Roger, p. 7; Thomas, p. 2; Thomas le (another), 385
Pulham (Poleham, Pullan), Jordan of, p. 5; 274
Pullus, Ralph, p. 7
Pultimor, see Poltimore
Punchardone (Punchardun), Alice de, 665; Richard de, p. 5; William de, p. 5
Purdeu, Henry, 263; Richard, 674; Robert, 368

Index of Persons and Places

Puridone, Richard de, p. 2
'Pusling', river, 564
Putiforde, see Pitford, Great
Putford (Putteford), Reginald of, 260
Putte, Robert de la, 16
Putteford, see Putford
Puttokescumbe, see Pittescombe

QUANTOXHEAD (Somerset), parson of, xxxi
Quarr (Quarrera, Isle of Wight), abbot of, 57
Quercu, Adam de, 95; Walter de, 443
Quinel, Peter, p. 6

RABSCOTT (ROBERDESCOTE), Richard of, p. 5
Rackenford, x, xxxiv, 373
Raddon (Raddone), 184, 185, 221, 775; East, 185; West, 221, 775
Raddon, Baldwin of, 182, 221, 775, 776; John of, 651; Roland of, 182; Stephen of, 182
Radershe, see Radge
Radeslo, see Ratsloe
Radge (Radershe), Ralph of, 607
Raggeshille, William de, 99
Ralegh, (Raleg', Ralege, Raleghe, Raleigh), Henry de, 385; William de, royal justice and treasurer of Exeter cathedral, xxiv, xxv, xxvi, 86, 445; William de, the elder, xxii, p. 1; 66, 315, 320, 325, 332, 385; William de, the younger, 320, 325, 418; Wymund de, 28, 221
Ralph, a groom, 545; Ralph son of, p. 3; Robert son of, 107
Rannulf, Geoffrey son of, 356; Richard son of, 592
Rashleigh Barton, 477
Ratsloe (Radeslo), Jordan of, p. 2
Rattery, 587
Raulestone, see Rolstone Barton
Rawenilda, Roger son of, 691; Geoffrey and Gilbert his brothers, 691
Rawridge (Rouerigge), 14
Rawstone Barton (Raulestone), 414
Redebert, Robert, 552
Redeman, Richard, 576
Redemore, see Ringmore
Redewei, see Rudway
Redvers (Revers, Rivers), Baldwin I de, earl of Devon, 57; Godfrey his clerk, 518; Baldwin III de, earl of Devon, xxv, xxvi, pp. 2, 3, 4; 3, 16, 103, 130, 515, 518, 532, 535, 543, 709, 751, 770; Richard I de, 47, 90, 130, 532, 543, 751; Richard II de, earl of Devon, 707, 751; Denise his wife, 707
Reeve (prepositus), Morinus the, 320; Patrick the, 284; Ralph the, p. 7
Reftone, see Rifton
Reginald, Henry son of, 345, 477
Reigni, John de, p. 5
Remstorre, Iwein de, 147
Rengot, Alice daughter of, 155

Revel, Robert, 78
Revers, see Redvers
Revetone, see Riverton
Rewe (Rewe), 512
Richard I, king, 23, 68, 123, 596, 636, 639, 707
Richard, earl, see Cornwall, Richard earl of
Richard, a beggar, 262; Durand, alias Durandus, son of, p. 3; 581, 633; Hamelin son of, 265; Sir William son of, 213
Richeman, Beatrice wife of John, of Exeter, 330, 753, 755; Edelota her maid, 755
Riddesforde, Adam de, 673
Riddlecombe (Ridelecumbe), 461
Ridel, Geoffrey, 88
Ridelecumbe, see Riddlecombe
Ridere, Roger son of Geoffrey le, 278
Ridone, John de, p. 3
Rifforde, see Rushford Barton
Rifton (Reftone), Jordan son of William of, 145
Riketrache, Robert, 104
Riley (Rileghe), Geoffrey of, 738; Walter his son, 738; Hugh of, 738
Ringeslade, see Ringslade
Ringmore (Redemore), Godus of, 568
Ringslade (Ringeslade), William of, p. 3
Risdon, Tristram, xiv
Ristivel, Roger, 430
Rivaux (Oryvalle), Peter de, xxii, xxiii, p. 1; 187
Rivers, see Redvers
Riverton (Revetone), William of, p. 5
Riwe, Richard de, p. 5
Rixdale (Rixtiville), Roger of, p. 3
Roberdescote, see Rabscott
Robert, a boy, 14; a stranger, 764
Roborough (Ruberghe, Rugheberghe), hundred, p. 4; 145, 520–33
Roc, William, 65
Rocforde, William de, 50
Roche, John de la, 29; Richard de la, 65
Rockbeare (Rokebere), 179
Rodeweie, Walter de la, lii, 114
Rof, John, 190; John, archdeacon of Cornwall, 221; Martin, p. 6; 112, 753, 754, 772; Thomas, p. 6
Roger, a boy, 22; Robert son of, 391
Rogerstone, Paris de, 638; Richard de, 653
Roges, Jordan son of, 146, 147
Rokebare, Reginald, 107
Rolland, Walter, of Pennicott, and Amice his wife, 184
Rolstone Barton (Raulestone), Hawise of, 412
Romillei, Robert de, 300; Cecily his daughter, 300
Roofer (coopertor), Richard the, 331
Rose, 133, see also Calverleigh
Rose Ash (Esse), 380
'Rostfeld', 361
Theobald of, 361
Rothebare, John de, p. 4
Rouen (dep. Seine-Maritime), France, dean and chapter of St. Mary's of, p. 2; 74
Rousdon, 46

Route, William de, p. 6
Ruche, see Ruffa
Rudone, Richard de, 607
Rudway (Redewei), Walter of, 494
'Rueberghe', 188
Ruffa (Ruche), Matilda, 140; p. 127; Robert her son, 140; p. 127
Ruffus, Gilbert, 430; John, 104; Ralph, 379, 385; Ralph (? another), 566; Reginald, 568, 575; William, 104
Rugberghe, Ralph de, 299
Rugeleon, Geoffrey, 403
Rugge, Geoffrey, p. 6; Reginald, 500; Richard, de la Penne, 704; Walter, 108
Ruggehulle, William, 97; Stephen his brother, 97
Ruglestdone, Stephen de, 117
Ruiwelin, Walter son of, 634; Matilda his mother, 634
Rus, Hugh le, 686; Ralph le, 127; Ralph le (? same), 776; Thomas le, p. 1; William le, p. 5
Rushford Barton (Rifforde), Adam of, p. 6 753; Ralph of, 70
Russeaus (Russelle), Peter de, xxii, p. 1
Russel, Stephen 521; Walter, p. 2; Walter (another), 316; Richard his son, 316 William, 290; William (another), 771; William, of Holcombe Rogus, 147
Russelle, see Russeaus
Ruwilin, William, p. 6
Ryme (Dorset), xlv

SAGKE, Thomas, 387
St. Dogmells (Pembrokeshire), abbot of, 587
St. Edmund, William de, ix, x
Saint Hill (Seinthille), Thomas of, and Beatrice his wife, 519
St.-Martin-les-Champs, Paris, priory of, 319
St. Mary Church, 3, 709
Sakiatone, Adam de, 418; Agnes de, 412
Salisbury (Salesbire, Wiltshire), bishopric of, 658
Saliur, John le, of Torrington, 359
Salterton (Saltertone), Alan of, 201; Philip of, 201
Sampford Courtenay (Samforde), 231, 232 Stephen Wainarde of, 232
Sampford Peverell, 581
Sampson, Ailward, 542
Sancto Albino, Stephen de, p. 5
Sancto Amando, Almaricus de, 708, 709
Sancto Dionisio, Robert de, 271
Sancto Stephano, William de, 587, 611
Sancto Vasto, Hugh de, 419
Sand Barton (Sande), William of, p. 2
Sangwin, William, p. 2
Santiago di Compostella (prov. Coruna), Spain, 46, 159, 269
Santone, Thomas de, 385
Sarah, Geoffrey son of, p. 6
Satterleigh (Saterleghe), Matthew of, 296
Saucey, Hugh de, 515
Saunton, 621
Sauser, William le, 271

Saxony, Jordan of, xlv
Schabecumbe, see Shapcombe
Sciria, Stephen, p. 7
Scopelake, Walter de, 542
Scot, Andrew le, p. 6
Scotia, Roger de, p. 3
Scottewrthe, William de, 269
Scurel, see Squirel
Scyredun, David de, 595; Oresia his daughter, 595
Seaton (Setona, Setone, Setune), 49; p. 126
Basilia of, 69; Luke of, p. 1
Seccheville, Secheville, see Sicca Villa
Segar, Swetricus, 21
Sege, Richard de la, 673
Segrave, Stephen de, xxvi
Sehive, Richard, p. 7
Seinthille, see Saint Hill
Selbirne, Martin de, 661
Sele, William de la, 443
see also Zeal, South
Seleda, see Slade
Selewrthe, see Silworthy
Sellake (Seglak), p. 127
Semechille, Roger de, p. 7
Semerus, 404; Richard his son, 404
Senewelle, Senewille, see Sowell Farm
Sepwassy, see Sheepwash
Serintone, Eudo de, p. 3
Serle, Richard, 462
Servant, Richard, 555
Serviens, John, p. 6; Luke, of Uffculme, 93, 99; Robert, of Tetcott, 263
Setona, Setone, see Seaton
Severe, Richard, 344
Seward, Henry, 140; p. 127; Goda his wife, 140
Sewennestone, see Simpson
Sewer (Sure), 603, 621
Seynte Mariecherch, Philip de, xliii
Shallaford (Shaldeford), Walter of, 616
Shanke, Robert, of Berrynarbor, 313; Roger, 574
Shapcombe (Schabecumbe), William of, 85
Shapley, 595
Shebbear (Safberghe, Sefberghe, Shefbere, Shefberghe), xliii
hundred, p. 4; 248, 424–52, 473
Sheepwash (Sepwassy), xxxiv
Thomas of, p. 5
Shene, Harding, 13
Shepherd (pastor), Roger the, 190
Sherborne (Shireburne, Dorset), abbot of, 221, 696, 709; see of, 417, 658; bishops of, see Forthhere
Sherford (Sireford), Oliver of, 78; William of, 78
Sheriff, Baldwin the, 343
see also Bath, Walter of
Sherwell (Shirewelle), John of, p. 6
Sherwood (Shirewode), Henry of, p. 4
Shete, see Shute
Shilstone (Selvestane), 515
Shiredone, see Skerraton
Shireve, Humphrey le, 406; William le, 406
Shirewelle, see Sherwell

Shirewode, *see* Sherwood
Shirvestone, John de, p. 3
Shirwell (Shirewelle, Shirewille), hundred, p. 5; 325, 336–43
Shopilande, Robert de, p. 5
Shorhame, William le Turnur, schepman of, 454, 750
Shorte, Roger le, 433
Shote, *see* Shute
Shropshire, x, 280, 291, 466; p. 128
Shute (Sheta, Shete, Colyton), 64
  Luke of, p. 8; 44, 64; Robert his son, 44
Shute (La Shote, Budleigh), 186
  John the miller of, 186
Sicca Villa (Seccheville, Secheville), Philip de, p. 2; Ralph de, 214, 221, 271, 477; Thomas his miller, 214
  Robert de, pp. 5, 7; Robert de (another), 301, 512; Robert de, de Strochille, 371; Warin de, p. 6; William de, 271
Sidbury (Siddebire, Sidebir, Sidesbire, Shiddebire), xxxiv, 53, 191, 193; p. 126
  Philip of, 107
Side, Walter, 643
Sidebire, *see* Sidbury
'Sidecume', 195
Sideham, *see* Sydeham, Sydenham
Sidelinche, Thomas de, 477
Sidford (Sideford), 191
Sidmouth (Sidemue), 195
Silkland (Silkelande), Thomas of, 430
Silverton (Sulfretona), 103
Silworthy (Selewrthe), Roger of, 269
Simon, Rogo son of, 721
Simpson (Sewennestone), Adam of, 702
Singhere, Osbert le, 433
Sireford, *see* Sherford
Siward, p. 6
  Richard, and Philippa his wife, 68
Skerraton (Shiredone), 588, 595
  Master Walter de, *alias* le Deveneis, *alias* de Novington, 595; William of, 588; Oliver his brother, 588
'Slade', 46
Slade (Seleda, Slad, Slade), 473
  Osmund of, 717; Robert of, xiii, xxxii, p. 5; 55, 472, 473, 750
Slote, Robert, 502
Slug, Seward, 542
Slutere, William le, 635
Smale, Adam le, 320; Reginald le, 748; Robert son of, 318
Smallake (Smalelake), Christopher of, 492
Smallbrook (Smalebrok), 421
Smallridge, 28
Smalprut, Roger, 201
Smetheam, Smetheham, *see* Smytham
Smethestone, *see* Smithson
Smith (*faber*), Geoffrey the, 520; Henry the, p. 7; John the, 542; Jolenta daughter of Adam the, 110; Nicholas the, 406; Nicholas son of Eustace the, and Gillian his wife, 555; Osbert the, 486; Philip son of Gilbert the, 575; Ralph the, 333; Reginald the, p. 6; Reginald the (another), 327; Richard

Smith—*cont.*
  the, p. 7; Robert the, p. 7; Robert the (another), p. 7; Robert the (another), 685; Robert Niger the (? same), p. 6; Roger the, p. 7; Roger the (another), p. 7; Roger the (another), 395; William the, 554
Smithincott (Smithenecote, Smithennecote), Erlemund, 99; Herlewin of (? same), 100; Rannulf of, 100, 125
Smithson (Smethestone), Elias of, 612
Smok, Henry, p. 7
Smytham (Smetheam, Smetheham), 433
  Rannulf of, 433; Richard of, 433
Snel, Richard, 691
Soler, Eustace del, p. 7
Somerset (Sumer', Sumers', Sumersette), xiii, xxii, xxiii, xxvii, xxxv, xxxvi, 3, 16, 81, 84, 160, 293, 301, 403, 451, 664, 759
Somerton (Sumertone Regis, Somerset), John le Blake of, 420
Sonbucke, William, 157
Soper (Sopere), Geoffrey le, 542; Robert le, 31
Soumoutone, *see* Molton, South
Southcott (Sucote), Michael of, p. 5; 395; Richard of, p. 6
Sowell Farm (Senewelle, Senewille), 99, 100
  William of, 99, 100, 101, 519
Spaiard, *see* Paiard
Sparke, Robert, 528
Speare, Walter, p. 6
Speccott Barton (Spekecote), Richard of, p. 4
Spelangre, Malerus de, p. 5
Spere, Walter, 51
Spicer, Jordan le, p. 4
Spichwik, Spicwik, *see* Spitchwick
Spigurnel, Richard, of Barnstaple, 334
Spilcombe Copse (Spillecumbe), Gilbert of, 64
Spileman, Roger, 730; Roger his father, 730; William, 744
Spillecumbe, *see* Spilcombe Copse
Spina, Amice daughter of Richard de, 241; Roger de, p. 3; William de, 688
Spineto, Gerard de, p. 3; 749
Spitchwick (Spichwik, Spicwik), Michael of, p. 3; 581
Spowe, Robert, p. 6
Sprei, *see* Sprytown
Spreyton (Spreitone, Spretone), 473, 501
Spriddlestone (Spridlestone), William of, p. 4
Spridelle, William, p. 3
Spridlestone, *see* Spriddlestone
Springan, Ralph, 221
Springe, 405
  Walter, 405
Sprot, Avice wife of Geoffrey, 227; William. 147
'Sprweie', 300
Sprytown (Sprei), 629
  Elias of, 630
Squirel (Scurel), Robert, 139; p. 127; Matthew, 139

Staddon (Stoddone), Richard of, 492; Robert of, p. 5
Stafford, see Stowford
Stake, Robert, 668
Stallenge Thorne (Stanlinche), 156
Thomas of, 156
Stanborough (Stainberghe, Stanberghe), hundred, xxvi, p. 3; 475, 583, 584–603, 611, 621, 684
Stancume, Roger son of Baldwin de, 370; William de, 370
Stanebire, Ralph de, p. 3
Stanforde, see Stowford
Stanhuse, see Stonehouse
Stanlinche, see Stallenge Thorne
Stanton, 475
'Stantone' (Churchstanton), 82
Stantor (Stantor), Elias of, p. 3
Stapestote, Robert de, p. 5
Steimur, Reginald le, p. 6; 396
Steinur, John le, 325
Stentwood, 80
Stevenhalle, see Stiniel
Stilbe, John, 459
Stiniel (Stevenhalle), Robert of, 403
Stockland (Stoklund, Dorset), 121
Stockleigh English, 221
Stockleigh Pomeroy, 221
Stoddone, see Staddon
Stodlegh, Matilda daughter of Gilbert de, xxx
Stoke, see Stokenham
Stoke Canon (Stokes, Stokes Cancellarii), 486
Stoke Gabriel (Stokes), Nicholas of, 704
Stokeinteignhead (Stoke, Stokes), 481, 510
'Stokeleg', 221
Stokenham (Stoke, Stokes), 677, 678, 679, 682
Geoffrey of, 685; Markerus of, 668
Stoke Rivers, 342
Stokes, William de, p. 3
see also Stoke Gabriel, Stokenham
Stokke, alias Wardrobe, Henry de la, 223
Stone (Lastane), 193
Stone, Geoffrey de la, p. 2
'Stoneforde', 591
Stonehouse (Stanhuse), Joel of, 525
Stork, Robert, 378
Stowford (Stafford, Stafforde, Lifton), 619
Robert the tithingman of, 629
Stowford (Stafford, Stafforde, South Molton), 290
Philip of, p. 5; Richard of, 290
Stowford (Stanforde, Black Torrington), 240
Jordan of, 240; Martin son of John of, 235; William of, 240
Strange (Stranga, Strange), Geoffrey, p. 6; John, 329, 754; Richard, p. 6; 329, 754; Richard (? another), 621
Stratton (Cornwall), hundred, 265
Strete, Philip de, alias Philip de la, p. 8; 16
Strethede, William de, p. 2
Strochille, Robert de Sicca Villa de, 371
Strode (Strode), Gervase of, 568, 574
Stur, Ralph, 107
Sturra, Roger son of William, p. 126

'Subrigge', 289
Sucote, see Southcott
Sucumbe, Baldwin de, p. 4
Suethogge (Swethog), Roger, p. 2; 75, 78
Suffolk, xxxiii
Sulfretona, see Silverton
Sulhand, Robert de, 655
Sulke, Richard, 767
Sulleie, Geoffrey de, 57
Sumerhille, see Summerhill
Sumertone Regis, see Somerton
Sumeter, Richard le, 212
Summerhill (Sumerhille), William of, p. 3
Sure, 71
Surreva, Walter, p. 125
Surrey, xlix, 1
Sussex, xxxviii
Sutton Lucy, 55
Swanecote, Martin de, p. 5
Swanekil (Swanekilda), Ralph son of, 574, 575
Swarteberge, Ailot de, 702
Swein, John, reeve of Bradninch, 370
Swethog, see Suethogge
Swetlache, Agnes de, 490
Swimbridge, 294
Swineherd (*porcarius*), Maurice the, 538
Swinespathe, Thomas de, 484
Sydeham, (Sideham, Sydeham), Robert of, x, 371, 373, 387
Sydenham (Sideham, Sidehame), Almaric of, xxxix, 613; Maurus of, 651
Syneker, Hugh le, 31

TAIL, Thomas, 409
Taillur (Taillor, Taliur), Guy le, 664; Henry le, p. 6; Henry le (another), 552; Hugh le, of Honiton, 30; John le, p. 6; Lawrence le, 756; Theophania his widow, 754, 756, see also Tailor, below; Nicholas le, de Boctone, 771; Robert le, p. 6; Roger le, p. 7; Walter le, p. 7
Tailor (*cissor, parmentarius, scissor*), David the, 557; Durandus the, p. 7; John the, 478; Nicholas a, 757; Thomas the, p. 6; Theophania widow of Lawrence the, 329; William the, p. 6
Taintone, William de, 607
Talaton (Talletone), Roger the clerk of, 104
Tale, Ralph, 107
Talebot, Philip, p. 4
Tailur, see Taillur
Talletone, see Talaton
Tanur, Walter le, p. 7
Tapeley (Tappeleghe), Robert of, p. 4
Tau (Tauwe), William de, p. 5; 472
'Taumowe', 434
Tautone, see Tawton
Tauwe, see Tau
Taverner (*tabernarius*), Geoffrey the, 272; Hugh the, 473; Richard the, 472
Taverner, Robert le, p. 7; Robert le (another), 422
Tavi Sancti Petri, see Petertavy

Index of Persons and Places

Tavistock (Tavistok, Tavistoke), 265
  burgh, xxviii, p. 7; 644–57; hundred, xxviii, p. 4; 644–57
  John Abbas of, 646, 649
Tavistock, abbot of, xxi, p. 4; 221, 243, 255, 265, 279, 650, 654, 657
  John abbot of, 265, 646
Taviton (Tavitone), Geoffrey of, 612
Tavy (Tavi, Thovi), river, 647; tithing, 712
Tawstock (Tavistoke), 287, 288
Tawton (Tautone Bishop's, North or South), 286, 287, 288, 457, 473
  Alexander of, 472; Richard de Toney, parson of, 405; William of, p. 7
Tawton, North (Nortautone), hundred, xxxii, p. 5; 453–79; manor, 473
Tawton, South (Sutautone), hundred, p. 5; 398–410, 473; manor, xlix, 410; tithing, 407, 408
Tayleboys, John, 145
Tedburn St. Mary (Teteburne, Tetteburne), Luke servant of the lady of, 503; Thomas of, 93, 419, 609
Teign, river, 720
Teignbridge (Teignebrigge, Teinebrigge), hundred, xxv, p. 3; 711–22
Teigne, Joyre de, p. 3
Teignemue, see Teignmouth
Teign George, 749
Teignmouth (Teignemue, Teingnemue), xxxiv, 731, 734, 737
  John Paz of, 542
Teing, William the miller of, 717
Teing Canonicorum, see Canonteign
Teigne, Richard de, 480
Teignemue, see Teignmouth
Teintone, Teitone, see Drewsteignton, Kingsteignton
Templars, Knights, 149, 154
Temple, Adam, 311
Templeton, 373, 390
Tennaton, 598
Teobald (Teubaud, Tibbaud, Tybaud), John, p. 2; 107, 364
Terri, Thomas, p. 5
Terrus, Robert son of, 391
Terry, Andrew, p. 1
Tetcott (Tetcote, Tettecote), 263
  Robert Serviens of, 263; Walter of, and Maisenta his wife, 239
Teteburne, Tetteburne, see Tedburn St. Mary
Tettecote, see Tetcott
Teubaud, see Teobald
Thethigmanne, Geoffrey, of Lewdon, 716
Thirletone, Walter de, 283
Thithene, John de la, p. 7
Thony, see Tony
Thornbury, parson of, xlv
Thorncombe, 28, 265
Thorne, Ralph de, 430; Robert de la, 82
Thornecumbe, John de, 607
Thorverton (Tholvertone, Thorvertone, Torvertone), xxxi, lii, 114, 494
  Nicholas the reeve of, 494
Throwleigh (Thruweleghe, Trualai, Truweleghe), 473, 499
  Richard of, 405

Thrudogge (Trudogge), Robert de la, 429; Walter, alias Walter de la, 429, 430
Thurlestone (Therlestane, Thirlestane, Thurlestane), 601, 621
Thurstan, Walter son of, 652
Tibbaud, see Teobald
Tidcombe (Tidecumbe), William Hals of, p. 127
Tideford (Tidewrthi), Henry of, p. 3
Tilleslow (Tullesho), Nicholas of, 257; Richard of, 257
Timme, Simon, 252
Tindel (Tyndel), Odo de, 528
Tirant (Tyrant), Richard le, p. 5; John, p. 7
Tirel, Henry, 509; John, p. 7
Tiuwe, Gilbert de, 702
Tiverton (Tuvertone, Twivertone, Twvertone, Twyvertone), burgh or vill, x, xiii, p. 6; 112, 136, 138, 141, 328; p. 126
  lepers of, p. 127; hundred, x, xi, xxxiii, lii, p. 2; 130–40, 141; pp. 126–7, 128; manor, 16; p. 126
  William the chaplain of, 135; p. 127
Tiwescumbe, see Wiscombe
Tolla, Richard, 542
Tonebire, John de, 169
Tony (Thony, Toney), Ralph, alias Ralph de, p. 5; 410; Roger his son, 410; Richard de, parson of Tawton, 405; Roger de, 410
Topsham (Toppesham), 210, 495, 500
Tor (Torre), 687
Torbryan (Torre Briane, Torre Brione), 687, 709
Toriton, Toritone, see Torrington
Torkeshege, Robert de, 703
Tormoham (Torre Briuwer), 695, 709
Torond, Thomas son of, 113
Torre (Torre), abbey/abbot/canons of, xxxvi, 161, 222, 700, 703
Torre, John de, 687; Martin de la, p. 3; Michael de la, 568; Robert son of Joce de, 572; Roger de la, p. 4
Torridge (Thoriz, Toriz), river, 264, 425, 439, 440, 463
Torrington, Black (Blaketoritone, Bleketoritone), hundred, xxiv, xxv, p. 4; 226–73, 279, 642; manor, 271, 273, 280; Adam Parvus of, 229; Henry Yerle of, 229; John the vicar of, 229
Torrington, Great (Toriton, Toritone), baron/barony of, 352, 477, 577
  Matthew of, lord of, 477; William of, lord of, and Avice his widow, 352; William III, baron of, 356
Torrington, Great or Little (Toritone), 351
  Joel of, 656
Torrington, Great (Toritone), burgh, p. 7; 356–9
  John le Saliur of, 359
Torrington, Little (Parva Toritone), 433
  Maisenta of, 450
Tosard, William, 419
Totedai, Richard, 447
Totefen, Andrew de, p. 3
Totnes (Toteneis, Totenes, Totenesse), burgh, p. 6; 587, 661, 683–5, 690

Totnes—*cont.*
    Geoffrey Brevel of, 684; Geoffrey of Cotmore of, 574; Geoffrey son of Sara of, 574; Joel, *alias* Juhel, of, 176, 319, 353
Totnes, honour of, xli, 176, 269, 566, 599, 638
Tottewrthe, Gerald de, 84
Toune, Osbert de la, 430
Trace, Roger, p. 4
Tracy (Traci), Eva de, 719; Henry de, lord of Barnstaple, xxv, xxxii, l, lii, p. 4; 114, 353, 494, 513; Roppe his ploughman, 494
    Henry de (another), 123; Oliver de, 719; William, p. 2; William (another), p. 6; William de (another), 123
Tranipreye, William, p. 7
Tranze, William, p. 6
Traty, William, 282
Travers, William, 746
Tredeluve, William, 450
'Treguz', 295
Treipas, Edmund, 498
Trematon (Cornwall), 176
Tremenet (Treminet, Treminettes), Richard de, p. 3; 738; William, p. 5
Trempestane, *see* Trimstone
Trempole, Elias de, 269
Trenchard, Nicholas, 607; Robert, 607, 608; William, 418, 477, 581, 608, 620, 625, 626; Michael and Robert his sons, 626
Treuerbi, Odo de, 603
Trill, Great (Tril), 28
    John of, 107
Trimstone (Trempestane), 316
    Roger of, 316
Tripling, Gervase, 776
Trove (Truve), Nicholas, 136; p. 127
Trualai, *see* Throwleigh
Trublevill (Trubleville), Henry de, xlvii, 123
Trudogge, *see* Thrudogge
Trusti, Gilbert, 461
Trutte, Vielus, 257
Truttup, Robert, p. 8
Truve, *see* Trove
Tuddecote, *see* Tythecott
Tudeham, Gundreda de, 473, 475; John her son, 473, 475
Tudhay, 67
Tug, Walter, 587
Tukebere, *see* Twigbear
Tulion, Thomas, 300
Tullesho, *see* Tilleslow
Tune, Hugh de la, 497
Tunnebrige, William de, of Bampton, 144
Turberne (Turbert), John, p. 6; 753, 754
Turberville (Turbeville), Gilbert de, xxv, xxvi, p. 5; 282, 283, 294, 295, 296; Pain de, 295; William de, 294
Turnehand, Richard, 201
Turnepain, Edward, 662
Turnur, Henry le, p. 6; Richard le, p. 6; Walter le, 605; William le, p. 7; 454;

Turnur—*cont.*
    William le (another), schepman of Shorhame, 454, 750
Turpin, Gilbert, p. 6
Turri, Gregory de, 168
Tuvertone, *see* Tiverton
Twichene, *see* Twitchen, Lower
Twigbear (Tukebere, Twikebere), 441
    Walter of, 443
Twiscombe (Tiwescumbe, Tyuwescumbe), Walter of, 503, 504
Twitchen, Lower (Twichene), Warin of, 430
Twivertone, *see* Tiverton
Tybaud, *see* Teobald
Tyndel, *see* Tindel
Tyrant, *see* Tirant
Tythecott (Tuddecote), Walter of, 429
Tyuwescumbe, *see* Twiscombe
Tywe, Gilbert de, p. 3

Uffculme (Uffculum, Uffeculum), hundred, x, p. 2; 92–102; manor, 102
    Luke Serviens of, 93, 99
Ugborough (Utkeberghe), 577, 582
Umberleigh (Umberleghe), 458, 477
Umfranville, Gilbert de, and Sibyl his wife, 477
Umfrei, Richard, 685
Underhille, Ralph, 575
Unetone, *see* Honiton
Upcott (Uppecote), 318
    Ivo of, 269; Robert of, 506, 507; Henry his son, 507; Thomas of, 395; Thomas of (? another), 506, 507
Up Exe (Uperexe, Uphexe), 494
    Bartholomew of, lii, 114, 494
Uphay (Huppehaie), Robert of, p. 1
Uphexe, *see* Up Exe
Uphill (Uphille), Reginald the reeve of, 520
Uphothedune, Reginald, 9
Uplowman (Lumene, Huplumene), pp. 126, 127
    Alice daughter of Goscelin of, p. 126
Uplyme (Uplim), 26, 28
Upottery (Uphoteri), 10, 28
Uppadone (Uppedone), Simon de, 386; Mabel his daughter, 386
    Stephen de, 185; William de, 184
Upton (Uptone, Cliston), Norman of, 175
Upton (Haytor), 700
Urcellus the Jew, 213; Camekinna his daughter, 213

Vaddicott (Faddecote), Adam of, p. 4
Vado, Gocius, *alias* Jocelin, de, p. 6; 554; James de, 688; Michael son of William de, 560; Alice his sister, 560
    Robert de, p. 4
Vaglefield (Faklefelde, Falklefelde), Roger of, xxxii, 267; Walter of, xxxii, 267
Valle Torta (Vautort), family, 103, 579
    Henry de, 263; Joel de, p. 5; 457, 473, 479, 581; Joel de (another), 479; Ralph de, p. 4; Reginald de, p. 1; 68, 176; Joan his wife, 68
    Roger de, 176, 641

Index of Persons and Places

Vallibus (Vaux), Adam de, 320; Hubert de, 57; Robert de, xxii, p. 1; 409, 513, 550; Matilda his widow, 513
Vassallus, Richard, 147
Vassel, Richard (? same), p. 5
Vaus, Nicholas de, 477
Vautort, see Valle Torta
Vaux, see Vallibus
Veg, Dolwyn, xxxii, 37; Thomas le, 635
Velwell (Falewille), Rannulf of, 587
Venn Ottery (Fenotri), 215
Venur, William le, p. 4
Ver, Roger de, p. 1
Veraby (Farebi), Walter of, 380
Vere, Ralph le, 548; Robert de, earl of Oxford, 176
Verge, John de la, p. 2
Vernun, William de, earl of Devon, 30, 141, 515, 535, 548; William de (another), 107
Veteri Ponte, Richard de, p. 4; 622, 638
Veutrer, alias le Mus, Richard le, 24
Via, Walter de, p. 4
Viel, Gervase de, 761; Roger, p. 6; 136; p. 127; Clarica, alias Claricia, his mother, 136; p. 127
Vielstone (Vielestone), Gilbert of, 429; John of, 429, 430; Ralph of, 429
Vilers, Gilbert de, 512
Vincent, Peter son of, p. 1
Vintner (*vinetarius*), Roger the, p. 7
Virga, Roger de, 700
Vito, Roger de, p. 6
Vitriaco, Thomas de, 147
Vivario, Walter de, 688
Vluesgrave, William, p. 7
Vuerlande, Walter de, 659
Vuingestone, Edward de, 662; Gilbert de, 662

WACHCUMBE (WATHKUMBE), Roger de, 39; p. 125; Susan his wife, p. 125
Wade, Walter, p. 2
Wadeheghe, Michael de, p. 2
Waiford, Baldwin de, 603
Wainarde, Stephen, of Sampford Courtenay, 232
Wakeman, 152
Walemere, Richard de, p. 3
Walensis, Henry, 477
Walerande (Walerant, Walrand, Walrande), Richard, 99, 101, 125; Richard (? another), 753, 773, 774; Walter or William son of, 99, 100
Wales (Wall'), xiv, 295, 611, 709
Walkhampton (Waltuntone), 530, 532
Walter, Alice daughter of, 699; Adam son of, 194; Richard son of, 486
Walwrthi, Roger de, 552
Wanci, Robert, p. 6
Wanford (Wangeforde, Waninforde, Waunford), family, 273
Hamelin de, 269, 273; Richard de, xxv, p. 4; 273; Richard son of Espus de, 273; Thomas his son, 273; Thomas de, xxvi
Wansley Barton (Wanteleghe), William of, p. 4

Warbrightsleigh Barton (Warbritteleghe), 390
Wardrobe, alias Stokke, Henry de la, 223
Ware, Adam le, 732
Warin, Walter p. 1
Waringstone (Waringgestone), 38, 80
Warkleigh (Wauercleghe), 277
Wartha, Richard, 575
Warthemore, Godfrey de, 147
Warwale, Ralph de, p. 7
Warwick (Warwicks), 291
Henry earl of, and Philippa his wife, 68
Warwik, Michael de, 584
Master Richard de, 646
Washbourne (Wasseburne), 663
Guy of, p. 3
Wasteper, Archibald, 597
Watchcombe, 57; see also 'Werdescumbe'
Wate, Jordan Du, 492
Watercombe (Watercumbe, Dorset), Rannulf of, 65
Watervale (Waterfalle), Jordan of, 627
Wathkumbe, see Wachcombe
Watta, John, 487
Waunford, see Wanford
Wayfrac, Robert, p. 6
Wdebire, see Woodbury
Wdehevese, see Woodovis
Wdelande, William de la, 441
Wdemanneswille, see Woodmanswell
Wdetune, John de, 221
Weaver (*textrix*), Alice the Cornish, xxxiv, 555; Beatrice or Margery, 531; Richard her son, 531
Weaver (Wevere), Nicholas of, 78; William of, 78
Weie (Weye), Richard de la, 220; William de la, pp. 4, 5; 284, 313; William de La (? another), 646
Welifed, Ralph, 152
Welitone (Wellintone, Willintone, Wylington), Ralph, alias Rannulf, de, 221, 342, 477; Ralph (another), 220
Wellangre, see Woolhanger
Wellintone, see Welitone
Welshman (*Walensis*), Alan the, 386; David the, 403; Elias, alias Eliot, the, 403; Gilbert the, 618; Godfrey the, 537; John the, 263; John the (another), 371; John the (another), 618; Lawrence the, 80; Matilda daughter of Robert the, 441; Roger the, 535; Walter the, 618; William the, 80
Wembury (Wembire, Wenbire), 539
Adam of, p. 4
'Werdescumbe' (Watchcombe), 60
Were, Hugh de la, 162; John son of William de, 494; Rannulf de la, p. 6; 416, 421
Werrington (Wlrintone, Wluretone, Wlurintone), xxxiv, 244, 245, 262, 265
Werwale, Martin de, p. 7
Westacott (Westcote, South Molton), Nicholas of, 290
Westacott (Westecote, Black Torrington), Walter of, 261
Westecot, 294

Westecote, *see* Westacott
Westicote, Richard de, 127
Westminster, xviii
West Mollande, Westmorlande, *see* Molland, West
Weston, 709
Weston Peverel (Westone), Isabel of, 525; William the smith of, 525
Wetecumbe, William de, 684
Wevere, *see* Weaver
Weycroft (Witecroft), Edmund of, 25
Weye, *see* Weie
Whaitemel, Osbert, 573
Wheie, Margaret daughter of William de la, 292
Whetistanne, Roger de, 738
Whimple (Wimple), 173
Whitchurch (Whitechurche), 522
White, Nicholas le, 104, 105; Richard le, 278; Richard le (another), 370, 379; Richard le (another), 557; Robert le, 107; Robert le (another), 440; William le, 308; William le (another), 730
Whitefelde, Peter de, 616
  see also Widefield
Whitefield (Whitefelde, Witafeld, Witefel, South Molton), 276
  Nicholas of, pp. 5, 7; Robert of, 276
Whitefield (Whitefelde, Witafelde, Braunton), Richard of, p. 5; 308
Whiteleghe, *see* Whiteley
Whiteleigh, 273
Whiteley (Whiteleghe), Iwanus of, 662
Whitepruvost, Adam, 104
Whiteside, Ralph, 575
Whiteslade, Robert de, 433; Geoffrey his son, 433
Whitesleghe, *see* Whitsleigh
Whitestane, Henry de, 453
Whitestone (Whitestane), 416, 502
  Brian of, and Mariota his wife, 502; Hugh de la Lake of, 504; Ralph son of Ralph of, 496
Whitetone, William de, 684
Whitford (Witeford, Witeforde, Whyteforde, Witford), burgh/manor/vill, p. 8; 37, 64, 71
  Philip of, 16; p. 125
Whitley (Witeleghe), 77
Whitley Farm (Whitteleghe), 57, 59
Whitsleigh (Whitesleghe), Robert of, p. 4; 345
Whitstone (Cornwall), vicar of, xxxi
Whorridge, 103
Wiche, Geoffrey de, 169
'Wicke', 660
Widdecombe in the Moor, 709
Widdewrthi, *see* Widworthy
Wideberghe, *see* Woodbeer
Widebrok, Stephen de, 269
Widecumbe, 84
Widefield (Whitefelde, Withefelde), Geoffrey of, 260; Robert of, 260
Widewell (Widewille), John of, 678
Widworthy (Widdewrthi, Widewothe, Widewrthe, Wydewrth), William of, p. 1; 29, 125, 147, 476
Wight, Isle of (Hants), 57, 59

Wike, Alexander de, p. 5; Alice wife of Ralph de la, 644; Amadas de, 528; Arlewin de, p. 7; Rannulf de, p. 5; Richard de, 405; William his son, 405, 407
  Robert de, 269; Roger de, p. 5; Walter de, p. 5; 472; Walter de (another), 528; William de, 567
Wikedone, Robert de, p. 5; 472
Wiking, Robert, 542
Wikoc, Baldwin, and Avice his wife, 744
Wile (Wyle), Angerus *alias* Augerus de, p. 4; 226, 251; Thomas de la, xxii, p. 1; 3, 187, 188, 265, 403, 409, 653
Willand (Willelande), 162
Wille, Odo, p. 4
Willey, 269
William I, king, xlvii, 13, 160, 168, 176, 265, 511; Matilda his queen, 168
William II, Rufus, king, 265, 397, 454
William, a boy, 76; a Welsh groom, 602
William, Geoffrey son of, 569; Hugh son of, p. 6; 260, 433, 448; Nicholas son of, 108; Ralph son of, 444; Richard son of, 212; Roger son of, 131; p. 126; Thomas son of, p. 7; Walter son of, 589; Warin son of, 661
Williamestone, *see* Wilmington
Willintone, *see* Welitone
Wilmington (Williamestone), Ralph of, 56
Wiltshire (Wiltes'), xxxv
  Thomas Capun from, 771
Wimund (Wymund), Martin son of Richard, 593
  Master Peter, 416
Winburnefort, *see* Womberford
Winchester (Hants), see of, xxvi
  bishop of, *see* Lucy, Godfrey de
Winesthorre, *see* Winstow Cottages
Winkleigh (Winkeleghe), hundred, p. 5; 295, 392-7, 473; vill, 392
  Alan son of the priest of, 392; John his brother, 392
Winnemer, Walter, 232
Winnescote, *see* Winscott Barton
Winscombe (Somerset), xxxvi
Winscott Barton (Winnescote, Fremington), John of, p. 4; 345
Winscott (Wynescote, Shebbear), Thomas of, p. 4
Winston (Winstone), Walter of, 537
Winstow Cottages (Winesthorre), Thomas of, p. 3
Winter, Robert, 463
Wintone, Roger de, 240
Wisar, Richard, 111
Wisdom, Germanus, p. 7; Osbert de, p. 4
Wishutkedune, Walter, 93
Witafeld, Witafelde, *see* Whitefield
Wite, Stephen le, 239
Witecroft, *see* Weycroft
Witefel, *see* Whitefield
Witefelde, John de, p. 4
Witeford, Witeforde, *see* Whitford
Withefelde, *see* Widefield
Witheleghe, *see* Withleigh
Wither, Alexander, p. 2

Index of Persons and Places

Witheridge (Wirigge, Wyrigge, Wytherigge), hundred, xxxii, xlii, xlix, p. 5; 183, 300, 368–91; manor, 300
Withleigh (Witheleghe), Clarica of, p. 127
Withulake, Hugh de, 269
Withycombe (Widecumbe), 209
Wittawere, William, 33
Wittinge, Wimund, 57
Wlf, Henry, 493
Wlfereswrthi, see Woolfardisworthy
Wllewelle, see Woolwell
Wlmar, Robert, alias Robert son of, 107
Wlneburg, see Wolborough
Wlnethecote, see Wollacott
Wlrinlande, Walter de, 239
Wlrivetone, William de, p. 4
Wlurintone, William de, 294, 373
Wnstone, see Wonson
Wodeburne, see Woodburn
Wodeham, William de, 768
Wodelande, Wodelond, see Woodland
Wodewis, see Woodhuish
Wolborough (Wlneburg) Elias of, 691
Wolford, 80
Wollacott (Wlnethecote), Robert of, 624
Wolmereswurthy, William de, xxx
Wombe, Thomas, 669
Womberford (Winburnefot), William of, p. 1
Wonford (Winforde, Wnforde, Woniford, Woniforde), hundred, xxi, p. 3; 393, 402, 405, 407, 410, 416, 473, 480–519, 770; p. 130
Stephen serjeant of, 483
Wonford (Waniforde, in Thornbury, Black Torrington), 266, 273
Wonson (Wnstone, Wunestone), Aenol of, 401; Luke of, 225, 401; Ralph of, 401; Thomas of, 401
Woodbeer (Wideberghe, Wudebere), William of, 78; William of (? another), 107
Woodburn (Wodeburne), Jordan of, p. 5
Woodbury (Wdebire), 222
William de Cumbe of, 204
Woodhuish (Wodewis), 9, 700, 709
Gilbert of, 686
Woodland (Wodelande, Wodelond), Andrew of, 569; Roger of, 569
Woodleigh, 603
Woodmanswell (Wdemanneswille), Robert of, 606
Woodovis (Wdehevese), Godfrey of, p. 4; Vivian of, p. 4
Woolfardisworthy (Wlfereswrthi), Robert of, p. 4
Woolhanger (Wellangre), Gilbert the miller of, 337
Woolwell (Wllewelle), Robert of, 688
Wotri, Henry, 362

Wrai, Reginald de, 464
Wray Barton (Wrei), William p. 3
Wrford, Richard de, 568
Wronke, Richard de, 127
Wrwildic, see Hurlditch
Wudebere, see Woodbeer
Wunestone, see Wonson
Wydewrth, see Widworthy
Wyle, see Wile
Wylington, see Welitone
Wymund, see Wimund
Wynescote, see Winscott

Ya (Yae, Iae), Alfred de la, 568; Alina de la, 587; Robert her son, 587 Geoffrey de la, 597; Geoffrey de la (another), 684; Hugh de la, 107; Nicholas de, p. 1; 29; Nicholas de la (another), p. 3; 601; Richard de la, 601
Yalberton, 709
Yalde Dune, Richard de, 225
Yale, Walter de, p. 1
Yalelande, see Yelland
Yarcombe (Ierttecumbe), manor, 13
prior of, 13; see also Otterton, prior of
Yarnescombe, Little (Petit Ernescumbe), 428
Yarnicombe (Iharnecumbe), Ralph of, p. 6
Yarty (Ierti), river, 20
Yate, Philip de la, 742
Yealmpton (Ialmetone, Yalmetone), manor, p. 7; 37, 604
Yein, Geoffrey le, 308, 309; Godfrey and Richard his sons, 309; Jordan le, 684
Yelland (Yalelande), Geoffrey son of Nicholas of, 395
Yeo, 419
Yeo (Iouwe), river, 415
Yepy, John de, p. 2
Yerle, Henry, of Black Torrington, 229
Yetminster (Dorset), xlv
Yolde, Alfred le, 390
Yolland (Yoldelande), Alan of, 622
York (Ebor'), William of, ix, x, p. 9; 37
Yorkshire, 50, 596
Yuli, Edward, 393

Zeal, South (Lasele, La Sele), 403
Reginald of, p. 5; 405, 472
Zuche (Zoche), Alan la, xxiv, xxv, p. 5; 271, 273, 279, 280; William his son, 271
Roger la, alias Roger de la, xxii, p. 1; 50, 271, 280, 300, 388; William de la, 388; William la (another), alias Belmeis, 300; William de, 300